# Essential Flies
## for the Great Lakes Region

Patterns, and Their Histories, for Trout, Steelhead, Salmon, Smallmouth, Muskie, and More

**INCLUDES** Minnesota, Michigan, Wisconsin, Indiana, Illinois, Ohio, Pennsylvania, New York, and Ontario, Canada

## JERRY DARKES
Fly Plate Photos by Jimmy Chang

## STACKPOLE BOOKS

Guilford, Connecticut

*To George Ayres, who left us recently.*
*An occasional fly angler and a good friend for many years,*
*he was a unique individual who left an impression on everyone*
*he met. George is missed by everyone who knew him.*

*Also, to Chris Helm, a longtime fixture in the world of fly fishing.*
*A Midwesterner, Chris was a true gentleman, a teacher, an*
*inspiration to many, and one of the best fly tiers ever.*

Published by Stackpole Books
An imprint of The Rowman & Littlefield Publishing Group, Inc.
4501 Forbes Blvd., Ste. 200
Lanham, MD 20706
www.rowman.com

Distributed by NATIONAL BOOK NETWORK

Copyright © 2020 Jerry Darkes

British Library Cataloguing in Publication Information available

Library of Congress Control Number: 2020939792

ISBN 978-0-8117-3962-7 (cloth: alk. paper)
ISBN 978-0-8117-6967-9 (electronic)

♾™ The paper used in this publication meets the minimum requirements of American National Standard for Information Sciences—Permanence of Paper for Printed Library Materials, ANSI/NISO Z39.48-1992.

# Contents

## Chapter 5: Warmwater Patterns

## Chapter 6: Patterns for Migratory Species

## Chapter 7: Apex Predator Patterns

# Foreword

While reviewing the discussion and extensive presentation of fly patterns contained within these pages, I couldn't help but reflect on the growth of fly tying over the last forty to fifty years. The advancements in materials and tying techniques is nearly staggering from the days when I learned to tie in the mid- to late 1970s. Don't worry, I won't bore you with stories of how we walked to school uphill both ways back in those olden days.

My tying bible at that time was *The Complete Book of Fly Tying* by Eric Leiser. Mr. Leiser was a master fly tier, and this was a very significant work at the time, providing a great resource for many upstart tiers. This book still sits on my shelf along with some other early classics, but now the flies contained within look so rudimentary compared to the daily presentation of new fly patterns on social media.

Not only have natural tying materials increased dramatically in quality thanks to genetic engineering, but so many superior synthetics have been developed that it is difficult to keep track. Combine this with ever-evolving techniques, and the subculture of fly tying has experienced rapid progression in recent years.

*Essential Flies for the Great Lakes States* captures this growth as it relates to the patterns of the region. This is an essential guide to the tried-and-true classics as well as innovative flies to pursue the myriad species that offer anglers a challenge throughout this diverse geographic area. Living in the Great Lakes region, I am often faced with the difficult decision of what direction to go and what species to fish for on any given day. When the prime time of year rolls around, it may be inland trout one day, steelhead the next, and bass or muskie the next. To take full advantage of what the Midwest and Great Lakes have to offer you need multiple fly boxes filled with an incredible variety of patterns, from size 22 dries for trout to twelve-inch-long concoctions for muskie and everything in between. This book provides the perfect reference to fill those boxes with essential patterns.

I first met Jerry over three decades ago while I was guiding in western New York. We connected instantly and quickly forged a friendship that included meeting in various parts of the Great Lakes region while exploring the tremendous opportunities that were emerging all around. At the time the Great Lakes did not portray the same fly-fishing image as more famous venues such as the western United States or the Catskills region. The lakes were on their way to recovery from blatant abuse and significant, well-documented water quality issues that had become evident decades before. The

Few places offer the variety of fly fishing opportunities that are found across the Midwest and Great Lakes regions. The flies can be very different depending on the situation. The patterns shown here can catch everything from trout and panfish to the largest Great Lakes predators. JERRY DARKES PHOTO

most visible indication was shorelines paved in dead fish that produced a nearly unbearable stench. Unethical angling practices and overcrowding of the more popular rivers as the lakes recovered also clouded the picture.

But I always appreciated the fishery as it recovered and developed through the late 1970s and 1980s, recognizing that its trajectory pointed toward something special. Jerry shared that same appreciation, and it was this common element that continued to allow our paths to cross even though we lived a couple of states apart. We met to fish along Lake Erie for steelhead and Lake Ontario for brown trout, and pursued native lake trout in the Niagara region. It was a blank canvas to explore with the only limit being one's imagination. We devised various hybrid lines and rigs to fish all types of water, including exploring the depths of the lakes and larger rivers—all at a time when variations in commercial lines were very limited. We regularly exchanged ideas to prepare for the next challenge and species.

While much of my involvement in the fly-fishing industry, along with much of my writing, focused on the lake-run element of the Great Lakes fishery, Jerry continued to push forward rooting out many unique opportunities and fisheries throughout the entire Great Lakes and Midwest. For years Jerry had the idea of documenting the opportunities that existed and were still developing in the region. I applauded his efforts, and on a few occasions he pitched me the idea of a book that documented these special fisheries with the offer of coauthorship. The timing was never right for me to join this journey, but in the end Jerry saw it through, producing the book titled *Fly Fishing the Inland Oceans*, published in 2013. This instantly became a go-to reference

for experiencing all the Great Lakes has to offer from a fly fisher's perspective.

It was Jerry's work as a fly-fishing industry sales representative that kept him so tightly connected through a career of commitment to the sport. Tireless effort and countless hours of travel kept many of the region's fly shops stocked and positioned to provide quality service to customers. But it was this connection that provided the opportunity to experience many of the inland fisheries throughout his territory in the Midwestern states in addition to the Great Lakes waters. This knowledge contributed significantly to the finished product. *Essential Flies for the Great Lakes States* truly represents a lifelong effort.

We often long to visit exotic and famous fly-fishing locations. Fortunately, the ability to travel to remote destinations has never been so accessible or attainable as it is today. The planning and preparation for a special trip can occupy a fly angler's mind for months. But when it comes to fly fishing, enjoyable outings often occur close to home. Great experiences are simply where you find them, and exploring your own backyard can result in unexpected results and pleasant surprises. While many anglers visit the Midwest and Great Lakes from great distances, the fishery largely serves the millions that live in rather close proximity to this unique resource. The spirit of taking advantage of what exists at your fingertips is at the very heart of this book that provides a range of flies to meet just about any fly-fishing challenge to be found in the region.

Rick Kustich
Grand Island, New York
June 27, 2019

# Introduction

## A BRIEF HISTORY OF FLY FISHING IN THE GREAT LAKES STATES

Other than the polar ice caps, the Great Lakes of North America present the largest, continuous source of fresh water on earth. Over 40 million people live in the region. Eight US states and the province of Ontario touch the lakes. The economic value of the lakes in terms of shipping, transportation, recreation, tourism, and natural resources is impossible to calculate.

The Great Lakes have over 11,000 miles of shoreline with hundreds of tributaries. North to south, the region encompasses several climatic zones. The lakes border wilderness as well as highly developed industrial areas. An amazing diversity of plant and wildlife species and ecosystems are found here. The overall importance of this region is almost beyond comprehension.

From an angling standpoint, this can be considered one of the premier sportfishing areas anywhere. Anglers have the lakes themselves, plus countless inland creeks, streams, rivers, ponds, and lakes at their doorstep. Both coldwater and warmwater opportunities abound, all found in a relatively small geographic area. An angler can fish smallmouth in the morning and then catch a hatch for trout in the afternoon and evening.

Fly fishing itself is defined by the flies we use—those accumulations of feathers, hair, fur, and synthetic materials attached to a hook and cast in hopes of attracting a fish to strike. The Great Lakes region has been a significant area for the development and evolution of fly patterns. A number of the "timeless" patterns we use are from this area and still work, unchanged from their original design.

The angling diversity found in the area has allowed us to expand our efforts from trout to a host of additional species. The creativity of fly tying and fly design is well established here and continues to be an ongoing process. It is important for us as both fly anglers and fly tiers to recognize the contributions of the Great Lakes region.

This area was an important stopping point in the westward progression of fly fishing, but in a sense has been "reborn" as perhaps the single most important region in North America for fly fishers. It is quite likely that you could fly-fish 365 days a year at multiple locations around the Great Lakes for a unique variety of species. If you are looking at an extensive range of fly patterns, just look in the fly bins of shops around the region.

In spite of being selective in the patterns presented, this book still contains well over 500 designs. The more I researched, the more layers of information I uncovered. Along with the well-known, recognized tiers, there are also many "unsung heroes," both past and present, who deserve recognition. In the end, these fly patterns reflect a combination of things—longevity, creativity, versatility,

The Great Lakes region has been a significant area for the development and evolution of fly patterns. A number of the "timeless" patterns we use are from this area and still work, unchanged from their original design.

Roberts Yellow Drake is a great example of a pattern that has stood the test of time. It can be fished anywhere fish are feeding on light-colored mayflies. The materials stay the same, but the size is adjusted as needed.

JERRY DARKES PHOTO

and practicality included. A lot of ground is covered by the patterns that are listed.

Looking back at the timeline, grayling were the starting point for fly anglers moving into the region of Michigan's Lower Peninsula. We know that this area was well known as the next stop beyond the eastern areas like the Catskills and Adirondacks, which are considered the birthplace of fly-pattern design in North America. The patterns that existed at the time were more than adequate for these fish. There were some local patterns being tied, but they were not a necessity to catch fish.

The northern peninsula of Michigan, northern Wisconsin, Minnesota, and Ontario saw a similar scenario as fly anglers pursued the local brook trout. Snelled flies with multiple flies on the leader got the job done. The Nipigon River in Ontario deservedly attracted a significant amount of interest, with some patterns being developed specifically for that area.

The introduction of brown trout fueled a whole new class of patterns that were more specific imitations of insects. This in turn led to a variety of new tying techniques and materials brought into the mix. Rivers like Michigan's AuSable and Manistee led this development, which still continues today. The Driftless area has become a subset of brown trout fishing in the region, with numerous patterns developed specifically for the area. Fly patterns, material, and techniques have migrated to other areas.

Fly fishing and flies for the migratory rainbows of the Great Lakes have gone through several evolutionary stages, starting with the realization that these fish would eat flies. From the earlier designs that mimicked western designs, there was a big move to natural patterns imitative of nymphs and eggs. Patterns that were imitative of an attractor

component were next. Most recently, streamers have come into the mix for both swung and stripped fly applications.

In the warmwater arena, smallmouth bass have become a major player for fly anglers. The sheer amount of water available across the area for this great gamefish is mind-boggling. From small streams to the open waters of the Great Lakes, smallmouth bass are a staple for both anglers and guides. No matter where you are across the whole area, it is likely that fishable smallmouth water is close by.

The apex predator of the region, the muskellunge, is now fair game on a fly and much pursued. Advances in equipment along with both tying materials and fly design allow anglers to take flies to where muskies live and do it for extended periods of time. The amazing thing is that muskie really like flies, and this is a legitimate method to catch them, not just a novelty.

The waters of the Great Lakes are no longer out of bounds to fly anglers. As discussed in my book, *Fly Fishing the Inland Oceans*, the lakes themselves and connecting waters provide endless opportunities for fly fishing. Here we can stalk and sight-fish on hard sand flats, throw flies to fish busting bait on the surface, find fish sipping mayflies gently on the surface, and probe the depths with sinking lines. Nearly any fly-fishing scenario can be found on the Great Lakes.

Yes, the lakes do have their problems—invasive species being the most prominent at present. But it's not all doom and gloom. The lake-dwelling coaster brook trout of Lake Superior, nearly wiped out by the mid-twentieth century, have rebounded quickly and in steadily increasing numbers due to special regulations. Wild lake trout populations are on the rise in all the lakes. Efforts at reintroducing Atlantic salmon are showing some signs of success.

Mayflies are the most recognized insect to Midwest fly anglers and are found in both moving water and stillwater environments. Most of the early dry fly development focused on mayfly imitations, and they still get the majority of interest in most situations. JON RAY PHOTO

A timeline of fly-fishing history: Here are a few of the many books used in researching information for this work. JERRY DARKES PHOTO

As we shall see, the area played a significant role in the development of fly fishing as we know it. This process is still continuing. Fly pattern evolution and development continue. Knowledge learned here is carried to all parts of the fly-fishing world. With an increasing population of fly fishers and diversity of fly-fishing opportunities, the region will continue as a primary influencer in the sport.

## The Early Period

We will never know for sure who was the first person to cast a fly to a fish on the waters of the Midwest or Great Lakes. Fish hooks made of bone have been found in archaeological sites in the area going back several thousand years. In the first part of the nineteenth century, there were reports of the indigenous peoples of the region dressing bone hooks with feathers, but no record of when this actually started.

What we do know is that fly fishing has been present in North America for over 250 years. European settlers brought their version of fly fishing with them across the Atlantic. Fishing with a fly was part of the food-gathering process, and a recreational aspect slowly became part of the activity as time went on. As settlers pushed west, a fly rod was part of the kit for many.

There is ample evidence that by the mid-1800s fly fishing was becoming established as a sport across eastern North America and working its way westward. There are a number of accounts from this time frame of wealthy "sports" traveling from larger cities such as New York, Boston, Philadelphia, or Chicago to the northern tier of the Great Lakes region. Further expeditions went into Ontario up to and beyond the rapids of the St. Marys River. Some ventured to the upper reaches of Lake Superior and even farther.

Robert Barnwell Roosevelt helped fuel interest in the region with his two books, *Game Fish of the North* (1862) and *Superior Fishing* (1865). We see that even as the Civil War raged, angling exploration was taking place. Up to this point, waterways were the main arteries of travel into the interior of the region. This began to change around 1870.

As railroad routes expanded, the north country became more accessible to anglers. Thaddeus Norris, perhaps the most noted American fly-fishing writer of the period, arrived in Grayling, Michigan, in the summer of 1874. His essay, *The Michigan Grayling*, was based on his explorations of the AuSable and Manistee Rivers. Norris wrote of vast numbers of easy-to-catch grayling coming to casts of three or four wet flies. At times, an angler would have a fish on each fly.

Found mainly in the upper portion of Michigan's Lower Peninsula, grayling thrived in the cold, pure waters of the area. Trout were found in very few of these rivers, and grayling were actually the native coldwater sportfish. Unfortunately, the same railroads that opened the north to angler access also allowed the white pine forests to be exploited. The Michigan grayling and the virgin pines would both be gone around the turn of the century.

Brook trout were found in Michigan's Upper Peninsula and in a very few Lower Peninsula streams, and across into northern Wisconsin and the province of Ontario. Logging had the same effect on the native brook trout populations as it did on the grayling. In addition, the lake-dwelling coaster brook trout, or "rock trout," of northern Lake Huron and Lake Superior also suffered from overfishing and habitat degradation.

In *Superior Fishing*, Robert Barnwell Roosevelt recounts an expedition to the Nipigon Bay area of Lake Superior focused on the brook trout of the lake. Other accounts from the late nineteenth and early twentieth centuries talk of the Nipigon brook trout that peak with the largest ever recorded brookie of 14½ pounds, caught in 1915. It may be that this distinct genetic strain is gone, but current fishing regulations are resulting in a noticeable increase in both numbers and size of these fish again.

Rainbow trout were first planted in Michigan at the mouth of the AuSable River near Oscoda in 1873. Subsequent stockings took place through the 1880s in other locations. These fish thrived, but disappeared from Great Lakes streams each summer, only to reappear again in the fall. It took several decades before biologists understood that this was an anadromous strain of rainbow; these fish were the ancestors of many of the migratory rainbows found across the Great Lakes today that are referred to generically as steelhead.

Rainbow stockings were successful across the northern tier of the Great Lakes by the early 1900s, and localized, self-sustaining populations were established and recognized by anglers. A young writer by the name of Ernest Hemingway wrote about the "world's best rainbow trout fishing" in the St. Marys River rapids for the *Toronto Star* newspaper in 1920. Today, natural reproducing populations of rainbows are found in all of the Great Lakes, but there are very few self-sustaining river populations.

*Superior Fishing* was published in 1865 and helped to spur interest in sportfishing in North America. Much of the book focuses on fly fishing the Great Lakes region. JERRY DARKES PHOTO

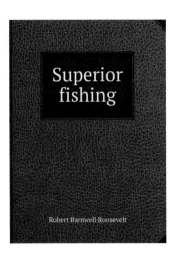

The Nipigon Historical Museum in Nipigon, Ontario, has an excellent exhibit recounting the history of fly fishing in the area. It focuses on the famous brook trout fishing and the story of the world-record fish. JERRY DARKES PHOTO

Many early bass flies were larger versions of trout patterns. These became commercially available by the late 1800s. JIMMY CHANG PHOTO

The first introduction of brown trout in the United States was in the Baldwin River, a tributary to Michigan's Pere Marquette River in 1883. This was the start of a significant shift in trout fishing around the region, which spread to other areas. Brown trout were much more tolerant of the warmer waters and sediment. They were also harder to catch and gradually became the dominant trout species in most of the area waters.

Stockings continued around the country through the 1880s, and browns gradually displaced the native trout species in many waters. By around 1920, they were the dominant trout of inland waters in the Midwest. Browns responded poorly to the flies and techniques used to catch brook trout, and fly anglers slowly developed patterns and methods for them. This process is still continuing today, as we will see. More than any other species, the brown trout embodies stream-based trout fishing across the region.

Theodore Gordon is considered by many as the "father of American fly fishing." From his base in New York's Catskill Mountains, Gordon spent the late 1880s developing patterns that would become the foundation of the dry fly in North America. Many of us recognize the Quill Gordon patterns as his creation.

As the railroads expanded and reached northern Michigan, Gordon traveled to the AuSable River and fished the traditional three wet fly casts for grayling. Gordon also contributed to the development of streamer flies with the development of his Bumblepuppy fly. There is evidence that Gordon was experimenting with this pattern as early as 1880.

There was also activity happening on the warmwater side of the equation. One of the earliest references to fly fishing in the New World was an account by a British army officer, one Robert Hunter, who wrote about fly fishing for smallmouth bass on the rivers around Montreal in 1785. Warmwater fishing received a significant boost with the 1881 publication of the *Book of the Black Basses* by Dr. James Henshall of Cincinnati, Ohio.

Henshall brought the sport of warmwater fly fishing into the forefront and is credited with creating one of the first fly patterns specifically designed to catch bass—the Henshall Bug. Prior to this, most bass fishing was done with over-sized versions of the brightly colored trout flies of the era. In her book *Favorite Flies and Their Histories* from 1892, Mary Orvis Marbury has a number of colored plates of bass-specific patterns. A state-by-state survey also lists patterns for various warmwater species as well as trout.

Interest in warmwater fly fishing continued to grow across the region due to several reasons. This was during the time when many of the trout waters were in decline due to the ravages of logging. Also, anglers were beginning to take more advantage of opportunities close to home. More fly patterns were developed specifically for bass, although cork-bodied flies appear to have come out of Arkansas and Missouri.

## The Formative Period: Twentieth Century

The Ft. Wayne Bucktail pattern appeared around 1900. The first commercial cork popper, called the Coaxer, came out of Chicago around 1910. The Wilder-Dilg was an early (1911) cork slider-style fly. Although developed in the Adirondacks, Tuttle's Devil Bug (1920) became an instant best-selling pattern in the region. By the 1920s fly fishing for smallmouth bass had become popular across much of the Midwest and Great Lakes area.

Around this same time, trout fly patterns began to change significantly. The earlier flies that were used for grayling and then brook trout were not productive. Catskill patterns were brought in and worked well on the finicky brown trout now dominant in many waters. Michigan tiers were quick to

With the establishment of brown trout in the waters of the Michigan, fly patterns evolved into Catskill-influenced designs. Many of these are still popular today and can be found in fly shop bins around the region. JERRY DARKES PHOTO

Early fly fishers took advantage of the species available to them. Due to the species diversity of the region, Midwest anglers developed patterns to catch multiple species. JIMMY CHANG PHOTO

mirror this style, and a number of patterns began to emerge. The Cabin Coachman by John Stephan, and Ernie Borchers's Drake series, reflect this design and are still catching fish today.

The original Adams dry was tied in 1922 by Len Halladay for use on Michigan's Boardman River. Perhaps the most popular dry fly ever created, this pattern has gone through numerous transformations and adaptations. In its current form, the standard Adams dry still echoes Catskill-style roots. Halladay's original version of the fly will still take fish today.

For fly tiers in the Midwest, the drawback to the Catskill designs was material cost and availability. When the Depression hit, this became even worse. There was no money to spare, even if materials could be found. Tiers had to use what they could find locally. Hackle came from barnyard chickens. Hair and fur were from locally harvested game animals. Sewing thread, bits of silk and wool, and even rubber strands from old truck seats all came into use.

Through the 1930s and into the 1940s, tying techniques and various patterns emerged across the region that are still in use today. The parachute-style of hackling was developed by William Avery Bush. Clarence Roberts and/or Earl Madsen tied deer hair parallel to and around the hook shank to form a dry fly body. Roberts also incorporated white deer belly hair for a parachute post. His Yellow Drake pattern imitates a number of light-colored mayflies, just by changing size.

Art Winnie started the use of turkey quill wings with his Michigan Hopper, later called Joe's Hopper. This pattern led to an ongoing series of grasshopper designs over the following decades by numerous tiers. One continuous feature characteristic of all these is the use of turkey quill wings.

Wisconsin contributed another classic fly pattern, the Hornberg. Named for game warden Frank Hornberg, this adaptable pattern can be tied as a dry fly, wet fly, or streamer. It is about as versatile as a fly can get and still remains extremely popular today.

Perhaps the single most important fly contribution out of this period was the Muddler Minnow. In terms of long-lasting influence, few fly patterns have had the significant impact the Muddler has. The version as we know it was originated by Don Gapen of Anoka, Minnesota, in 1936 for use on Ontario's Nipigon River. It may have been a modification of a simpler design used by local natives, but the clipped-hair head gave rise to an entire new class of streamer patterns that still continues today.

A number of significant fly tackle manufacturers and suppliers were based across the region, including names such as Cumings, Heddon, Millsite, Pflueger, Shakespeare, and South Bend. Rod makers included Lyle Dickerson, Paul Young, and Morris Kushner, who were based in Michigan.

The Muddler Fly

This Muddler fly was tied by Don Gapen who created it in 1936 while fishing the Nipigon River in Ontario, Canada. It's a fly created to represent the sculpins minnow. Today it's the leading trout fly

Gapen's ™

Authenticated by Dan Gapen Sr. son of Don Gapen

A Muddler Minnow tied by Dan Gapen, from the Nipigon Historical Museum. This nondescript fly led to a revolution in streamer fly design that continues to this day. JERRY DARKES PHOTO

Frost Flies began in the late 1800s and helped make the Midwest the fly-tying capital of the world. Stevens Point, Wisconsin, became a focal point of this activity. It continued well into the twentieth century. JIMMY CHANG PHOTO

It was in Stevens Point, Wisconsin, that fly tying was turned into an industry. This started in the late 1890s when a fly fisher by the name of Carrie Frost trained and hired several local girls to tie flies commercially for sale. Prior to this, the majority of flies sold in the United States came from Great Britain or were tied by first-generation immigrants from England, Ireland, or Scotland.

Frost had 150 girls working for her by 1919. The business was sold and became the Weber Tackle Company around 1920. By 1940, Weber, Worth, and a number of smaller, local companies employed over 500 local tiers and sold over 10 million flies annually. Frost is recognized as the founder of the American fly-tying industry, and Stevens Point was the fly-tying capital of the world for several decades.

During the late 1920s, Wisconsin native Helen Shaw began to make her mark as a fly tier. Shaw never received formal training, but was engaged in commercial tying while still in high school. She partnered with Sheboygan fishing tackle retailer Art Kade and tied an extensive assortment of patterns for sale. A single *Art Kade Fly Crafters* catalog

Frost Flies offered one of the first-ever crayfish patterns on the commercial market. This helped show the evolution of bass flies from the earlier brightly colored designs toward more imitative patterns.
JIMMY CHANG PHOTO

was printed in 1938, and Shaw tied every fly that was sold by Kade.

Shaw relocated to New York after meeting and marrying Hermann Kessler, the art director for *Field and Stream* magazine. By combining their talents, a breakthrough book, simply titled *Fly Tying*, was published in 1963. Each step of the tying process was shown in a photograph, and easily understood text accompanied each photo. *Fly Tying* still remains one the definitive publications of this art.

In the 1930s, George Leonard Herter out of Waseca, Minnesota, became a significant part of the fly-fishing business. Despite all of Herter's personal claims and exaggerations, his book *Professional Fly Tying, Spinning and Tackle Making* (1941) went through numerous editions and may be the most successful fly-tying book ever. Herter's catalogs were popular for several generations of anglers, and the arrival of the latest edition was an eagerly anticipated event.

After World War II, things were fairly quiet on the fly-fishing stage. The introduction of spinning tackle definitely had an impact as it swept across the country. Fly fishing

was not forgotten, but it did take a backseat. However, some significant events still occurred.

In 1945 angling friends Leon Martuch, Clare Harris, and Paul Rotiers founded a company called Scientific Anglers (SA) in Midland, Michigan. From their experience working for Dow Chemical, they developed the first PVC fly lines and, by the mid-1950s, the first truly modern floating fly lines. This was followed by the first modern sinking lines in 1960. In its 60-plus-year history, SA has stayed based in Midland and is a driving force in fly line coating, core advancement, and design.

Ernie Schwiebert was born in Chicago and caught his first trout from the Pere Marquette River in Michigan. His book *Matching the Hatch*, published in 1955 when Schwiebert was in his early twenties, set the bar for later angling entomology books. Schwiebert earned his bachelor's degree from Ohio State University. Parts of his angling observations came from time spent on Ohio's Mad River and the spring creeks near Castalia, Ohio.

Schwiebert's additional works including the massive *Nymphs* and two-volume *Trout*. Looking at the numerous articles he wrote for a variety of publications, Schwiebert is one of the leading fly-fishing writers ever. A pioneer in fisheries conservation, Schwiebert was involved in the founding of Trout Unlimited, the Theodore Gordon Fly Fishers, and the Federation of Fly Fishers.

In 1959 a group of concerned anglers met near Grayling, Michigan, to address the continuing decline of trout habitat on the main stream of the AuSable. Headed by George Griffith of Griffith Gnat fame, they formed an organization called Trout Unlimited. Now generally referred to as TU, this organization has celebrated 50-plus years of coldwater conservation across North America.

In 1966 coho salmon were stocked in Lake Michigan in an effort to help control populations of the invasive alewife, whose numbers had exploded to a point where die-offs led to lake shorelines covered with millions of rotting fish. The coho returned as mature fish in 1967 and started an angling craze that has continued since.

Salmon stockings had occurred periodically before this, but none had been successful. Chinook salmon stockings followed, which also took hold, and a whole industry developed around them. Fly anglers were drawn to these fish as they returned to rivers to spawn. The northwest side of Michigan, in particular, was the beneficiary of this phenomenon. Rivers like the Pere Marquette and Manistee lured anglers from around the world to their waters.

An important offshoot was the rediscovery of the steelhead that had been present in these rivers for decades. The fish were there, but little emphasis was put on fishing for them. Anglers targeting salmon began to take notice of the large trout that were showing up through the months of October and into November.

Although the salmon were often reluctant to take flies consistently, the big rainbows seemed to relish them. Anglers paid more attention to these migratory trout and took time to learn how to catch them. The late 1960s and early 1970s started a renaissance in Great Lakes steelhead. Although there were a number of locations where steelhead reproduced naturally, they again became part of the stocking programs of all the states bordering the lakes as well as the province of Ontario.

With the advent of better gear—graphite rods, disc-drag reels, and more technical fly lines—anglers had better tools to chase steelhead. The development of layering systems for clothing and breathable/waterproof fabrics allowed them to stand the rigors of typical Great Lake steelhead weather. Fly patterns evolved quickly from designs that copied West Coast examples to more natural imitations of the eggs and nymphs the fish fed on.

## Steps to the Present Day and Beyond

Through the last several decades of the twentieth century and into the present day, the steelhead has reigned as the crown jewel for Great Lakes and Midwest fly fishers. Traditional techniques using a swung fly and two-hand rods have returned to the scene. Switch rods were developed that allow several fly presentation styles from one rod. Fly lines have become very sophisticated and an integral part of taking the fly to the fish instead of relying on a chunk of lead.

There are a host of talented guides and fly tiers who helped to advance this fishery to its present state. Names such as Kevin Feenstra, Walt Grau, John Kluesing, Rick Kustich, Jeff Liskay, Dave Pinczkowski, Ray Schmidt, Greg Senyo, Matt Supinski, and numerous others span over four decades. They are familiar across the lakes and well beyond for their contributions to this fishery. Today, Great Lakes steelheading draws anglers from around the world and is an industry all its own that contributes millions of dollars to the regional economy.

Trout fishing also received a similar regeneration in 1970. Fishing writer Joe Brooks had an article in the August issue of *Outdoor Life* magazine about a new style of fly that two young anglers, Doug Swisher and Carl Richards, had developed after extensive research, much of which took place on Michigan's AuSable River. *Selective Trout* was published the year after and became an instant classic in fly-fishing literature.

A number of books had previously discussed entomology and imitation, but this was the first to present both insects and flies in large color photographs. The most important mayfly hatches were presented for a number of regions. Several distinctive fly styles were presented. Although Swisher and Richards were not the first to develop no-hackle, parachute, or emerger patterns, they brought them into the mindset of trout anglers everywhere.

Several other works followed from the Swisher-Richards duo. This spurred a number of entomology-based angling works from around the country that went into more detail about mayflies and also paid attention to caddis and stoneflies. All major classes of trout stream insects were finally being recognized.

In 1979 and 1980, Wisconsin biology professor Gary Borger presented several works—*Nymphing* and *Naturals*—that were true to the scientific veracity of entomology but presented everything in layman's terms. Borger has continued to be a major contributor to fly-fishing education for

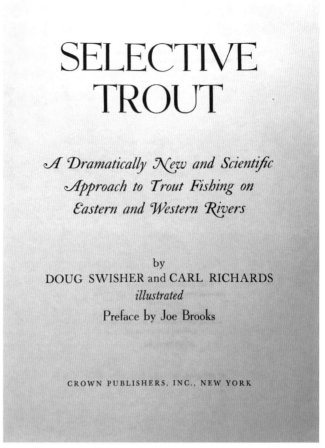

*Selective Trout*, published in 1971, became an instant fly-fishing classic and helped to highlight the Midwest as a leading area in trout fly development. Many of the concepts presented in the book are still in use today and continue to influence fly design and construction. JERRY DARKES PHOTO

Through the use of large color photographs, *Selective Trout* taught entomology to the average trout fly fisher. Much of the book is scientifically based, but presents information in an easily understood format. It also brought an assortment of fly-tying concepts together under one cover and introduced no-hackle dry flies to anglers. JERRY DARKES PHOTO

The public library in Grayling, Michigan, has a large area devoted to fly fishing and fly tying. The focus in on local waters, but there are books covering all aspects of fly fishing. It is well worth a stop and spending several hours.
JERRY DARKES PHOTO

nearly 50 years. His son, Jason, has followed in his father's footsteps.

In 1999, Michigan anglers/guides Kelly Galloup and Bob Linsenman wrote a revolutionary book, *Modern Streamers for Trophy Trout*. This work took the practice of streamer fishing to an entirely new plateau. Fly anglers now had a blueprint on how to target the largest fish in a river system all the time. The concepts presented in this book have spread to wherever trout are found. In addition, a whole genre of fly tying emerged based on the concepts Galloup and Linsenman presented. Guides like Russ Maddin and Alex Lafkas are on the cutting edge of continuing this work.

As we look to the present day, trout fishing and fly design innovation continues. Night fishing for brown trout has developed a significant following, spurred by guides such as Tommy Lynch. Called "mousin'," this technique focuses on the largest fish in a system and has migrated to other trout fishing areas.

On the warmwater side of the aisle, the quest for targeting the apex predators in a system has also developed. Wisconsin guides Bill Sherer, Larry Mann, and Wendy Williamson, along with Michigan's Brian Meszaros, pioneered early fly fishing and guiding for muskellunge. *Muskie on the Fly* (2008) by Robert Tomes and the recent *Hunting Musky with a Fly* (2017) by Rick Kustich focus specifically on targeting muskie. A host of younger guides and fly tiers are

following this lead, and catching muskie on flies has become a mainstream activity across the region.

Smallmouth bass are also receiving well-deserved recognition as a key fly-fishing target.

Tim Landwehr and his crew are significant promoters of this on Wisconsin's Menominee River. Mike Schultz and his guide staff have opened up awareness of the warmwater rivers of central Michigan. A number of trout and steelhead guides are also shifting to smallmouth during the warmest months of the summer.

Tim Holschlag's *Smallmouth Fly Fishing* (2006) is a truly comprehensive look at smallmouth. Nearly all the information is based on Holschlag's experience fishing the waters of the Midwest and Great Lakes. *Smallmouth: Modern Fly Fishing Methods, Tactics & Techniques* (2017) by Dave Karczinski features the latest in fly patterns and techniques from the top guides in the Midwest.

Even the open waters of the Great Lakes are home to fly anglers. The late Roger LaPenter pioneered smallmouth fishing on Lake Superior's Chequamegon Bay. Kevin Morlock and his Indigo Guide Service have brought fly anglers from around the globe to chase carp in the waters around Lake Michigan's Beaver Island. Karl Weixlmann works the Lake Erie shoreline near Erie, Pennsylvania. Brian Meszaros was a fixture on Lake St. Clair and the Detroit River, and Eric Grajewski has assumed that role.

I combined my 30-plus years of personal Great Lakes experience along with information from a unique group of fly fishers to write my first book, *Fly Fishing the Inland Oceans* (2013). We have shown that most of the fish in the Great Lakes can be taken on a fly. The surface has barely been scratched here, and there is still much work to be done.

Much of modern fly fishing as we know it has roots in the Midwest and Great Lakes regions. After early stages of development in the Catskills and Poconos, subsequent innovation and progress took place in the Midwest. Michigan has played a major role and is still a major contributor.

Some of our most recognized and enduring fly patterns originated here, and a significant cottage industry of independent fly tiers supplying area shops still exists. Cane rod building is thriving, with numerous custom makers across the region. Fly fishing is alive and well.

Trout populations are stable and steelhead are present in significant numbers in all five of the Great Lakes. Warmwater awareness continues to grow as more anglers focus on this resource. This region will continue to be a significant workshop for the development of new fly patterns and fishing techniques. The purpose of this book is to provide a look into the past, see what is happening now, and open a window to the future.

## A Special Note on Fly Patterns, Recipes, and Components

Each of the following chapters presents a cross section of significant flies either from or for use in the Midwest and

Great Lakes regions. The United States and Canada are both represented. There are contributions from both professional and hobby tiers. The fly pattern categories presented cover the full range of fly-fishing opportunities available. There are few places where such a broad range of waters and species is available to so many anglers.

Mention is made of both influential patterns and their creators in each chapter. Patterns little known outside the area are also listed. If I have missed a significant person or pattern, please accept my apologies. The more research that took place, the more patterns and tiers I uncovered. This could have continued endlessly, and there had to be a stopping point to stay within the parameters of this book.

Please understand that many patterns have variations in their recipes. When a specific recipe was given by the tier, it was listed that way. If no recipe was received or not found, I interpreted the materials as accurately as possible—50-plus years of fly-tying experience supports this. For these I listed a usable hook, thread, or material and also substituted for an item that may no longer be available. Fly tying is a continuously evolving process, and new products come into use while others go away or may no longer be available. This is part of both the challenge and the fun.

As you review the recipes as they are written, there are a few things to keep in mind. For consistency, the parts of the fly are listed in the sequence that they are typically tied in. The materials listed under a certain category for a pattern will also be listed in the sequence they would be secured. For example, if you see "Wing: Olive Arctic fox,

Fly-tying thread has gotten more specialized through the years. New, stronger materials are available in a wide range of colors for all tying applications. JERRY DARKES PHOTO

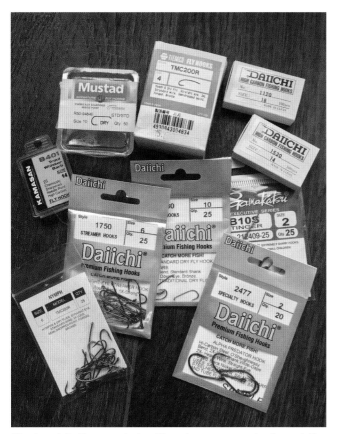

The hook is the most significant component of most fly patterns. Selecting the proper hook is a primary step in fly construction. There are hooks for generalized use as well as for special applications. JERRY DARKES PHOTO

pearl Flashabou, peacock herl," it means the wing of the fly has olive Arctic fox tied in first, then pearl Flashabou over, with peacock herl on top.

Please note that this is not meant to be a beginner fly-tying manual. I assume that most readers will have at least rudimentary tying skills. With the sequence of materials as listed in the recipe and the photograph, most tiers should be able to interpret the fly assembly. Many of the notes will contain information on the fly construction. Some of this is from the pattern originator, and some is additional information from me to help in the construction. Certain critical techniques will be presented in detail.

If you don't have a particular material that a pattern calls for, fear not. There is likely an acceptable substitute in most cases. This may be a more critical factor with hook size and color in matching specific insects with dry flies, but do the best with what you have to work with. It seems that dry fly size is often more of a determining factor than color when it comes to success.

At present there is no sizing standard between thread brands, and each has its own unique system. For most of our fly-tying history, thread selection was quite limited. A number of earlier patterns did not show a particular brand, but have a size such as 6/0 listed. This likely refers to Danville thread, which was the primary brand available for many years, so it is listed as such. Monocord is also a Danville product. An 8/0 listing is likely a Uni product, and so on. I have listed a single thread type for each pattern, but substitiution is certainly doable.

There is now a host of tying threads on the market. Threads are found in very small diameters with amazing strength in a variety of colors. These make it easier for most tiers to work on hook sizes like #18 and smaller. Some of the recipes present the latest in threads.

A similar scenario occurs with hooks. For many years Mustad was the primary hook brand available. Partridge and several other English hooks were available through some outlets, but difficult to locate. TMC and Daiichi fly hooks appeared around 30 years ago and have taken over as leading brands. More recently Gamakatsu, Ahrex, and several other brands have become available and are favored in several specialty applications.

The hook is the "heart" of most patterns, and all assembly takes place around it. Older pattern recipes often listed hooks very generically, such as "standard dry fly" or "4xl streamer." In these situations, I replaced it with a modern, readily available equivalent. The tier can certainly substitute a similar hook as desired.

The brown trout is the staple for dry fly anglers across the Midwest and Great Lakes. Whether on the famous AuSable in Michigan, the Driftless area of Wisconsin, Minnesota, and Iowa, or Ohio's Mad River—the brown trout is the primary target. JIMMY CHANG PHOTO

# Dry Flies

## INTRODUCTION

The dry fly has reached much of its present state of development through the efforts of Midwest and Great Lakes anglers and tiers. Many of the patterns, current material applications, and tying techniques had their origins in this region. Various early designs were generalists or attractors, but as knowledge of the entomology of the area grew, specific imitations began to appear.

The mayfly rules across the region as the most recognized and imitated insect. They are abundant in all moving waters as well as many lakes. A full range of species has been presented, from the tiny Trico to the giant Hex. The primary mayfly species are shown in various stages of development. This allows many options to create flies for "selective trout."

The various tiers show different paths to reach similar conclusions. Pattern templates are presented where, by varying hook size and material coloration, a full range of mayfly species can be imitated. Jerry Reagan's spinners, Ed McCoy's duns, along with emergers tied by Charlie Chlysta and Dennis Potter, are great examples of this.

Caddis and stoneflies are less represented. This is not to diminish their importance; they just do not share the same status as the mayfly across the region. Their application is often more localized. Terrestrials are an important category, first given recognition in this area. Night flies have turned into an art form all their own.

Finally, I want to emphasize again that I have tried to give all pattern recipes in their original form with as much detail as possible. Some of the descriptions are quite generic, so it will be up to the tier to select a usable item. Hook, thread, and material substitutions can be made if a particular item is not available. Let logic rule here.

The Adams may be the most recognized dry fly worldwide. This pattern was developed for use on Michigan's Boardman River. The original version (left) has a Catskill-design influence that has carried into the modern version (right). Few trout anglers will venture onstream without some version of the Adams in their fly box.
JIMMY CHANG PHOTO

## Group 1: Adams Family

It would be difficult to go fly fishing for trout anywhere in the world and open an angler's fly box without finding some version of an Adams dry fly. Few flies have the universal acceptance by both anglers and trout of the Adams.

(**Left to right**) Row 1: Halladay Adams, Standard Adams, Parachute Adams; Row 2: Half Adams, Flat Wing Adams, Adams Midge. JIMMY CHANG PHOTO.

## HALLADAY ADAMS

*Originated by Len Halladay, tied by Jerry Darkes*

- **Hook:** #10-20 Mustad 94840
- **Thread:** Black 6/0 Danville
- **Tail:** Golden pheasant tippets
- **Body:** Coarse gray wool yarn
- **Wings:** Barred Plymouth Rock rooster hackle tips, oversized, three-quarters spent
- **Hackle:** Barred Plymouth Rock and Rhode Island Red rooster hackle, oversized and full

**Notes:** This is the original Adams pattern as tied by Len Halladay in 1922 for his friend Charles F. Adams. It was first used on the Boardman River near Traverse City, Michigan.

## STANDARD ADAMS

*Originator unknown, tied by Jerry Darkes*

- **Hook:** #10-20 Daiichi 1180
- **Thread:** Black or gray 70-denier UTC
- **Tail:** Grizzly and brown hackle fibers, mixed
- **Body:** Muskrat underfur or gray dry fly dubbing
- **Wings:** Grizzly hackle tips, upright and divided
- **Hackle:** Grizzly and brown, mixed

**Notes:** Perhaps the most recognized dry fly pattern worldwide, the modern Adams tempts trout everywhere they are found. It imitates nothing specific, but has a buggy look that can work during a hatch or just fishing the water.

## PARACHUTE ADAMS

*Originator unknown, tied by Jerry Darkes*

- **Hook:** #10-20 Daiichi 1180
- **Thread:** Black or gray 70-denier UTC
- **Tail:** Grizzly and brown hackle fibers, mixed
- **Body:** Muskrat underfur or gray dry fly dubbing
- **Wing:** Single upright post of calf tail, Hi-Viz, or similar material in white, orange, or chartreuse
- **Hackle:** Grizzly and brown, mixed

**Notes:** The parachute version of the Adams (and all dry flies) work best on smooth, flat water. Tiers will often substitute cree tail fibers and hackle in the modern version of the Adams in place of the mixed grizzly and brown. This simplifies the tying process and doesn't seem to affect the productivity of the fly.

## HALF ADAMS

*Originated and tied by Jerry Darkes*

- **Hook:** #10-20 Daiichi 1180
- **Thread:** Gray 70-denier UTC
- **Tail:** Variant hackle fibers
- **Body:** Muskrat underfur
- **Wings:** Mallard flank fibers, upright and divided
- **Hackle:** Variant

**Notes:** Back in my early days of fly tying, there was not a consistent supply of good grizzly dry fly hackle and any that could be found was pricey. The same for grizzly hackle tips. There were capes found in various mixed-color shades called "Variant," and many had a barred brown color base. Mallard flank was already used in many dry patterns and easy to get. This pattern produced a lot of fish and still does today.

## FLAT WING ADAMS

*Originated and tied by Jerry Darkes*

- **Hook:** #14-16 Daiichi 1310
- **Thread:** Gray 70-denier UTC
- **Body:** Gray dry fly dubbing
- **Wings:** Grizzly hackle tips, tied flat
- **Hackle:** Grizzly and brown, mixed, or cree

**Notes:** I'm not certain that I was the first to make this version of the Adams, but I have never seen anyone else tie it. This goes back to the early 1970s, and I have tied and used this fly for many years. It is a good pattern to try when rising fish will not respond to other flies and no hatch is visible. It can also be fished as a terrestrial pattern. The Daiichi 1310 hook has a 1X short shank, so you can present a smaller fly on an extra-wide gap hook. In theory, this hooks better and is easier to remove.

## ADAMS MIDGE

*Originator unknown, tied by Jerry Darkes*

- **Hook:** #20-24 Daiichi 1100
- **Thread:** Gray 70-denier UTC
- **Tail:** Grizzly and brown, mixed, or cree
- **Body:** Gray dry fly dubbing
- **Hackle:** Grizzly and brown, mixed, or cree

**Notes:** Setting the grizzly hackle tip wings on small hooks can be a daunting task. This simplified version of the Adams is doable for most tiers. Using cree hackle makes it even easier. This hook has a wider gap than standard, giving more positive hooking and easier removal.

## Group 2: Midwest Classics

This is an assortment of patterns with true Midwestern roots, coming out of both northern Michigan and Wisconsin. Going forward you may find that a number of these flies could be in multiple groups, so please excuse me if you feel I placed a pattern incorrectly. The ultimate goal is to give an overview of pattern history, development, and application of use.

(Left to right) Row 1: Madsen's Skunk Dry, Cabin Coachman, Corey's Calftail, Borchers Drake Parachute, Roberts Yellow Drake; Row 2: Madsen's Barber Pole, Hornberg, Hornberg Variation, Pass Lake Special, Hairwing No-Hackle; Row 3: Close Carpet Fly, Calf Hair Downwing; Row 4: Duck Quill No-Hackle (2 colors). JIMMY CHANG PHOTO

### MADSEN'S SKUNK DRY

*Originated by Earl Madsen, tied by Jerry Darkes*

- **Hook:** #8 Mustad 94840 or 94831
- **Thread:** Black 6/0 Danville
- **Tail:** Gray squirrel
- **Body:** Black chenille
- **Wing:** White or natural deer hair
- **Legs:** White rubber strands or rubber hackle

**Notes:** Earl Madsen was a Grayling, Michigan, guide and fly tier. This historical pattern was created in the 1940s and thought to be the first to incorporate rubber legs. This fly is also called the Michigan Skunk and AuSable Skunk. A black or dark brown hackle can be added to increase floatability. In addition to trout, it is also a good pattern for bluegill and other warmwater species.

### CABIN COACHMAN

*Originated by John Stephan and George Mason, tied by Jerry Darkes*

- **Hook:** #10-14 Mustad 94840
- **Thread:** Black 6/0 Danville
- **Tail:** Red hackle fibers
- **Body:** Peacock herl
- **Wings:** Andalusian (blue dun) hackle tips
- **Hackle:** Brown and grizzly, mixed

**Notes:** This pattern was developed in the mid-1930s by AuSable fly fishers John Stephan and George Mason. It reflects the Catskill school of tying dry flies. Another impressionistic pattern, it has been catching fish in northern Michigan for many decades.

## COREY'S CALFTAIL

*Originated by Ralph Corey, tied by Jerry Darkes*

- **Hook:** #8-16 Mustad 94840
- **Thread:** Black 6/0 Danville
- **Tail:** White calf tail
- **Body:** Yellow, red, or gray dubbing or chenille
- **Rib:** Gold or silver wire
- **Wing:** A single bunch of white calf tail
- **Hackle:** Brown

**Notes:** Another early to mid-twentieth-century pattern, this design is by Ralph Corey. It was created to target the brook trout of northern Michigan, but was also used in larger sizes to target big browns at night. Larger sizes, #8-10, are palmered with a brown hackle.

## BORCHERS DRAKE

*Originated by Ernie Borchers, tied by Jerry Darkes*

- **Hook:** #8-16 Mustad 94840
- **Thread:** Black 6/0 Danville
- **Body:** Mottled turkey quill fibers
- **Wings:** Blue dun hackle tips
- **Hackle:** Grizzly and brown, mixed

**Notes:** This pattern by AuSable River guide Ernie Borchers dates back to the 1940s and is still popular today. The initial version was tied in a size 10 to imitate the Brown Drake mayfly. Various sizes gradually came into the mix to imitate the various dark-bodied mayflies of the area.

Borcher's Drake. JERRY DARKES PHOTO

## BORCHERS DRAKE PARACHUTE

*Originated by Ernie Borchers, tied by Old AuSable Fly Shop*

- **Hook:** #10-16 Daiichi 1180
- **Thread:** Black 70-denier UTC
- **Tail:** Moose mane
- **Body:** Natural turkey quill fibers
- **Wings:** Fine deer hair
- **Hackle:** Grizzly and brown, mixed

**Notes:** This is a modern variation of the pattern created by Ernie Borchers to imitate various brown-colored mayflies. It is important to note that the parachute-style hackling technique was originated around 1930 by William Avery Brush.

## ROBERTS YELLOW DRAKE

*Originated by Clarence Roberts, tied by Old AuSable Fly Shop*

- **Hook:** #8-16 Daiichi 1180
- **Thread:** Yellow 70-denier UTC
- **Tail:** Pheasant tail fibers
- **Body:** Natural deer hair
- **Wing/Post:** White deer belly hair
- **Hackle:** Ginger

**Notes:** A game warden from Grayling, Michigan, Clarence Roberts developed this pattern in the 1950s. In this original coloration it mimics a variety of light-colored mayflies, from the giant *Hexagenia* to various Sulphur species by tying on different size hooks. By altering the thread and hackle colors, an extensive range of mayflies can be imitated. Other than updating hooks and thread, this pattern has not really changed since its introduction.

## MADSEN'S BARBER POLE

*Originated by Earl Madsen, tied by Old AuSable Fly Shop*

- **Hook:** #8-10 Mustad 94840
- **Thread:** Black 6/0 Danville
- **Tail:** Woodchuck guard hairs
- **Body:** Yellow poly yarn
- **Rib:** Maroon embroidery yarn
- **Wings:** Grizzly hackle tips
- **Hackle:** Grizzly and brown, mixed

**Notes:** Another pattern from Earl Madsen that goes back nearly 100 years. Over time there have been a number of variations of this pattern. The body/ribbing combination gives a distinct imitation of a segmented body.

## HORNBERG

*Originated by Frank Hornberg, tied by Jerry Darkes*

- **Hook:** #8-12 Mustad 94840
- **Thread:** Black 6/0 Danville
- **Body:** Flat silver tinsel
- **Underwing:** Yellow calf tail or bucktail
- **Wings:** Mallard flank feather tips, tied parallel to the hook shank
- **Cheeks:** Jungle cock
- **Hackle:** Grizzly

**Notes:** Wisconsin game warden Frank Hornberg developed this pattern in the 1920s. The Weber Tackle Co. offered it as a commercial pattern through the 1940s. It is a unique fly in that it can be fished dry as a grasshopper or caddis/stonefly imitation. It can also be a baitfish imitation when fished subsurface.

## HORNBERG VARIATION

*Originator unknown, tied by Jerry Darkes*

- **Hook:** #10-14 Daiichi 1180
- **Thread:** Black 70-denier UTC
- **Body:** Pearl Krystal Flash
- **Wing:** Yellow hackle fibers or bucktail, mallard flank fibers
- **Hackle:** Grizzly and brown, mixed

**Notes:** As with many older, classic patterns, numerous variations of the Hornberg evolved over time. This is a productive searching pattern suggestive of either a caddis or stonefly.

## PASS LAKE SPECIAL

*Originated by E. Stubenvoll, tied by Jerry Darkes*

- **Hook:** #10-14 Mustad 94840
- **Thread:** Black 6/0 Danville
- **Tail:** Mallard flank fibers
- **Body:** Black chenille or peacock herl
- **Wing:** White calf tail
- **Hackle:** Brown

**Notes:** This classic Wisconsin pattern came from the vise of Rev. E. Stubenvoll in the mid-1930s, and was originally used for chasing big brook trout in Ontario. It was found to be a productive pattern when fished locally. This is another fly that adapts well as a dry, wet, or streamer pattern.

## HAIRWING NO-HACKLE

*Originated by Doug Swisher and Carl Richards, tied by Jerry Darkes*

- **Hook:** #10-20 Mustad 94840
- **Thread:** 6/0 Danville, to complement body color
- **Tail:** Deer body hair fibers
- **Body:** Fine poly or fur dubbing, specific to the insect being imitated
- **Wing:** Deer body hair, tied upright and fanned out

**Notes:** With the publication of their book *Selective Trout* in 1971, Doug Swisher and Carl Richards expanded the concept of specific insect imitation with the use of dry flies. From 1965, this was likely the first hackle-less dry fly of a new era in fly fishing and tying. Focused on mayflies, hook size and body color are adjusted as needed.

## CLOSE CARPET FLY

*Originated by George Close, tied by Jerry Darkes*

- **Hook:** #10-14 TMC 2312
- **Thread:** Black 6/0 Uni
- **Tail/Abdomen:** Deer body hair
- **Wing:** Deer body hair
- **Thorax:** Coarse Antron yarn

**Notes:** This Wisconsin pattern imitates the larger tan to dark-colored mayflies such as March, Brown, Gray Fox, Brown Drake, and *Isonychia*. It is an interesting combination of techniques. It has the deer hair body developed by Earl Madsen and Clarence Roberts. The wing reflects the original no-hackle design of Swisher and Richards. The wing is set upright and fanned per their Hairwing No-Hackle. Antron carpet fibers are spun in a loop and wrapped both behind and in front of the wing for support.

## CALF HAIR DOWNWING

*Originator unknown, tied by Jerry Darkes*

- **Hook:** #14 TMC 100
- **Thread:** Yellow 8/0 Uni
- **Tail:** Bleached elk hock
- **Body:** Yellow synthetic or fur dubbing
- **Wing:** White calf tail
- **Hackle:** Dun

**Notes:** Another Wisconsin pattern, this is suggestive of the Little Yellow Stonefly. These insects are found across much of the Midwest through the late spring and early summer.

## DUCK QUILL NO-HACKLE (2 COLORS)

*Originated by Doug Swisher and Carl Richards, tied by Jerry Darkes*

- **Hook:** #12-18 Mustad 94840
- **Thread:** 6/0 Danville (use finer thread on #16 and smaller), to complement body color
- **Tail:** Split hackle fibers or synthetic Microfibbetts, specific to the insect being imitated

- **Body:** Fine synthetic or fur dubbing, specific to the insect being imitated
- **Wings:** Duck wing quill sections

**Notes:** This design dates back to 1967 as a refinement to the Hairwing No-Hackle pattern. It was introduced with the publication of Richards and Swisher's book *Selective Trout*. Also called the Sidewinder No-Hackle, this fly works best on smooth, flat water with super-selective fish. The wings are quite fragile, but a small touch of Flexament on the tips will help protect them.

## Group 3: AuSable Specials

These patterns are mainly found in the Grayling, Michigan, area and used throughout the AuSable River system. They certainly have use on other waters. The late Calvin (Rusty) Gates created the majority of these and should be both recognized and remembered for his many contributions to fly tying and fly fishing, along with being a tireless advocate for the AuSable River.

**(Left to right)** Row 1: Dust Bunny, Awesome, Smock's Sulphur, Rusty's White Knot; Row 2: Rusty's Spinner, Rusty's Orange Sedge, Rusty's SRB. JIMMY CHANG PHOTO

## DUST BUNNY

*Originated by Rusty Gates, tied by Gates Lodge*

- **Hook:** #12 Daiichi 1180
- **Thread:** Brown 8/0 Uni
- **Tail:** Dun snowshoe hare foot guard hair
- **Body:** Mix of one-third each brown olive SLF, gray SLF, and gray beaver dubbing
- **Wing:** Dun snowshoe hare foot guard hair

**Notes:** This pattern from the late, great Rusty Gates is an offshoot of the Fran Betters Usual fly. The wing is made with the hair being tied in to form a "V." The recipe given here is specific as an *Isonychia* emerger, and Josh Greenburg of Gates Lodge calls it the "ugliest fly they sell." Size and color can be varied to imitate a number of different mayflies.

## AWESOME

*Originator unknown, tied by Gates Lodge*

- **Hook:** #12-16 Daiichi 1180
- **Thread:** Orange 8/0 Uni
- **Tail:** Moose fibers
- **Body:** Peacock herl
- **Wings:** Grizzly hackle tips
- **Post:** White Hi-Viz, trimmed short
- **Hackle:** Grizzly, parachute-style

**Notes:** This is the current version of a pattern that originated in the 1950s. It is a good deerfly imitation and a general summertime searching pattern.

## SMOCK'S SULPHUR

*Originated by Bob Smock, tied by Gates Lodge*

- **Hook:** #14-18 Daiichi 1180
- **Thread:** Yellow 8/0 Uni
- **Tail:** Two tangerine-dyed hackle fibers, 2 times length of shank
- **Body:** Yellow dubbing
- **Post:** Fine white deer hair
- **Hackle:** Tangerine-dyed, parachute-style

**Notes:** This pattern is from the early 1980s and is also called the Tangerine Dun or Tangerine Dream. Bob Smock used Rit #40 Tangerine Dye for the hackle. Modern sulphur-colored dubbings often have a hint of orange in them. This is likely the effect Smock created with the dye color he used.

## RUSTY'S WHITE KNOT

*Originated by Rusty Gates, tied by Gates Lodge*

- **Hook:** #10-12 Daiichi 1180
- **Thread:** Dark brown 6/0 Danville
- **Tail:** Moose fibers
- **Body:** Reddish brown deer hair
- **Post:** White deer hair
- **Hackle:** Dark dun, parachute-style

**Notes:** This popular summer pattern from the early 1990s is another *Isonychia* imitation. It evolved from Rusty Gates's original Spinner pattern (below).

## RUSTY'S SPINNER

*Originated by Rusty Gates, tied by Gates Lodge*

- **Hook:** #8-18 Daiichi 1180
- **Thread:** Rusty brown 6/0-8/0 Uni
- **Tail:** Three moose fibers
- **Body:** Reddish brown deer hair parallel to hook shank
- **Wings:** Grizzly hackle tips, tied three-quarters spent
- **Hackle:** Grizzly and brown, mixed

**Notes:** Another pattern from Rusty Gates, this is from the mid-1980s and imitates a wide range of mayfly spinners. The body hair was colored with Rit #20 Cocoa Brown Dye. It may be one of the best spinner patterns ever created and can be fished on trout streams anywhere. This is a fly to have in your box all the time!

## RUSTY'S ORANGE SEDGE

*Originated by Rusty Gates, tied by Gates Lodge*

- **Hook:** #10-12 Daiichi 1180
- **Thread:** Orange 6/0 Uni
- **Body:** Pale orange dubbing, brown hackle
- **Wing:** Natural deer body hair
- **Hackle:** Brown

**Notes:** Through the AuSable River system and across much of the Midwest, mayflies receive the majority of interest for dry fly fishing. This is a pattern for the late summer and fall that draws topwater attention when mayfly activity has started to slow down. The larger caddis are not found in abundance, but seem to attract a lot of surface interest.

## RUSTY'S SRB

*Originated by Rusty Gates, tied by Gates Lodge*

- **Hook:** #12-16 Daiichi 1180
- **Thread:** Black 6/0 Danville
- **Body:** Peacock herl
- **Back:** 2 mm foam strip
- **Wings:** Grizzly hen hackle tips, flat
- **Hackle:** Grizzly

**Notes:** Another Rusty Gates pattern from the 1980s. This deerfly imitation continues to catch fish. It is an effective searching pattern and is likely also taken as an ant or beetle. The foam strip is tied in at the back of the hook and pulled over the top of the peacock herl.

# Group 4: Hatch Matchers, Hendrickson

In many areas of the Midwest, *Ephemerella subvaria* is the first major mayfly hatch of the season and highly anticipated by anglers. Time varies considerably depending on latitude. On Ohio's Mad River, Hendricksons may start showing up in late March. On the northern edge of their range, they may not show until late May.

Males and females differ in both coloration and size, with trout showing a preference for one or the other at times. Look for emergence in the afternoon and duns often hatching during periods of inclement weather. Mated females will have a visible yellow egg sac. Spinners usually fall in the evening, but a period of cold weather may push this until morning.

**(Left to right)** Row 1: The Hendrickson Usual, Hendrickson Cripple/Quigley-Style; Row 2: Female Hendrickson Comparadun, Male Hendrickson Comparadun; Row 3: Red Quill Stacker, Riverhouse Hendrickson Spinner.
JIMMY CHANG PHOTO

## THE HENDRICKSON USUAL

*Originated by Fran Betters, tied by Gates Lodge*

- **Hook:** #12-14 TMC 101 or equivalent
- **Thread:** Burnt orange 6/0 Uni
- **Tail:** Dun snowshoe rabbit foot guard hair
- **Body:** Snowshoe rabbit foot underfur cut with Hendrickson pink dubbing
- **Wing:** Dun snowshoe rabbit foot guard hair

**Notes:** This is a very effective emerger pattern. It differs slightly from the standard Usual in that colors are adjusted a bit to closer match a Hendrickson mayfly. The tail and wing should be dun or gray colored and the body dubbing should have a hint of pink. The Usual can be adjusted for size and color to match a number of mayflies.

## HENDRICKSON CRIPPLE/QUIGLEY-STYLE

*Originated by Bob Quigley, tied by Gates Lodge*

- **Hook:** #14 TMC 100
- **Thread:** Burnt orange 8/0 Uni
- **Tail:** Brown Antron over wood duck flank fibers
- **Thorax:** Tan turkey biot
- **Abdomen:** Hendrickson pink dubbing, dun hackle
- **Wing:** Fine deer hair or yearling elk hair

**Notes:** The Hendrickson is a mayfly where fish can become very selective to specific stages of the hatch. The Quigley Cripple template is specific to those bugs that get caught in their nymph shuck and never fully emerge, becoming easy prey for trout. Be sure to trim the hackle on the bottom. Again, by varying size and color, a number of mayflies can be imitated.

## FEMALE HENDRICKSON COMPARADUN

*Originated by Al Caucci and Bob Nastasi, tied by Gates Lodge*

- **Hook:** #14 Daiichi 1100 or 1110
- **Thread:** Tan 8/0 Uni
- **Tail:** Dun hackle fibers or Microfibbetts
- **Abdomen:** Pink turkey biot
- **Thorax:** Tan or Hendrickson pink dry fly dubbing
- **Wing:** Fine deer hair

**Notes:** Again we see a specific fly design or template in a color scheme specific to the Hendrickson mayfly. The wing hair is tied upright and spread into a 180-degree arc. Here the split tail and wing work to hold the fly upright on the surface. The Comparadun is best on flat-water applications to target selective fish. They do not float well on broken water.

Fly shop bins tell what insects are currently hatching. Looks like it's Hendrickson time! JERRY DARKES PHOTO

Hendrickson time! This well-stocked fly box shows a full lineup of Hendrickson dries in the middle-right rows. Emerger to spinner phases are all well covered, along with several other mayfly patterns. JERRY DARKES PHOTO

## MALE HENDRICKSON COMPARADUN

*Originated by Al Caucci and Bob Nastasi, tied by Gates Lodge*

- **Hook:** #14 Daiichi 1100 or 1110
- **Thread:** Brown 8/0 Uni
- **Tail:** Split dun hackle fibers or Microfibbets
- **Abdomen:** Tan dry fly dubbing, tied thin
- **Thorax:** Tan dry fly dubbing
- **Wing:** Fine deer hair

**Notes:** As mentioned above, the male Hendrickson mayfly is a bit larger and colored different than the female. The Comparadun template has been adjusted specific to this.

## RED QUILL STACKER

*Originated and tied by John Sheets*

- **Hook:** #14 Daiichi 1180
- **Thread:** Burnt orange 70-denier UTC
- **Tail:** Moose body hairs
- **Body:** Stripped dark ginger hackle quill (soaked in water)
- **Post/Wing:** Rust-colored Antron yarn, medium dun saddle hackle

**Notes:** Northern Michigan native John Sheets has been a fly angler and tier for a number of decades. This design

was created from his disappointment in conventional spinner patterns. He feels this design gives a more realistic spent-wing imprint on the surface film. It also increases both flotation and visibility—both are important advantages for the angler. The yarn is tied in opposite the hook point, wrapped with hackle, then tied down over the body.

## RIVERHOUSE HENDRICKSON SPINNER

*Originated and tied by Dennis Potter*

- **Hook:** #14 TMC 100
- **Thread:** Brown 70-denier UTC
- **Egg Sac:** Yellow Superfine dubbing, in a ball
- **Tail:** Light dun Microfibbets, tied long
- **Body:** Tying thread
- **Thorax:** Brown Superfine dubbing
- **Wings:** Clear crinkled Z-Lon
- **ID post:** Fluorescent yellow yarn

**Notes:** We will see more from Dennis Potter. The egg sac is a standard feature on a number of Hendrickson spinner patterns, and fish may be selective to feeding on spinners with the egg sac. The ID post makes it easier to spot the fly as it sits flush in the water.

## Group 5: Hatch Matchers, Sulphur

*Ephemerella invaria* is one of the most widespread of all upper Midwest mayfly hatches. The *invaria* species hatches mid-to late afternoon May into July. It often overlaps with the later hatching, smaller-size *Ephmerella dorthea*, which begins in the latter part of May. These two are often generically referred to as "sulphurs." The *invaria* will be a size 12-14, while *dorthea* is size 16-18. Actual color of these insects can vary from stream to stream, but the *dorthea* species is always a more pale yellow color.

   Spinners come back to the water in the evening the day after hatching. At times, both duns and spinners will be on the water at the same time. Careful observation is required, and fish may switch from feeding on duns to spinners. If this occurs with both *invaria* and *dorthea* present, the angler has a dilemma deciding which to imitate.

**(Left to right)** Row 1: Ted's Sulphur CDC Emerger, Sulphur Usual Variant; Row 2: Sulphur Thorax; Row 3: Sulphur Hackled Comparadun; Row 4: Small Sulphur Spinner, Large Sulphur Spinner. JIMMY CHANG PHOTO

## TED'S SULPHUR CDC EMERGER

*Originated and tied by Ted Kraimer*

- **Hook:** #14-16 Daiichi 1130
- **Thread:** Yellow 70-denier UTC
- **Tail:** Rust-colored Antron fibers
- **Abdomen:** Sulphur yellow turkey biot
- **Thorax:** Yellow Superfine dubbing, sparse dun hackle
- **Wing:** Looped gray CDC feather

**Notes:** For some reason known only to them, trout often prefer the emerger stage of the Sulphur hatch. They may still deliberately focus on emergers as dun numbers increase, so watch feeding fish carefully. This is an effective, durable pattern that has proven itself on the AuSable, Manistee, and other Midwestern rivers.

## SULPHUR USUAL VARIANT

*Originated by Fran Betters, tied by Gates Lodge*

- **Hook:** #14-16 Daiichi 1180
- **Thread:** Pale yellow 6/0 Uni
- **Tail:** Four to five wood duck fibers
- **Abdomen:** Yellow turkey biot
- **Thorax:** Yellow dry fly dubbing
- **Wing:** Hair from a snowshoe rabbit foot

**Notes:** This pattern imitates the almost-hatched dun. It goes a step beyond the true emerger, as the wing is upright and the body is almost fully out of the shuck.

## SULPHUR THORAX

*Originated by Vince Marinaro, tied by Jon Uhlenhop*

- **Hook:** #12-18 Daiichi 1180
- **Thread:** Dun 14/0 Veevus
- **Tail:** Dun hackle fibers or Microfibbetts, split
- **Body:** Orange yellow to pale yellow dry fly dubbing. Fly-Rite #33 Orange Sulphur is a popular material for the *invaria* species.
- **Wing:** Dun Sparkle yarn
- **Hackle:** Two medium to light blue dun dry fly hackles

**Notes:** The thorax-style dry fly was first introduced in 1950 by Vince Marinaro for use on the limestone streams of southeast Pennsylvania. The concepts behind this style of tying are presented in his book, *A Modern Dry Fly Code*. A single wing is set more toward the middle of the hook. The hackles are wound behind and in front of the wing to form an "X" and then clipped flat. This style of tying remains popular in locales with plenty of smooth, flat flows and selective-feeding trout, as the fly sits into the surface film. By varying size and color, numerous mayfly species can be imitated

## SULPHUR HACKLED COMPARADUN

*Originator unknown, tied by Gates Lodge*

- **Hook:** #14-16 Daiichi 1180
- **Thread:** Yellow 6/0 Uni
- **Tail:** Dun hackle fibers or Microfibbetts
- **Body:** Orange yellow to pale yellow dry fly dubbing
- **Wing:** Fine deer body hair
- **Hackle:** Blue dun

**Notes:** By adding the hackle behind the deer hair wing, this fly floats better but still provides the distinctive wing of the original Comparadun pattern. Trim the hackle flat on the bottom. This is a good fly to use when both duns and spinners are present, as it provides features of both.

## SMALL SULPHUR SPINNER

*Originator unknown, tied by Gates Lodge*

- **Hook:** #16-18 Daiichi 1180
- **Thread:** Pale yellow 8/0 Uni
- **Tail:** Dun hackle fibers or Microfibbetts
- **Body:** Pale yellow dry fly dubbing
- **Wing:** White Hi-Viz

**Notes:** This pattern is specific to the *Ephemerella dorthea* mayfly. On smaller-size hooks, it is difficult and time consuming to try and split the tails. The fish don't seem to notice.

## LARGE SULPHUR SPINNER

*Originator unknown, tied by Gates Lodge*

- **Hook:** #14-16 Daiichi 1100
- **Thread:** Yellow 6/0 Uni
- **Body:** Yellow to pale yellow dry fly dubbing
- **Tail:** Dun hackle fibers or Microfibbetts
- **Wing:** White Hi-Viz or similar synthetic

**Notes:** It pays to carry spinner patterns for *Ephemerella dorthea* in several sizes and color variations in case the fish are being selective. Try to match the specific size and color to the location you are fishing, as coloration often varies from stream to stream.

Fishing a mayfly spinner fall is a popular activity for Midwest fly anglers. Most of this activity occurs in the evening and can last into darkness. Careful observation is required to match the insect correctly. JON RAY PHOTO

## Group 6: Hatch Matchers, Mahogany and *Isonychia*

These two have been grouped together because they often overlap in hatch timing. The Little Mahogany and Great Mahogany (*Paraleptophlebia* and *Leptophlebia*) usually appear on late April or early May afternoons and may be found sporadically throughout the season. They are very similar in appearance but significantly different in size. The Little Mahogany is size 16-18, while the Great Mahogany is size 12-14. A Borchers Drake in these sizes is good insurance to have in addition to the patterns below.

*Isonychia* mayflies are also called Slate Drakes and are found from May through the entire season into September. All stages of this insect can be important—nymph, dun, and spinner. This is a large mayfly, size 8-10, and often attracts large fish to feed on the surface. Both the emergence and spinner fall is in the late afternoon, and fish may selectively feed on only one stage, so it pays to have both.

(**Left to right**) Row 1: Mahogany Parachute, Real McCoy All-Purpose Mahogany Dun, Real McCoy All-Purpose Drake Spinner; Row 2: Mahogany Comparadun, McCoy's Isonychia Spinner; Row 3: Tilt-Shoot Iso, Hi-Viz Iso Spinner; Row 4: McCoy's Iso Paraspinner, McCoy's Isonychia Dun, McCoy's Stillborn Isonychia Emerger. JIMMY CHANG PHOTO

## MAHOGANY PARACHUTE

*Originated and tied by Kelly Galloup*

- **Hook:** #10-14 TMC 103BL
- **Thread:** Wine or claret 6/0 Uni
- **Tail:** Three moose body hair fibers, from making body
- **Body:** Natural moose body hair, 2 times length of hook shank
- **Wing:** Fine white deer belly hair
- **Hackle:** Brown

**Notes:** This pattern goes back to Kelly Galloup's Midwestern roots. The tying process reflects the original Roberts Yellow Drake. Moose body hair replaces the deer body hair of Roberts's pattern, and the thread color helps reflect the actual color of the insect.

## REAL McCOY ALL-PURPOSE MAHOGANY DUN

*Originated and tied by Ed McCoy*

- **Hook:** #10-14 TMC 100
- **Thread:** Wine 6/0 Uni
- **Tail:** Moose body hair fibers, 3 to 4 per side
- **Body:** Stacked moose body hair, 1.5 times hook length
- **Wing:** White deer belly hair
- **Hackle:** Grizzly and brown

**Notes:** Ed McCoy guides in northern Michigan. He is a dry fly design and tying specialist with degrees in zoology and fisheries and wildlife. His time at college allowed him to make in-depth studies of notable northern Michigan rivers and their insects.

The wing is back over the body. When the hackle is wrapped, it will sit upright with an angle to the back, similar in appearance to a floating mayfly. The tail on McCoy's patterns is made by trimming out the center hairs from the body.

## REAL McCOY ALL-PURPOSE DRAKE SPINNER

*Originated and tied by Ed McCoy*

- **Hook:** #10-14 TMC 100 or standard dry fly
- **Thread:** Wine 6/0 Uni
- **Tail:** Moose body hair fibers, 4 to 6 per side
- **Body:** Stacked moose body hair, 1.5 times length of hook shank
- **Post:** Fluorescent yellow Para Post
- **Hackle:** Oversized grizzly, parachute-style

**Notes:** This Ed McCoy pattern imitates several of the Midwestern "drake" mayfly spinners as well as the Mahogany spinners in the smaller size. It can be fished during the spinner fall and used as a searching pattern.

## MAHOGANY COMPARADUN

*Originated by Al Caucci and Bob Nastasi, tied by Gates Lodge*

- **Hook:** #10-14 1180 Daiichi
- **Thread:** Dark brown 6/0 Uni
- **Tail:** Dun hackle fibers or Microfibbetts
- **Body:** Reddish brown dry fly dubbing
- **Wing:** Fine, dark-colored deer body hair

**Notes:** This is the standard Comparadun template, colored and sized to the Mahogany mayflies.

## McCOY'S ISONYCHIA SPINNER

*Originated and tied by Ed McCoy*

- **Hook:** #10-14 TMC 100 or equivalent
- **Thread:** Dark Brown 8/0 Uni
- **Tail:** Reddish-brown deer hair from body
- **Body:** Reddish-brown deer hair
- **Wing:** Gray Hi-Viz
- **Hackle:** Medium dun tied parachute-style

**Notes:** The Isonychia spinner color scheme can also work for the mahogany spinner. This #14 (pictured) would be specific to the mahogany mayflies found across the Midwest.

## TILT-SHOOT ISO

*Originated and tied by Ted Kraimer*

- **Hook:** #10-14 TMC 5212
- **Thread:** Wine 6/0 Uni
- **Tail:** Moose body hair
- **Body:** Moose body hair
- **Thorax:** Isonychia Fine and Dry Dubbing
- **Wing:** White deer belly hair
- **Hackle:** Grizzly dyed dun

**Notes:** This mayfly may also be referred to as the Slate Drake or Maroon Drake. Ted Kraimer of Current Works Guide Service in Traverse City, Michigan, notes that this pattern covers several *Isonychia* mayfly species. He fishes this pattern from June to mid-September. Kraimer observed that the size of the insect decreases through the summer.

## HI-VIZ ISO SPINNER

*Originator unknown, tied by Gates Lodge*

- **Hook:** #10-12 Daiichi
- **Thread:** Dark brown 8/0 Uni
- **Tail:** Dun hackle fibers or Microfibbetts
- **Abdomen:** Brown turkey biot
- **Thorax:** Brown dry fly dubbing with grizzly hackle on top
- **Wings:** Light gray synthetic yarn (Antron, poly, Z-Lon)
- **Post:** Loop of fluorescent orange Hi-Viz yarn

**Notes:** This pattern floats well on broken water and is easy to spot in fading evening light. It is an updated version of Rusty's Spinner (from Group 3) created by Rusty Gates.

## McCOY'S ISO PARASPINNER

*Originated and tied by Ed McCoy*

- **Hook:** #10-12 TMC 100 or standard dry fly
- **Thread:** Dark brown 6/0 Uni
- **Tail:** Deer hair fibers, 4 to 6 per side
- **Body:** Stacked burgundy deer hair, 1.5 to 2 times the length of hook shank
- **Post:** White Para Post
- **Hackle:** Medium dun

**Notes:** This pattern is specific to the *Isonychia bicolor* spinner fall.

## McCOY'S ISONYCHIA DUN

*Originated and tied by Ed McCoy*

- **Hook:** #10-12 TMC 100 or standard dry fly
- **Thread:** Olive 6/0 Uni
- **Tail:** Gray deer body hair, 4 to 6 fibers per side
- **Body:** Gray deer body hair, 1.5 times the length of the hook
- **Wing:** White or gray deer belly hair
- **Hackle:** Grizzly dyed dun

**Notes:** This pattern is specific to the *Isonychia bicolor* dun emergence. Here the wing is set in front of the hackle, and the hackle is trimmed on the bottom so the fly sits flat in the surface film.

## McCOY'S STILLBORN ISONYCHIA EMERGER

*Created and tied by Ed McCoy*

- **Hook:** #10-12 Klinkhammer dry fly hook
- **Thread:** Olive 6/0 Uni
- **Tail:** Tips of fibers used for body
- **Body:** Natural turkey tail feather fibers
- **Rib:** Wine Ultra Wire, fine
- **Wing:** Gray or natural deer body hair
- **Hackle:** Dun or gray CDC, wrapped over thorax area
- **Overwing:** Gray or white 3 mm foam

**Notes:** As mentioned before, trout may get specific to a certain stage of mayfly emergence. In this case, the insect gets stuck in the nymph case and does not become a full-formed dun. They never leave the water and become an easy meal for feeding trout.

## Group 7: Hatch Matchers, Brown Drake

The Brown Drake mayfly, *Ephemera simulans*, is found across much of the Midwest. For many anglers this large mayfly is one of the most anticipated hatches of the year, often more so than the fabled *Hexagenia*, which appears a few weeks later. These mayflies hatch in the fairly short time frame of two to three weeks starting in early June. Duns start to emerge in the late afternoon into the evening. Spinners appear in the evening, often in massive clouds above the river. If conditions are right for mating and the spinners drop to the water, it can be a memorable fishing experience. This is one of the key hatches and will draw the largest fish to the surface.

**(Left to right)** Row 1: Brown Drake Comparadun; Row 2: Bob's Brown Drake Cripple, Bob's Brown Drake Spinner; Row 3: Riverhouse Brown Drake Parachute, McCoy's X-Factor Brown Drake Dun, Brown Drake Stacker. JIMMY CHANG PHOTO

### BROWN DRAKE COMPARADUN

*Originated by Al Caucci and Bob Nastasi, tied by Gates Lodge*

- **Hook:** #10 TMC 5212
- **Thread:** Tan 6/0 Uni
- **Tail:** Moose body fibers
- **Abdomen:** Tan dry fly dubbing, wrapped thin
- **Thorax:** Tan dry fly dubbing
- **Wing:** Gray deer body hair, length of hook shank

**Notes:** This is the maximum size for a Comparadun-style dry fly. If tied any bigger than this, both balance and flotation become an issue. Again, this pattern is best fished on smooth water. The dubbing at the thorax is wrapped tightly in back and front of the wing to provide support.

### BOB'S BROWN DRAKE CRIPPLE

*Originated and tied by Bob Linsenman*

- **Hook:** #10 TMC 5212, bent 30 degrees at middle
- **Thread:** Gray 6/0 Uni
- **Tail:** Brown hackle fibers or pheasant tail fibers
- **Body:** Mixed brown and gray dry fly dubbing
- **Wing:** Natural deer body hair, short
- **Hackle:** Short brown in front of wing
- **Head:** Light tan or cream dry fly dubbing

**Notes:** Longtime AuSable River guide Bob Linsenman developed this pattern a number of years ago, and it has proven productive on fussy trout. Linsenman favors the "big water" stretch of the AuSable below Mio.

Brown Drake mayflies bring large browns to feed on the surface. This hefty fish took a McCoy dun pattern.
JON RAY PHOTO

## BOB'S BROWN DRAKE SPINNER

*Originated and tied by Bob Linsenman*

- **Hook:** #10 TMC 5212
- **Thread:** Cream 6/0 Uni
- **Tail:** Moose body fibers plus 2 strands of pearl Krystal Flash
- **Body:** 1 mm brown foam
- **Wings:** Light tan poly yarn
- **Hackle:** Brown

**Notes:** This is Linsenman's favored pattern when Brown Drake spinners drop. The bit of flash in the tail attracts attention when there are numerous bugs on the surface. The body foam is tied forward and then pulled back and tied down over the hook shank, extending ⅜ inch beyond the hook bend, palmered with brown hackle the width of the hook gap. The hackle is then wrapped in an "X" over the wings.

## RIVERHOUSE BROWN DRAKE PARACHUTE

*Originated and tied by Dennis Potter*

- **Hook:** #10 TMC 100
- **Thread:** Brown 70-denier UTC
- **Tail:** Pheasant tail fibers
- **Body:** Yellow deer body hair
- **Post:** Clear crinkled Z-Lon or Hi-Viz
- **Hackle:** Brown

**Notes:** Dennis Potter feels a parachute-style is the most versatile of dry fly designs. They are particularly well suited to mayfly imitations. The body hair is stacked and tied parallel to the shank, with tips extending just past the bend. This fly is a great update of the classic Roberts Drake design.

## McCOY'S X-FACTOR BROWN DRAKE DUN

*Originated and tied by Ed McCoy*

- **Hook:** #10-12 TMC 100 or standard dry fly
- **Thread:** Yellow 6/0 Uni
- **Tail:** Three to four fibers moose body hair from trimming fly body
- **Body:** Elk body hair tied in 1.5 times length of hook shank, moose body hair over top
- **Wing:** White or gray deer belly hair
- **Hackle:** Brown and grizzly dyed golden straw, tied conventional-style then trimmed flat on the bottom.

**Notes:** McCoy's X-Factor design template can be applied to a number of different mayfly species. It gives a super-realistic profile on the surface, floats well, and is very durable. Putting the moose hair over the elk hair gives a noticeable two-toned look to the body. The wing is set in front of the hackle, which is trimmed flat.

## BROWN DRAKE STACKER

*Originated and tied by John Sheets*

- **Hook:** #12 Daiichi 1180
- **Thread:** Yellow 6/0 Uni
- **Tail:** Natural elk body hair fibers, 3 each side, left from body
- **Body:** Natural elk body hair, 2 times length of hook shank
- **Post/Wing:** Rust-colored Antron yarn
- **Hackle:** Brown and grizzly, mixed

**Notes:** This unique design has a great profile and surface imprint. The yarn is tied in opposite the hook point, wrapped with hackle, then pulled down over the body. The pattern is super effective and works when both duns and spinners are on the water.

## Group 8: Hatch Matchers, Hex

One of the largest mayflies found anywhere (size 6-8) is the famed *Hexagenia limbata*. They begin to appear in mid-June in southern parts of the Midwest and can continue through mid-July in more northern areas. Both dun emergence and spinner falls start at dark and continue into the night. When the Hex is on, there will be plenty of bleary-eyed anglers in places like Traverse City and Grayling, Michigan, after spending much of the night on the water.

Anglers often stake out a spot in the evening and wait until dark for activity to begin. The spinners may fall right after dusk, but warmer weather can delay this well into the night. On some nights they may not fall at all. When everything comes together it can be an epic experience, as the largest trout in a section of water may take a floating fly only a few feet away from you.

If night fishing is not of interest, covering water with a Hex pattern at daybreak and over the next few hours will often tempt a good fish or two. Another species, *Hexagenia atrocaudata*, also called the Red Hex, appears mid-August into September and is found across much of the region. This bug often appears when there is still daylight.

*Hexagenia* duns molting into spinners. Both stages of this largest of mayflies are important to anglers. They are found in both coldwater and warmwater environments. JERRY DARKES PHOTO

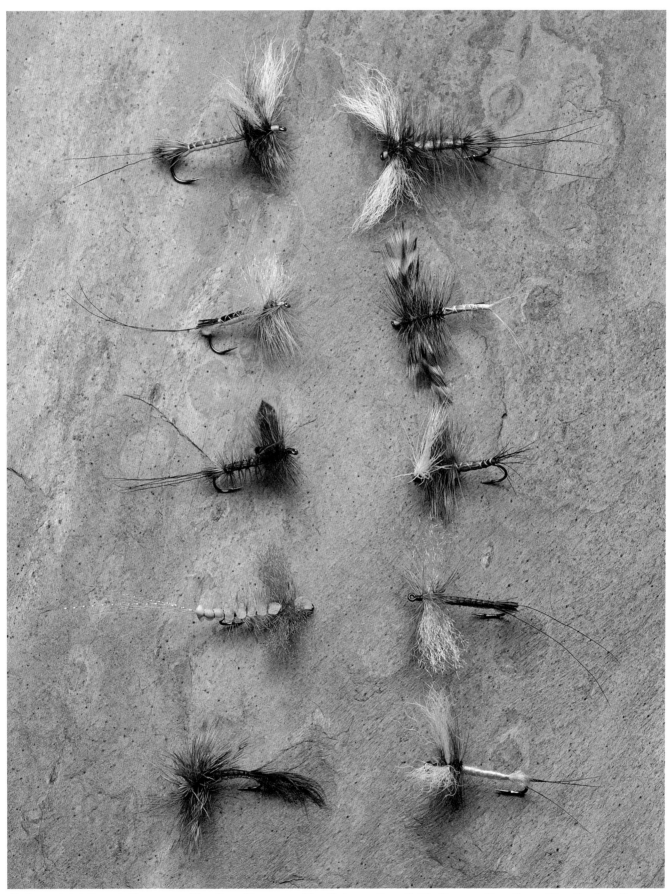

**(Left to right)** Row 1: Troutsman Hex Dun, Troutsman Hex Spinner; Row 2: Fly Factory Hex, Super Hex Stacker; Row 3: Burck Spinner, McCoy's X-Factor Hex Dun; Row 4: Bob's Hex Spinner, Red Hex; Row 5: Numb Nuts Hex Emerger, Jo's Hex. JIMMY CHANG PHOTO

## TROUTSMAN HEX DUN

*Originated and tied by Kelly Galloup*

- **Hook:** #6 Daiichi 2461, TMC 5212, TMC 2312
- **Thread:** Yellow 6/0 Uni
- **Tail:** Moose mane fibers
- **Underbody:** Yellow bucktail
- **Overbody:** Natural deer hair
- **Wing:** White calf tail, upright and divided
- **Hackle:** Brown and grizzly, mixed

**Notes:** This was one of the first commercially available Hex patterns and dates back to the late 1970s. It remains a best-seller to this day. When this fly was first tied, a 4xl streamer hook was used. There were no lighter wire hooks available in the size and configuration needed. The TMC 5212 and 2312 hooks also work.

## TROUTSMAN HEX SPINNER

*Originated and tied by Kelly Galloup*

- **Hook:** #6 Daiichi 2461, TMC 5212, TMC 2312
- **Thread:** Yellow 6/0 Uni
- **Tail:** Moose mane fibers
- **Underbody:** Yellow bucktail
- **Overbody:** Natural deer hair
- **Wings:** White calf tail, tied spent and slightly forward
- **Hackle:** Grizzly and brown, mixed

**Notes:** This complements the dun pattern and is used at the latter part of the hatch when spinners begin to drop to the surface. The hackle is wrapped over the body and should be the width of the hook gap.

## FLY FACTORY HEX

*Originated and tied by Dirk Fischbach*

- **Hook:** #6 TMC 5212
- **Thread:** Yellow 6/0 Uni
- **Tail:** Moose mane fibers left after trimming the body
- **Body:** Pale yellow poly yarn with egg loop at hook bend
- **Overbody:** Moose mane, 2 times length of hook shank
- **Wings:** White poly, Antron, or Hi-Viz
- **Hackle:** Badger or cream

**Notes:** This is another popular pattern named after the Fly Factory fly shop that was in Grayling, Michigan, for many decades. Dirk Fischbach is a Michigan guide and fly tackle sales rep.

## SUPER HEX STACKER

*Originated and tied by John Sheets*

- **Hook:** #6 Daiichi 1280
- **Thread:** Chartreuse 3/0 Uni
- **Tail:** Elk hair fibers from body, 3 per side
- **Abdomen:** Elk body hair, 2 times length of hook shank
- **Thorax:** Tan fox fur or poly dubbing
- **Wings:** Grizzly hackle tips
- **Post:** Yellow poly yarn
- **Hackle:** Grizzly and brown, mixed

**Notes:** A bit difficult and time consuming to tie, this pattern by John Sheets may be one of the best Hex designs there is. It is very realistic with a great imprint in the surface film. The yellow poly yarn is tied in halfway up the shank, wrapped with hackle, then pulled forward and tied down. Fish consistently eat this fly.

## BURCK SPINNER

*Originated and tied by Dennis Burck*

- **Hook:** #8 Daiichi 2220
- **Thread:** Black 6/0 Uni
- **Tail:** Moose fibers
- **Body:** Natural deer hair, parallel to hook shank
- **Wings:** Large mottled hackle tips
- **Hackle:** Brown

**Notes:** Dennis Burck ties flies commercially for Gates Lodge. This pattern will work for both Hex emergences, but is one of the few available imitations of the Red Hex, which hatches later in the summer.

## McCOY'S X-FACTOR HEX DUN

*Originated and tied by Ed McCoy*

- **Hook:** #6 TMC 5212 or 2xl dry fly hook
- **Thread:** Yellow 6/0 Uni
- **Tail:** Moose body fibers, 3 to 4 each side
- **Body:** Elk body hair tied in 1.5 times the length of the hook, moose body hair over top
- **Wing:** White or gray deer belly hair
- **Hackle:** Brown and grizzly dyed golden straw

**Notes:** Another variation of the X-Factor series template from Ed McCoy, this is a consistent fish taker. Set the wing in front of the hackle and trim the hackle flat on the bottom.

## BOB'S HEX SPINNER

*Originated and tied by Bob Linsenman*

- **Hook:** #6 Daiichi 1280
- **Thread:** Brown 6/0 Uni
- **Tail:** Moose mane mixed with 2 strands of pearl Krystal Flash
- **Body:** 1 mm yellow foam strip
- **Wing:** Gray poly yarn

**Notes:** This flat-riding pattern sits flush in the surface film and is a favorite of Linsenman's on the "big water" of the AuSable. The foam strip is tied forward, then pulled back and tied down to extend ½-inch beyond the bend of the hook. Palmer with grizzly hackle sized to the hook gap. The hackle is wrapped in an "X" pattern over the wings. The flash in the tail helps attract feeding fish when there are numerous bugs on the water.

## RED HEX

*Originated by Dirk Fischbach, tied by Jerry Darkes*

- **Hook:** #6-8 Daiichi 2461 or 2460
- **Thread:** Wine or claret 70-denier UTC
- **Tail:** Moose fibers from overbody
- **Underbody:** Cream poly yarn with egg loop at hook bend
- **Overbody:** Moose body fibers
- **Wings:** White poly yarn, clear Antron, or Hi-Viz
- **Hackle:** Grizzly and brown, mixed

**Notes:** This is basically the Fly Factory Hex with a different color thread giving the body a reddish hue. The Daiichi 2461 or 2460 is a great hook for larger dries. It is light, but very strong and sharp.

## NUMB NUTS HEX EMERGER

*Originated and tied by Ted Kraimer*

- **Hook:** #10 Partridge Klinkhamer Extreme
- **Thread:** Camel 6/0 Uni
- **Tail/Shuck:** Brown marabou and brown Antron
- **Body:** Cream dubbing with moose body hair tied on top
- **Wing:** Fine deer body hair
- **Hackle:** Brown and grizzly, mixed

**Notes:** There are not many Hex emerger patterns that see regular use. The duns and spinners get nearly all the attention. This is a good pattern to try early in the hatch, when you see fish rising but there are few, if any, bugs on the water.

## JO'S HEX

*Originated by Josephine Sedlecky-Borsum, tied by Jerry Darkes*

- **Hook:** #6-8 Mustad 9762
- **Thread:** Black 6/0 Danville
- **Tail:** Three pheasant tail fibers
- **Body:** Yellow yarn with egg loop at hook bend
- **Wing:** White calf tail, upright and divided
- **Hackle:** Brown

**Notes:** This is another pattern that could have been put into several groups, but I added it here as a number of Hex pattens are likely based on this design. From the 1950s, it is a bit unique in that it was created for use on the Pere Marquette River rather than the AuSable or Manistee systems.

# Group 9: Hatch Matchers, Miscellaneous

There are various additional mayfly species present across the Midwest that are of more local importance. Referred to as Blue-Winged Olives or just plain Olives, these are usually of the *Baetis* genus and may appear on just about any day of the year depending on conditions. Cool, cloudy, drizzly conditions usually trigger their activity. Olives are typically the first hatch of the year, and also the last in many areas. They are usually quite small, size 16-22, but trout seem to savor them.

Several species of *Siphnolurus*, referred to as Gray Drakes, are very important on a number of Midwest rivers, including the Pere Marquette and Muskegon in Michigan and the Wolf River in Wisconsin. Another nighttime event, the spinner fall of this large (size 10-12) mayfly happens quickly at dusk starting in mid-May and continuing into June.

*Tricorythodes* are found across the region, with a near daily emergence from mid-July through September. This is an early to mid-morning opportunity, as fish feed on the freshly molted male spinners and hatching females. Tricos are a challenging hatch to fish due to the small size (#20-24) of this mayfly. Light tippet and a good presentation are needed for success.

*Ephoron leukon*, the White Mayfly, makes its appearance in August and continues into September as temperatures begin to cool down. Another nighttime occurrence, both duns and spinners appear at the same time, and fish are rarely particular to either stage. This hatch is locally important and is also found on a number of warmer rivers where it draws smallmouth bass to the surface, which will sip insects as delicately as any brown trout.

There are also other mayflies present such as the March Brown, Gray Fox, and various Cahill species. Rather than carrying flies specific for these, they can usually be imitated with other patterns. The Borchers Drake in size 10-12 works for the darker mayflies, and a larger-size (#14) Sulphur imitation serves well for the Light Cahill.

## GRAY PARADRAKE/PARADUN

*Originated by Doug Swisher and Carl Richards, tied by Gates Lodge*

- **Hook:** #12 Daiichi 1180
- **Thread:** Yellow 6/0 Uni
- **Tail:** Moose body hair fibers
- **Body:** Gray deer hair
- **Post:** Fine natural deer hair
- **Hackle:** Grizzly dyed yellow

**Notes:** This Swisher/Richards pattern template dates back to the early 1970s. The deer hair is tied forward, then pulled back and tied down parallel to the hook shank and extended past the bend of the hook. It is a bit time consuming and difficult to tie, but provides a great silhouette on the water. Idaho's Mike Lawson used this design in many of his patterns for larger mayflies. Well-known Colorado fly tier Charlie Craven simplified the tying process.

## GRAY DRAKE PARACHUTE

*Originator unknown, tied by Pacific Fly Group*

- **Hook:** #12 Daiichi 1180
- **Thread:** Gray 6/0 Uni
- **Tail:** Moose body fibers
- **Body:** Gray dry fly dubbing with yellow thread rib
- **Post:** Black Antron yarn
- **Hackle:** Grizzly

**Notes:** This is a good general-purpose pattern for the various *Siphnolurus* species around the country. The dark wing post actually provides good visibility to track the fly in twilight.

## GRAY DRAKE SPINNER

*Originated and tied by Ted Kraimer*

- **Hook:** #12 TMC 101
- **Thread:** Gray 6/0 Uni
- **Tail:** Clear Microfibbetts, split
- **Abdomen:** Gray turkey biot
- **Thorax:** Gray Fine and Dry Dubbing
- **Post/Spotter:** 1 mm white foam strip
- **Hackle:** Grizzly

**Notes:** This is an effective pattern when fish are focused on Gray Drake spinners. The white foam spotter helps the angler spot the fly on the water.

There are several *Siphnolurus* mayfly species referred to as Gray Drakes. They are locally important on a number of Midwest waters. JON RAY PHOTO

**(Left to right)** Row 1: Gray Paradrake/Paradun, Gray Drake Parachute, Gray Drake Spinner; Row 2: Ephron Parachute, Ephron Spinner; Row 3: Olive Thorax, Olive Parachute; Row 4: Trico Spinner, Opal Butt Trico Spinner. JIMMY CHANG PHOTO

## EPHRON PARACHUTE

*Originator unknown, tied by Jerry Darkes*

- **Hook:** #10 Daiichi 1100
- **Thread:** White 70-denier UTC
- **Tail:** White hackle fibers
- **Body:** White dry fly dubbing
- **Post:** Clear Hi-Viz
- **Hackle:** White or cream

**Notes:** This is another nighttime emergence, and there can be so many insects in the air it looks like a blizzard. This hatch crosses over to warmer rivers that hold smallmouth bass, which feed heavily during this emergence.

## EPHRON SPINNER

*Originator unknown, tied by Jerry Darkes*

- **Hook:** #10 Daiichi 1280
- **Thread:** White 70-denier UTC
- **Tail:** Clear Microfibbetts
- **Body:** White dry fly dubbing
- **Wings:** White poly yarn

**Notes:** Both duns and spinners are usually on the water at the same time during the Ephron hatch. It is typically of short duration, but features intense activity on the water. Most river smallmouth anglers don't know if it happens on their favorite water, as they do not stay long enough to find out.

## OLIVE THORAX

*Originated by Vince Marinaro, tied by Gates Lodge*

- **Hook:** #14-20 Daiichi 1100
- **Thread:** Olive 8/0 Uni
- **Tail:** Dun hackle fibers or Microfibbetts
- **Body:** Olive dry fly dubbing
- **Wing:** Dun hen hackle fibers
- **Hackle:** Dun

**Notes:** I apologize to those of you who feel these insects should have received more attention. In reality, a whole chapter and more could probably have been devoted to these delicate mayflies. A number of species fall under this umbrella. Both wing and body color vary locally, so knowledge of your local waters is beneficial to properly match them.

## OLIVE PARACHUTE

*Originator unknown, tied by Gates Lodge*

- **Hook:** #16-22 Daiichi 1110
- **Thread:** Olive 8/0 Uni or smaller
- **Tail:** Dun hackle fibers or Microfibbetts
- **Body:** Olive dry fly dubbing
- **Post:** Clear Hi-Viz or gray poly yarn
- **Hackle:** Dun

**Notes:** The parachute-style may be better suited to the smaller Olive mayflies, being easier for many tiers. Also, a simple conventional-hackled fly, trimmed flat on the bottom, works well for the smallest of these.

## TRICO SPINNER

*Originator unknown, tied by Jerry Darkes*

- **Hook:** #22-24 Daiichi 1110
- **Thread:** Black 10/0 Veevus
- **Tail:** Clear Microfibbetts or white hackle fibers, tied long
- **Abdomen:** Tying thread
- **Thorax:** Black dry fly dubbing
- **Wings:** Clear Hi-Viz, white poly yarn

**Notes:** This mid- to late summer hatch is usually an early morning occurrence and is very temperature driven. It takes a unique breed of angler to fish this with regularity, as many factors—pinpoint casting, light tippet, correct fly size, drag-free drift, gentle presentation—come into play for success. Landing several fish in a morning is considered a great success.

## OPAL BUTT TRICO SPINNER

*Originated and tied by Dennis Potter*

- **Hook:** #22-24 TMC 2488
- **Thread:** Black 8/0 Uni
- **Tail:** Dun Microfibbetts, extra long
- **Abdomen:** Opal tinsel
- **Thorax:** Black Superfine dubbing
- **Wing:** Light gray poly yarn
- **Spotter:** Fluorescent orange or pink egg yarn

**Notes:** Another creation from Dennis Potter and Riverhouse Fly Co. The short, wide-gap hook aids in both hooking and then unhooking fish for an easier, quicker release. The use of the tinsel abdomen allows this fly to get noticed when there are numerous naturals on the water. The fluorescent spot allows the angler to track the fly on the water.

# Group 10: Reagan Spinners

Jerry Reagan is an angler and fly tier from Swartz Creek, Michigan, who provides a direct link from the early days of fly development on Michigan's AuSable River to today. At 75 years old, Reagan still ties commercially for several shops in the Grayling area. Anglers in the know are great fans of his series of spinner patterns, which are presented here. These are often the "last resort" patterns that will trick a stubborn brown that has refused everything else.

Reagan developed a unique hackling style for his spinners that allows the wings to sit flush on the surface, but still provides good flotation and visibility on the water. These flies were developed in the 1980s and have been catching fish ever since.

This book is not meant to be an instructional tying manual, but the process of tying Reagan's spinners is not well known outside the area and is well worth sharing. Here is the Hex spinner:

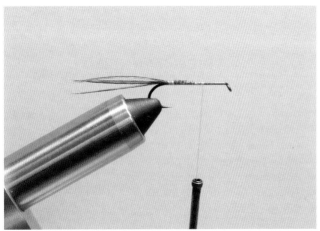

**1.** Take a half dozen or so pheasant tail fibers and tie them in at the bend of the hook. The fibers should extend back one to one-and-a-half times the length of the hook shank. Wrap over the butt ends of the fibers forward to halfway up the shank, and trim any remaining fiber ends.
JERRY DARKES PHOTO

**3.** Pull the butt ends of the deer hair straight up and wrap the thread in front of the hair so that it stands up at 90 degrees. Then wrap thread around the base of the hair just above the body to form the parachute post for the hackle. Make the post wraps up a bit above the body.
JERRY DARKES PHOTO

**2.** Cut a bunch of natural deer body hair about the diameter of a pencil at the hide. The hair should be longer than the shank of the hook. Clean out any short hair or fuzz, then even the ends of the hair (use a hair tamper or do it by hand). Measure a point on the deer hair where the ends will be just past the bend of the hook. Tie in the hair a bit in front of the midpoint on the hook shank. Wrap the thread back to the bend in spaced-out, even wraps, then wrap forward so that there is a series of X-wraps over the deer hair to form the body. JERRY DARKES PHOTO

**4.** Select two brown dry fly hackles with fibers about twice the gap of the hook in length. Prep them and tie them down in front of the parachute post and extending to the rear of the fly, with the shiny side of the hackles up.
JERRY DARKES PHOTO

**5.** Select two hen hackles and even up the tips.
JERRY DARKES PHOTO

**6.** Separate out fibers on the hen hackles to a point about the length of the hook shank. Tie in the two feathers together in front of the parachute post, shiny side up. **Note:** On larger-size patterns (#6, #8), keep the wings shorter than the hook shank to minimize spinning when casting and twisting up the tippet. JERRY DARKES PHOTO

**7.** Trim off the butt ends of the hen hackles. Separate the hackles to form wings on each side of the shank. Use a series of X-wraps to set the wings. JERRY DARKES PHOTO

**8.** Wrap both hackles at the same time around the deer hair post. Start at the highest thread wraps on the post and then wrap the hackles down toward the body. Each wrap should be below the previous. Four to six wraps of hackle should be used. JERRY DARKES PHOTO

**9.** Tie off the hackle and trim the excess. Form the head of the fly, then whip finish and trim the thread. Trim the parachute post just above the hackle so that it flares out slightly. JERRY DARKES PHOTO

**10.** Bottom view. JERRY DARKES PHOTO

**(Left to right)** Row 1: Bat Fly, Sulphur/Pale Evening Dun Spinner; Row 2: Brown Drake Spinner, Hex Spinner; Row 3: Rusty Spinner (*Isonychia*), Female Hendrickson Spinner; Row 4: Gray Drake Spinner. JIMMY CHANG PHOTO

## BAT FLY

- **Hook:** #14 Mustad 94840 or equivalent
- **Thread:** Gray 6/0 Danville
- **Tail:** Dun hackle fibers
- **Body:** Deer hair
- **Wings:** Dun hen
- **Hackle:** Dun

**Notes:** This pattern imitates several different species of *Baetisca* mayfly spinners. Give it a try if standard patterns are being refused during the Hex hatch. It is also a good pattern to try during the day in Hex season. Keep the body short and fat and the wings long.

## SULPHUR/PALE EVENING DUN SPINNER

- **Hook:** #14 or #16 Mustad 94840
- **Thread:** Yellow 6/0 Danville
- **Tail:** Dun hackle fibers
- **Body:** Deer hair
- **Wings:** Dun hen
- **Hackle:** Dun

## BROWN DRAKE SPINNER

- **Hook:** #10 Mustad 9672
- **Thread:** Dark brown 3/0 Danville
- **Tail:** Pheasant tail fibers
- **Body:** Yellow poly yarn, deer hair
- **Wings:** Dun hen
- **Hackle:** Brown

## HEX SPINNER

- **Hook:** #6 Mustad 9672
- **Thread:** Yellow 3/0 Danville
- **Tail:** Pheasant tail fibers
- **Body:** Deer hair
- **Wings:** Grizzly or dun hen
- **Hackle:** Brown

**Notes:** The same pattern in a size 8 works well to blind fish during the day when the Hex hatch is on.

## RUSTY SPINNER (*ISONYCHIA*)

- **Hook:** #12 or #14 Mustad 94831
- **Thread:** Dark brown Danville
- **Tail:** Three pheasant tail fibers or black moose fibers
- **Body:** Rusty brown deer hair
- **Wings:** Dun hen
- **Hackle:** Brown and grizzly, mixed

**Notes:** This pattern can be used to imitate a wide range of mayfly spinners by adding size 16 along with size 12 and 14.

Jerry Reagan sets the wings on a Hex spinner pattern. The unique hackling style allows his patterns to present a great silhouette on the water and still have hackle support. JERRY DARKES PHOTO

## FEMALE HENDRICKSON SPINNER

- **Hook:** #14 Mustad 94840 or equivalent
- **Thread:** Reddish brown 6/0 Danville
- **Egg Sac:** Yellow poly yarn, cut short
- **Tail:** Three dark moose body fibers
- **Body:** Turkey tail feather fibers
- **Wings:** Dun hen
- **Hackle:** Dun

**Notes:** This is the only one of Reagan's patterns that does not use deer hair for the body. Twist the turkey tail fibers when wrapping and combine with the moose hair to make the wing post. Be sure to cross the thread down and back over the body to help strengthen it. The thread color helps give the fly the color of the natural insect. This can also be tied without the egg sac. It is important to note that the hackle feathers are tied in above the wing with the shiny side up.

## GRAY DRAKE SPINNER

- **Hook:** #10 Mustad 9672
- **Thread:** Green 3/0 Danville
- **Tail:** Three black moose body hairs
- **Body:** Dun deer hair
- **Wings:** Dun hen
- **Hackle:** Yellow grizzly and grizzly, mixed

**Notes:** Reagan has continued with the hooks used when these patterns were originally designed. You could update by substituting more modern hooks. Other than that, no changes are needed.

## Group 11: Packing Foam Emergers

This series of patterns is tied by Charles Chlysta, a retired biology teacher from Ohio. Chlysta is an excellent all-around fly fisher and fly tier with a special affection for Michigan's AuSable system. If you have read Josh Greenburg's book, *Rivers of Sand*, Chlysta is the person referred to as "Picket Pin." He has spent a lifetime fishing the AuSable system.

He ties this style of dries for the stubborn, selective brown trout of the AuSable, but they will catch trout anywhere these bugs appear. Color and size can also be adjusted to cover most any mayfly hatch. Several of these are "half-hatched" variations incorporating the nymph abdomen color with the dun color at the thorax.

(**Left to right**) Row 1: PFE Isonychia, PFE Male Hendrickson; Row 2: PFE Sulphur Emerger; Row 3: PFE Female Hendrickson, PFE Brown Drake. JIMMY CHANG PHOTO

When there is an abundance of insects, trout can become super-selective feeders. Being able to properly imitate various emergence stages can often be a key to success. This series of patterns has been effective on selective-feeding browns. JERRY DARKES PHOTO

## PFE ISONYCHIA

- **Hook:** #10-12 Daiichi 1160
- **Thread:** Olive brown 70-denier UTC
- **Tail:** Rust-colored Antron yarn
- **Abdomen:** Dark brown Fine and Dry Dubbing
- **Thorax:** Tan Fine and Dry Dubbing
- **Post:** Loop of white packing foam, dun snowhoe rabbit guard hairs
- **Hackle:** Dun and dark brown, mixed

## PFE MALE HENDRICKSON

- **Hook:** #12-14 Daiichi 1160
- **Thread:** Burnt orange 70-denier UTC
- **Tail:** Rust-colored Antron yarn
- **Abdomen:** Dark brown Fine and Dry Dubbing, sparse
- **Thorax:** Tan Fine and Dry Dubbing
- **Post:** Loop of white packing foam with dun snowshoe rabbit guard hairs in front
- **Hackle:** Dun

## PFE SULPHUR EMERGER

- **Hook:** #14-18 Daiichi 1160
- **Thread:** Yellow 70-denier UTC
- **Tail:** Rust-colored Antron yarn
- **Body:** Sulphur yellow Fine and Dry Dubbing
- **Post:** Loop of white packing foam with gray poly or Antron yarn in front
- **Hackle:** Cream or pale yellow

**Notes:** There are several different variations of Sulphur dubbing. All of them will work depending on the shade of the insects locally. This can also be an effective imitation of the Pale Morning Dun of the western United States.

## PFE FEMALE HENDRICKSON

- **Hook:** #12-14 Daiichi 1160
- **Thread:** Brown 70-denier UTC
- **Tail:** Coq de Leon hackle fibers or barred wood duck flank fibers
- **Abdomen:** Light gray Fine and Dry Dubbing
- **Thorax:** Hendrickson pink Fine and Dry Dubbing
- **Post:** Loop of white packing foam with dun snowshoe rabbit guard hairs in front
- **Hackle:** Dun and brown, mixed

**Notes:** At times fish will show a noticeable preference for either the male or female Hendrickson as well as either the emerger or fully hatched dun. It pays to carry a full complement of all phases when fishing this hatch.

## PFE BROWN DRAKE

- **Hook:** #10 Daiichi 1160
- **Thread:** Brown 70-denier UTC
- **Tail:** Moose hair fibers
- **Abdomen:** Dark reddish brown Fine and Dry Dubbing
- **Thorax:** Natural hare's ear dubbing
- **Post:** Loop of white packing foam with dun snowshoe rabbit foot guard hairs in front
- **Hackle:** Grizzly

# Group 12: Rivergod Emergers

The moniker "Rivergod" refers to emerger patterns from the vise of Michigan's Dennis Potter. Potter operates Riverhouse Fly Company and offers a full range of fly patterns for the Midwest and beyond. He incorporates a unique mix of modern materials and design with the classic foundations from northern Michigan into a series of productive patterns of unmatched quality and durability.

Potter gives tying demonstrations at shows across the region and offers a series of videos highlighting his unique patterns. Potter dyes his Z-Lon to get the colors he needs. You can view and purchase all of Potter's patterns from his website, riverhouseflyco.com.

## SLATE WING OLIVE EMERGER

- **Hook:** #18-20 TMC 101
- **Thread:** Olive 70-denier UTC
- **Tail:** Rusty brown EP Fibers, wood duck flank fibers
- **Abdomen:** Olive thread
- **Thorax:** Olive Superfine dubbing
- **Wing:** Crinkled Z-Lon, dyed gray

## HENDRICKSON EMERGER

- **Hook:** #14 TMC 100
- **Thread:** Tan 70-denier UTC
- **Tail:** Rusty brown EP Fibers, wood duck flank fibers
- **Abdomen:** Tan thread
- **Thorax:** Hendrickson pink Superfine dubbing
- **Wing:** Crinkled Z-Lon, dyed gray

## SULPHUR EMERGER

- **Hook:** #16 TMC 101
- **Thread:** Yellow 70-denier UTC
- **Tail:** Rusty brown or light yellow EP Fibers, wood duck flank fibers
- **Abdomen:** Yellow thread
- **Thorax:** Sulphur yellow dubbing
- **Wing:** Crinkled Z-Lon, dyed gray

## ISONYCHIA EMERGER

- **Hook:** #12 TMC 100
- **Thread:** Brown 70-denier UTC
- **Tail:** Rusty brown EP Fibers, pheasant tail fibers
- **Abdomen:** Brown Superfine dubbing, sparse
- **Rib:** Opal tinsel
- **Thorax:** Brown Superfine dubbing
- **Wing:** Crinkled Z-Lon, dyed gray

## BROWN DRAKE EMERGER

- **Hook:** #10 TMC 100 or equivalent
- **Thread:** Tan 70-denier UTC or equivalent
- **Tail:** Rusty brown EP Fibers over light yellow EP Fibers, pheasant tail fibers in center
- **Abdomen:** Tan Superfine dubbing
- **Rib:** Opal tinsel
- **Thorax:** Tan Superfine dubbing
- **Wing:** Crinkled Z-Lon, dyed gray

## BROWN DRAKE EMERGER VARIANT

- **Hook:** #10 TMC 100
- **Thread:** Brown 70-denier UTC
- **Tail:** Rusty brown EP Fibers over light yellow EP Fibers, pheasant tail fibers
- **Abdomen:** Yellow deer hair
- **Thorax:** Tan Superfine dubbing
- **Wing:** Crinkled Z-Lon, dyed gray

**Notes:** Crinkled Z-Lon is a hard material to find, and Potter preps it himself for texture and color. It is still his favorite material for the wing. With a bit of research, the tier can find substitute materials that perform adequately, such as EP Fibers, Sparkle Emerger Yarn, Hi-Viz, etc.

**(Left to right)** Row 1: Slate Wing Olive Emerger, Hendrickson Emerger, Sulphur Emerger; Row 2: Isonychia Emerger; Row 3: Brown Drake Emerger, Brown Drake Emerger Variant. JIMMY CHANG PHOTO

## Group 13: Assorted Caddis and Stoneflies

The mayfly certainly gets top billing across the region as the most important trout stream insect for dry fly applications. Likely this follows the precedent established in the Catskills and Poconos, which migrated to the Great Lakes and Midwest. Both caddis and stoneflies are important categories of insects for the area, but we see only a fraction of the number or variation in patterns as with mayflies. Where we see both caddis and stoneflies become much more important is with nymph patterns for steelhead anglers.

There have been some works focusing more on caddis and stonefly species and distribution for the region, but for most anglers, imitation of these is in a much more generalist application.

Most of these patterns are grouped by size and color; however, there are some specific species—the Little Black Caddis, Grannom Caddis, Little Black Stone, and Yellow Stone—that receive special attention and are included in the fly plate photo and recipes.

The lack of patterns here should not diminish the significance of either of these groups of insects. What it points out is that for these insects more generalist patterns normally get used. The venerable Elk Hair Caddis will certainly catch its share of trout across the region, but the patterns here have also earned a place in Midwest anglers' fly boxes.

(**Left to right**) Row 1: Little Black Caddis, Grannom Caddis, Butch Caddis (2 colors); Row 2: Updowner Caddis Emerger (Grannom), Updowner Caddis Parachute (Grannom), Gray Stone; Row 3: Lawson Spent Caddis, Little Black Stone Parachute; Row 4: Yellow Stone, Slow Water Sally, McCoy's Ultimate Stimulator. JIMMY CHANG PHOTO

## LITTLE BLACK CADDIS

*Originated by unknown, tied by Jerry Darkes*

- **Hook:** #16-18 TMC 100
- **Thread:** Black 8/0 Uni
- **Body:** Black Superfine dubbing or beaver underfur
- **Wing:** Dark gray duck quill
- **Hackle:** Black

**Notes:** This is an early hatching insect across much of the upper Midwest. In the spring creeks of the Driftless region, it can appear as early as late winter. It is also productive tied in an emerger style as described below.

## LITTLE BLACK CADDIS EMERGER

- **Hook:** #16-18 TMC 2487
- **Thread:** Black 8/0 Uni
- **Tail:** Tan/gray poly yarn, sparse
- **Body:** Black SLF Finesse or Ice Dub
- **Head:** Black Superfine dubbing
- **Legs:** Gray partridge fibers
- **Wing:** Short dark gray duck quill or gray poly yarn

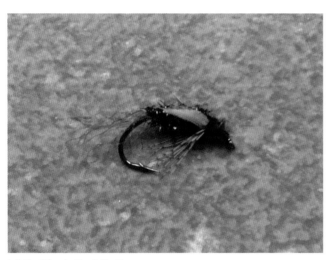

Little Black Caddis Emerger. JERRY DARKES PHOTO

## GRANNOM CADDIS

*Originator unknown, tied by Jerry Darkes*

- **Hook:** #14 TMC 100
- **Thread:** Olive 70-denier UTC
- **Body:** Gray Superfine dubbing
- **Egg Sac:** Bright green Superfine dubbing
- **Wing:** Light gray duck quill
- **Hackle:** Dun

**Notes:** Also called the Mother's Day Caddis due to its general emergence date, the appearance of Grannoms often coincides with the start of the Hendrickson mayfly hatch. Careful observation may be needed to determine which insect the fish are feeding on.

## BUTCH CADDIS

*Originated by Kelly Galloup, tied by Steve May*

- **Hook:** #12-16 TMC 100 or equivalent
- **Thread:** 8/0 Uni to match naturals
- **Tail:** Amber Antron yarn
- **Body:** Dubbing to match naturals
- **Rib (optional):** Fine silver wire
- **Underwing:** Amber Antron yarn
- **Wing:** Deer hair or elk hair, color to match naturals
- **Legs (optional):** Centipede hackle or rubber legs, size to hook

**Notes:** This Kelly Galloup pattern presents a great caddis template that can be sized and colored as desired. It is a great fly in broken water and will float like a cork. The wing is reverse-tied forward and then pulled back and tied down to form a head. Trim straight across the top. Fish it in rough water in combination with a pupa pattern.

## BUTCH CADDIS #2

**Notes:** This is a simple color variation with the addition of white foam at the head to make the fly more visible under low-light conditions.

## UPDOWNER CADDIS EMERGER (GRANNOM)

*Originated and tied by Jon Uhlenhop*

- **Hook:** #14-20 TMC 2087 (#14)
- **Thread:** 14/0 Veevus, to match color of insect (tan)
- **Tail:** Antron yarn to match (light olive)
- **Body:** Superfine or similar dubbing to match (tan or ginger)
- **Wing:** Cow elk hair
- **Hackle:** Color to match naturals (silver badger)

**Notes:** Jon Uhlenhop created this pattern for the spring creeks of the Wisconsin Driftless area, but it can be used anywhere as a caddis emerger by simply adjusting size and color. It is extremely rugged and versatile. The recipe as shown in parenthesis is specific to the Grannom caddis.

## UPDOWNER CADDIS PARACHUTE (GRANNOM)

*Originated and tied by Jon Uhlenhop*

**Notes:** This variation of the Updowner Caddis has the hackle tied around the base of the wing parachute-style with a bit of the elk hair butts showing. It sits better in the film and can be more effective on slower, flat water. I suspect that this is also taken by fish as an emerging mayfly. Again, the Grannom coloration is shown, but size and color is easily adjusted as needed.

## GRAY STONE

*Originated and tied by Jerry Reagan*

- **Hook:** #8 Mustad 9672
- **Thread:** Yellow 6/0 Danville
- **Tail:** Yellow poly yarn for egg sac
- **Body:** Gray poly dubbing
- **Underwing:** Deer hair
- **Wings:** Cream hen hackles
- **Post:** Butts from deer hair underwing
- **Hackle:** Grizzly

**Notes:** Reagan has found this to be a good searching pattern to draw fish to the surface during the day. Though not in big numbers anywhere, the *Paragnetina*, or golden stone, is found across the region, and fish seem to favor this fly. The wings and hackle are set similar to his mayfly spinner patterns.

## LAWSON SPENT CADDIS

*Originated by Mike Lawson, tied by Steve May*

- **Hook:** #12-20 TMC 100
- **Thread:** Black 8/0 Uni
- **Abdomen:** Superfine dubbing, color to match naturals
- **Wings:** Matched partridge body feathers
- **Thorax:** Peacock herl
- **Hackle:** Grizzly

**Notes:** Developed by Idaho's Mike Lawson, this western-born pattern imitates a caddis that has laid its eggs and fallen to the surface. It has proven to be an effective pattern for Midwest waters. Body color and size can be varied to match naturals as needed. Favored colors are black, tan, olive, and a peacock body. The hackle can be trimmed flat on the bottom if needed for the fly to sit right in the surface film.

## LITTLE BLACK STONE PARACHUTE

*Originated and tied by Jerry Reagan*

- **Hook:** #12-16 Mustad 94840
- **Thread:** Black 6/0 Danville
- **Body:** Black Superfine dubbing or similar
- **Wing:** Deer hair
- **Post:** Deer hair butts from wing tied upright
- **Hackle:** Grizzly

**Notes:** Another Jerry Reagan creation, this early season pattern can kick off dry-fly fishing on numerous Midwest waters. It is simple and quick to tie and super durable.

## YELLOW STONE

*Originated by unknown, tied by Jerry Darkes*

- **Hook:** #14 Daiichi 1260
- **Thread:** Yellow 70-denier UTC
- **Tail:** Cream or light yellow hackle fibers
- **Abdomen:** Pale yellow dry fly dubbing
- **Underwing:** Yellow Antron fibers
- **Wing:** Bleached elk or deer hair
- **Thorax:** Yellow dubbing
- **Hackle:** Cream or pale yellow

**Notes:** This generic pattern may imitate several different insects. It can cover the widespread yellow stonefly that begins hatching in mid-May in the southern parts of the region and continues through the summer. I suspect fish also take this fly as the yellow crane fly, which is common across much of the Midwest.

## SLOW WATER SALLY

*Originated and tied by Brad Befus*

- **Hook:** #16-18 TMC 200R or equivalent
- **Thread:** Tan 70-denier UTC
- **Egg Sac:** Red or orange fine Antron
- **Tail:** Ginger goose biots
- **Underbody:** Pale yellow Superfine dubbing
- **Body:** Ginger goose biots
- **Wing:** Yellow-dyed Medallion Sheeting
- **Thorax:** Pale yellow Superfine dubbing
- **Hackle:** Grizzly
- **Sight Spot (optional):** Orange yarn

**Notes:** When yellow stones are found on flat water, trout can get super selective when eating them. Developed by Scientific Anglers president Brad Befus, this pattern covers that situation.

## McCOY'S ULTIMATE STIMULATOR

*Originated and tied by Ed McCoy*

- **Hook:** #4 TMC 200R
- **Thread:** Yellow 70-denier UTC
- **Underbody:** Peacock herl
- **Body:** Black foam
- **Rib:** Dun hackle
- **Underwing:** Gray poly yarn with pearl Krystal Flash on top
- **Wing:** Elk hair
- **Thorax:** Sulphur yellow dubbing
- **Legs:** Black rubber legs
- **Hackle:** Dun

**Notes:** On the other end of the size spectrum, this pattern is used to draw attention to the surface when no hatch is present. This pattern from Michigan guide Ed McCoy is a bit time consuming to tie, but can draw big fish to the top. It is good one to try when the water is up and off-color a bit. Twitch it on the surface and hang on.

## Group 14: Assorted Insects

**(Left to right)** Row 1: Furled CDC Cranefly, Driftless Cranefly, Cosmic Cranefly; Row 2: Griffith's Gnat, Indicator Gnat, Emerger Gnat; Row 3: JR Damsel (2 colors); Row 4: Adult Damsel. JIMMY CHANG PHOTO

## FURLED CDC CRANEFLY

*Originated and tied by Jon Uhlenhop*

- **Hook:** #12-18 Daiichi 1180
- **Thread:** Tan 14/0 Veevus
- **Body:** 2 mm foam, ginger Sparkle Yarn
- **Wing:** Gray CDC
- **Thorax:** Ginger dry fly dubbing
- **Legs:** Knotted barred Microfibbetts
- **Hackle:** Cree

**Notes:** This pattern from John Uhlenhop is a bit involved to tie, but is very productive. The yarn on the body is twisted or furled. This involves twisting two materials and then letting them wrap back over each other. If you are not familiar with this technique, it is shown on several YouTube videos. The book, *Tying Furled Flies: Patterns for Trout, Bass, and Steelhead*, by Ken Hanley, presents this in detail.

## DRIFTLESS CRANEFLY

*Originated and tied by Jon Uhlenhop*

- **Hook:** #16 TMC 206 BL
- **Thread:** Tan or gray 8/0 Uni
- **Body:** 2 mm tan foam tied on a needle, extended body style, with ginger Sparkle Yarn pulled over
- **Wing:** Amber Antron fibers
- **Thorax:** Ginger dry fly dubbing
- **Hackle:** Cree
- **Legs:** Coq de Leon hackle fibers on each side, 2 times body length

**Notes:** Though overlooked by many anglers, craneflies are a significant food source on many Midwest waters. This is particularly true in the Driftless region of Wisconsin and Iowa. They emerge starting in May and continue through most of the summer. Look for them in the evenings. This pattern from Jon Uhlenhop is fairly simple to tie and effective.

## COSMIC CRANEFLY

*Originated and tied by Charlie Piette*

- **Hook:** #17 TMC 102Y
- **Thread:** Burnt orange 8/0 Uni
- **Body:** Sulphur yellow Fine and Dry Dubbing
- **Wings:** Narrow strips of thin packing foam
- **Legs:** Hungarian partridge
- **Hackle:** Yellow grizzly

**Notes:** Craneflies are part of the order Diptera. They are non-biting two-winged insects. Midges and mosquitoes are also grouped here. The yellow crane fly is the most common color found across the region. This pattern comes from Charlie Piette, who was manager of Tight Lines Fly Fishing in DePere, Wisconsin. Size and color can be easily adjusted as needed.

## GRIFFITH'S GNAT

*Originated by George Griffith, tied by Jerry Darkes*

- **Hook:** #16-26 Daiichi 1180 or similar
- **Thread:** Black 10/0 Veevus
- **Body:** Peacock herl
- **Hackle:** Grizzly

**Notes:** By rights this pattern could have been listed under the AuSable Classics group, as it was born on the banks of the AuSable River by George Griffith, the founder of Trout Unlimited in the 1940s. Because of its continued use since then in the original form, it has been grouped as a contemporary pattern. This is the universal midge imitation and can catch trout around the world. When the trout are eating small, this fly usually gets the job done. The only updating I've done is a current hook and a strong, fine-diameter thread to make tying easier.

## INDICATOR GNAT

*Originator unknown, tied by Gates Lodge*

- **Hook:** #16-26 Daiichi 1180 or similar
- **Thread:** Black 8/0 Uni (switch to a finer thread as hook size decreases)
- **Body:** Peacock herl
- **Sighter/Wing:** Orange or chartreuse Hi-Viz
- **Hackle:** Grizzly

**Notes:** The standard Griffith's Gnat can be hard to see in low light or when there is glare on the water. A bit of bright color added to the fly makes it much easier to spot and doesn't seem to bother fish. Most any bright yarn can be used as a sighter. Trim it slightly longer than the hackle.

## EMERGER GNAT

*Originator unknown, tied by Gates Lodge*

- **Hook:** #16-26 Daiichi 1180 or similar
- **Thread:** White 10/0 Veevus
- **Tail:** Clear Antron fibers as a shuck
- **Rear Body:** White thread on back half of hook
- **Front Body:** Peacock herl
- **Hackle:** Grizzly on front body

**Notes:** At times an emerging midge produces better. If the standard Griffith's Gnat isn't working, give this version a try. Again, you can reduce thread diameter as the hook size gets smaller.

## JR DAMSEL (2 COLORS)

*Originated and tied by Jon Ray*

- **Hook:** #12 Daiichi 1260
- **Thread:** Black 70-denier UTC
- **Rear Body:** Thin green or blue mylar tubing
- **Front Body:** Peacock herl
- **Head:** Black foam
- **Wing:** White calf tail over black calf tail
- **Legs:** Black rubber hackle

## ADULT DAMSEL

*Originated and tied by Glen Wisener*

- **Hook:** #8 TMC 212Y
- **Thread:** Blue 70-denier UTC
- **Rear Body:** Barred Adult Damsel Body
- **Front Body:** Blue Damsel Fine and Dry Dubbing
- **Head:** Thin blue foam
- **Wings:** Badger hackle
- **Eyes:** Black plastic bead chain, small

**Notes:** The blue foam forming the head serves as a post to wrap the hackle parachute-style. It is then pulled forward and tied down in front of the eyes. The hackle is pulled together on each side to form the wings.

# Group 15: Terrestrials

Land-based insects that either fall, jump, or get blown into the water are a significant source of food for fish in waters across the Midwest. Called terrestrials, they can vary significantly in size and are most often used during the heat of the summer when these insects are most active. This is usually thought of as a trout-water phenomenon, but don't overlook terrestrial patterns on warmwater rivers. Smallmouth bass love to eat them, too!

## JOE'S HOPPER

*Originated by Art Winnie, tied by Jerry Darkes*

- **Hook:** #6-10 Daiichi 1280
- **Thread:** Black 6/0 Danville
- **Tail:** Red hackle fibers
- **Body:** Yellow yarn or foam
- **Rib:** Brown hackle, trimmed
- **Wing:** Mottled turkey or synthetic substitute
- **Hackle:** Brown

**Notes:** This is another classic AuSable pattern dating back to the 1940s that still enjoys popularity today. It is also called the Michigan Hopper and is one of the earliest specific terrestrial patterns. It was originally tied on a streamer hook, as those were the only longer-shank hooks available. Today we have many hook options. Art Winnie was also possibly the first tier to use turkey wing quills in a fly. This design has been the foundation for a host of hopper patterns. This fly is also effective when fished sunken, below the surface.

## ZUDDY'S DARTH HOPPER

*Originated and tied by Matt Zudweg*

- **Hook:** #6-10 Daiichi 2220
- **Thread:** Yellow 70-denier UTC
- **Body:** Caddis green Ice Dub
- **Back:** Tan closed-cell foam, formed from a Beavertail Cutter sized to hook
- **Legs:** Chartreuse/black Centipede Legs
- **Wing:** White Hi-Viz
- **Head:** Foam from body

**Notes:** Muskegon River guide Matt Zudweg fishes this pattern through the summer months. High floating and super durable, it is effective for both trout and smallmouth bass. The color can be altered as desired. The head is formed from extending the foam over the front of the fly and folding it back, then tying it down.

## FIRETIGER HOPPER

*Originated and tied by Ted Kraimer*

- **Hook:** #8 TMC 200R
- **Thread:** Chartreuse 70-denier UTC
- **Body:** Chartreuse foam, marked with a Sharpie
- **Underwing:** Pearl Angel Hair
- **Top Wing/Head:** Deer hair
- **Legs:** Chartreuse/black and red rubber hackle
- **Sighter:** Orange foam

**Notes:** Another great fly from Ted Kraimer of Current Works. This realistic pattern is best when green-colored hoppers are on the water. The body segments are made with the tying thread. The top wing and head are formed by tying the deer hair forward, then pulling it back and tying it down to form a bullet-head shape. It is then trimmed on the bottom. You can alter the foam to match hopper color as needed.

## SANDWICH HOPPER

*Originated and tied by Jerry Darkes*

- **Hook:** #8-10 Daiichi 1280
- **Thread:** Hopper yellow 70-denier UTC
- **Body/Head:** Foam strip cut from sheet
- **Underbody (optional):** Yellow Superfine dubbing
- **Legs:** Barred Silicone Micro Legs, knotted to form the rear legs

**Notes:** The Sandwich series of terrestrial patterns utilizes both dark and light colors of foam sheeting for bodies and visibility. The foam sheets are glued using 3M 77 spray adhesive. For this size fly, cut the foam strip 3/16 inch wide and then into sections just over 1 inch long. Lay a base of thread on the hook shank with a drop of Super Glue gel at the hook bend and just behind the hook eye. Lay the foam strip on the hook so it extends just past the bend and forward past the eye. Secure with thread to form body segments, just behind the eye. Fold back the foam and secure to form the head, trim off any excess foam in back, then tie in the legs. The rear of the foam can be trimmed into a rounded shape. The colored foam can be altered as needed—tan, orange, or green. A wing of white EP Fibers can be added right before folding the foam back for the head.

## CHUBBY CHERNOBYL HOPPER

*Originator unknown, tied by Steve May*

- **Hook:** #6-12 TMC 5263 or equivalent
- **Thread:** Tan 8/0 Uni
- **Tail:** Tan or pearl Krystal Flash
- **Underbody:** Tan Aunt Lydia's Sparkle Yarn
- **Body:** 2 mm tan foam
- **Legs:** Tan or brown rubber hackle
- **Wings:** White poly yarn

**Notes:** This western-created pattern has multiple uses across the Midwest. It can be a hopper or stonefly and is great for a hopper/heavy nymph combo. It will catch trout, smallmouth and largemouth bass, and panfish. Adjust size and color as desired.

**(Left to right)** Row 1: Joe's Hopper, Zuddy's Darth Hopper, Firetiger Hopper; Row 2: Sandwich Hopper, Chubby Chernobyl Hopper, Crowe Beetle; Row 3: Fathead Beetle, Wiggle Float Beetle, Sandwich Beetle; Row 4: SOB (Son of Beetle), Loco Beetle, Flying Carpenter Ant; Row 5: Cinnamon Flying Ant Parachute, Indicator Ant, Sandwich Cricket; Row 6: Glenn River Cricket, Glenn River Lady Bug (2 colors). JIMMY CHANG PHOTO

The evolution of pattern design. Here is a look at one of the original terrestrials, Joe's Hopper, contrasted with the author's Sandwich Hopper. Advances in materials have allowed many patterns to go through various development stages. JIMMY CHANG PHOTO

## CROWE BEETLE

*Originated by John Crowe, tied by Buck Juhasz*

- **Hook:** #12-16 Daiichi 1180 or equivalent
- **Thread:** Black 6/0 Uni
- **Body/Back/Legs:** Black deer hair
- **Sighter (optional):** Bright-colored egg yarn or foam

**Notes:** This pattern comes out of Pennsylvania where it has been catching trout for decades. I have been familiar with it from the late 1960s. It is a great fish-catching pattern, but lacks durability. It's worth keeping a couple of these in your box during the summer for when foam patterns are not working. Foam patterns are not always as effective, as many lack the distinctive fish-attracting "plop" when they hit the water.

## FATHEAD BEETLE

*Originated and tied by Dennis Potter*

- **Hook:** #12 TMC 100
- **Thread:** Black 70-denier UTC or similar
- **Body:** Peacock herl
- **Back:** Black foam strip
- **Head:** Black foam from back
- **Legs:** Fine black rubber hackle
- **Wings:** Gray poly yarn
- **Sighter:** Glo Bug Yarn

**Notes:** Another great pattern from Dennis Potter. According to Potter: "This fly has it all; peacock belly, foam body and head, wings, legs, and an indicator." Fish this for trout and panfish.

## WIGGLE FLOAT BEETLE

*Originated and tied by Ted Kraimer*

- **Hook:** #12-14 TMC 100B
- **Thread:** To match foam color 8/0 Uni
- **Body:** Midge Cactus Chenille or similar material
- **Back:** 1 mm yellow, black, brown, green foam strip
- **Wing:** Deer hair
- **Head:** Foam from back
- **Legs:** Sili Legs
- **Sighter:** Orange foam

**Notes:** This is another multipurpose beetle imitation that works for both trout and panfish. You can change the color as desired.

## SANDWICH BEETLE

*Originated and tied by Jerry Darkes*

- **Hook:** #10-14 Daiichi 1310
- **Thread:** Black 70-denier UTC
- **Body:** 2 mm black foam with 1 mm yellow foam over top
- **Legs:** Fine black rubber hackle, 2 strands per side

**Notes:** This was the first of my Sandwich series terrestrials. The idea was to duplicate the "plop" of the Crowe beetle and improve both durability and visibility on the water. I like the wide gap on the Daiichi 1310 for holding fish and making it easier to unhook fish. The sheets of foam are glued with 3M 77 spray adhesive and then cut into strips with a razor. Size as follows for the 1310 hook: #10: 5 mm wide x 15 mm long, #12: 4 mm wide x 13 mm long, #14: 3 mm wide x 11 mm long.

From midsummer on, terrestrial patterns become important. Both trout and warmwater species will feed actively on land-based insects that fall, jump, or get blown into the water. JERRY DARKES PHOTO

## SOB (SON OF BEETLE)

*Originated and tied by Jerry Darkes*

- **Hook:** #12 Daiichi 1310
- **Thread:** Black 70-denier UTC
- **Body:** Black peacock Ice Dub, 2 mm black/1 mm yellow foam (cut body with River Road #14 Beetle Cutter)
- **Legs:** Montana Fly Company Barred Sexi Floss

**Notes:** This is an updated version of the original Sandwich beetle design. In hand it has a more buggy look to it. The size 12 Daiichi 1310 hook is 1x short so it matches up with the size 14 cutter. This has proven to be the most productive size for this fly.

## LOCO BEETLE

*Originated by Harrison Steeves (I think), tied by Glenn Weisner*

- **Hook:** #14 TMC 206BL
- **Thread:** Black 8/0 Uni
- **Body:** Black dry fly dubbing
- **Back:** Peacock Loco Foam
- **Legs:** Black brush bristles
- **Head:** Peacock Loco Foam, pulled back and tied down

**Notes:** I believe Virginia fly fisher Harrison Steeves was the first to use Loco Foam in this application. The legs are formed by heating brush bristles and bending them to shape. Substituting rubber hackle for the legs makes the fly easier to tie and also more durable.

## FLYING CARPENTER ANT

*Originated and tied by Ted Kraimer*

- **Hook:** #10-12 TMC 100
- **Thread:** Black 6/0 Uni
- **Body:** Peacock herl
- **Back:** 2 mm black foam
- **Wing:** Gray CDC
- **Legs:** Fine black rubber hackle
- **Sighter:** White 2 mm foam

**Notes:** Here is another great ant pattern for when these large, flying insects are active. They may be found along an extensive stretch of water or in just a short section. When present, fish relish them. The foam is tied down three times to form abdomen, thorax, and head. The legs are tied on at the abdomen and thorax.

## CINNAMON FLYING ANT PARACHUTE

*Originator unknown, tied by Gates Lodge*

- **Hook:** #12-16 Daiichi 1180
- **Thread:** Tan 70-denier UTC
- **Body:** Reddish tan or reddish brown dry fly dubbing
- **Wing:** White Hi-Viz
- **Post:** White Hi-Viz segment
- **Hackle:** Brown

**Notes:** Ants come in assorted sizes and black, brown, or a combination of both. A general assortment of sizes and colors should be carried for summertime fishing. Knowing which are most common on your favorite rivers can simplify this process. The body segments should be tied in two distinct bumps. The post is a forward continuation of the wing tied upright and secured by the front body.

## INDICATOR ANT

*Originated and tied by Jon Uhlenhop*

- **Hook:** #12-16 TMC 206BY
- **Thread:** Black 8/0 Uni
- **Body:** Black Superfine dubbing
- **Back:** 1 mm black foam
- **Post:** Orange Hi-Viz or similar material
- **Hackle:** Grizzly

**Notes:** As you have hopefully figured out, the importance of ants as a summertime food source for trout and panfish across the Midwest should not be overlooked. I have also seen and caught large river smallmouth gently sipping ants beneath hanging tree branches, as cautious as any brown trout. The first time it happened, the rise indicated a small fish, but a 17-inch river smallmouth was hooked, and an important lesson learned. In this pattern, each body segment is covered with foam, and the Hi-Viz post is tied in between the segments.

## SANDWICH CRICKET

*Originated and tied by Jerry Darkes*

- **Hook:** #10-14 Daiichi 1280
- **Thread:** Black 70-denier UTC
- **Body:** 2 mm black foam with 2 mm yellow foam strip
- **Underbody (optional):** Black dry fly dubbing
- **Head:** Foam strip
- **Legs:** Fine black rubber hackle

**Notes:** This is the final fly in the Sandwich series of terrestrial flies. It is constructed the same as the hopper. The same foam sheets are used as for the hopper, but tied down opposite. Crickets usually start a size smaller and go a size smaller than hoppers. As you go down in hook size, you may find it easier to use 1 mm foam.

## GLENN RIVER CRICKET

*Originated and tied by Glen Wisener*

- **Hook:** #10-12 TMC 206BY
- **Thread:** Black 8/0 Uni
- **Tail:** Black goose biots
- **Body:** 2 mm black foam strip with black peacock over top
- **Wing:** Black deer hair
- **Legs:** Knotted black poly yarn
- **Head:** 2 mm black foam

**Notes:** This is a great-floating, durable, fish-catching pattern. Fish it close to the bank and underneath overhanging branches. It is a bit difficult to see on the water, so the addition of a bright-colored foam sighter or bit of Glo Bug Yarn will increase visibility significantly.

## GLENN RIVER LADY BUG (2 COLORS)

*Originated and tied by Glen Wisener*

- **Hook:** #16 TMC 206BY
- **Thread:** Black 8/0 Uni
- **Body:** Black peacock Ice Dub
- **Back:** Red or orange 2 mm foam, marked with a black Sharpie
- **Head:** Fine black dry fly dubbing
- **Eyes:** Black mono, small

**Notes:** This is a precise imitation of a ladybug and is great for selective trout. Again, it is very durable, floats well, and is easy to see despite the small size.

# Group 16: Attractors

Attractor dry flies come in two versions: There are those that rely on color contrasts or bright colors to attract fish. Others have a buggy, lively look to them, imitating nothing in particular but resembling a number of things. Both applications are represented below. A number of the patterns shown in earlier groups could also fall into this category. The patterns shown here are found across the area with regularity.

## PATRIOT PARACHUTE

*Originated by Charles Meck, tied by Gates Lodge*

- **Hook:** #12-18 Daiichi 1180
- **Thread:** Red 70-denier UTC
- **Tail:** Brown hackle fibers
- **Body:** Smolt blue Krystal Flash, tying thread
- **Post:** White Hi-Viz
- **Hackle:** Brown

**Notes:** This has been a popular pattern for nearly 30 years and has caught trout everywhere. It imitates nothing, but fish love it. It is also tied with upright divided white calf tail wings and brown hackle. Using the blue Krystal Flash for the body is considered a key element of the fly's success.

## BURNT WULFF

*Originator unknown, tied by Damian Wilmot*

- **Hook:** #8-16 Daiichi 1180
- **Thread:** Black or orange 6/0 Uni
- **Tail:** Moose mane fibers
- **Body:** Peacock herl, burnt orange floss or orange tying thread
- **Wings:** Orange calf body hair
- **Hackle:** Brown

**Notes:** This Wisconsin pattern is also called the Brule River Wulff because of its popularity on the upper part of that river for brook trout. Variations of it have been around for many decades, and it is a true Midwest original. It can be used in place of the Royal Wulff if desired.

## SUGAR CREEK SPECIAL, REGULAR AND PARACHUTE

*Originator unknown, tied by Jerry Darkes*

- **Hook:** #12-#16 Daiichi 1180 or equivalent
- **Thread:** Black or gray 70-denier UTC or similar
- **Tail:** Grizzly and brown, mixed, or Coq de Leon fibers
- **Body:** Peacock herl
- **Wings/Post:** Grizzly hackle tips, white calf body hair, or Hi-Viz for parachute
- **Hackle:** Grizzly and brown, mixed, or cree

**Notes:** This fly is of Pennsylvania origin and is also called the Peacock Adams. It would be hard to argue against the iridescence of a peacock body with an Adams wing and hackle combo. This is a fun fly to tie, and its results on the water may surprise you.

## NORTH BRANCH DRAKE

*Originated by Hank Vesey, tied by Gates Lodge*

- **Hook:** #14-16 Daiichi 1180
- **Thread:** Black 6/0 Uni
- **Tail:** Natural deer hair
- **Body:** Natural deer hair
- **Wing:** Natural deer body hair
- **Hackle:** Grizzly and brown, mixed

**Notes:** This Michigan pattern dates back to the late 1950s and reflects the use of deer hair and thread to make a body that came out of the Grayling, Michigan, area. This fly does not imitate any particular insect, but has a super-buggy look to it on the water. The name would suggest it was developed for use on the North Branch of the AuSable. The same section of deer hair is used for the tail and body. The body hair is secured with a series of crisscross wraps and the tops flared at the bend to form the tail.

**(Left to right)** Row 1: Patriot Parachute, Burnt Wulff; Row 2: Sugar Creek Special, Regular and Parachute; Row 3: North Branch Drake. JIMMY CHANG PHOTO

## Group 17: Night Flies

Northern Michigan has been one of the primary areas in the growth of night fishing for trout. This developed partly from the need to fill time before and after significant hatches like the *Hexagenia* mayfly. One of the earliest flies associated with night fishing in Michigan was the Houghton Lake Special, which is actually presented in the Streamers section of this book due to its primary function in that role. This multipurpose pattern likely emerged in the late 1930s, as there was some night activity going on then.

In his book, *Rivers of Sand*, Josh Greenburg devotes a full chapter to night fishing, now often generically referred to as mousin'. Greenburg credits a person nicknamed Picket Pin (Charlie Chlysta, who we met earlier in this chapter) as a primary influence in the development of the "mousin' game" as it is practiced today. "Pin's greatest contribution to night fishing," Greenburg states, "was introducing the rest of us to the Gartside Gurgler. The Gurgler has changed not only the flies we fish at night, but also the way we fish them."

Over time, Chlysta came up with various Gurgler hybrids, but the original Gurgler design has held its own as a top producer. This is a pattern that deserves mention twice in this book. It is presented here and also in the Warmwater Patterns chapter. Our buddy Picket Pin also loves to catch smallmouth, and the Gurgler is one of his favorites for that, too.

### GARTSIDE GURGLER

*Originated by Jack Gartside, tied by Charles Chlysta*

- **Hook:** #2 Daiichi 2461
- **Thread:** Color to scheme of fly 3/0 Danville or Monocord
- **Tail:** Marabou plume or sparse bucktail (optional: Krsytal Flash, Sili Legs)
- **Body:** Estaz or Cactus Chenille to match color scheme of fly (optional: grizzly saddle)
- **Back:** 2 mm closed-cell foam
- **Legs:** Sili Legs

**Notes:** This is the favored Gurgler variation for nighttime use. The foam for the back is pulled over the top of the body and tied down just behind the eye. Trim the foam to leave around ½ inch extended beyond the eye, giving it a curved shape. The River Road Creations (riverroadcreations.com) Frog Cutter works well for this. Various types of rubber hackle can be added in the tail and used for the legs. Darker colors—olive, brown, black—are preferred for this application. This pattern can be skated across the current, dead-drifted, and twitched as needed. Work the fly as tight as possible to cover, using a short, heavy leader.

The Gartside Gurgler. JERRY DARKES PHOTO

The patterns listed here are those specific to night-fishing applications across the region. In the recent decade or so, night fishing for big browns has turned into an art form in itself. The flies and techniques used have been slowly migrating to those areas where big brown trout are prevalent, including Arkansas, Missouri, and numerous locations out West.

### MONGOOSE

*Originator unknown, tied by Jerry Reagan*

- **Hook:** #2 Mustad 9674
- **Thread:** Black Monocord
- **Tail:** Gray squirrel tail
- **Body:** Gray squirrel tail
- **Hackle:** Grizzly

**Notes:** This pattern dates back numerous decades. The body is made by adding separate clumps of gray squirrel tail, going around and forward up the hook shank. Increase the size of the squirrel tail clumps as you advance forward. Leave the bottom of the shank open. The body should have a distinctive wedge shape to it when viewed from below. Putting the squirrel tail on in individual groups also likely helps trap air and aid flotation. This pattern pushes a big wake when swung across the current to help attract attention to it.

### WHITE-BELLIED MOUSE

*Originated and tied by Tommy Lynch*

- **Rear Hook:** #2 Gamakatsu Finesse Wide Gap
- **Thread:** Gray or olive 140-denier UTC
- **Tail:** 3 mm wide rubber band
- **Rear Body:** White rabbit strip, sand- or variant-colored rabbit strip, bright-colored Centipede Legs
- **Connector:** 30 lb. Fireline Braid
- **Front Hook:** #1/0 Daiichi 2441
- **Front body:** White rabbit strip, sand- or variant-colored rabbit strip, Centipede Legs
- **Back:** Black or brown ⅛-inch Evasote foam

**(Left to right)** Row 1: Mongoose, White-Bellied Mouse; Row 2: Gurgling Mouse, Midnight Creeper; Row 3: Moorish Mouse, Gator Bait. JIMMY CHANG PHOTO

**Notes:** Tommy Lynch is a night-fishing specialist. This pattern shows the current "state-of-the-art" in night flies for big brown trout. It has produced giant browns all across the country, in addition to bass and other species. It is a bit difficult and time consuming to tie, but worth the effort. To go beyond this basic recipe, Schultz Outfitters (schultzoutfitters.com) has a great YouTube video showing the proper steps.

## GURGLING MOUSE

*Originated and tied by Ted Kraimer*

- **Hook:** #2 Gamakatsu B10S
- **Thread:** Tan 3/0 Uni
- **Tail:** Tan marabou plume, gold Angel Hair
- **Body:** Tan synthetic yarn, tan schlappen
- **Back:** 5 mm closed-cell foam
- **Legs:** Tan rubber hackle

**Notes:** This night pattern is relatively simple to tie and probably a good choice for a starting tier and angler. It is also a consistent big-trout producer. Be sure to tie a few in darker colors, too, and give it a try for bass!

## MIDNIGHT CREEPER

*Originated and tied by Ed McCoy*

- **Hook:** #2 TMC 8089
- **Thread:** Black 6/0 Uni
- **Tail:** Red Flashabou, black bucktail, two black rabbit strips
- **Body:** 2 mm black foam, black rabbit strip
- **Legs:** Orange Centipede Legs

**Notes:** This is another great pattern that has tricked plenty of big trout and is relatively simple to tie. Use a frog-shaped foam cutter to simplify the construction. The rabbit strip is wrapped to form the body. Do this one in true frog colors, too, and fish it for bass and pike!

## MORRISH MOUSE

*Originated by Ken Morrish, tied by Old AuSable Fly Shop*

- **Hook:** #1-4 Daiichi 1750
- **Thread:** Black 140-denier UTC or equivalent
- **Tail:** Brown or black Zonker strip, 2 times body length
- **Body:** Elk body hair
- **Back:** Black 3 to 4 mm closed-cell foam strip

**Notes:** This is one of the best-known mouse patterns and catches fish everywhere. It works great for trout and bass. I usually tie this on the Daiichi 2461 hook, as it has a wider hook gap. Trim the hair off the front half of the rabbit strip for the tail. The elk body hair is spun and packed tightly, covering the length of the hook shank. Trim on the top and bottom. When fishing it during the day, I like to add a spotter of fluorescent orange yarn at the tied-down point of the yarn behind the eye. This makes it easier to track on the surface, as this fly sits very low in the water.

Michigan angler Phil Cook with a big nighttime brown trout taken while mousin'. Night fishing has become a favored activity across the Midwest and beyond to target the largest brown trout in a system. It has also proven effective for both largemouth and smallmouth bass. PHIL COOK PHOTO

## GATOR BAIT

*Originated and tied by Ed McCoy*

- **Front Hook:** #2 TMC 8089
- **Rear Hook:** #4 TMC 300
- **Thread:** White 6/0 Uni
- **Connector:** 50 lb. Fireline Braid
- **Rear tail:** Copper Flashabou ginger rabbit strip secured and left long in front.
- **Rear Body:** Root beer Cactus Chenille
- **Rear Collar:** Tip-wrapped ginger marabou, then brown marabou
- **Rear Back:** Front part of ginger rabbit strip
- **Front Body:** Ginger rabbit strip from back, bleached deer body hair two-thirds up hook shank, 2 sets of orange black-barred Sili Legs in front, black deer body hair

**Notes:** This is another pattern that is a bit time consuming to make, but has produced many large browns at night and is also a good warmwater pattern. Keep in mind that any of these patterns that incorporate a lot of rabbit strips will pick up significant water weight. Be sure the outfit you are casting them with is up to the task—at minimum a 7-weight, with an 8-weight probably better.

# Wets and Nymphs

**2**

## INTRODUCTION

Wet flies had certainly been used in the Midwest and Great Lakes areas as early as the 1860s. The first fly fishermen to traverse the region fished the multi-wet fly rigs of the day with the flies on gut snells. This has been presented in a number of historical works. The traditional English patterns swung down and across certainly caught their share of fish, typically either brook trout or grayling.

During the mid- to late 1800s, British anglers were beginning to add more natural-looking designs to their creations. Entomology was in a rudimentary stage, but the connection between subaquatic stream life and surface insects was being made. Patterns such as the Woodcock and Brown, Grouse

and Green, or Grouse Spider came into being and were the forerunners of current soft-hackle designs. These patterns were fished upstream in addition to down and across.

Catskill anglers practiced and preached the use of the dry fly for trout. Fly anglers were taught that fishing dries was a more difficult and a superior way to catch trout. But we know that many of these same anglers journeyed to northern Michigan and fished wet flies for grayling. Theodore Gordon and others also fished subsurface patterns on their home waters.

James Leisenring had considerable influence on fishing both wets and nymphs as we practice it today. Vernon Hidy, Roy Ovington, and John Atherton all published books in the early 1950s that focused on these subsurface patterns.

Early fly anglers in the Midwest fished the patterns available to them. The gut-snelled, multi-rig flies of the era were used for both brook trout and grayling through the late 1800s and lasting into the early twentieth century. JIMMY CHANG PHOTO

A modern nymph pattern, the Tungsten Choked Mayfly, in contrast to an old pattern, the Hare and Copper. As in all fly tying, innovations in materials and information has led to a new generation of nymph designs. JIMMY CHANG PHOTO

In 1955, Sid Gordon published *How to Fish from Top to Bottom*. This book focused on his observations of nymphs in the waters of Michigan, Minnesota, and Wisconsin. In 1960, Jim Quick presented *Fishing the Nymph*, essentially a primer on how to fish nymphs.

In addition to its dry fly contributions, *Selective Trout* by Doug Swisher and Carl Richards presented a number of sub-surface concepts for nymph and pupae design. *Nymphing* by Gary Borger expanded on the basic concepts of Jim Quick. Schwiebert's *Nymphs* was an amazing presentation on the nymphs, larva, and pupa of much of North America. All of these works have a foundation in the streams of the Midwest.

Research has shown that trout feed below the surface 75 to 95 percent of the time. In spite of this, fishing wet flies or nymphs is not a focus for a large number of Midwest trout anglers. Instead, time is spent waiting for hatch periods, sleeping during the day in order to mouse at night, or casting streamers. Things are a bit different in the Driftless area of Wisconsin and Iowa, where a distinct nymph fishery and series of patterns have emerged.

Where we do see nymphs play a significant role is in the steelhead fishery of the Great Lakes. Here nymphs receive top billing as the most fished and most productive flies to catch these oversized migratory rainbows. As we shall see, some of these are very specific to certain insects, some are oversized versions of generic trout patterns, and others show a mix of standard nymph design with an attractor component.

The use of nymph patterns for steelhead came with the realization that although these fish do not have to feed in order to survive until spawning, they will readily utilize available food. Most of these fish are fall/winter run and spring spawners. They are present in Great Lakes tributaries when water temperatures and insect activity are at their lowest, so they have minimal opportunity to feed on the surface. There are some exceptions to this, but in general opportunities are very limited.

The latest Euro-nymph techniques and fly patterns have made their way into the area and have their proponents. This method definitely works, and there has been slow growth among anglers with this approach. However, the dry fly and streamer traditions of northern Michigan and Wisconsin are hard to break. Again, the Driftless area shows a more progressive attitude toward welcoming recent developments.

## Group 1: Midwest Classics

### HORNBERG WET

*Originated by Frank Hornberg, tied by Jerry Darkes*

- **Hook:** #8-12 Mustad 3096B
- **Thread:** Black 6/0 Danville
- **Body:** Silver tinsel
- **Underwing:** Yellow bucktail
- **Overwing:** Mallard flank feathers
- **Cheeks (optional):** Jungle cock
- **Hackle:** Grizzly

**Notes:** This is basically the same as the Hornberg Dry recipe. To adjust as a true wet fly, a heavier wire hook is used and a grizzly hackle with softer fibers.

### PASS LAKE WET

*Originated by Rev. E. Stubenvoll, tied by Jerry Darkes*

- **Hook:** #12-16 Mustad 3906
- **Thread:** Black 6/0 Danville
- **Tail:** Mallard flank or golden pheasant tippets
- **Body:** Peacock herl or black chenille
- **Wing:** White calf tail
- **Hackle:** Brown

**Notes:** Again, we see two versions of a pattern, which are changed mainly by using a heavier hook and softer hackle.

Nymph patterns are fished extensively across the Great Lakes for migratory trout and salmon. Numerous unique designs have been created that combine both natural and attractor components. Steelhead, in particular, are targeted with these flies. JERRY DARKES PHOTO

(**Left to right**) Row 1: Hornberg Wet, Pass Lake Wet; Row 2: Wet Skunk (Modern), Wet Skunk (Original).
JERRY DARKES PHOTO

## WET SKUNK (MODERN)

*Originated by Earl Madsen, tied by Jerry Darkes*

- **Hook:** #8-12 Daiichi 1710
- **Thread:** Black 6/0 Danville
- **Tail:** White calf tail or gray squirrel tail
- **Body:** Black or yellow chenille
- **Back:** Natural deer hair
- **Legs:** Black-barred white rubber legs

**Notes:** There are several "modern" versions of this pattern. This is the one I have seen most often.

## WET SKUNK (ORIGINAL)

*Originated by Earl Madsen, tied by Jerry Darkes*

- **Hook:** #8 Mustad 75980
- **Thread:** Black 6/0 Danville
- **Tail:** Gray squirrel tail
- **Body:** Black chenille
- **Legs:** Two sets of white rubber legs

**Notes:** This fly will still move its share of trout and is a good choice in early season when the water is up. There are a number of popular western patterns with the same basic design to them.

## Group 2: Borger Nymphs

Gary Borger has been involved in entomology and fly design since the early 1970s when he was working on his PhD at the University of Wisconsin. The nearby streams of Wisconsin's Driftless area served as a perfect laboratory. His first book, *Nymphing*, published in 1979, was one of the first to show how to tie specific patterns and then provide detail on how to rig and fish them effectively.

Borger has spent a lifetime as a fly angler, fly tier, instructor, presenter, and more. He is considered one of the world's foremost fly-fishing educators, with numerous books and magazine articles to his credit, and was a pioneer in fly-fishing video education.

(**Left to right**) Row 1: Beadhead Red Brown Nymph—Red Brown Nymph (Original); Row 2: Hair Leg Woolly Worm, Mono Stonefly Nymph; Row 3: Hair Leg Scud. JIMMY CHANG PHOTO

## RED BROWN NYMPH—BEADHEAD

*Originated by Gary Borger, tied by Jerry Darkes*

- **Hook:** #10-18 Daiichi 1260
- **Thread:** Dark brown 70-denier UTC
- **Bead:** Copper or gold, size to hook
- **Tail:** Pheasant tail fibers
- **Body:** Rusty brown dubbing
- **Legs:** Rabbit fur guard hairs
- **Wing Case:** Peacock herl

**Notes:** This is a slight change from the recipe listed by Gary Borger in his book *Nymphing*. The various types and sizes of nymph hooks and brass beads were not on the market when the book came out in 1979. This fly represents an updated version of the original.

## RED BROWN NYMPH (ORIGINAL)

*Originated by Gary Borger, tied by Jerry Darkes*

- **Hook:** #6-18 Mustad 94840
- **Thread:** Dark brown 6/0 Danville
- **Tail:** Rusty brown pheasant tail fibers
- **Weight (optional):** 015 inch-diameter lead wire (.010 inch on #16-18)
- **Body:** Dark, rusty brown dubbing or Mohlon yarn
- **Legs:** Guard hairs from back of bleached cottontail rabbit pelt
- **Covert (Wing Case):** Peacock herl

**Notes:** This fly is more exact to Borger's original recipe for this pattern. It is imitative of a wide range of mayfly species by altering the hook size and length. Borger describes the bleaching process for the cottontail rabbit in *Nymphs*.

## HAIR LEG WOOLLY WORM

*Originated by Gary Borger, tied by Jerry Darkes*

- **Hook:** #2-18 Mustad 9672
- **Thread:** Dark brown Danville Monocord (go to 6/0 Danville for #10 hook and smaller)
- **Tail:** Black calf tail, short
- **Body:** Dark brown Mohlon or mohair yarn
- **Rib:** Medium to fine silver wire
- **Weight (optional):** Lead wire, gauge to hook size
- **Thorax:** Dark brown Mohlon or mohair yarn
- **Legs:** Black calf tail in loop

**Notes:** It is likely this pattern, as is, imitates crane fly larva. Pick or brush out the yarn for a buggy look. Various modern coarse dubbings could replace Mohlon yarn. By varying size and colors, this design template is representative of a wide range of aquatic insects.

## MONO STONEFLY NYMPH

*Originated and tied by Jerry Darkes*

- **Hook:** #2-6 Mustad 9672
- **Thread:** Black Monocord
- **Tail:** Black goose biots
- **Underbody:** .025-inch-diameter lead wire
- **Abdomen:** Flat monofilament, dyed gray
- **Thorax:** Black dubbing
- **Wing Case:** Dark turkey quill section
- **Legs:** Black calf tail

**Notes:** Borger based this pattern on a design by George Grant of Butte, Montana, from the early 1930s. This pattern is for the large *Pteronarcys* species. For the underbody secure a section of lead wire to each side of the hook shank, then wrap with pink floss and color the top with a Sharpie. The dubbing in the thorax is in a loop and picked out after being wrapped. The amber-colored *Perlidae* species is imitated by adjusting colors of materials and using smaller hook sizes (#6-10).

## HAIR LEG SCUD

*Originated by Gary Borger, tied by Jerry Darkes*

- **Hook:** #8-16 Mustad 94840
- **Thread:** Light brown Danville
- **Tail:** Wood duck or mallard dyed wood duck flank feather fibers (from back)
- **Body:** Bleached cottontail rabbit
- **Rib:** 28- to 32-gauge copper wire
- **Back:** Wood duck or dyed mallard flank
- **Legs:** Bleached cottontail rabbit guard hairs

**Notes:** The flank feather fibers for the back are tied in at the hook eye, then pulled down over the hook and secured by wrapping the ribbing forward and over the top. This adds the tail as well as the back. It's evident that the modern fly tier has plenty of conveniences not available when these patterns were developed: pre-bleached furs and hairs, synthetic dubbing and shell backs, curved scud hooks, and more.

## Group 3: Schwiebert Patterns

In the introduction to his most popular book, *Nymphs*, Ernie Schwiebert wrote, "*Nymphs* attempts to provide a foundation for nymph fishing techniques on American waters, firmly based upon the living subaquatic naturals." This was taking a step beyond the basic information that had only recently begun to appear in the fly-fishing community. Borger and Schwiebert were among the first to thoroughly present this most effective fly-fishing technique to American anglers.

Published in 1973, it is doubtful the exact pattern materials and tying minutia presented in this book are truly necessary. However, it is well worth a look just to see the plates of the insects that were painted by Schwiebert. The amount of time and effort that went into this is quite amazing.

As hard as I searched, I was not able to find any samples—drawings, photos, etc.—of patterns tied based on the recipes given in *Nymphs*. I selected a short assortment and tied them as closely to the originals as I could determine from the recipes given by Schwiebert. One thing for sure, the availability of materials today made this easier than back when the book was originally published.

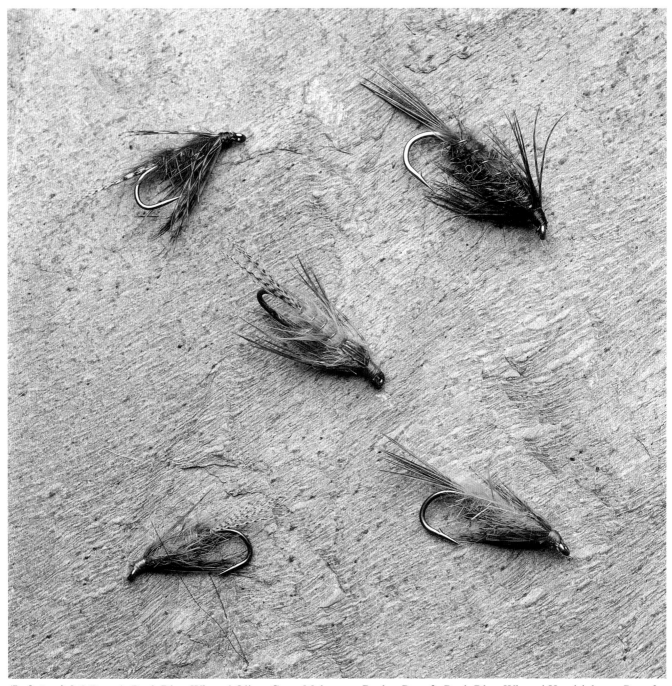

**(Left to right)** Row 1: Dark Blue-Winged Olive, Great Mahogany Drake; Row 2: Dark Blue-Winged Hendrickson; Row 3: Light Blue-Winged Olive, Pale Sulphur Dun. JIMMY CHANG PHOTO

## DARK BLUE-WINGED OLIVE

*Originated by Ernie Schwiebert, tied by Jerry Darkes*

- **Hook:** #14-16 Orvis Premium 1xl
- **Thread:** Black 6/0 Danville
- **Body:** Dark black brown hare's mask underfur
- **Gills:** Dark black brown marabou
- **Rib:** 7X mono
- **Thorax:** Dark blackish brown hare's mask
- **Wing Case:** Dark olive brown feather section
- **Legs:** Dark olive partridge

**Notes:** This recipe is specific to the *Ephemerella attentuata* mayfly, which is widespread across much of the Midwest. The Daiichi 1560 is a substitute for the hook.

## GREAT MAHOGANY DRAKE

*Originated by Ernie Schwiebert, tied by Jerry Darkes*

- **Hook:** #10-12 Mustad 9672
- **Thread:** Dark brown 6/0 Danville
- **Tail:** Dark pheasant tail fibers
- **Underbody:** Lead wire, similar diameter to shank
- **Body:** Dark purplish brown dubbing mixed with hare's ear guard hairs spun on purple silk
- **Gills:** Olive brown marabou
- **Rib:** Fine gold wire
- **Thorax:** Dark purplish dubbing mixed with hare's ear guard hairs on purple silk
- **Wing Case:** Dark purplish brown feather section
- **Legs:** Dark mottled brown partridge

**Notes:** This is specific to the *Isonychia sadlieri* mayfly. It is the largest of the *Isonychia* species found in the Midwest and lacks the white stripe found on the *bicolor* nymph. The lead wire is secured on each end of the hook. Rather than purple silk, I spun the dubbing on purple 140-denier UTC thread. The gills are secured to the sides of the body with the gold rib wire.

## DARK BLUE-WINGED HENDRICKSON

*Originated by Ernie Schwiebert, tied by Jerry Darkes*

- **Hook:** #12-14 Orvis Premium 1xl
- **Thread:** Brown 6/0 Danville
- **Tail:** Medium brown pheasant tail
- **Body:** Dark brownish yellow dubbing mixed with hare's mask guard hairs
- **Gills:** Pale yellowish brown marabou
- **Rib:** Fine gold wire
- **Thorax:** Dark brownish yellow dubbing mixed with hare's mask guard hairs
- **Wing Case:** Dark brown mottled feather section
- **Legs:** Dark brown partridge

**Notes:** This is specific to the *Ephemerella invaria* mayfly nymph, which is widely distributed from Quebec to North Carolina. As mentioned in the previous chapter, this is one of the first significant hatches to draw large fish to the surface. You can substitute with the Daiichi 1560 hook. Again, the gills are secured to the side of the body with the rib wire.

## LIGHT BLUE-WINGED OLIVE

*Originated by Ernie Schwiebert, tied by Jerry Darkes*

- **Hook:** #14-16 Orvis Premium 1xl (standard nymph)
- **Thread:** Olive 6/0 Danville
- **Tail:** Pale barred wood duck flank
- **Body:** Medium olive dubbing, mottled brown
- **Gills:** Pale olive gray marabou
- **Rib:** Fine gold wire
- **Thorax:** Medium olive dubbing, mottled brown
- **Wing Case:** Brownish olive mottled feather section
- **Legs:** Pale brown partridge, dyed olive

**Notes:** This recipe represents *Ephemerella lata*, another widespread mayfly and an important summer hatch on many rivers. The body and thorax are mottled with a brown Sharpie marker. Again, substitute the Daiichi 1560 hook.

## PALE SULPHUR DUN

*Originated by Ernie Schwiebert, tied by Jerry Darkes*

- **Hook:** #12-16 Orvis Premium 1xl (standard nymph)
- **Thread:** Burnt orange 6/0 Danville
- **Tail:** Amber pheasant tail
- **Body:** Medium brown dubbing mixed with hare's ear guard hairs spun on pale yellow silk
- **Gills:** Pale amber marabou, secured at sides of body with fine gold wire
- **Rib:** Fine gold wire
- **Thorax:** Medium brown dubbing with hare's ear guard hair on pale yellow silk
- **Wing Case:** Mottled amber feather section
- **Legs:** Light brown partridge

**Notes:** *Ephemeralla dorthea* is an important summer hatch across the Midwest and from Quebec to North Carolina. The dubbing was spun on yellow 140-denier UTC thread and tied on the Daiichi 1560 hook.

# Group 4: Driftless Specials

The Driftless covers an area of southwest Wisconsin, northeast Iowa, southeast Minnesota, and a small bit of Illinois. We call it a trout Shangri La. It is a land of cold, clean water isolated by the warm waters of the Midwest. The glaciers of the last ice age missed this area, leaving a series of forested ridges and deeply carved valleys with numerous coldwater streams. It features a karst geology, with limestone bedrock and an extensive underground drainage system.

There are thousands of miles of spring creeks dissecting the area and over 600 natural springs. Brook trout are the original natives and still present in the coldest, cleanest flows. Brown trout dominate most waters and can reach surprising proportions given the size of many of the streams.

Even though being close to several large metropolitan areas including Minneapolis and Chicago, fishing pressure is relatively light. This is one area of the Midwest where nymph patterns and nymphing techniques have become an important part of the game. Standard trout patterns work, but a number of patterns unique to the region have been developed.

## SIMPLER SQUIRREL

*Originated by John Bethke, tied by Jerry Darkes*

- **Hook:** #12-16 Daiichi 1120
- **Bead:** Gold, size to hook
- **Thread:** Black 70-denier UTC
- **Tail:** Two strands of pearl Krystal Flash
- **Body:** Fox squirrel dubbing blend
- **Rib:** Gold wire
- **Thorax:** Medium fluorescent pink chenille

**Notes:** The Pink Squirrel nymph is a must-have for Driftless area anglers. This pattern incorporates a commercial dubbing blend of fox squirrel cut with Antron fibers, a simpler option to blending your own dubbing.

## BETHKE PINK SQUIRREL

*Originated by John Bethke, tied by Jerry Darkes*

- **Hook:** #12-16 Mustad 3906
- **Thread:** Black 6/0- 8/0 Uni
- **Bead:** Gold, size to hook
- **Tail:** Two strands of pearl rainbow Krystal Flash
- **Body:** Fox squirrel body fur mixed with Lureflash amber Antron and olive Ice Dub
- **Rib:** Red wire
- **Thorax:** Medium fluorescent shrimp pink chenille (Hareline CHM 140)

**Notes:** This is the original Pink Squirrel recipe per wiflyfisher.com. My best guess is that it imitates an egg-carrying scud. The Pink Squirrel has migrated to other trout waters and has proven its effectiveness elsewhere. It is a good steelhead nymph when upsized a bit. As we shall see, there are numerous clones and hybrids of this great fish-catching pattern.

## TUNGSTEN CHOKED MAYFLY NYMPH

*Originated and tied by Jon Uhlenhop*

- **Hook:** #12-16 TMC 2457
- **Thread:** Brown 10/0 Veevus
- **Bead:** Gold tungsten, size to hook
- **Collar:** Pink Bug Collar
- **Tail:** Coq de Leon fibers
- **Abdomen:** Tying thread
- **Rib:** Fine copper wire
- **Thorax:** Golden brown Ice Dub, dark-barred ginger hen hackle

**Notes:** This hybrid pattern uses the tungsten collar for its added sinking and eye-catching characteristics. It has a mayfly nymph silhouette with added features of the Pink Squirrel.

## LUND'S HOT PINK SQUIRREL

*Originated by Brian Stewart, tied by Lund's Fly Shop*

- **Hook:** #12-16 TMC 2457
- **Thread:** Black 8/0 Uni
- **Bead:** Brass, size to hook
- **Tail:** Two strands of pearl Krystal Flash
- **Abdomen:** Black squirrel dubbing blend
- **Rib:** Fine gold wire
- **Thorax:** UV fluorescent pink Ice Dub

**Notes:** This pattern brings a different color scheme into the Pink Squirrel lineup. There are times when the dark variation is more productive.

**(Left to right)** Row 1: Simpler Squirrel, Bethke Pink Squirrel, Tungsten Choked Mayfly Nymph, Lund's Hot Pink Squirrel, B'Smo's Pink Princess; Row 2: B'Smo's Deep Purple, Biot BWO, Lund's Pink Squirrel, Trigger Caddis Olive; Row 3: Trigger Caddis Tan, Driftless Cased Caddis, Jigged Driftless Cased Caddis; Row 4: Hot Spot Czech Scud, Czech Scud; Row 5: Flashback MFG, CDC Mayfly Nymph, Glass Bead Caddis Larva. JIMMY CHANG PHOTO

## B'SMO'S PINK PRINCESS

*Originated and tied by Brain Smolinski*

- **Hook:** #14 TMC 2457
- **Thread:** Fluorescent pink 70-denier UTC
- **Bead:** Black nickel tungsten, 7/64 inch
- **Tail:** Pink Veevus Iridescent Thread
- **Body:** Blend of dark olive Hare's Ear Plus and peacock Ice Dub
- **Rib:** Pink Veevus Iridescent Thread
- **Thorax:** Blend of fluorescent pink Hareline Dubbin and UV fluorescent hot pink Ice Dub
- **Wing:** White goose biots

**Notes:** Brian Smolinski runs Lund's Fly Shop in River Falls, Wisconsin. He has a number of unique and effective patterns for fishing area waters. The Pink Princess combines properties of two great patterns: the Pink Squirrel and Prince Nymph.

## B'SMO'S DEEP PURPLE

*Originated and tied by Brian Smolinksi*

- **Hook:** #16 Gamakatsu J20 Jig Nymph Hook
- **Thread:** Black 6/0 Uni
- **Tail:** Silver Veevus Iridescent Thread
- **Bead:** Black nickel slotted tungsten, 7/64 inch
- **Weight:** .020-inch-diameter lead wire
- **Body:** Dubbed mixture of black Hare's Ear Plus and black rabbit fur
- **Rib:** Silver Veevus Iridescent Thread
- **Thorax:** Mixture of purple Ice Dub and purple rabbit fur
- **Collar:** Black Ice Dub

**Notes:** This pattern is suggestive of a variety of dark-colored larva. It is designed to be fished through deep, fast flows Euro nymph–style. The hint of purple helps attract attention.

## BIOT BWO

*Originated and tied by Jon Uhlenhop*

- **Hook:** #16-20 TMC 2457
- **Thread:** Olive 14/0 Veevus
- **Tail:** Fine-barred wood duck flank fibers or mallard dyed wood duck
- **Abdomen:** Tan turkey biot
- **Thorax:** Bead sized to hook, olive SLF in front and back
- **Wing Case:** Wood duck flank fibers or dyed mallard
- **Legs:** Wood duck or dyed mallard fibers

**Notes:** Various Blue-Winged Olive mayflies are present in Driftless streams, often found in significant numbers. These nymphs will take fish year-round. Putting the bead in the thorax provides a natural-looking pattern with extra weight to sink quickly. After the wing case is pulled over the top and tied down, leave a few fibers on each side, pulled back and tied off as legs.

## LUND'S PINK SQUIRREL

*Originated by Brian Stewart, tied by Lund's Fly Shop*

- **Hook:** #12-16 TMC 2457
- **Thread:** Gray or tan 8/0 Uni
- **Tail:** Two strands of pearl Krystal Flash
- **Abdomen:** Fox squirrel dubbing blend
- **Rib:** Red wire
- **Thorax:** Blend of shell pink and fluorescent shell pink dubbing

**Notes:** This variation of the Pink Squirrel is the go-to version sold at Lund's Fly Shop.

## TRIGGER CADDIS OLIVE

*Originated and tied by Jon Uhlenhop*

- **Hook:** #12-16 Gamakatsu J20 or equivalent
- **Thread:** Olive 14/0 Veevus
- **Bead:** Gold slotted tungsten, 1/8 inch
- **Tag:** Fluorescent orange 10/0 thread, opal tinsel
- **Body:** Olive SLF blend
- **Rib:** Small opal tinsel
- **Hackle:** Dark mottled partridge or hen
- **Collar:** Dark SLF blend

**Notes:** This Euro-style pattern is designed to initiate or "trigger" a responsive strike. It is best fished in deep, fast flows where trout have to react quickly to any food that drifts by.

## TRIGGER CADDIS TAN

*Originated and tied by Jon Uhlenhop*

- **Hook:** #12-16 Gamakatsu J20
- **Thread:** Tan 14/0 Veevus
- **Bead:** Gold slotted tungsten, 1/8 inch
- **Tag:** Fluorescent orange 10/0 thread, opal tinsel
- **Body:** Blend of UV tan Ice Dub and tan SLF
- **Rib:** Small opal tinsel
- **Hackle:** Gray partridge
- **Collar:** UV tan Ice Dub and tan SLF

**Notes:** This color scheme covers several types of insects and is suggestive of a light-colored caddis larva or scud.

## DRIFTLESS CASED CADDIS

*Originated and tied by Jon Uhlenhop*

- **Hook:** #10-16 TMC 2487
- **Thread:** Olive 10/0 Veevus
- **Bead:** Gold tungsten, size to hook
- **Tag:** Opal tinsel, chartreuse Uni-Stretch, chartreuse Ice Dub
- **Body:** Peacock herl, gray ostrich fibers
- **Rib:** Fine copper wire
- **Hackle:** Gray partridge
- **Collar:** Peacock herl

**Notes:** This pattern is a "peeking" caddis design where the head of the larva is seen just at the end of the larval case. The chartreuse head would suggest one of the numerous *Rhyacophila* species abundant throughout the Midwest.

## JIGGED DRIFTLESS CASED CADDIS

*Originated and tied by Jon Uhlenhop*

Same as the previous pattern, except tied on the Gamakatsu J20 hook in the same size range.

## HOT SPOT CZECH SCUD

*Originated and tied by Jon Uhlenhop*

- **Hook:** #12-16 TMC 2487
- **Thread:** Tan 14/0 Veevus
- **Tag:** Opal tinsel
- **Tail:** Gray partridge fibers
- **Weight (optional):** Lead wire
- **Body:** Sowbug gray Whitlock SLF blend
- **Egg Spot:** UV pink Ice Dub
- **Legs:** Gray partridge
- **Shellback:** Clear ¼-inch Scud Back
- **Rib:** 6X mono rib to form body segments

**Notes:** Scuds are abundant in the streams of the Driftless region. This is a super-realistic representation of a pregnant scud, which is often preferred by trout when present. The partridge feather is secured at the eye and then pulled over the top of the body and secured at the hook bend with dubbing to form the tail. The rib separates the leg fibers and ties down the shellback to form body segments.

Scuds are abundant in most Driftless region streams. There are a number of different species, and both size and color can vary. These patterns can be very effective, especially when there is minimal insect activity. JON RAY PHOTO

## CZECH SCUD

*Originated and tied by Jon Uhlenhop*

- **Hook:** #12-16 TMC 2487
- **Thread:** Tan 14/0 Veevus
- **Tag:** Opal tinsel
- **Tail:** Tip fibers from gray partridge feather used for legs.
- **Body:** Rainbow Scud Dub with UV gray Ice Dub
- **Legs:** Gray partridge feather
- **Shellback:** Clear ¼-inch Scud Back
- **Rib:** 6X mono rib to form body segments

**Notes:** Pulling the partridge feather over the top of the hook to create the legs adds to the realistic look of this pattern. This can be used to create a scud pattern for use anywhere. Scud colors vary widely depending on species, type of aquatic vegetation, and water chemistry.

## FLASHBACK MFG

*Originated and tied by Charlie Piette*

- **Hook:** #12-16 Daiichi 1120
- **Thread:** Brown 6/0-8/0 Uni
- **Bead:** Copper, brass, or tungsten, size to hook
- **Tail:** Brown hackle fibers, tied short
- **Body:** Fox squirrel body fur spun into a dubbing loop
- **Back:** Strand of pearl Flashabou
- **Rib:** Red wire

**Notes:** Charlie Piette of Tight Lines Fly Fishing in DePere, Wisconsin, spends numerous days fishing the streams of the Driftless region each year. This simple-to-tie pattern has been one of his most consistent producers when there is no surface activity showing.

## CDC MAYFLY NYMPH

*Originated and tied by Jon Uhlenhop*

- **Hook:** #12-16 TMC 2457
- **Thread:** Brown 10/0 Veevus
- **Bead:** Hot pink, size to hook
- **Tail:** Coq de Leon fibers
- **Body:** Brown tying thread ribbed with fine copper wire
- **Thorax:** Olive brown Ice Dub
- **Hackle:** Gray CDC, sparse

**Notes:** This pattern is size specific to the most common mayflies found in Driftless streams. The pink bead is to attract attention to the fly. The CDC fibers hold air bubbles similar to the gas bubble formed by various emerging insects.

## GLASS BEAD CADDIS LARVA

*Originator unknown, tied by Steve May*

- **Hook:** #12-16 TMC 2487 or equivalent
- **Thread:** Black 6/0 Uni
- **Tag:** Neutral-colored 6/0 thread
- **Body:** Glass beads slid onto hook, color to match natural larva
- **Collar:** Black Ice Dub spun on black 6/0 thread
- **Head:** Black glass beads

**Notes:** The idea of using glass beads to represent body segments has been around for quite a while, but has never achieved a lot of popularity. I'm not sure why this is, as these patterns are simple to make and allow a multitude of color schemes and variations.

# Group 5: Standard Nymphs

This grouping mainly contains well-recognized patterns. These are recipes as I know them or how they were sent to me from the originator. Several primary pattern templates or designs can be adjusted easily with material substitutions to create different patterns—a theme that we will see repeated often.

I am especially pleased to present Frank Sawyer's original Pheasant Tail pattern to start things off, for a few reasons. First, there is the historical context of this time-proven pattern and how it has evolved over time. Next, even in a time of limited materials, tiers worked with the materials at hand to achieve a particular appearance, such as a translucent body. I hope this again shows tiers how fortunate we are to have the tying resources that are available today.

## SAWYER PHEASANT TAIL

*Originated by Frank Sawyer, tied by Jerry Darkes*

- **Hook:** #12-18 wet fly or standard nymph hook
- **Tail:** Pheasant tail fibers
- **Body:** Base of copper wire with pheasant tail fibers over tip, then ribbed with copper wire
- **Thorax:** Copper wire
- **Wing Case:** Pheasant tail fibers

**Notes:** This is the original pattern as Sawyer presented it in 1958 in his book *Nymphs and the Trout*, although the pattern is likely to have been created a bit earlier. Sawyer was a riverkeeper on the River Avon, just north of Salisbury in Great Britain. What makes this pattern unique is that it is tied without thread. The copper wire is used for weight and to secure the pheasant tail to the hook. Sawyer felt that the shine of the copper with the sparseness of the pheasant tail matched the translucency of the natural insect.

Sawyer Pheasant Tail. This pattern led to the development of one of today's most recognized nymph designs. JERRY DARKES PHOTO

(**Left to right**) Row 1: Beadhead Hare's Ear, Hare's Ear Nymph, Hare and Copper; Row 2: HE Gray Drake, HE Hendrickson, HE Brown Drake; Row 3: HE Stone Fly Nymph, Beadhead HE Stone Nymph, Beadhead Pheasant Tail Nymph; Pheasant Tail Nymph; Row 4: Beadhead Half and Half Nymph, Half and Half Nymph, Beadhead Prince Nymph, Prince Nymph; Row 5: Beadhead Black Prince, Black Prince, Bob's Swimming Iso Nymph, Iso Bugger. JIMMY CHANG PHOTO

## BEADHEAD HARE'S EAR

*Originator unknown, tied by Jerry Darkes*

- **Hook:** #10-18 Daiichi 1560
- **Thread:** Gray 70-denier UTC
- **Bead:** Gold, size to hook
- **Tail:** Wood duck, mallard flank fibers, hare's ear guard hairs
- **Abdomen:** Hare's ear dubbing blend (natural, black, olive, brown)
- **Rib:** Gold tinsel or medium wire
- **Thorax:** Hare's ear dubbing blend, colored to match abdomen
- **Wing Case:** Section from mottled turkey or pheasant tail feather

**Notes:** This may be the best all-around nymph pattern ever created. It imitates nothing particular, but by varying color, and hook length and size, it is representative of a wide range of subsurface insects. There are multiple variations of how it is tied. This is the version I usually make. The abdomen is finger dubbed and tied thin, while the thorax is done in a dubbing loop so it is larger and the fur can be picked out.

## HARE'S EAR NYMPH

*Originator unknown, tied by Jerry Darkes*

Same as the previous pattern but without the bead. You can wrap lead wire in the thorax area before tying in to add weight. I like to use wire of a similar diameter to the hook shank when adding weight this way.

## HARE AND COPPER

*Originator unknown, tied by Jerry Darkes*

- **Hook:** #10-18 Daiichi 1550
- **Thread:** Dark brown 70-denier UTC
- **Tail:** Pheasant tail fibers, hare's ear guard hairs
- **Body:** Coarse hare's ear dubbing
- **Rib:** Copper wire

**Notes:** This pattern is originally from New Zealand. Be sure to do the dubbing in a loop and pick out all the fibers. Usually tied in the natural hare's ear color, this super-buggy design is suggestive of a variety of subaquatic life. You can weight it with wire or add a bead. This pattern works on trout streams everywhere and is open to various interpretations.

**Please note:** For all the HE patterns listed here, the thorax fur is finger dubbed and the abdomen is done in a dubbing loop and picked out. This is to emphasize the natural shape of the insect. If weight is desired, wrap lead wire in the thorax area.

## HE GRAY DRAKE

*Originator unknown, tied by Jerry Darkes*

- **Hook:** #10-12 Daiichi 1710
- **Thread:** Gray 70-denier UTC
- **Tail:** Gray marabou plume tip
- **Abdomen:** Natural hare's ear blend
- **Rib:** Gold tinsel
- **Thorax:** Natural hare's ear blend
- **Wing Case:** Section of mottled turkey or pheasant

**Notes:** The Hare's Ear Nymph design template can be adjusted easily by material substitution. These nymphs are excellent swimmers, and the marabou tail adds plenty of life and movement to the fly. Retrieve it with short, jerky strips.

## HE HENDRICKSON

*Originator unknown, tied by Jerry Darkes*

- **Hook:** #14 Daiichi 1560
- **Thread:** Brown 70-denier UTC
- **Tail:** Wood duck flank fibers
- **Abdomen:** Reddish brown nymph blend
- **Rib:** Copper wire
- **Thorax:** Dark brown hare's ear blend
- **Wing Case:** Dark brown feather section

**Notes:** This is an easy-to-tie, productive pattern. You can add a bit of weight in the thorax area if desired. This same pattern can also work for the larger Sulphur nymphs.

## HE BROWN DRAKE

*Originator unknown, tied by Jerry Darkes*

- **Hook:** #8-10 Daiichi 1720
- **Thread:** Tan 70-denier UTC
- **Tail:** Tan or cream marabou plume tip
- **Body:** Tan hare's ear blend ribbed with gold tinsel
- **Rib:** Gold tinsel or medium gold wire
- **Thorax:** Natural hare's ear blend
- **Wing Case:** Mottled turkey or pheasant tail section

**Notes:** This is slow-swimming nymph, and the marabou adds movement. Use a hand-twist retrieve. This nymph is usually only fished in late May and early June prior to emergence.

## HE STONE FLY NYMPH

*Originated by Rick Kustich, tied by Jerry Darkes*

- **Hook:** #10-16 Daiichi 1560
- **Thread:** Black 70-denier UTC
- **Tail:** Black goose biots
- **Abdomen:** Black Haretron blend
- **Rib:** Copper or gold wire
- **Thorax:** Black Haretron blend
- **Wing Case:** Mottled turkey or pheasant tail section

**Notes:** Also called the Simple Stone Nymph, this is essentially a Hare's Ear with a biot tail. This is a key pattern for use in the Midwest. I usually only tie this in black, but have had good success with a golden stone coloration for spring steelhead. It catches everything—trout, steelhead, smallmouth, carp, and more.

## BEADHEAD HE STONE NYMPH

*Originated by Rick Kustich, tied by Jerry Darkes*

Same recipe as above but with a black bead and tied on a 2xl hook. Another winner!

## BEADHEAD PHEASANT TAIL NYMPH

*Originated by Al Troth, tied by Jerry Darkes*

- **Hook:** #12-20 Daiichi 1560 or equivalent
- **Thread:** Brown 6/0-10/0 or smaller, depending on hook size
- **Bead:** Gold or copper, size to hook
- **Tail:** Pheasant tail fibers
- **Abdomen:** Pheasant tail fibers
- **Rib:** Copper wire
- **Thorax:** Peacock herl
- **Wing Case/Legs:** Pheasant tail fibers pulled over thorax, tied down then pulled back on each side and tied down and trimmed for legs

**Notes:** This is the modern "American" version and most-often-found recipe that is attributed to Al Troth. To form the wing case and add legs, pheasant tail fibers are pulled over the thorax, tied down then pulled back on each side and tied down and trimmed for legs. There are a number of variations. It is imitative of a multitude of mayfly species and has application on trout waters everywhere. Be sure to have these in black, too, especially in smaller sizes.

## PHEASANT TAIL NYMPH

*Originated by Al Troth, tied by Jerry Darkes*

Same as above without the bead. This was actually the original recipe for the American version of the Pheasan Tail Nymph. The bead was a later add-on to the fly.

## BEADHEAD HALF AND HALF NYMPH

*Originated by Jeff Stanifer, tied by Jerry Darkes*

- **Hook:** #10-14 Daiichi 1560 or equivalent
- **Thread:** Tan 70-denier UTC
- **Bead:** Gold or copper, size to hook
- **Tail:** Pheasant tail fibers
- **Abdomen:** Pheasant tail fibers
- **Rib:** Copper wire
- **Thorax:** Haretron blend
- **Wing Case:** Mottled turkey tail feather section

**Notes:** There are several Half-and-Half fly patterns. To my knowledge, this version is Midwest originated. Obviously, it is a combination of a Pheasant Tail and Hare's Ear. It has proven effective on trout and especially steelhead. It can be altered as desired by changing the hook size and the colors of the abdomen, thorax, and ribbing wire.

## HALF AND HALF NYMPH

*Originated by Jeff Stanifer, tied by Jerry Darkes*

Same as previous recipe, but without the bead.

## BEADHEAD PRINCE NYMPH

*Originated by Doug Prince, tied by Pacific Fly Group*

- **Hook:** #10-16 Daiichi 1560
- **Thread:** Black or brown 70-denier UTC
- **Bead:** Gold, size to hook
- **Tail:** Brown goose biots
- **Body:** Peacock herl
- **Rib:** Oval gold tinsel
- **Hackle:** Brown or mottled brown
- **Topping:** White goose biots

**Notes:** The Prince Nymph we know today is not the same as the one that Doug Prince originally tied in the 1930s; this pattern is actually the Brown Forked Tail Nymph, which over time became known as the Prince. Not that it really matters. This is just one fish-catching fly that imitates nothing specific, but looks like a lot of different things.

## PRINCE NYMPH

*Originated by Doug Prince, tied by Jerry Darkes*

Same as above without the bead.

## BEADHEAD BLACK PRINCE

*Originated and tied by Jerry Darkes*

- **Hook:** #10-14 Daiichi 1560 or equivalent
- **Thread:** Black 70-denier UTC
- **Bead:** Black, size to hook
- **Tail:** Black goose biots
- **Body:** Black Haretron dubbing
- **Rib:** Black wire
- **Hackle:** Black
- **Topping:** White goose biots

**Notes:** There are a multitude of Prince Nymph variations tied at present. The basic "Prince" template has biots for the tail and then biots tied flat on top of the body. Body materials and colors vary along with biot color. I have tied this color scheme for over 20 years and had not seen it prior to this. It has proven particularly effective for steelhead. I believe that the contrast of the black body color with the white biots attracts attention, and the stonefly nymph silhouette seals the deal.

## BLACK PRINCE

*Originated and tied by Jerry Darkes*

Same as above without the bead

## BOB'S SWIMMING ISO NYMPH

*Originated by Bob Linsenman, tied by Pacific Fly Group*

- **Hook:** #10 Daiichi 1260
- **Thread:** Black 70-denier UTC
- **Bead:** Black, size to hook
- **Tail:** Medium dun hackle fibers
- **Body:** Peacock herl, white dental floss
- **Rib:** Black wire
- **Wing:** Gray poly yarn
- **Hackle:** Grizzly hen

**Notes:** This pattern is specific to the *Isonychia bicolor* mayfly nymph. The white stripe on the back is a distinct feature on this bug. They are strong swimmers found in rocky areas with fast current. Let the fly swing tight and rise at the end of the drift, and give it a few strips. Linsenman fishes this fly extensively on the big-water areas of Michigan's AuSable River. You can also tie this without the bead.

## ISO BUGGER

*Originated and tied by Matt Zudweg*

- **Hook:** #10-12 Daiichi 1110
- **Thread:** Black 6/0 Uni
- **Bead:** Gold or copper, size to hook
- **Tail:** Peacock black Ice Dub
- **Body:** Peacock black Ice Dub
- **Hackle:** Brown saddle
- **Wing Case:** Black Ice Dub, strand of yellow glow-in-the-dark Flashabou

**Notes:** Is this a nymph or a streamer? The answer is . . . yes. This fly can be fished both ways to duplicate the swimming characteristics of the Iso nymph. Matt Zudweg is a year-round guide on Michigan's Muskegon River and surrounding waters and has caught both trout and steelhead on this pattern.

The *Isonychia bicolor* nymph is easily recognized by the white stripe down its back. This mayfly is well distributed across Midwest trout waters and often targeted by feeding fish. JON RAY PHOTO

# Group 6: Hex Nymphs

The *Hexagenia limbata* mayfly nymph is well known to most Midwest fly fishers. Its importance goes beyond the realm of the trout angler, being found in a variety of warm- to coldwater environments. Hex nymphs, also called "wigglers," are harvested commercially in some areas and sold as live bait for yellow perch and steelhead. Hex nymph flies are probably most fished by steelhead anglers, but have also proven effective to sight-fish for carp on Great Lakes flats. In addition, big-water fly fishers can catch both smallmouth and walleye by slowly stripping Hex patterns when the nymphs start emerging from silty lake bottoms.

## SCHMIDT'S HEX

*Originated and tied by Ray Schmidt*

- **Hook:** #6 Daiichi 1710
- **Thread:** Tan 70-denier UTC
- **Tail:** Natural gray ostrich
- **Abdomen:** Possum Hex dubbing, gray ostrich, pheasant tail over top
- **Rib:** 6X mono
- **Thorax:** Possum Hex dubbing, brown hen hackle
- **Wing Case:** Pheasant tail
- **Eyes:** Mono, small

**Notes:** This is one of the most popular Hex nymph designs on the market. The abdomen is formed by layering the materials on top of each other. Ray Schmidt has legendary status among Great Lakes anglers as an outfitter and guide. He has developed numerous patterns designed for Midwest and Great Lakes fisheries.

## JOE'S WIGGLE HEX

*Originated and tied by Joe Penich*

### Abdomen
- **Hook:** #6 TMC 200R, cut off at bend after fly is completed
- **Thread:** Dark brown 6/0 Uni
- **Tail:** Three strands of natural ostrich
- **Body:** Fine sulphur yellow dubbing
- **Gills:** Natural pine squirrel
- **Back:** Light brown ¼-inch Scud Back, tied in 4 segments
- **Rib:** Tying thread
- **Connector:** 20 lb. mono

The large size of the *Hexagenia* mayfly allows the fly to be tied in both standard and articulated designs. Is one more effective than the other? Some anglers swear by the articulated versions, while others say it doesn't matter.
JIMMY CHANG PHOTO

**(Left to right)** Row 1: Schmidt's Hex, Joe's Wiggle Hex; Row 2: Full-Motion Hex, Possum Hex; Row 3: Sexy Hexy, Weighted Sexy Hexy. JIMMY CHANG PHOTO

## Thorax

- **Hook:** #4 Kamasan B-174
- **Thread:** Black 6/0 Uni
- **Body:** Fine sulphur yellow dubbing
- **Legs:** Gold variant rabbit fur
- **Wing Case:** Light brown ¼-inch Scud Back, tied in 3 segments
- **Rib:** Tying thread
- **Eyes:** Mono, medium

**Notes:** Ontario, Canada, fly tier Joe Penich should more be referred to as a fly artist. His designs and tying techniques are flawless. Both the gills and legs are made by putting the furs in a dubbing loop. Penich is equally at home tying small dries, a large nymph such as this, or a full-dressed Atlantic salmon pattern. We will see more of his creations.

## FULL-MOTION HEX

*Originated and tied by Steve May*

- **Hook:** #6-8 Daiichi 1560
- **Thread:** Black 6/0 Uni
- **Bead:** Brass, size to hook
- **Tail:** Cream, tan, or ginger rabbit strip, partridge hackle
- **Body:** Tan Sow-Scud Dubbing, ribbed
- **Rib:** Opal tinsel
- **Collar:** Partridge hackle, black rabbit dubbing

**Notes:** This super-versatile pattern is another contribution out of Canada. Ontario-based tier Steve May created this fly to mimic the undulating movement of a swimming Hex nymph. All the materials bring this fly to life—drift it, swing it, or strip it. This fly is also a great imitation of a baby sculpin.

## POSSUM HEX

*Originated by Kevin Feenstra, tied by Jerry Darkes*

- **Front Hook:** #6-8 Daiichi 1120
- **Thread:** Tan 70-denier UTC
- **Rear Hook:** #8 Daiichi 1750 (optional: cut off at bend when fly is completed)
- **Tail:** Clump of Australian opossum fur
- **Abdomen:** Sulphur Possum Plus dubbing, Australian opossum fur
- **Connector:** 20 lb. mono
- **Thorax:** Sulphur Possum Plus dubbing, grizzly or mottled hen over top
- **Wing Case:** Peacock herl
- **Eyes:** Mono or plastic bead chain, small

**Notes:** This is my take on a favorite pattern of well-known Michigan guide Kevin Feenstra. This simple-to-tie, super-durable pattern catches about anything you can think of. To form the abdomen, alternate sections of dubbing and fur. As well as a Hex nymph, it is likely also taken as a small baitfish.

## SEXY HEXY

*Originated and tied by Jerry Darkes*

- **Front Hook:** #6-8 Daiichi 1120
- **Thread:** Tan 70-denier UTC
- **Rear Hook:** #8 Daiichi 1260 (optional: cut off at bend when fly is completed)
- **Tail:** Natural, tan, or light brown grizzly marabou
- **Body:** Sulphur Possum Plus dubbing, grizzly marabou
- **Connector:** 20 lb. mono
- **Thorax:** Sulphur Possum Plus dubbing, grizzly hen hackle
- **Wing Case:** Peacock herl
- **Eyes:** Mono or plastic bead chain, small

**Notes:** Yes, this is total knockoff of the previous pattern from Feenstra. Australian opossum fur on the pelt can be hard to find. Grizzly marabou is an easy-to-find substitute.

## WEIGHTED SEXY HEXY

*Originated and tied by Jerry Darkes*

**Notes:** This is the same as the previous pattern except the front hook is inverted, and instead of mono eyes, extra-small black barbell eyes or small, black metal bead chain is used for the eyes. You can leave off the wing case. This has been a good pattern for carp on Great Lakes flats.

## Group 7: Soft Hackles

Soft hackles were some of the earliest flies created. They are suggestive of many types of insects, both aquatic and terrestrial. Soft-hackle patterns were brought back into the mainstream in the United States in 1975 with the publication of *The Soft Hackle Fly* by Sylvester Nemes. The late Dick Walle of Toledo, Ohio, was a recognized proponent of soft-hackle patterns and preached their use extensively.

Soft hackles can be fished in variety of methods including dead-drifted, swung down and across, or with a slow hand-over-hand retrieve. They can imitate emerging insect, cripples and stillborns, or spent insects. They are often overlooked by anglers and popularity across the Midwest is quite localized, but they will catch fish everywhere.

(**Left to right**) Row 1: Black Soft Hackle, Yellow Crane Fly, Partridge and Yellow, Hendrickson Soft Hackle; Row 2: Soft Hackle Sow Bug, Gray Drake Soft Hackle; Row 3: All-Purpose Soft Hackle. JIMMY CHANG PHOTO

## BLACK SOFT HACKLE

*Originator unknown, tied by Jerry Darkes*

- **Hook:** #12-16 Daiichi 1550
- **Thread:** Black 70-denier UTC
- **Body:** Black Haretron dubbing
- **Back (optional):** Black Krystal Flash
- **Hackle:** Black wet fly

**Notes:** This is about as basic as a fly can get. It may be a drowned beetle or ant, an emerging black caddis, possibly even a snail if dead-drifted in the surface film. Whatever it is, it catches fish!

## YELLOW CRANE FLY

*Originator unknown, tied by Jerry Darkes*

- **Hook:** #14-18 TMC 2487
- **Thread:** Chartreuse 70-denier UTC
- **Body:** Chartreuse dry fly dubbing
- **Rib:** Fine silver wire
- **Hackle:** Tan or light ginger hen hackle

**Notes:** This is another pattern that overlaps several insects. Crane flies are abundant across the Driftless region as well as other areas. This pattern covers a greenish color phase of this insect. There are also some rivers such as the Kinnickinnic in Wisconsin and others where the Sulphur mayfly actually changes to a greenish hue as the hatch progresses.

## PARTRIDGE AND YELLOW

*Originator unknown, tied by Steve May*

- **Hook:** #12-18 Daiichi 1550 or equivalent
- **Thread:** Yellow 8/0 Uni
- **Body:** Tying thread, ribbed with fine gold tinsel
- **Rib:** Fine gold tinsel
- **Hackle:** Gray partridge

**Notes:** This is the classic wet-fly known to many anglers, and there are many variations. It can be fished as a crane fly or Sulphur emerger. A multitude of insects can be duplicated by changing hook size and design or thread color from this simple design template. You can also add a thorax of peacock herl if desired.

## HENDRICKSON SOFT HACKLE

*Originator unknown, tied by Jerry Darkes*

- **Hook:** #14 Daiichi 1560
- **Thread:** Brown 70-denier UTC
- **Tail:** Pheasant tail fibers
- **Abdomen:** Pheasant tail fibers
- **Rib:** Fine copper wire
- **Thorax:** Hendrickson pink dubbing
- **Hackle:** Partridge

**Notes:** This fly is specific to the Hendrickson mayfly emerger. Again, we have a basic pattern template and by adjusting hook size, thorax materials, and thread color, a wide range of mayflies can be covered. The pheasant tail and abdomen remain unchanged.

## SOFT HACKLE SOW BUG

*Originator unknown, tied by Jerry Darkes*

- **Hook:** #14-16 Daiichi 1560
- **Thread:** Brown 6/0 Danville
- **Body:** Cinnamon Haretron dubbing
- **Rib:** Opal tinsel
- **Hackle:** Gray partridge or mottled gray hen
- **Head:** Fluorescent red or orange thread

**Notes:** This pattern came to the Driftless region by way of the Bighorn River in Montana. Body color can be varied, but a key feature is the brightly colored head of the fly. When there are a lot of naturals present, a bit of color gets the fly noticed. It works great as an attractor when paired with another smaller larva or pupa pattern.

## GRAY DRAKE SOFT HACKLE

*Originated and tied by Kevin Feenstra*

- **Hook:** #12 Daiichi 1560
- **Thread:** Gray 70-denier UTC
- **Tail:** Two strands of pearl or silver Krystal Flash
- **Body:** Natural deer hair, sparse
- **Hackle:** Partridge or grouse

**Notes:** Feenstra ties this pattern specific to the Gray Drake hatch on Michigan's Muskegon River. By simple adjustments in color and size, it can cover a wide range of mayflies. The tail helps make the fly stand out when there are large numbers of naturals present.

## ALL-PURPOSE SOFT HACKLE

*Originated and tied by Matt Supinski*

- **Hook:** #10 Daiichi 1260
- **Thread:** Gray 6/0-8/0 Uni
- **Bead:** Black, size to hook
- **Tail:** Partridge hackle tip
- **Abdomen:** Gray fur dubbing
- **Rib:** Darker thread to show body segments
- **Wing:** A few strands of UV Minnow Belly, pearl Krystal Flash
- **Thorax:** Peacock Ice Dub
- **Hackle:** Partridge

**Notes:** Matt Supinksi has written a number of books and dozens of magazine articles, and has been a fixture on Michigan's Muskegon River for many years. The AP Soft Hackle described here is for the prolific Gray Drake hatch on the Muskegon, but again we see that a number of mayfly emergers can be imitated with this pattern template by adjusting size and color. This can be tied all the way down to a #16 hook.

## Group 8: Assorted Nymphs

These patterns are some that did not fit well into other categories but still need to receive their due recognition. They imitate a diverse range of aquatic insects.

### JOE'S DAMSEL

*Originated and tied by Joe Penich*

- **Hook:** #10-14 TMC 300
- **Thread:** Olive 8/0 Uni
- **Weight:** Four to five turns of .015-inch-diameter lead wire at thorax
- **Tail:** Olive grizzly marabou
- **Abdomen:** Olive floss
- **Rib:** Fine silver wire
- **Thorax:** Brown olive squirrel dubbing
- **Legs:** Olive grizzly marabou
- **Wing Case:** Olive floss
- **Eyes:** Mono, small

**Notes:** This super-realistic pattern looks fragile, but is constructed to be extremely durable. Swim this in slow current and stillwaters for trout and in warmwater situations for a host of species.

### KILLER BUNNY RABBIT

*Originated by Larry McGratton, tied by Steve May*

- **Hook:** #8-12 Daiichi 1560
- **Thread:** Black 6/0 Uni
- **Tail:** Olive rabbit fur, strands of pearl Flashabou
- **Body:** Olive rabbit dubbing
- **Rib:** Pearl Flashabou
- **Hackle:** Olive partridge or hen
- **Collar:** Peacock black Ice Dub

**Notes:** This generic pattern doesn't imitate anything in particular, but resembles a variety of forms such as crayfish, dragonfly nymphs, and more. It can also be tied in natural rabbit and black to cover an extensive range of food organisms. Steve May says, "It is effective on most anything with fins."

### STEVE'S LEATHERWORM

*Originated and tied by Steve May*

- **Hook:** #6-10 TMC 200R
- **Thread:** Red 6/0 Uni
- **Bead:** Brass or gold, size to hook
- **Weight (optional):** .015-inch-diameter lead wire
- **Back:** Red, brown, or black Ultra Suede
- **Rib:** Tying thread

**Notes:** There are many species of aquatic worms. They are common in freshwater habitats and are found in a wide range of water conditions, with some species being very pollution tolerant. They have a color range of red, tan, brown, and black and may be up to 5 inches in length.

### IAN'S BUZZER

*Orignated and tied by Ian Colin James*

- **Hook:** #8-14 Kamasan B420
- **Thread:** Black 6/0 Uni
- **Abdomen:** Copper wire
- **Thorax:** Black goose biots
- **Thorax Stripe:** Copper Flashabou
- **Coating:** Epoxy or UV Fly Finish

**Notes:** This pattern is from the late Ian Colin James of London, Ontario. Larger midges (chironomids) are known as "buzzers" in the UK. Size range and color varies considerably. You can substitute the Daiichi 1120 or TMC 2457 hooks, among others. These patterns have proven effective for carp in moving water and also steelhead in larger sizes.

### ZEBRA MIDGE

*Originated by Ted Welling, tied by Jerry Darkes*

- **Hook:** #16-20 Daiichi 1120
- **Thread:** Black, brown, olive, gray, or red 70-denier UTC or similar
- **Bead:** Gold, copper, or clear glass, size to hook
- **Body:** Thread
- **Rib:** Fine silver wire
- **Thorax (optional):** Peacock herl or black dubbing

**Notes:** This pattern imitates a midge pupa and originally came from the Lee's Ferry tailwater in Arizona. It is now a standard pattern in tailwaters across the country and will catch fish wherever midges are found. The common colors of this pattern are listed. Black with a silver rib is the most popular combination.

### UFO

*Originated and tied by Damian Wilmot*

- **Hook:** #12-#14 Daiichi 1110 or equivlent
- **Tail:** Grizzly and tan grizzly hackle tips
- **Body:** Peacock herl
- **Hackle:** Grizzly and tan grizzly

**Notes:** This "unidentified fly-like object" is a wet fly when fished in the film or allowed to sink. It may also be fished dry before it soaks up and sinks. Dead-drift it, fish down and across, or work it with a hand-over-hand retrieve. It looks like a wide range of natural insects, but nothing particular.

**(Left to right)** Row 1: Joe's Damsel, Killer Bunny Rabbit, Steve's Leatherworm; Row 2: Ian's Buzzer, Zebra Midge (assorted colors), UFO; Row 3: Dragon Dropper, Miss Pinky. JIMMY CHANG PHOTO

This large spring creek brown took a Zebra Midge variation. Most use of smaller nymph patterns takes place in the Driftless area, but they can be locally effective elsewhere. JERRY DARKES PHOTO

## DRAGON DROPPER

*Originated and tied by Charlie Piette*

- **Hook:** #6 Daichi 2461
- **Thread:** Brown olive 70-denier Uni
- **Tail:** Olive grizzly marabou
- **Body:** Olive Sparkle Yarn
- **Rib:** Clear medium Half Round Rib
- **Legs:** Olive partridge or hen hackle
- **Head:** Olive Sparkle Yarn
- **Eyes:** Black mono, large

**Notes:** Dragonflies are likely more important in warmwater applications, but they do appear in slower sections or backwater areas of trout streams. Charlie Piette from Tight Lines Fly Fishing finds this a good pattern to work in those areas, as well as in rivers and lakes for bass and panfish.

## MISS PINKY

*Originated and tied by Damian Wilmot*

- **Hook:** #10 TMC 200R
- **Thread:** Black 6/0 Uni
- **Body:** Pink floss, clear Vinyl D-Rib
- **Rib:** White ostrich spun in a dubbing loop
- **Hackle:** Hungarian partridge
- **Head:** Peacock herl

**Notes:** This pattern is a favorite of Wisconsin guide Damian Wilmot on the upper part of Wisconsin's Brule River. What this fly actually imitates is not known, but trout take this larva pattern readily and it may work elsewhere.

# Group 9: Crossover Nymphs

These patterns serve in a double-duty role. They will work for both stream trout and the migratory trout of the Great Lakes. The migratory fish are mainly steelhead, but there are lake-run browns that show up in a number of tributaries and take nymphs at times, too. There are numerous rivers and streams around the Great Lakes that have both resident and migratory trout populations.

## SPARROW NYMPH

*Originated by Jack Gartside, tied by Jerry Darkes*

- **Hook:** #6-12 Daiichi 1550
- **Thread:** Color to match body 6/0 Danville
- **Tail:** Pheasant rump marabou
- **Body:** Squirrel/rabbit dubbing mix
- **Hackle:** Pheasant rump feather wound as a collar
- **Head:** Pheasant aftershaft feathers

**Notes:** There are numerous variations of this impressionistic pattern. The materials have a lot of movement in the water, and this fly just looks alive. Put the body dubbing in a loop and pick out the fibers after it is wrapped. The original had an olive body, but a tan or even cream body has proven to be effective across the Midwest. Whatever the fish think it is, they certainly eat it. Because the aftershaft feathers are so fragile, I now tie the collar feather in at the tip and wrap the feather all the way to the marabou material at the base to give a similar look. Grizzly marabou can also be substituted for the tail.

## HEX SPARROW

*Originated and tied by Jerry Darkes*

- **Hook:** #6-10 Daiichi 1710
- **Thread:** Tan or yellow 70-denier UTC
- **Tail:** Three to four natural gray ostrich feather fibers or grizzly marabou
- **Body:** Sulphur yellow nymph dubbing
- **Collar:** Ringneck pheasant rump feather
- **Head:** Sulphur yellow nymph dubbing
- **Eyes:** Black mono, small

**Notes:** I started tying this pattern about 30 years ago. It combines features of both a Hex nymph and the Sparrow nymph. It has caught many trout and steelhead, along with salmon, around the Great Lakes in numerous tributaries. I suspect it is also taken as a small baitfish, too. Wrap dubbing in a figure 8 around the eyes to form the head.

These stonefly nymphs by Ontario tier Joe Penich are super realistic in appearance and constructed for extreme durability. Penich is well known for his tying abilities and creative designs. PHOTOS BY JERRY DARKES

**(Left to right)** Row 1: Sparrow Nymph, Hex Sparrow; Row 2: Beadhead Easy Stone (2 sizes); Row 3: Joe's Black Stone Nymph; Row 4: Joe's Golden Stone Nymph. JIMMY CHANG PHOTO

## BEADHEAD EASY STONE (2 SIZES)

*Originated and tied by Jerry Darkes*

- **Hook:** #10-14 Daiichi 1530
- **Thread:** Black 70-denier UTC
- **Bead:** Black, size to hook
- **Tail:** Black goose biots
- **Body:** Black Haretron dubbing
- **Rib:** Small silver or black wire
- **Collar:** Black Haretron dubbing

**Notes:** There are several different stonefly species, generically referred to as Early Black or Early Brown Stones, that are on the small side. Most stonefly nymphs are fairly involved to tie. This didn't make much sense to me in the smaller sizes. This simplified pattern is a quick tie and catches fish. Spin the fur in a dubbing loop, then pick or brush out at the front for the collar. It is particularly effective on steelhead. Using the Daiichi 1530 hook allows a small-profile nymph to be tied on a 2X strong hook capable of holding a large fish in moving water without springing open. You can tie this on longer hooks up to a size 10.

## JOE'S BLACK STONE NYMPH

*Originated and tied by Joe Penich*

- **Hook:** #4-10 TMC 200R
- **Thread:** Black 70-denier UTC
- **Tail:** Black goose biots
- **Underbody:** Lead wire, same diameter as hook shank
- **Body:** Black medium Vinyl Rib
- **Rib:** Fine copper wire
- **Thorax:** Dark brown squirrel dubbing, black hen hackle
- **Wing Case:** Black ¼-inch Scud Back
- **Eyes:** Black mono
- **Antennae:** Black goose biots

**Notes:** Here we see the other extreme in a beautiful stonefly nymph that is nearly a piece of art from Joe Penich. In the larger sizes it is likely that more realism is important for the fly to be effective. The lead wire for the underbody is a section tied on each side of the hook shank. This pattern covers all features of the natural—split tail, segmented body, multiple wing cases, legs, and antenna.

## JOE'S GOLDEN STONE NYMPH

*Originated and tied by Joe Penich*

- **Hook:** #4-10 TMC 200R
- **Thread:** Brown 8/0 Uni
- **Tail:** Ginger goose biots
- **Underbody:** Lead wire, diameter of hook shank
- **Body:** Gold medium Vinyl Rib
- **Rib:** Fine copper wire
- **Thorax:** Golden brown Ice Dub, ginger hen hackle
- **Wing Case:** Light brown ¼-inch Scud Back
- **Eyes:** Black mono
- **Antennae:** Ginger goose biots

**Notes:** Similar to the previous pattern. Again, when imitating larger insects, it is likely important to include all major body features. As size decreases, the need to duplicate each body part diminishes. However, matching the size of the insect can still be important.

# Group 10: More Crossover Nymphs

These are additional patterns that have both trout and Great Lakes migratory fish applications. It is a bit difficult to place some of these in a specific category. Chapter 6, Patterns for Migratory Species, will describe an assortment of nymphs specifically designed for and focused on these fish.

## SULPHUR WIGGLE NYMPH

*Originated and tied by Matt Supinksi*

- **Front Hook:** #14-16 Daiichi 1120
- **Thread:** Brown 8/0-10/0 Uni
- **Bead:** Copper, 3/32 inch
- **Rear Hook:** Straight-eye dry fly, cut off at bend after fly is completed
- **Tail:** Partridge feather fibers
- **Abdomen (rear hook):** Pheasant tail fibers, wrapped
- **Rib:** Copper wire
- **Connector:** 10 lb. mono
- **Thorax (front hook):** Peacock Ice Dub, extra-small J:Son Mayfly Nymph Legs over top
- **Hackle:** Brown partridge feather
- **Eyes:** Black mono, small
- **Wing Case:** Brown partridge or grouse

**Notes:** There are times when extra movement makes a fly more effective. Several nymph patterns here incorporate this into their design. Matt Supinski designed this pattern for use on the Muskegon River where there are populations of both resident and migratory trout.

## BLACK STONE WIGGLE NYMPH

*Originated and tied by Matt Supinksi*

- **Front Hook:** #10-14 Daiichi 1120
- **Thread:** Black 6/0 Uni
- **Bead:** Black, size to hook
- **Rear Hook:** Straight-eye dry fly, cut off at bend after fly is completed
- **Connector:** 10 lb. mono
- **Tail:** Black goose biots
- **Abdomen (rear hook):** Black V-Rib or similar material
- **Thorax (front hook):** Peacock black Ice Dub with small J:Son Stonefly Nymph Legs
- **Hackle:** Gray partridge
- **Eyes:** Black mono, small
- **Wing Case:** Black 1/4-inch Scud Back

**Notes:** Again, the extended body gives extra movement to the fly. Stoneflies do not emerge to the surface the way mayflies or caddis do. Instead they crawl to the shore and out of the water prior to changing to the adult.

## WIGGLE STONE

*Originated and tied by Greg Senyo*

- **Front Hook:** #10-14 Daiichi 1120
- **Thread:** Black 6/0 Uni
- **Rear Hook:** Standard down-eye dry fly, #12 or #14, cut off at bend after fly is completed
- **Tail:** Black goose biots
- **Abdomen (rear hook):** Black rabbit dubbing
- **Rib:** 5X mono
- **Connector:** 8 lb. mono
- **Thorax (front hook):** Steelie blue or peacock Ice Dub
- **Wing Case:** Black 1/4-inch Scud Back, pearl tinsel, or Flashabou
- **Legs:** Black goose biots

**Notes:** Greg Senyo grew up fishing the Lake Erie tributaries for steelhead. The thorax color works as a trigger to attract fish. This pattern is a must-have for steelhead across the Great Lakes and is also a great trout fly.

## WIGGLE PRINCE

*Originated and tied by Greg Senyo*

- **Front Hook:** #10-14 Daiichi 1120
- **Thread:** Black 6/0 Uni
- **Rear Hook:** Standard down-eye dry fly, #12-#14
- **Tail:** Brown goose biots
- **Abdomen (rear hook):** Peacock herl
- **Rib:** 5X mono
- **Connector:** 8 lb. mono
- **Thorax (front hook):** Peacock herl or peacock Ice Dub
- **Wing Case:** Pearl tinsel or Flashabou
- **Legs:** Brown and black biots

**Notes:** The Prince Nymph is another great pattern for both trout and steelhead. This version throws extra movement into the mix to add to its appeal.

**(Left to right)** Row 1: Sulphur Wiggle Nymph, Black Stone Wiggle Nymph; Row 2: Wiggle Stone, Wiggle Prince; Row 3: Dr. Mike (3 colors); Row 4: Soft-Hackle Stone; Row 5: Superior X Legs, Beadhead Superior X Legs. JIMMY CHANG PHOTO

## DR. MIKE (3 COLORS)

*Originated and tied by Jerry Darkes*

- **Hook:** #12-14 Daiichi 1120
- **Thread:** 70-denier UTC, to match body color
- **Bead:** Copper, size to hook
- **Body:** Caddis cream Brite Blend, peacock Brite Blend, or chartreuse Ice Dub
- **Hackle:** Grouse, partridge, or mottled hen
- **Head:** Peacock herl

**Notes:** The late Mike Bennett, aka Dr. Steelhead, was a longtime friend and guide on the Ohio and Pennsylvania tributaries of Lake Erie. Turning over rocks in both Elk Creek and Conneaut Creek showed an abundance of a pale yellow caddis larva. I used the caddis cream Brite Blend on yellow thread that looked to be a good match for these, and the steelhead loved the fly (and still do). It became one of Bennett's favorites, and we added a bright and dark color into the mix to cover various water conditions. The fly has caught plenty of stream trout, too.

## SOFT-HACKLE STONE

*Originator unknown, tied by Jerry Darkes*

- **Hook:** #8-14 Daiichi 1530
- **Thread:** Black 70-denier UTC
- **Tail:** Black goose biots
- **Body:** Black Haretron dubbing
- **Rib:** Black wire or V-Rib
- **Hackle:** Black-dyed pheasant rump or hen hackle, tied in at the tip, keep some of the marabou from the base of the feather

**Notes:** We know that soft hackles were some of the earliest flies. The earliest mention of them for stoneflies (also called "water crickets") goes back to the 1750s. In 1976, Charles Brooks published *Nymph Fishing for Larger Trout*. Brooks described stonefly nymphs tied "in the round," where the hackle is wound around the hook and no wing cases are on the pattern. The concept is that in turbulent water, stonefly nymphs tumble in the current and trout do not have time to inspect for exact imitation. All sizes and colors of stoneflies can be tied in this manner, but the smaller black stone seems the best suited for Midwest application.

This steelhead hit a Soft-Hackle Stone nymph swung across the current. A dead drift is usually the most productive nymph presentation, but it pays to swing a nymph at times also. Changing the movement of the fly can trigger a strike at times. JERRY DARKES PHOTO

## SUPERIOR X LEGS

*Originated by Jim Pollock, tied by Jerry Darkes*

- **Hook:** #7 Mustad 9671
- **Thread:** Brown 6/0 Danville
- **Weight (optional):** .020-inch-diameter lead wire
- **Tail:** Brown grizzly marabou
- **Abdomen:** Kaufmann brown Stonefly Blend
- **Rib:** Medium copper wire
- **Thorax:** Kaufmann brown Stonefly Blend
- **Legs:** Brown with orange flake Sili Legs

**Notes:** This pattern comes out of Duluth, Minnesota, and has been a staple on Lake Superior tributaries of the region. Weight is added over the thorax area only. Also be sure to brush out the dubbing on the thorax. Both color and size can be varied as desired. This fly has caught trout across the country and is a good pattern for smallmouth, too!

## BEADHEAD SUPERIOR X LEGS

*Originated by Jim Pollock, tied by Jerry Darkes*

Same as above, but add a copper bead sized to the hook.

# 3

# Streamer Patterns

## INTRODUCTION

To me a streamer fly is an artificial fly that is given movement either by the current or the angler moving it, and that imitates a living aquatic organism such as a baitfish, leech, or crayfish or features color and flash to attract fish to strike it. I feel comfortable with this description because, as we shall see, streamers can vary greatly in size, color, and manner of construction.

Looking at the fly-fishing history here in North America, Theodore Gordon, who we consider the father of dry-fly fishing in the United States, was experimenting with streamers as early as 1880. He may also be considered the "father of the modern streamer," as his Bumblepuppy was well known in his lifetime and the first pattern of its type to gain recognition. This pattern went through stages of development over a period of years, and Gordon wrote about catching pike, salmon, striped bass, and other gamefish on it.

Modern line technology combined with creative fly patterns allows fly anglers to expand their range beyond streams and rivers. Large sections of water can be covered efficiently, targeting active fish. Many modern streamer designs, as well as ways to fish them, were developed in the Midwest and Great Lakes areas. JEFF LISKAY PHOTO

Here is the version of Gordon's preferred dressing of this pattern:

## BUMBLEPUPPY

*Originated by Theodore Gordon, tied by Jerry Darkes*

- **Hook:** Wet fly or 2xl-4xl streamer (long shanks were not available in Gordon's time)
- **Thread:** Black
- **Tail:** Small bunch red hackle fibers, rather long
- **Body:** White wool or chenille, rather heavy
- **Rib:** Single strand or red wool
- **Throat:** Two turns of a red and white neck hackle, mixed
- **Wing:** White bucktail clipped on lower half, matched narrow brown turkey tail feather sections

The Bumblepuppy. JERRY DARKES PHOTO

The Great Lakes contributed what is considered to be the single most influential streamer pattern ever developed. Dan Gapen's Muddler Minnow was born on Ontario's Nipigon River in 1937. What made the fly unique was its spun deer hair head. Although the technique of spinning hair was not new, the manner it was used as the head of the fly was revolutionary.

The spun hair head design opened the door to an ongoing list of patterns that continues to this day. The Midwest also continues to be a major influencer in the use of streamer flies through innovations in application and presentation as well as the patterns themselves. Just as with dry flies, we see the roots of development in the Catskills and the Midwest taking this to a higher level.

*Modern Streamers for Trophy Trout* by Bob Linsenman and Kelly Galloup was published in 1999 and has become the "bible" for modern streamer anglers. These Michigan-based fishermen presented in detail a whole system for targeting the largest trout. As with Swisher and Richards's work with dry flies, the AuSable River proved to be a primary laboratory for this pair's work. The concepts Galloup and Linsenman presented are used worldwide to pursue trophy trout, and have also expanded warmwater fly-fishing opportunities.

Dan Gapen's Muddler Minnow is one of the best-known of all streamer patterns. This pattern has Great Lakes roots and helped to create a trend in fly design that continues today. JERRY DARKES PHOTO

The Muddler Minnow and Zoo Cougar are two classic streamer designs. The Great Lakes and Midwest continue to be key areas in the development of streamer fly designs. Both inland and big-water environments provide the perfect laboratories for fly research. JIMMY CHANG PHOTO

A new generation of streamer anglers has emerged who have expanded this style of fishing and the flies used. Names such as Blane Chocklett, Alex Lafkas, Russ Maddin, and Mike Schultz are recognized across the fly-fishing community for their roles in this process. I am happy to be able to present some of the most recent developments in this genre of flies and fly tying.

# Group 1: Classic Patterns

These patterns span a time frame from the 1930s to the 1960s, and each reflects a different concept of tying. One of them may not even really be a streamer. During the post–World War II period, fly-fishing attention began to shift to the western states as that region was being developed. Also, the introduction of spinning tackle captured a significant portion of the attention that had previously been directed to fly fishing.

There are certainly other patterns that could have been included here, but these few were selected for their distinct characteristics.

## MUDDLER MINNOW

*Originated by Don Gapen, tied by Jerry Darkes*

- **Hook:** #2-12 Daiichi 1720
- **Thread:** Black 3/0-8/0 Uni, depending on hook size
- **Tail:** Small section of natural turkey wing quill
- **Body:** Flat gold tinsel
- **Wing:** Gray squirrel tail, mottled turkey wing quill on each side
- **Head:** Natural deer body hair

**Notes:** This recipe reflects Gapen's original dressing. It was designed to imitate a cockatouche minnow, another name for sculpin, to target the large brook trout of Ontario's Nipigon River. It is tied on a 3xl-4xl streamer hook, of which there are presently many options. When the wing is set, it should be at an upward angle of about 30 degrees. The deer hair is spun, then trimmed.

The Muddler is to streamers what the Adams is to dry flies—a multitude of variations have emerged over time. The defining characteristic is the spun and clipped deer hair head, which has become an important element of a host of successful streamer patterns.

## THE BUZZ SAW

*Originated by Earl Madsen, tied by Old AuSable Fly Shop*

- **Front Hook:** #4-6 Daiichi 1720
- **Rear Hook:** #4-6 Daiichi 1720
- **Thread:** Red Monocord
- **Tail:** Tuft of red saddle hackle feather
- **Rear Body:** Red floss
- **Rib:** Flat silver tinsel
- **Connector:** 20 lb. mono, rear hook attached inverted and tight to the front hook, with minimal movement
- **Front Body:** Red floss
- **Rib:** Flat silver tinsel
- **Wing:** White bucktail, black bucktail (original pattern called for black-and-white skunk, which is not readily available or desired these days)

**Notes:** While this is often referred to as an articulated fly, this is not accurate, as the rear body is not constructed to move. What this pattern does bring, however, is one of the earliest streamers with a stinger-style hook that is designed to catch short-striking fish that miss the front hook. The Buzz Saw is still a popular fly today in the Grayling, Michigan, area.

Sculpin are found in the faster sections of rivers and streams across the Great Lakes and Midwest. They hide around rocks and other bottom cover. Whenever sculpins are present, they are favored prey of gamefish. JERRY DARKES PHOTO

## BEAMAN'S GHOST

*Originated by Hugh Beaman, tied by Jerry Darkes*

- **Hook:** #4-8 Daiichi 1710
- **Thread:** Black 6/0 Danville
- **Weight (optional):** Lead wire, same diameter as hook shank
- **Body:** Black wool
- **Rib:** Flat gold tinsel
- **Wing:** White hackle feathers
- **Throat:** Red or yellow hackle fibers, sparse

**Notes:** This is one of the few Midwestern streamer patterns reflective of the earlier feather wing designs from New England. Designed to target brook trout, it is a "bare bones" design lacking the fancy trimmings of earlier patterns, such as topping, cheeks, or eyes. Nonetheless, it works well for the brook trout of the area.

**(Left to right)** Row 1: Muddler Minnow; Row 2: The Buzz Saw, Beaman's Ghost; Row 3: Thunder Creek (3 colors); Row 4: Houghton Lake Special. JIMMY CHANG PHOTO

## THUNDER CREEK (3 COLORS)

*Originated by Keith Fulsher, tied by Jerry Darkes*

- **Hook:** #8-10 6x1 ring eye (this style hook is now hard to locate, so the Daiichi 1750, 4xl straight-eye streamer hook is shown)
- **Thread:** Red 70-denier UTC
- **Body:** Flat silver tinsel
- **Back:** Bucktail, reverse-tied
- **Belly:** Bucktail, reverse-tied
- **Gills:** Tying thread
- **Eyes:** Painted on, or 3D stick-on (3D eyes used here to add more realism)
- **Head:** Bucktail from back and belly

**Notes:** This is an important fly series for a number of reasons. Although he was from New York State, these were first tested by Fulsher in the 1960s in a small stream in Wisconsin, Thunder Creek. They were one of the first streamers to focus on realistic imitation, and also introduced the technique of reverse-tied bucktail. Here the bucktail is tied forward, then pulled back and tied down.

The original pattern calls for a 6xl ring-eye hook, which is nearly impossible to find. By only altering the back bucktail color and leaving the belly white, these three flies represent a creek chub, emerald shiner, and silver shiner, respectively. The head size can be increased if needed by building up with a neutral-color dubbing on the thread prior to pulling the bucktail back. The head is then coated with Hard As Nails, epoxy, or UV cure. Fulsher created a complete series of baitfish patterns by altering body materials and colors of bucktail for the back and belly.

Reverse-tying bucktail and other materials such as Craft Fur helps to add a larger profile. It is an important technique in the construction of many modern streamers. It can be used in any part of the fly by cutting the material to length and securing to the hook shank at the butt ends with the tips extending forward. JERRY DARKES PHOTO

The section of hair is pulled back and then thread-wrapped to hold in position. At the front, thread can be wrapped farther back to create a head and a large area to attach eyes. JERRY DARKES PHOTO

## HOUGHTON LAKE SPECIAL

*Originated by Bob Jewell, tied by Jerry Darkes*

- **Hook:** #2-8 Daiichi 1720
- **Thread:** Black 3/0 Danville
- **Tail:** Red yarn
- **Body:** Black chenille
- **Rib:** Flat silver tinsel
- **Wing:** White or brown over white bucktail
- **Hackle:** Brown, heavily wrapped

**Notes:** This pattern can fall into several categories. It was originally tied as a nighttime dry fly for trout, and was both dead-drifted and quartered downstream and swung across the current. On the swing, it often got pulled under the surface—no longer a true dry fly. It was then found that this fly can be cast and stripped during the day and will attract fish. Much like the Hornberg, this pattern can be fished different ways and will produce. You can still find it in Grayling, Michigan, area fly shops today. I have substituted a modern hook model in the recipe. Any 3x1 to 4x1 streamer hook is usable.

## Group 2: Important Influencers

Similar to the previous group, these streamer patterns move a little farther up the timeline in creativity. These patterns are from the late 1980s through the 1990s and show a number of additional features and characteristics that are now found in nearly all contemporary streamer patterns.

### ZOO COUGAR

*Originated and tied by Kelly Galloup*

- **Hook:** #2-4 TMC 300
- **Thread:** Black 100-denier GSP
- **Tail:** Yellow marabou
- **Body:** Pearl Sparkle Braid
- **Wing:** Mallard flank dyed wood duck yellow
- **Underwing:** White calf tail
- **Collar:** Olive yellow deer body hair
- **Head:** Olive yellow deer body hair

**Notes:** This is the original color scheme of this legendary fly. It can be tied and fished in a number of different colors. Galloup stresses that "the flank feather placement is very important to make the fly swim properly. Make sure the feather is directly on top." The head should be trimmed wide and rounded on top, flat on the bottom. Also, this is a neutral-density fly designed to be fished on a sinking or sinking-head line, maybe the first pattern to be specifically designed this way. The combination of the almost-floating fly paired with the sinking line allows the fly to be worked at a wide range of speeds and with all types of action on the retrieve.

### CIRCUS PEANUT

*Originated and tied by Russ Maddin*

- **Front Hook:** #2-4 TMC 9395
- **Rear Hook:** #2-4 TMC 5262
- **Thread:** Black 6/0 Uni
- **Tail:** Sculpin olive marabou
- **Rear Body:** Olive or root beer Estaz, barred Sili Legs (chartreuse or pumpkinseed), brown or black schlappen
- **Connector:** 30 lb. Maxima monofilament
- **Front Body:** Olive or root beer Estaz, barred Sili Legs (chartresue or pumpkinseed), brown or black schlappen
- **Eyes:** Barbell-style, tied on bottom of hook shank

**Notes:** Russ Maddin is another well-known "streamer freak" and a top-notch fly designer whose patterns are proven fish-catching designs. Northern Michigan has been his testing ground for many years. The "Nut," as Maddin calls it, came about from the need for a large fly with lots of movement that could be cast without tangling. It also eliminates the leverage from a long-shank hook that helps large, twisting trout work loose. Connecting two shorter-shank hooks solved these problems. The connector mono is looped through the rear hook eye, then doubled over and secured to the front by wrapping the mono nearly the length of the front hook, then coated with Zap-A-Gap or Krazy Glue.

The Circus Peanut may be the first truely articulated streamer and was the inspiration for a host of patterns to follow. Colors can be altered as desired.

### CONRAD'S SCULPIN

*Originated by Jeff Conrad, tied by Pacific Fly Group*

- **Front Hook:** #2 Mustad 3366
- **Rear Hook:** #6 Mustad 3366
- **Thread:** Black 140-denier UTC or similar
- **Tail (rear hook):** A ball of chartreuse Ice Dub, 2 black schlappen feather sections, black and chartreuse marabou tips
- **Connector:** 40 lb. mono with 3 or 4 red glass beads
- **Body (front hook):** Black marabou plume, chartreuse marabou plume over top, black deer body hair
- **Eyes:** Chartreuse barbell-style, large

**Notes:** This was one of the first true "big trout" streamers commercially on the market and has accounted for numerous trophy fish. Both trout and bass love this fly, and I'm sure other species will eat it. Colors can be altered as desired, and you can add flash and rubber legs, too. This is a great pattern template to work with.

For the tail, put the ball of chartreuse Ice Dub at the bend of the hook; add the two schlappen feather sections about ¾ inch long, tied down in front of the dubbing, curving out on each side into a "V" shape; then the tip of a black, then a chartreuse marabou plume over top. The 40-pound mono is looped through the eye of the rear hook and doubled over, then three or four red glass beads are slid onto the mono and secured to the front hook with thread wrapped the length of the hook and coated with Zap-A-Gap. Trim the deer hair flat on top and bottom, leaving a wide head, then add chartreuse barbell eyes to the top of the front hook shank so the top hook is inverted when fishing and the black is on top.

**(Left to right)** Row 1: Zoo Cougar, Circus Peanut; Row 2: Conrad's Sculpin, Rattlesnake; Row 3: Yellow Butt Monkey, Mad Pup. JIMMY CHANG PHOTO

## RATTLESNAKE

*Originated and tied by Ray Schmidt*

- **Front Hook:** #6 TMC 105
- **Rear Hook:** #6-8 TMC 2457, snelled to 20 lb. Maxima, with 3 to 5 copper or brass beads
- **Thread:** Black 100-denier GSP
- **Wing:** Rabbit strip, Holographic Flashabou
- **Body:** Two wraps of Estaz
- **Collar:** Deer body hair
- **Head:** Deer body hair

**Notes:** This pattern dates back to 1998 and is one of the first with a short-shank hook extended to the back. It is a great choice when larger streamers are not getting looks. It sinks and swims well and color can be adjusted to a number of natural baitfish or just as an attractor.

Slide the copper or brass beads onto the mono, then secure the rear hook to the front hook so that the rear hook is inverted, the mono should go through the eye of the front hook, then lashed down on the top and bottom of the hook shank, wrapping thread back to the bend, then trim the mono and coat with cement. Trim the head flat on the sides with a taper down to the hook eye.

## YELLOW BUTT MONKEY

*Originated by Scott Smith and Bob Linsenman, tied by Pacific Fly Group*

- **Hook:** #2-4 TMC 300 or 5236
- **Thread:** Tan 3/0 Uni
- **Tail:** Yellow marabou plume tip (optional: add 4 to 6 strands of gold Flashabou)
- **Body:** Root beer Estaz
- **Rib:** Medium copper wire
- **Wing:** Rusty orange rabbit strip
- **Throat:** Red wool
- **Collar:** Pheasant rump
- **Eyes:** Barbell-style, large
- **Head:** Tan ram's wool, spun and clipped

**Notes:** This is another pattern from the north shore of Lake Superior, and it takes the Zonker to a whole new level. The rabbit strip is secured to the top of the body with the wire rib. It was created for the oversized brook trout ascending tributaries from Lake Superior, but has worked on a variety of species including trout, bass, and salmon. This is another great pattern template open to a wide range of color variations.

## MAD PUP

*Originated by Russ Maddin, tied by Pacific Fly Group*

- **Hook:** #2-4 TMC 300 or similar
- **Thread:** 140-denier UTC, color to match fly
- **Tail:** Rabbit strip, tied long with front part used to create half of the body
- **Body/Head:** Rabbit strip from tail, ram's wool
- **Eyes:** Barbell-style, large, on bottom of hook shank

**Notes:** Multiple color schemes can be created with this pattern, which attracts a variety of large gamefish. Tying a loop of mono horizontally at the hook bend prior to adding the wing helps minimize fouling. Maddin has an updated version of this where two schlappen feathers replace the rabbit strip and a collar of bucktail is added prior to the head. He also alternates colors of wool for the head.

This is the updated version of the Mad Pup streamer. The schlappen feathers do not hold as much water weight and are less apt to tangle into the hook when cast. Many fly patterns evolve over time as updates in materials take place. JERRY DARKES PHOTO

# Group 3: Bugger Hybrids

The Woolly Bugger may be the most recognized fly pattern worldwide. Although a woolly worm fly is mentioned in Walton's *The Compleat Angler* (1653), the Woolly Bugger as we know it is generally credited to Russell Blessing, a Pennsylvania fly fisher, who put the pattern together in 1967. Blessing's fly was designed to imitate the Dobson fly larva, also called a hellgrammite, for smallmouth bass. Blessing's original pattern had a black marabou tail, olive chenille body, and black hackle palmered over the body. This is still one of the most popular colors of this fly.

## WOOLLY BUGGER (ORIGINAL PATTERN)

*Originated by Russell Blessing, tied by Jerry Darkes*

- **Hook:** #4-8 Daiichi 2220
- **Thread:** Black 6/0 Uni
- **Tail:** Black marabou plume tip, approximately length of hook shank
- **Weight (optional):** Lead wire, same diameter as hook shank
- **Body:** Medium olive chenille
- **Hackle:** Black saddle

**Notes:** By varying hook size and length, along with materials and colors, this fly can simulate a wide range of things. The Woolly Bugger looks like nothing, but imitates everything. I have always tied the saddle hackle in by the tip so that the fibers angle backward and get longer toward the eye of the hook. The hackle should be palmer wrapped the length of the hook shank. which gives it a more streamlined look.

If there is a weakness to this fly, it is that after a few fish the hackle often breaks where it is tied in at the hook bend and unwinds, making the fly useless. There are several ways to minimize this. First, after the hackle is wound, counter-wrap over the hackle with wire or 3X mono. Another option is to twist the hackle and chenille together and wind forward as a single piece. With each wrap, pull the hackle fibers back to position them pointing to the rear of the fly.

The Woolly Bugger is everything a fly tier could want: easy to tie with simple materials, and it catches fish everywhere. Few fly patterns are as well recognized. By varying size and color, it imitates a host of organisms that fish feed on. JERRY DARKES PHOTO

## LION BUGGER

*Originated and tied by Jon Uhlenhop*

- **Hook:** #4-6 Daiichi 1710
- **Thread:** Brown 70-denier UTC
- **Tail:** Tan or olive grizzly marabou over orange grizzly marabou, 2 orange or chartreuse Sili Legs
- **Body:** Olive or root beer Estaz or Cactus Chenille, brown saddle hackle
- **Legs:** Yellow Centipede Legs
- **Collar:** Tan or olive grizzly marabou
- **Head:** Black nickel Cross-Eyed Cone, size to hook

**Notes:** This is a great crayfish imitation and can also be used to imitate small gobies and sculpin. It has great movement and is often taken dead-drifted or on the drop. The saddle hackle is palmer wrapped over the body, and the marabou for the collar is wrapped behind the cone.

## BAIT BUGGER

*Originated and tied by Tim Pearson*

- **Hook:** #4 Daichi 1710
- **Thread:** Olive brown 70-denier UTC
- **Tail:** Olive grizzly marabou
- **Body:** Golden brown Ice Dub, natural or yellow-dyed grizzly saddle feather
- **Flash:** Perch Flashabou
- **Head:** Large gold cone

**Notes:** Tim Pearson is an artist and guide on Minnesota's North Shore area. This pattern imitates a host of darker-colored baitfish. Its mottled appearance and flash bring it to life in the water. Tie in the Perch Flashabou at the front, extending forward, then pull back several strands at a time over the body with each wrap of the hackle. This allows the flash to spread evenly on top of the body, not waving around in one big clump.

## CRAW BUGGER (2 COLORS)

*Originated and tied by Jerry Darkes*

- **Hook:** #4-8 Daiichi 1710
- **Thread:** 70-denier UTC, to match body
- **Tail:** Sculpin olive marabou plume tip
- **Eyes:** Mono, small
- **Body:** Brown or olive Craw Dub, or similar coarse dubbing
- **Rib:** Brassie wire, to match body color
- **Hackle:** Olive- or brown-dyed mallard flank

**Notes:** This simple fly was deigned to target carp and smallmouth in clear-water situations. It has a slim profile and sinks well, with a great translucent look in the water. Wrap the body dubbing in a loop and then brush out on the bottom for the best effect.

## QUICK BUGGER

*Originated and tied by Scott Gobel*

- **Hook:** #4-6 TMC 200R
- **Thread:** 70-denier UTC, color to match body
- **Tail:** Tip from marabou plume, 4 to 6 strands of Flashabou
- **Weight (optional):** Lead wire, size to hook shank
- **Body:** Cross-cut rabbit
- **Bead:** Vary size and color as desired

**Notes:** Indiana angler Scott Gobel shares this pattern. It meets all the criteria of a "guide fly," being quick and easy to tie and catches fish. It can be colored to represent a wide range of aquatic organisms or fished as an attractor.

**(Left to right)** Row 1: Lion Bugger, Bait Bugger; Row 2: Craw Bugger (2 colors); Row 3: Quick Bugger, Stonebugger, Pepperoni Yum Bug JIMMY CHANG PHOTO

## STONEBUGGER

*Originator unknown, tied by the Orvis Company*

- **Hook:** #6-10 Daiichi 1710
- **Thread:** Brown 6/0 Uni
- **Tail:** Brown marabou
- **Weight:** Lead wire, size to hook shank
- **Body:** Kaufmann brown Stonefly Blend
- **Legs:** Brown grizzly or mottled hen
- **Wing Case/Back:** Turkey tail section

**Notes:** This pattern is a proven fish catcher around the region. Brook trout in northern lakes especially seem to like it. It is a bit time consuming to tie, but worth the effort! This fly can be stripped or swung, and it catches trout, smallmouth, carp, and more. Usually seen in brown, but tan, olive, and black are also productive colors. Each body section is tied in this sequence from the tail and then repeated: Dub body, tie in wing case section, then feather by the butt end; pull down legs and tie down; then pull down wing case and tie down. Three leg sections are enough to give this pattern its super-buggy look.

## PEPPERONI YUM BUG

*Originated and tied by Charlie Chlysta*

- **Hook:** #4 Daiichi 2461
- **Thread:** Brown 70-denier UTC
- **Tail:** Brown Mottlebou
- **Weight:** Lead wire, same diameter as hook shank
- **Abdomen:** Black chenille, tied heavy
- **Legs:** Black and white Centipede Legs, 2 pairs each side
- **Thorax:** Orange or burnt orange chenille
- **Hackle:** Cree or ginger grizzly

**Notes:** Our friend Picket Pin returns here with one of his favorite smallmouth patterns. This is his "improved" version of the western Yuk Bug. Just like the original Woolly Bugger, this fly bridges the gap between nymph and streamer, as it can be dead-drifted, swung, or stripped and still catch fish.

# Group 4: General Purpose #1

Here is a group of home-grown, Midwest patterns that borrow from a few different tying themes. These all feature a clipped deer hair head that can be done a few different ways to create a "vortex" behind the head to help movement of materials or help add movement of the fly itself.

## CROSS-EYED MUDDLER (2 COLORS)

*Originated and tied by Jon Uhlenhop*

- **Hook:** #4-8 Daiichi 1710 or similar
- **Thread:** Black 70-denier UTC
- **Tail:** Marabou, silver Holographic Flashabou
- **Body:** Holo silver Lite Brite dubbing
- **Wing:** Two rabbit strips, pearl Krystal Flash
- **Legs:** Two Sili Leg strands on each side
- **Throat:** Red Krystal Flash
- **Collar:** Natural deer body hair
- **Head:** Natural deer body hair
- **Cone:** Silver Cross-Eyed Cone, size to hook

**Notes:** This pattern template has tons of movement and plenty of flash. The twin rabbit strips give a crayfish-type silhouette when stripped. This can be done in all primary colors—add in white, yellow, and tan. Some of the newer barred rabbit strip colors give this fly a great lifelike appearance.

## Z'S SUPER STREAMER

*Originated and tied by Matt Zudweg*

- **Hook:** #6 TMC 8089
- **Thread:** White 140-denier UTC
- **Tail:** Barred rabbit strip (do not trim front)
- **Body:** Front of barred rabbit strip from tail

- **Flash:** DNA HoloFlash
- **Collar:** Mallard flank feather
- **Head:** Deer belly or elk body hair, one large clump

**Notes:** Rabbit strips plus elk or deer hair make a great combination, as we will see multiple times. Wrap the front part of the tail rabbit strip over the hook shank for the body. Trim the deer/elk hair in front, but leave plenty of longer hairs. Multiple color combinations are possible with this pattern, and it will catch pretty near anything.

## Z'S FLUX CAPACITOR

*Originated and tied by Matt Zudweg*

- **Hook:** #1-2 Daiichi 2460
- **Thread:** White or yellow 100-denier Lagartun XX or equivalent
- **Tail:** Bucktail
- **Body:** Front of bucktail from the tail
- **Underwing:** Gold or copper Flashabou
- **Overwing:** Bucktail
- **Head:** Yellow deer body hair

**Notes:** This fly can be fished just under the surface on a floating line or taken to mid-depth and stripped with a sinking-head line. Use a loop knot to attach this fly to the leader for maximum movement. Color combinations are endless!

**(Left to right)** Row 1: Cross-Eyed Muddler (2 colors); Row 2: Z's Super Streamer, Z's Flux Capacitor; Row 3: Mini D (2 colors); Row 4: Short Striker. JIMMY CHANG PHOTO

## MINI D (2 COLORS)

*Originated and tied by Tommy Lynch*

- **Front Hook:** #2 Daiichi 1710 or similar
- **Rear Hook:** #4 Gamakatsu B10S
- **Thread:** White 100-denier GSP or 140-denier UTC colored to fly
- **Tail:** Holo Flashabou or New Age Holo Flash
- **Rear Body:** UV Polar Chenille, wrapped rabbit strip, mallard flank
- **Connector:** 30 lb. bite wire with one 3D bead
- **Front Body:** Holo Flashabou or New Age Holo Flash, wrapped rabbit strip, UV Polar Chenille
- **Overwing:** Two mallard flank feathers, Flashabou
- **Collar:** Wrapped rabbit strip, deer body hair
- **Head:** Spun deer hair
- **Eyes:** 3D, coated with Clear Cure Goo Hydro

**Notes:** This is a sized-down version of the original Drunk and Disorderly by Tommy Lynch, with the rattle removed. It is important to note the materials sequence as given for both the front and back sections. The deer hair head is trimmed flat bottom and top, slightly cupped on top, then coated with Clear Cure Goo Hydro.

The smaller size is easier to cast and manipulate for most anglers. It is designed have a crankbait-type action and catches a wide range of fish species. Colors are endless, but a selection should have light (white, gray), dark (black, olive), and bright (orange, chartreuse, yellow) base colors.

## SHORT STRIKER

*Originated and tied by Jerry Darkes*

- **Front Hook:** #2 Gamakatsu B10S
- **Thread:** Gray 140-denier UTC
- **Rear Hook:** #4 Daiichi Octopus
- **Connector:** 50 lb. braid
- **Tail/Wing:** White-barred black rabbit strip
- **Flash:** Pearl Krinkle Mirror Flash or Krystal Flash
- **Belly:** White bucktail
- **Collar/Head:** Gray or olive deer belly hair
- **Eyes (optional):** 3D

**Notes:** This pattern came about from fishing the large, lake-dwelling brook trout of Lake Superior known as coasters. These fish are notorious for following and nipping at the back end of a fly. The stinger hook noticeably increases the number of fish hooked. This has been my favorite color scheme, but other colors are definitely usable, and everyone will have their favorite.

This pattern is a bit time consuming to tie, but not technically difficult. The final length when complete will be around 4 inches, an ideal size to imitate a wide range of forage species.

For the hook size listed, cut a length of braid around 4 inches. Attach the braid to the rear hook by doubling it over and inserting the tag ends through the hook eye. Push the hook through the loop created and pull the braid tight

behind the hook eye, keeping the tag ends even in length. To attach to the front hook, lay the braid on top of the front hook shank. Insert a short piece of braid down through the front hook eye and pull back from the eye onto the bottom of the hook shank. With the thread at the front hook eye, secure the braid to the top and bottom of the front hook by wrapping with thread six to eight times. Then wrap to the bend of the hook and back up to the eye, and tie off. This secures the rear hook with no chance to pull loose.

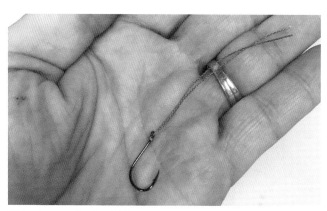

This shows the braid looped and secured to the hook. This technique carries over to a large number of current fly patterns. JERRY DARKES PHOTO

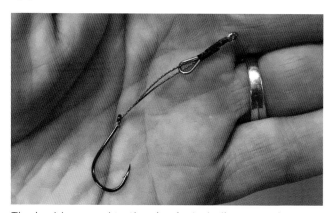

The braid secured to the shank. A similar procedure is used whenever braid is attached to a shank. JERRY DARKES PHOTO

The rear hook is then put into the vise, and the thread is started in the middle of the shank. Put a drop of Super Glue gel on the thread and lay the rabbit strip on top.

Create an open spot on the rabbit strip right over the thread by stroking the hair forward and exposing just the hide. Wrap the thread over the open area four to six times. Leave the thread bobbin hanging to maintain pressure and cut the front part of the rabbit strip to about halfway up the front hook. Tie off the thread on the rear hook and cover with a bit of Super Glue.

The thread is restarted on the front hook and the rabbit strip secured. The flash material is then added in front of the rabbit strip. Turn over and tie in the belly, then turn back so the hook is upright and add collar and head. Trim the head into a tapered shape.

Brown trout are not always the biggest trout in the system. This PB brookie came from Ontario's Nipigon River on a Stripped-Down Muddler. GORD ELLIS PHOTO

## STRIPPED-DOWN MUDDLER

*Originated and tied by Jerry Darkes*

- **Hook:** #1 or #2 Aqua Talon or similar
- **Thread:** 140-denier UTC, match color scheme of fly
- **Hook Loop:** 40-50 lb. braid (optional: add beads to the braid)
- **Shank:** Flymen 20 mm Articulated Shank
- **Wing:** Zonker strip, Krystal Flash or Krinkle Mirror Flash
- **Collar:** Mallard flank feather or schlappen
- **Head:** Deer body hair
- **Weight (optional):** Tungsten bead
- **Eyes (optional):** Barbell-style

**Notes:** This pattern has emerged as a more versatile version of the previous Short Striker. It is constructed in the same sequence except the Flymen Shank takes the place of the front hook. Weight can be added by sliding a tungsten bead onto the loop of the shank before wrapping it closed with thread. Or barbell eyes can be attached to the bottom of the shank in front of the loop prior to adding the deer hair head. I have fished this fly extensively and caught fish from one end of North America to the other— Labrador, the Great Lakes, the inland Midwest, and Alaska. It has become my favorite streamer pattern.

Stripped-Down Muddler. JERRY DARKES PHOTO

# Group 5: General Purpose #2

These patterns vary in appearance, but all use Craft Fur as a primary item in their construction. Most tiers opt for the "Extra Select" version of this great material that is now used extensively in both freshwater and saltwater applications.

## BAY TOAD

*Originated and tied by Ted Kraimer*

- **Hook:** #4 Daiichi 2450 or 2451
- **Thread:** Olive dun 6/0 Uni
- **Tail:** Golden olive Extra Select Craft Fur, barred with black or brown Sharpie marker
- **Body:** Olive Ice Chenille, pheasant rump feather
- **Head:** Black, then olive EP Fibers
- **Eye:** Large black bead chain

**Notes:** Ted Kraimer designed this scaled-down version of the saltwater Toad pattern for use on Lake Michigan's Grand Traverse Bay. It is a great mini goby and sculpin imitation, or dragonfly nymph. Do a tan/brown version and you have a Hex nymph. Its targeted use is for smallmouth and carp, but other species will eat it, too!

## PERCH FRY

*Originated and tied by Austin Adduci*

- **Hook:** #4 TMC 811S
- **Thread:** Dark brown 70-denier UTC
- **Back/Belly:** Tan Extra Select Craft Fur

**Notes:** It doesn't get much simpler than this. Reverse-tie the Craft Fur and mark with a Sharpie. Illinois guide Austin Adduci fishes this in the early summer in southern Lake Michigan when young-of-the-year yellow perch are abundant. Smallmouth, walleye, pike, and even brown trout will also target these when present.

## BAD HAIR DAY SCULPIN

*Originated and tied by Dave Pinczkowski*

- **Hook:** #2-4 Gamakatsu B10S
- **Thread:** Olive 70-denier UTC
- **Tail:** Olive Extra Select Craft Fur, june bug Flashabou
- **Body:** Olive and brown mixed Extra Select Craft Fur, gold Angel Hair
- **Collar:** Copper Flashabou
- **Head:** Olive Ice Dub

**Notes:** The Bad Hair Day streamer is well known to Great Lakes anglers and has been steadily migrating to other areas. This creation by Wisconsin angler/guide Dave Pinczkowski will catch most anything that swims. Color can be varied and accenting materials added as desired. This version is best in darker or tannic-colored water. Add barring with a Sharpie.

Reverse-tying the Craft Fur gives this pattern its great movement and translucency in the water. After cutting the fur off the sheet, leave most of the shorter hairs in the bunch. Tie to the shank at the bottom of the bunch with the tips facing forward. Then pull all the Craft Fur back and secure by wrapping thread in front. Three to four sections of Craft Fur should fill the hook shank. For the final step, after the thread has been trimmed off, give the hook a finger "flick" and the Craft Fur will flare out noticeably.

A big-water smallie that took a Bad Hair Day with eyes added. This pattern can be adjusted in a number of ways. Adding eyes can enhance its effectiveness at times. JERRY DARKES PHOTO

(**Left to right**) Row 1: Bay Toad, Perch Fry; Row 2: Bad Hair Day Sculpin, Bad Hair Day Emerald Shiner; Row 3: Wool Ease Minnow (2 colors); Row 4: Articulated BHD, Crafty Minnow. JIMMY CHANG PHOTO

## BAD HAIR DAY EMERALD SHINER

*Originated and tied by Dave Pinczkowski*

- **Hook:** #2-4 Gamakatsu B10S
- **Thread:** Chartreuse 70-denier UTC
- **Tail:** White Extra Select Craft Fur, pearl Krinkle Mirror Flash or Lateral Scale
- **Body:** White Extra Select Craft Fur, silver Angel Hair
- **Head:** Chartreuse Extra Select Craft Fur

**Notes:** This is the favorite color scheme of this great pattern for the open waters of the Great Lakes or anywhere emerald shiners are abundant. As in the previous patterns, reverse-tie the Craft Fur. Colors can be adjusted as needed or desired. By following the basic recipe and tying process, an endless number of imitative or attractor variations are possible.

## WOOL EASE MINNOW (2 COLORS)

*Originated and tied by Charlie Chlysta*

- **Hook:** #1-4 Daiichi 2461
- **Thread:** 8/0 Euro, to match color of minnow back
- **Weight (optional):** .015-.020-inch-diameter lead wire
- **Body:** White Lion brand "Wool-Ease" yarn
- **Underwing:** Light-colored Icelandic Sheep Wool, sparse
- **Flash:** Ice Dub Shimmer Fringe or similar material
- **Overwing:** Extra Select Craft Fur
- **Collar:** Hen hackle

**Notes:** There are times when a streamer with a slender profile and subdued flash works better. This pattern can be tied to imitate a variety of smaller baitfish found across the Midwest and Great Lakes. Here we see an emerald shiner and black-nosed dace. When wrapping the body yarn, pull the longer fibers back with each wrap. Then brush out the fibers to create a translucent body. If you are weighting the fly, wrap the wire on the front half of the hook.

## ARTICULATED BHD

*Orignated by Dave Pinzkowski, tied by Kory Boozer*

- **Front Hook:** #2/0-1 Partridge Universal Predator
- **Thread:** 140-denier UTC, per fly color scheme
- **Rear Hook:** #1-4 Partridge Universal Predator
- **Tail:** Holographic Flashabou
- **Rear Body:** Brown Extra Select Craft Fur
- **Connector:** Senyo Intruder Wire with two 3D beads
- **Front Body:** Two sections brown Extra Select Craft Fur, bronze Holographic Flashabou
- **Belly:** Tan Extra Select Craft Fur
- **Head:** Brown Senyo Laser Yarn

**Notes:** The length of the Extra Select Craft Fur limits size to a single-hook pattern. To make a larger version of the Bad Hair Day streamer, Indiana guide/angler Kory Boozer combines two single-hook versions. To create the head, a clump of Senyo Laser Yarn is spread around the hook eye and secured in the middle. It is then pulled back over and around the Craft Fur and thread-wrapped in front to secure in place. Again, both imitative and attractor color variations can be made.

## CRAFTY MINNOW

*Originated and tied by Steve May*

- **Hook:** #1-4 Gamakatsu SC15
- **Thread:** White 70-denier UTC
- **Tail:** Red synthetic yarn, pearl Krystal Flash
- **Belly:** White Extra Select Craft Fur or Polar Fiber
- **Back:** Olive Extra Select Craft Fur or Polar Fiber
- **Sides:** Grizzly saddle hackle tips
- **Eyes:** 3D

**Notes:** This is an easy-to-tie, smaller, slender baitfish imitation for use anywhere. When tying in the back and belly, leave a bit extending forward, then pull it back, tie down, and trim. This helps give the fly a more realistic silhouette. This is the original color scheme, but it is open to a wide range of variation. Color it to the primary baitfish in the area you will be fishing.

## Group 6: General Purpose #3

These are additional patterns that utilize Extra Select Craft Fur as a primary material. Several are quite simple, and two are quite involved in their construction. Here we see how a different hook and additional materials can significantly alter both the look and application of a streamer pattern.

(Left to right) Row 1: Jigawatt Minnow, DP Baitfish; Row 2: CF Smelt; Row 3: Chartreuse and White Glow, Craft & Craft Minnow—Firetiger. JIMMY CHANG PHOTO

### JIGAWATT MINNOW

*Originated and tied by Matt Zudweg*

- **Hook:** #6 TMC 8089
- **Thread:** White 140-denier UTC
- **Tail:** White Extra Select Craft Fur
- **Body:** Pearl Estaz Grande
- **Collar:** White Craft Fur Brush
- **Wing:** White Extra Select Craft Fur, gray olive Extra Select Craft Fur, EP 3D Minnow Fibers, pearl Flashabou
- **Eyes:** 5/16-inch 3D
- **Head:** Hot glue

**Notes:** This a super-fishy pattern to imitate silvery baitfish in this color scheme. The olive gray Craft Fur is one to keep in mind. It is not seen very often, but is a productive color in both fresh- and saltwater patterns. The hot glue is used to secure the eyes and fill any gaps. Clear Cure Goo or a similar UV cure material can also be used.

### DP BAITFISH

*Originated and tied by Dave Pinczykowski*

- **Hook:** #1-4 Gamakatsu B10S
- **Thread:** White 140-denier UTC
- **Wing:** White Extra Select Craft Fur, mix of silver Angel Hair and pearl Flashabou, olive gray Extra Select Craft Fur
- **Eyes:** 3D

**Notes:** Another great imitation of medium-size baitfish. This color imitates an alewife, an invasive species in the Great Lakes that is targeted by salmon and trout. To give a different profile, this pattern could have the Craft Fur reverse-tied as in the Bad Hair Day. Secure the eyes with Liquid Fusion.

## CF SMELT

*Originated and tied by Jerry Darkes*

- **Hook:** #2 Mustad Signature Stinger
- **Thread:** Gray 140-denier UTC
- **Tail:** Light purple Steve Farrar SF Blend
- **Belly:** Light purple Steve Farrar SF Blend, sparse
- **Back:** Gray Extra Select Craft Fur, olive Krinkle Mirror Flash
- **Head:** Flymen Fish Mask, #5 with 3D eyes

**Notes:** This color scheme is specific as a smelt imitation, but this pattern can be colored as desired. The SF Blend is a great belly material, having a nice subtle flash to it. Make sure to keep the belly sparse for the slender profile of a smelt. The Fish Mask works wherever you want 3D eyes placed without having to use epoxy or hot glue.

## CHARTREUSE AND WHITE GLOW

*Originated and tied by Ted Kraimer*

- **Hook:** #1/0 Gamakatsu 60-degree jig hook
- **Thread:** Bright green Flymaster Plus
- **Tail:** Mix of green glow-in-the-dark Flashabou and pearl Flashabou
- **Body:** Silver UV Polar Chenille, white schlappen
- **Belly:** White Extra Select Craft Fur
- **Legs:** Chartreuse-barred black Sili Legs
- **Wing:** Chartreuse bucktail, chartreuse Extra Select Craft Fur
- **Eyes:** Chartreuse 3D barbell-style

**Notes:** This pattern works well for Great Lakes chinook salmon when they are staged in harbors and estuary areas. Fish it at night or pre-dawn. Flash a camera to charge the fly.

## CRAFT & CRAFT MINNOW—FIRETIGER

*Originated and tied by Ted Kraimer*

- **Hook:** #1/0 Gamakatsu 60-degree jig hook
- **Thread:** Chatreuse Flymaster Plus Danville
- **Tail:** Firetiger Holographic Flashabou
- **Body:** Gold Holographic Cactus Chenille, chartreuse schlappen
- **Belly:** Chartreuse Extra Select Craft Fur
- **Legs:** Chartreuse-barred black Sili Legs
- **Wing:** Orange Extra Select Craft Fur barred with a black Sharpie, black Extra Select Craft Fur

**Notes:** This is a great fly for bass, pike, and even walleye. Fish it into pockets in cover or along ledges and drop-offs. With these last two flies, we see that a similar pattern template gives a variety of applications by changing materials.

## Group 7: General Purpose #4

Here are a series of patterns that use a rabbit strip as a primary component. This makes a durable pattern that has plenty of movement. These days rabbit strips are available in a multitude of colors. If there is a downside to rabbit, it would be that it soaks up water and becomes difficult to cast with a light line weight. Seven-weight outfits and heavier work best to carry patterns like this.

### GALLOUP'S MADONNA

*Originated by Kelly Galloup, tied by Jerry Darkes*

- **Hook:** #2-8 TMC 300
- **Thread:** Black 100-denier GSP
- **Body:** Mylar tinsel or Flat Braid
- **Underwing:** A few strands of pearl Flashabou
- **Wing:** Single rabbit strip on #6 or #8 hook, double rabbit strip on #2 or #4 hook
- **Collar:** Deer body hair, color to match wing bottom
- **Head:** Deer body hair, color to match wing
- **Cone:** Gold, size to hook

**Notes:** The Madonna leads the way in a still-continuing parade of rabbit strip patterns. Galloup calls this a "must-have" pattern. Colors are per personal preference, but white, yellow, olive, black, and tan are key. The two-tail version is a great crayfish imitation in olive, tan, or a rusty brown. To minimize the rabbit strip wrapping in the hook when casting, keep the length of the hide barely past the bend of the hook. The collar hair should be in a 180-degree arc on the top of the fly, not the bottom. The hair for the head should surround the cone and be trimmed flat on the bottom.

Madonna. JERRY DARKES PHOTO

### DOUBLE BUNNY

*Originated by Scott Sanchez, tied by Pacific Fly Group*

- **Hook:** #2-8 TMC 5263
- **Thread:** UTC 140-denier, to match back color
- **Belly:** Light-colored rabbit strip
- **Back:** Dark-colored rabbit strip
- **Flash:** Three to four strands of Krystal Flash on each side
- **Eyes:** 3D

**Notes:** This multi-use pattern catches a wide range of species. It can be single or dual colored. The rabbit strips are joined "skin to skin" with Tear Mender fabric glue to create a single strip. If using two colors, the darker one goes on top. The olive/tan combination shown here is a Midwest favorite. The eyes are secured with Liquid Fusion or Super Glue gel.

### PANCORA CRAB

*Originated and tied by Ray Schmidt*

- **Hook:** #2-6 Daiichi 1750
- **Thread:** Olive 140-denier UTC
- **Tail:** Orange marabou
- **Rib:** Medium copper wire
- **Weight:** Lead wire, same diameter as hook shank
- **Body:** Olive Estaz
- **Legs:** White round rubber
- **Wing:** Olive-barred brown or black Zonker strip
- **Collar:** Olive Ice Dub
- **Cone:** Copper, size to hook

**Notes:** Ray Schmidt originally designed this for the rivers of Chile and Argentina. It imitates the pancora crab, which is indigenous to those waters. It is also an excellent crayfish imitation for the waters of the Midwest. Lead wire should be wrapped on the front half of the hook. The copper wire is used to secure the rabbit strip to the top of the body. The rabbit fur is separated with each wrap so that the wire goes down to the hide. Five or six wraps should be used.

### SHORT STRIKER II (2 COLORS)

*Originated and tied by Jerry Darkes*

- **Front Hook:** #2 Gamakatsu B10S
- **Thread:** 140-denier UTC, color to match rabbit strip
- **Rear Hook:** #4 Gamakatsu B10S
- **Connector:** 40-50 lb. braid
- **Wing:** Barred rabbit strip with a few strands of similar color Krinkle Mirror Flash, matching color small bunch of bucktail
- **Belly:** Small bunch of lighter colored bucktail
- **Head:** 2 clumps Senyo Laser Dub to match color scheme of fly
- **Eyes:** 3D

**Notes:** This is another version of the Short Striker presented earlier. Construction is the same except the Laser Dub replaces the deer hair head. The eyes are secured with Liquid Fusion.

**(Left to right)** Row 1: Double Bunny, Pancora Crab; Row 2: Short Striker II (2 colors); Row 3: Autumn Defender, Simpleech Baitfish. JIMMY CHANG PHOTO

## AUTUMN DEFENDER

*Originated and tied by Ted Kraimer*

- **Hook:** #4 Gamakatsu S11-4L2H
- **Thread:** Camel 6/0 Uni
- **Tail:** Black-barred sand variant or brown-barred tan rabbit strip
- **Body:** Large olive brown Krystal Hackle, rusty copper UV Palmer Chenille
- **Collar:** Yellow marabou plume, golden brown marabou plume, a few strands of kelly green and copper Holographic Flashabou, mallard dyed wood duck flank feather
- **Head:** Golden brown Ice Dub
- **Cone:** Large copper

**Notes:** Rabbit and marabou together is a great fish-catching combination. Wrap the body materials together and tie the marabou feathers for the collar in at the tip. This color scheme resembles sculpin, creek chubs, or a juvenile brown trout. I also expect it may look like a lamprey, a seldom-mentioned food species in many Great Lakes tributaries. Despite the name, this fly will catch fish year-round.

## SIMPLEECH BAITFISH

*Originated and tied by Dave Pinczykowski*

- **Hook:** #4 Gamakatsu B10S
- **Thread:** White 140-denier UTC
- **Wing:** White rabbit strip, a bit of silver Angel Hair on top
- **Eyes:** White barbell-style

**Notes:** Total fish-catching simplicity here. The rabbit strip is pushed through the hook and then secured at the hook eye. The eyes are wrapped on the top of the hook shank so the fly rides inverted. You could add a tail of some sort and body material if desired, but it really isn't necessary. White rabbit with a bit of flash will do the job. Don't make the rabbit too long behind the hook, or you can miss strikes or have it tangle while casting.

# Group 8: General Purpose #5

Here are more rabbit strip designs in a range of sizes and material combinations. All of these are fish catchers and will work for a variety of species.

## RED OCTOBER

*Originated and tied by Mike Schmidt*

- **Front Hook:** #4-6 Daiichi 2220
- **Thread:** 140-denier UTC, color to match fly
- **Rear Hook:** #2-4 Daiichi 1750 or similar
- **Tail:** Rabbit strip
- **Rear Body:** Crystal Chenille, schlappen, marabou
- **Connector:** .018-inch-diameter Beadalon wire with two 3D beads
- **Front Body:** Marabou plume tip, Crystal Chenille, schlappen, marabou in front of rear body
- **Color:** Single color of Senyo Laser Dub
- **Head:** Flymen Fish-Skull

**Notes:** Mike Schmidt of Anglers Choice Flies is famous for his streamer patterns. This one has a slim profile and sinks quick once it soaks up water. There are numerous color schemes, but the tan shown here, along with olive and brown, are most often used.

## LAFKAS'S FISH SKULL DECEIVER (BABY BROWN TROUT VARIATION)

*Originated and tied by Alex Lafkas*

- **Front Hook:** #1 Gamakatsu B10S
- **Rear Hook:** #2 Gamakatsu B10S
- **Tail:** Natural Brown strung rooster saddle
- **Flash:** Copper Holographic Flashabou
- **Rear Body:** Brown Chocklett Filler Flash, brown bucktail, yellow bucktail
- **Connector:** Nylon-coated braided wire with 1 orange 3D bead
- **Front Body:** Brown bucktail, yellow bucktail
- **Topping:** Peacock herl
- **Head:** Gold Flymen Fish-Skull, small or medium

**Notes:** Michigan-based guide Alex Lafkas is known for his big-fish-catching skills and created this updated version of Lefty's Deceiver. Hook size can be adjusted as desired, as well as substituting stainless versions for saltwater use. The bucktail on the front body is reverse-tied, with each clump ¼ inch longer than the previous one. Start at 1¼ inch for a 6- to 7-inch fly. This color is one of Lafkas's favorites for big trout, but it can be changed as desired for a variety of applications

## MEAT WAGON

*Originated and tied by Jerry Darkes*

- **Hook:** #1-4 Daiichi 2151
- **Thread:** 140-denier UTC, to match rabbit strip
- **Tail:** Barred rabbit strip with 6 to 8 strands of Krinkle Mirror Flash
- **Belly:** Light-colored bucktail, similar color marabou plume tip
- **Back:** Darker bucktail, similar color marabou plume tip
- **Collar:** Red schlappen, Palmer Chenille
- **Eyes:** 3D

**Notes:** This has been a good pattern for river trout and smallmouth, having lots of flash and movement to it. The bucktail is added to keep the rabbit strip from wrapping into the hook. Attach the eyes with Liquid Fusion or Super Glue gel. I usually tie this with black-barred olive, black-barred brown, or black-barred white rabbit strips and match the overall color pattern of the fly to the rabbit.

## JOE'S GOLDEN SCULPIN

*Originated and tied by Joe Penich*

- **Hook:** #2/0-2 Kamasan B-940
- **Thread:** Brown 8/0 Uni, tan 70-denier UTC at tail
- **Tail:** End of gold variant rabbit strip, tied down at bend of hook with UTC thread
- **Weight (optional):** Lead wire, same diameter as hook shank
- **Body:** Olive brown Pseudo Hackle
- **Wing:** Remainder of rabbit strip, tied down over body, then wrapped twice
- **Pectoral Fins:** Light brown or tan grizzly marabou
- **Throat:** Red marabou
- **Head:** Dark olive pine squirrel strip

**Notes:** This elegant pattern has a super-lifelike profile in the water with plenty of material movement. It is quite simple to tie and will catch a host of species. Additional base colors include olive and brown.

**(Left to right)** Row 1: Red October, Lafkas's Fish Skull Deceiver; Row 2: Meat Wagon, Joe's Golden Sculpin, Mike's Meal Ticket; Row 3: Red Neck Rabbit (2 colors), Amarillo; Row 4: Nipigon River Leech, Mike's Strip Leech; Row 5: Mike's Red Rocket, Robinson's Munchable Minnow. JIMMY CHANG PHOTO

White rabbit strip is a great material for bright baitfish imitations. This Lake Superior coaster brook trout found white rabbit with some flash and rubber legs an irresistible combination. JERRY DARKES PHOTO

## MIKE'S MEAL TICKET

*Originated and tied by Mike Schmidt*

- **Front Hook:** #1 Mustad 34007
- **Thread:** Olive 140-denier UTC
- **Rear Hook:** #2 Mustad 34007
- **Rear Body:** Pearl EP Sparkle Brush, 2 gold flecked Sili Legs on each side
- **Rear Back:** Olive rabbit strip
- **Connector:** .018-inch-diameter nylon-coated wire with two ⅛-inch glass beads
- **Front Body:** Pearl EP Sparkle Brush
- **Front Back:** Olive rabbit strip, olive ram's wool
- **Belly:** White ram's wool
- **Legs:** Gold-flecked Sili Legs
- **Eyes:** Barbell-style, large

**Notes:** This is a great pattern to imitate a crippled baitfish. The eyes are tied on, so the front hook should be tied inverted, while the back hook is down. The rabbit strip on the rear body is secured at both the bend of the hook and the eye. The front hook is pushed through the rabbit strip leaving approximately 1 inch extending back to cover the connection, then tied down both back and front. Gamakatsu B10S or similar hooks could be substituted for the stainless hooks in the recipe.

## RED NECK RABBIT (2 COLORS)

*Originated by Grand River Troutfitters, tied by Steve May*

- **Hook:** #2-#6 3Xl streamer
- **Thread:** Black 6/0 Uni
- **Body:** UV Polar Chenille
- **Wing:** Rabbit strip
- **Throat:** Wrapped webby red hackle
- **Eyes:** Red barbell-style, large or medium

**Notes:** This pattern is tied so that the hook rides inverted. The eyes are secured first on top of the hook. After the body is wrapped, the hook is pushed through the rabbit strip from the bottom (hide) side. Leave enough of the rabbit strip forward to tie it off at the eye in front of the body and throat. The eyes will be on the bottom. This pattern will catch a variety of species. Natural or attractor colors can be used to create a wide range of different looks.

## AMARILLO

*Originated and tied by Austin Adduci*

- **Hook:** #6 TMC 200R
- **Thread:** 70-denier UTC, color to match wing
- **Body:** Pearl Estaz
- **Wing:** Yellow rabbit strip twice the length of the hook shank
- **Belly:** White rabbit fur
- **Eyes:** 3D

**Notes:** This is a good pattern when there are lots of smaller baitfish present. The rabbit strip is tied down in front only and should extend just a bit past the hook bend. This makes it flutter and gives the appearance of a crippled minnow. This is one of Adduci's favorite colors, but there are plenty of options. Again, secure the eyes with Liquid Fusion or Super Glue gel.

## NIPIGON RIVER LEECH

*Originated by Bill Boote, tied by Jerry Darkes*

- **Hook:** #2-8 Daiichi 2220
- **Thread:** Olive 3/0 Uni
- **Weight:** Lead wire, size to hook shank
- **Tail:** Chartreuse marabou, pearl Krystal Flash
- **Body:** Dark olive Uni Mohair Yarn
- **Rib:** Medium silver wire
- **Wing:** Olive chinchilla rabbit strip 2 times length of hook
- **Throat:** Red marabou
- **Collar:** Olive-dyed pheasant rump

**Notes:** Weight the front half of the hook only. The rabbit strip back is secured to the body with the silver wire rib. This is a favored pattern for the Ontario shoreline of Lake Superior and is popular in the lower Nipigon River. It has caught big brook trout, lake trout, steelhead, and salmon. I expect a lot of other fish will eat it, too.

## MIKE'S STRIP LEECH

*Originated and tied by Mike Verhoof*

- **Hook:** #1/0-#4 Daiichi 2441
- **Thread:** Olive 70-denier UTC
- **Body:** Olive Ice Dub
- **Wing:** Olive rabbit strip, pearl Krystal Flash
- **Legs:** White round rubber
- **Collar:** Wrapped red schlappen, olive schlappen, olive rabbit fur in a dubbing loop

**Notes:** This is the favorite color of Ontario guide Mike Verhoof for both steelhead and salmon on Lake Huron tributaries. This template allows for a wide range of color combinations. All the components of a successful streamer are here.

## MIKE'S RED ROCKET

*Originated and tied by Mike Schmidt*

- **Front Hook:** #1 Gamakatsu B10S
- **Thread:** 70-denier UTC, color to match rabbit strip
- **Rear Hook:** #2 Gamakatsu B10S
- **Tail:** Rabbit strip, Holographic Flashabou
- **Rear Body:** Cactus chenille, schlappen, marabou plume
- **Connector:** .018 inch-diameter Beadalon wire with two ⅛-inch glass beads
- **Front Body:** Holographic Flashabou, Cactus Chenille, marabou plume
- **Legs:** Two strands of Sili Legs on each side
- **Cheeks:** Grizzly marabou
- **Head:** Two bunches of Senyo Laser Dub, same or different colors
- **Eyes:** 3D

**Notes:** Another great pattern from Angler's Choice Flies. Brown or tan over yellow is a favorite color and makes a great golden shiner imitation. Other key combinations are black over blue, olive over tan, and burnt orange over black. For both the front and back bodies, the schlappen feathers are palmered over the Cactus Chenille, and the marabou feather is tip-wrapped in front. Attach the eyes with Liquid Fusion or Super Glue gel

## ROBINSON'S MUNCHABLE MINNOW

*Originated and tied by Patrick Robinson*

- **Hook:** #1/0 Daiichi 2441 or similar
- **Thread:** Black 210-denier Danville Flat Waxed Nylon
- **Tail:** Orange chinchilla rabbit strip, pearl Krystal Flash
- **Body:** Orange chinchilla rabbit strip
- **Collar:** Orange schlappen
- **Head:** Brown Senyo Laser Dub, tan Senyo Laser Dub, orange Ice Dub in front
- **Eyes:** 3D

**Notes:** Patrick Robinson is the head guide for Steelhead Alley Outfitters. He ties this fly in a number of different color combinations depending on location and time of year. This is the "Creeky Crawfish" variation that is designed mainly for river smallmouth. The rabbit strip for the body is wrapped, or cross-cut rabbit can be used and wrapped. Secure eyes with Liquid Fusion or Super Glue gel.

# Group 9: General Purpose #6

This grouping covers a wide range of applications, from the shoreline waters of Lake Erie to the Grand River in Ontario to the smallmouth rivers of Wisconsin. Some of these are quite simple, expressing basic functionality in a streamer, while others are more artistic.

## LITTLE PRECIOUS

*Originated and tied by Karl Weixlmann*

- **Hook:** #8-10 Mustad 9672
- **Thread:** Fluorescent red 3/0 Danville
- **Bead:** Brass, size to hook
- **Back:** Pearl Flashabou, olive Arctic fox
- **Belly:** White Arctic fox

**Notes:** Pennsylvania-based guide Karl Weixlmann covers the Lake Erie shoreline and tributaries. This is a "guide fly" that covers several uses. An emerald shiner imitation, it can be cast and stripped in shoreline and estuary areas or swung and stripped in current. Steelhead and smallmouth are the primary targets.

## TED'S LITTLE BROOK TROUT

*Originated and tied by Ted Kraimer*

- **Hook:** #2-6 TMC 300
- **Thread:** Olive dun 6/0 Uni
- **Weight:** Four to six turns of .035-inch-diameter lead wire
- **Tail:** Golden brown marabou
- **Body:** Golden olive Tri Lobal or Estaz
- **Wing:** Golden brown marabou
- **Topping:** Peacock herl
- **Throat:** Orange calf tail
- **Collar:** Mallard flank dyed wood duck

**Notes:** This pattern reflects a "kinder, gentler" streamer. The wire for weight should be on the front half of the hook. The oversized articulated patterns that are so prominent today do not always work. Instead of lamenting that "they are off the streamer bite today," switching to a smaller, realistic pattern may trigger strikes. Brook trout are scattered across the northern tier of the region and a target of bigger brown trout.

## MIKE'S DAMINO

*Originated and tied by Mike Schmidt*

- **Hook:** #6 Daiichi 1120
- **Thread:** Olive 140-denier UTC
- **Back:** Light olive SF Blend
- **Belly:** White marabou
- **Gills:** Red McFly Foam yarn
- **Eyes:** 3D

**Notes:** A number of different baitfish can be imitated by varying the color of the SF Blend used for the back. This version is of the emerald shiner, a widespread species across the Great Lakes and Midwest. Using gray or brown for the back covers a host of other baitfish. Secure eyes with Loctite or Super Glue gel.

## JOE'S RAINBOW TROUT

*Originated and tied by Joe Penich*

- **Hook:** #2-4 Kamasan B-17S or similar
- **Thread:** White 70-denier UTC
- **Body:** Minnow belly Ice Dub, sparse
- **Wing:** Olive Polar Fiber over light pink Polar Fiber, marked with olive and pink Sharpie
- **Belly:** White Polar Fiber
- **Sides:** A single strand of pink Flashabou on each side
- **Eyes:** Silver 3mm 3D

**Notes:** Rainbow trout and steelhead are present in many Great Lakes tributaries, and some have significant natural reproduction. The fingerlings are targeted by all the larger fish in the system. This pattern covers that application well. Secure eyes with Super Glue gel.

## JOE'S GOLDEN DARTER

*Originated and tied by Joe Penich*

- **Hook:** #4-8 Kamasan B-17S
- **Thread:** White 70-denier UTC
- **Body:** Olive brown Ice Dub, sparse
- **Wing:** Dark brown Polar Fiber over light brown Polar Fiber
- **Belly:** Yellow Polar Fiber
- **Sides:** A single cree hackle on each side with a strand of copper or bronze Flashabou
- **Eyes:** Gold 3mm 3D

**Notes:** Darters are small, perch-like fish found across the streams and rivers of North America. There are a number of species referred to generically as golden darters. They require clean, fast-moving water and develop bright colors during spawning season, when they are often targeted by gamefish. Secure eyes with Super Glue gel.

JIMMY CHANG PHOTO

**(Left to right)** Row 1: Little Precious, Ted's Little Brook Trout, Mike's Damino; Row 2: Joe's Rainbow Trout, Joe's Golden Darter, Joe's Emerald Shiner; Row 3: Tubular Smelt, Polar Shiner, Emerald Candy; Row 4: Ian's Epoxy Minnow (2 colors), Ian's Smack 'Em; Row 5: Pat's Fur Ball (2 colors), Lil Big Eyes; Row 6: Pat's Laser Minnow (2 colors).

Two variations of a Polar Shiner–style pattern. Small baitfish streamers can be very effective when recently hatched fry are present. These can also be dead-drifted under an indicator rig with great success. JERRY DARKES PHOTO

## JOE'S EMERALD SHINER

*Originated and tied by Joe Penich*

- **Hook:** #2-8 Kamasan B-17S
- **Thread:** White 70-denier UTC
- **Body:** Minnow body Ice Dub
- **Tail:** White Polar Fiber
- **Wing:** Olive over white Polar Fiber
- **Belly:** White Polar Fiber
- **Sides:** A strand of pearl Flashabou on each side
- **Eyes:** Silver 3mm 3D

**Notes:** The emerald shiner is distributed across North America from Canada to the Gulf of Mexico. It is normally found in larger lakes and rivers and is abundant in the Great Lakes. We have seen a number of patterns that imitate this important forage species. Secure eyes with Super Glue gel.

## TUBULAR SMELT

*Originated and tied by Karl Weixlmann*

- **Hook:** #2-8 Mustad Signature Stinger
- **Thread:** Fluorescent red 3/0 Danville
- **Belly/Back:** Pearl/white Metz Deadly Dazzle with pink Deadly Dazzle, pink Flashabou Mirage, silver Flashabou, blue Krystal Flash, purple Krystal Flash (all sparse), topped with gray Deadly Dazzle and peacock herl

- **Body:** Pearl mylar epoxied, then colored with red permanent marker
- **Eyes:** Painted

**Notes:** Rainbow smelt are an invasive species in the Great Lakes. They became an important forage species through much of the twentieth century, but numbers have been declining in recent decades. In spite of this, smelt patterns continue to catch fish. This fly does a great job of imitating the multiple colors of the rainbow smelt.

## POLAR SHINER

*Originated and tied by Geoff Kowalczyk*

- **Hook:** #6 TMC 105
- **Thread:** White 70-denier UTC
- **Body:** Red wool, wrapped thin, leaving a tuft for a tail
- **Wing:** White Polar Fiber, black peacock Krystal Flash, olive Polar Fiber
- **Eyes:** 3D

**Notes:** Capt. Geoff Kowaczyk fishes this pattern in Lake St. Clair, mainly for smallmouth bass that are feeding on young-of-year emerald shiners. By changing the color of the Polar Fiber material and Krystal Flash, a number of other forage species can be imitated. For example, gray on top would be a silver shiner, while brown on top would be a creek chub or black nosed dace. Eyes are secured with Super Glue gel.

## EMERALD CANDY

*Originated and tied by Karl Weixlmann*

- **Hook:** #4-8 Daiichi 1750
- **Thread:** Fluorescent red 3/0 Danville
- **Belly/Back:** White Fish Hair, gold and pearl Flashabou, olive Fish Hair, peacock herl (all sparse)
- **Body:** Pearl Mylar tubing, colored green on top
- **Eyes:** Silver 3mm 3D

**Notes:** This pattern is based on Bob Popovics's Surf Candy but with a freshwater twist. It is easy to cast, sinks well, and is super durable. It works wherever emerald shiners are found. The body is epoxied, and the eyes can be set before the epoxy hardens.

## IAN'S EPOXY MINNOW (2 COLORS)

*Originated and tied by Ian Colin James*

- **Hook:** #10 Daiichi 1560 or equivalent
- **Thread:** Black 6/0 Danville
- **Tail:** Short tuft of wool yarn
- **Body:** Diamond Braid
- **Back:** Same yarn used at tail
- **Coating:** Epoxy or UV cure material
- **Eyes:** Extra-small stick-on

**Notes:** From the late Ian Colin James, the Epoxy Minnow can be done in a wide range of colors. It is a deadly pattern for a variety of panfish and will work when larger gamefish are feeding just-hatched baitfish. When the tail is tied in, wrap it forward leaving the same material extending forward of the hook eye. The fly is then tied backward. Tie in the Diamond Braid at the eye, take thread back to the tail, wrap the Diamond Braid back, and tie off. Then pull the wool back over the body, and tie off and finish at the tail. Coat with epoxy; when hardened add the eyes.

## IAN'S SMACK 'EM

*Originated and tied by Ian Colin James*

- **Hook:** #6-8 Daiichi 1560 or equivalent
- **Thread:** Brown or black 6/0
- **Body:** Pearl Lite Brite or Ice Dub
- **Belly:** White marabou
- **Back:** Fox or gray squirrel tail

**Notes:** This is another multi-species-attracting pattern. The two kinds of squirrel tail give distinctly different color patterns. Each imitates an assortment of smaller baitfish.

## PAT'S FUR BALL (2 COLORS)

*Originated by Pat Ehlers, tied by Rainy's Flies*

- **Hook:** #4 Gamakatsu B10S or Daiichi 2546 for saltwater use
- **Thread:** 6/0 Uni, color to match fly
- **Tail:** CCT Fibers with grizzly saddle hackle tip on each side
- **Body:** CCT Body Fur
- **Eyes:** ¼-inch 3D

**Notes:** Pat Ehlers is a well-known figure in the fly-fishing industry. He is based in Milwaukee, Wisconsin, where he runs The Fly Fisher's fly shop. This simple pattern has caught a wide variety of species in both fresh water and salt water. After the CCT Body Fur is wrapped, it is then trimmed into the desired shape. Secure the eyes with Tuffleye epoxy.

## LIL BIG EYES

*Originated and tied by Austin Adduci*

- **Hook:** #6 TMC 200R
- **Thread:** White or chartreuse 140-denier UTC
- **Tail/Body:** Two large grizzly hackle tips, with pearl Krystal Flash on each side
- **Head:** Pearl Senyo Laser Dub
- **Eyes:** 6 mm 3D

**Notes:** This fly is mainly used to target smallmouth. Adduci says, "It will catch anything that eats little fish." He likes to fish this on an intermediate line. Dyed grizzly can be used for different colors and then matched with the Laser Dub. As in previous patterns, a section of Laser Dub is tied down in the middle, then pulled back and tied off. It can be brushed or combed out before securing the eyes with Liquid Fusion or a similar material.

## PAT'S LASER MINNOW (2 COLORS)

*Originated by Pat Ehlers, tied by Rainy's Flies*

- **Hook:** #1/0 Gamakatsu B10S
- **Thread:** Chartreuse or gray 6/0 Uni
- **Tail:** Chartreuse or natural wide grizzly hackle, with pearl Flashabou or Krystal Flash over top
- **Head:** Two bunches of chartreuse or gray Senyo Laser Dub
- **Eyes:** ¼-inch 3D

**Notes:** These are the two main colors of this pattern that Ehlers favors, but others can be easily created. Again, this will catch a wide range of fish species. The Laser Dub is tied down in the middle, then pulled back, secured, and brushed. The eyes are attached with Liquid Fusion.

## Group 10: General Purpose #7

Lots of marabou in these patterns. Just a reminder here: Most of the times when we say marabou is being used, it means either the tip part of a plume as a tail or the plume wrapped like a hackle. Individual marabou fibers are not pulled off the feather and tied in because they are much too fragile.

### BOOGIE MAN (2 COLORS)

*Originated and tied by Steve May*

- **Front Hook:** #6 TMC 8089
- **Thread:** 3/0 Danville, color to match fly
- **Rear Hook:** #4 TMC 9395
- **Tail:** Marabou plume tip
- **Rear Body:** UV Polar Chenille, then saddle hackle, Sili Legs in front
- **Connector:** Beadalon wire with 2 red glass beads
- **Front Body:** Marabou plume, then UV Polar Chenille, marabou plume top and bottom, then a few strands of Flashabou
- **Pectoral Fins:** Grizzly marabou
- **Legs:** Sili Legs
- **Throat (optional):** Red Polar Chenille fibers
- **Eyes:** Red barbell-style, medium
- **Head:** CCT Body Fur, colored on top with Sharpie marker

**Notes:** Ontario fly angler Steve May ties a series of "full motion" patterns that are constructed to provide maximum amount of movement in the fly. All the materials used and manner of assembly contribute to this concept. The CCT Body Fur is wrapped and trimmed for a head. White and yellow are two popular color schemes, but tie in your favorite colors.

### JUNK YARD DOG

*Originated and tied by Mike Schmidt*

- **Front Hook:** #2/0 Gamakatsu B10S
- **Thread:** Dark brown 140-denier UTC
- **Rear Hook:** #1 Gamakatsu SP11 3L3H
- **Tail:** Tan marabou
- **Body:** UV Polar Chenille
- **Wing:** Tan marabou, tan Arctic fox
- **Connector:** Beadalon nylon-coated wire with two 3D beads
- **Front Body:** Two tan marabou plumes
- **Collar:** Tan Arctic fox tail
- **Head:** Dark tan Senyo Laser Dub
- **Eyes:** Large 3D

**Notes:** This fly has a big profile in the water, with plenty of movement. It is lightweight and easy to cast because the materials compress when out of the water. When fished on a sinking-head line, it really comes to life. On both the rear and front bodies, the Arctic fox is reverse-tied. The marabou on the front body is tip-wrapped. For the head a large bunch of Laser Dub is used, and after being secured, is trimmed to shape. Tan/yellow (pictured here)

is a popular color combination, dark brown/tan, and gray/white are also used, or you create your own favorite.

### GREMLIN BUGGER

*Originated and tied by Nate Sipple*

- **Hook:** #1/0 Daiichi 2461
- **Thread:** Orange 70-denier UTC
- **Weight (optional):** .025-inch-diameter lead wire
- **Tail:** Sculpin olive marabou, olive Krinkle Mirror Flash
- **Body:** Olive/black variegated chenille, olive schlappen
- **Collar:** Olive marabou wrapped, barred brown duck flank feather (merganser shown)
- **Head:** Sculpin olive Senyo Laser Dub in a loop
- **Eyes:** Silver/red 6 mm Jurassic Eyes

**Notes:** From Wisconsin guide Nate Sipple, this pattern could have also gone under the Bugger Hybrid grouping. It is designed as a sculpin imitation with a focus on warmwater species, but trout have no problem eating it, too. If weight is added, it is wrapped on the front half of the hook only. There are a number of duck species with similar barred feathers that could be used. Barred mallard flank feathers can be found dyed in a wide range of colors. The Laser Dub is put into a dubbing loop to form the head, the first time we have seen it used this way.

### RIVER PUFF

*Originated and tied by Austin Adduci*

- **Hook:** #4 TMC 200R
- **Thread:** Chartreuse 140-denier UTC
- **Tail/Underbody:** White bucktail
- **Collar:** One white and one yellow marabou plume, yellow schlappen
- **Head:** #6 Flymen Fish Mask, with eyes

**Notes:** This pattern can be worked slowly and still has lots of movement. It works well for fish in a neutral mood, which are not willing to chase a fast-moving fly, but can still be tempted to hit. Lots of color combinations can be created, but this is Adduci's favorite. Tie the bucktail in about halfway up the hook shank. A bit of pearl Krystal Flash or Flashabou can be added over the bucktail if desired. The marabou is then tip-wrapped in front, and the schlappen is wrapped.

**(Left to right)** Row 1: Boogie Man (2 colors); Row 2: Junk Yard Dog; Row 3: Gremlin Bugger, River Puff; Row 4: Mike's Schwartz, Conehead Trick or Treat. JIMMY CHANG PHOTO

## MIKE'S SCHWARTZ

*Originated and tied by Mike Schmidt*

- **Front Hook:** #1 Daiichi 2461
- **Thread:** Dark brown 140-denier UTC
- **Rear Hook:** #2 Daiichi 2461
- **Tail:** Tan grizzly marabou
- **Rear Body:** Brown UV Polar Chenille
- **Connector:** 40 lb. Fireline
- **Front Body:** Tan grizzly marabou, brown UV Polar Chenille
- **Collar:** Tan Senyo Laser Dub, natural mallard flank
- **Head:** Golden brown Ice Dub
- **Eyes:** Black plastic bead chain

**Notes:** This pattern can work as either a brown sculpin or a round-nosed goby, a widespread Great Lakes invasive species that most gamefish relish. Interestingly, gobies turn a purplish brown color when spawning. The brown UV Polar Chenille mimics this shade well.

## CONEHEAD TRICK OR TREAT

*Originated by Kelly Galloup and Bob Linsenman, tied by Pacific Fly*

- **Hook:** #2-#4 TMC 300
- **Thread:** Black 3/0 Uni
- **Tail:** One each brown, olive, and tan grizzly marabou feathers mixed, 4 strands of gold Krystal Flash, 2 pumpkin Sili Legs
- **Body:** Brown medium Sparkle Chenille, brown saddle hackle
- **Wing:** Orange, then brown, then olive grizzly marabou feather
- **Throat:** Tan grizzly marabou feather
- **Legs:** Pumpkin Sili Legs, 2 each side
- **Head:** Black nickel cone

**Notes:** This is both a crayfish and a sculpin imitation. The mixed colors of grizzly allow it to blend in with the different colors of bottom substrate. It can also be tied without the cone, but be sure to weight the body a bit.

# Group 11: General Purpose #8

These patterns cover an assortment of materials and applications. They can be used to target a wide range of species including smallmouth, steelhead, and stream trout.

## THE HAMMER

*Originated and tied by Scott Gobel*

- **Hook:** #2 Gamakatsu B10S
- **Thread:** Tan 140-denier UTC
- **Tail:** Two wide olive saddle hackle tips, gold Krystal Flash
- **Body:** Olive copper UV Polar Chenille
- **Eyes:** Red barbell-style, large or medium
- **Head:** Sculpin olive Senyo Laser Dub

**Notes:** This is a great imitation of a small rock bass, also called redeye or goggle eye. They are found in warmer waters across the Great Lakes and Midwest and serve as a food source for many larger gamefish such as largemouth bass, walleye, and pike. The Laser Dub is secured in the middle, pulled back, and tied off.

## THE FISHSTRESS

*Originated by Craig Amacker, tied by Pacific Fly Group*

- **Hook:** #4-8 Daiichi1720
- **Thread:** White 140-denier UTC
- **Tail:** White marabou, pearl Krystal Flash
- **Body:** Pearl Ice Dub or pearl green Lite Brite
- **Collar:** Mixed white and red saddle hackle
- **Head:** Silver cone, size to hook

**Notes:** Wisconsin angler and guide Craig Amacker developed this as a crippled baitfish imitation. Fish it

with a jerky retrieve, letting it fall periodically. Most fish will hit it on the drop. The body is made by putting the material in a dubbing loop and then wrapping over the hook shank.

## GRAU'S TIGER

*Originated by Walt Grau, tied by Jerry Darkes*

- **Hook:** #2-4 Daiichi 1750
- **Thread:** Black 140-denier UTC
- **Body:** Silver mylar tinsel
- **Wing:** Red and orange mixed bucktail, pearl Flashabou, yellow bucktail, green bucktail on top
- **Throat:** Red hackle fibers
- **Sides:** Yellow grizzly hackle
- **Eyes (optional):** Painted or 3D

**Notes:** Walt Grau is a longtime guide on Michigan's Pere Marquette River system. The Tiger has been catching big brown trout and steelhead in the area for a number of decades. This pattern has proven productive wherever big trout are found.

**(Left to right)** Row 1: The Hammer, The Fishstress; Row 2: Grau's Tiger, Kluesing's Blueberg; Row 3: Driftless Obsession (2 colors); Row 4: Queen of Muddy Waters, Tongue Depressor. JIMMY CHANG PHOTO

## KLUESING'S BLUEBERG

*Originated by John Kluesing, tied by Jerry Darkes*

- **Hook:** #4-8 TMC 105
- **Thread:** Fluorescent red 6/0 Danville
- **Tail/Body:** Blue Flashabou
- **Wing:** Curved mallard flank feather
- **Collar:** Grouse or pheasant hackle

**Notes:** Another long-tenured pattern with Pere Marquette River origins, this was one of the first Great Lakes patterns to imitate a salmon fry. Big resident trout and steelhead will both eagerly target recently hatched fry. The Blueberg can be dead-drifted and then swung across the current where the curve of the feather will give a bit of a wobble.

## DRIFTLESS OBSESSION (2 COLORS)

*Originated and tied by Craig Amacker*

- **Hook:** #4-8 Daichi 1720
- **Thread:** Danville 6/0, to match body color
- **Tail:** Short yellow marabou, copper Krystal Flash, olive marabou
- **Body:** Olive or golden olive Sparkle Chenille or Estaz
- **Legs:** Yellow or chartreuse rubber hackle
- **Bead:** Gold or copper, size to hook

**Notes:** Amacker fishes this during high-water periods on Driftless area streams. The same pattern will catch trout, smallmouth, and more everywhere they are found. These are favored colors, but other combinations can certainly work. Note that for the tail the olive marabou goes over the top of the yellow. To tie in the legs, a single strand of the rubber hackle is secured to the hook shank in the middle, then each end is pulled back and the thread wrapped in front to secure. This is a fun fly to tie and fish!

## QUEEN OF MUDDY WATERS

*Originated and tied by Kevin Feenstra*

- **Hook:** #6 Daiichi 2220
- **Thread:** Gray 6/0 Uni
- **Wing/Body:** Copper Flashabou, curved mallard flank feather, fluorescent pink Ice Dub
- **Collar:** Mallard flank feather

**Notes:** Feenstra uses this for both trout and steelhead in high springtime flows on the Muskegon River. The wing/body materials are tied in two times. The mallard flank for the collar is wrapped. Similar to the Blueberg, this is a salmon smolt imitation. It can be both swung or slowly stripped and swung across the current. Of special note: Copper Flashabou shows up well in dirty water and can be used to enhance streamers for those conditons.

## TONGUE DEPRESSOR

*Originated by Bill Sherer, tied by Pacific Fly Group*

- **Hook:** #4-6 Daiichi 1730
- **Thread:** Red or orange 3/0 Uni
- **Weight:** Lead wire, similar diameter to hook shank
- **Tail:** Olive marabou
- **Body:** Olive Estaz or Cactus Chenille

**Notes:** Northern Wisconsin guide Bill Sherer targets smallmouth bass and walleye with this pattern, although it has caught many other species. To weight this fly, a section of lead wire is secured to each side of the hook shank instead of being wrapped. Trim the body on top and bottom. The curved shape and flattened body of this pattern give it wobble motion. Be sure to fish it attached with a loop knot to give maximum movement. Other favored color combinations are white tail/pearl body, black tail/black body, and chartreuse tail/chartreuse body.

Rarely used for stream brook trout these days, small, flashy streamers often work very well. They can be fished effectively on short, light rods that are better suited to small-stream applications. KEVIN FEENSTRA PHOTO

# Group 12: Deep Minnows and Variations

If you had to pick one fly pattern to fish for the rest of your life, Bob Clouser's Deep Minnow would likely be at the top of the list. Although designed for smallmouth bass, I'm not sure there is a species out there that's catchable on a fly, in freshwater or saltwater, that has refused this pattern. It is the single most important fly for the waters of the Great Lakes and will work everywhere across the Midwest.

The placement of the eyes on the underside of the hook is the key to this fly. This gives a jig-like, hopping motion on the retrieve, which can be enhanced by using a loop knot to attach to the tippet. Use Loctite or Super Glue gel to help secure the eyes to the top of the hook shank and keep them from twisting and killing the action of the fly. Most tiers have settled on the Gamakatsu B10S as the primary hook for freshwater use, but others are usable. In smaller sizes (#8-12) a nymph hook such as the Daiichi 1710 is a good choice. If the fly is also being used in salt water, try the Daiichi 2546.

## DEEP MINNOW

*Originated by Bob Clouser, tied by Jerry Darkes*

- **Hook:** #1-6 Gamakatsu B10S
- **Thread:** 140- or 70-denier UTC, color to match back
- **Eyes:** Barbell-style, size to hook
- **Belly:** Bucktail, sparse, 2 to 3 times length of hook shank
- **Back:** Ten to twelve strands of Krystal Flash, bucktail over top

**Notes:** As simple as the pattern looks, there are several main points to keep in mind to tie this pattern properly. First, the barbell eyes are tied on the top of the hook shank so it rides inverted in the water. Start the thread about one-third the length of the hook behind the eyes. Put a drop or two of Super Glue gel over the thread and then lay the barbell eyes on the shank. Secure the eyes with a series of crisscross wraps, with several circular wraps below the eyes but above the hook shank to tighten the crisscross wraps. The goal is to keep the eyes in place sitting perpendicular to the hook shank and level on top of the shank.

Keep the bucktail for the back and belly sparse. Most tiers tend to overdress this fly, which is detrimental to the fly's movement. To best secure the Krystal Flash, tie it down in the middle and secure to keep it from slipping out. It can then be easily trimmed to the correct length, extending just past the belly hair. The bucktail for the back should then be tied in to extend a bit past the Krystal Flash.

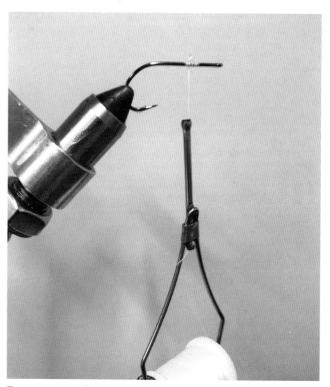

To construct the Deep Minnow correctly, it is essential to secure the barbell eyes. Lay a short thread base one-third of the hook shank length behind the hook eye and add a drop of Loctite or Super Glue gel on top.
JERRY DARKES PHOTO

**(Left to right)** Row 1: Deep Minnow, Half and Half, Double Deep Minnow, Flashtail Deep Minnow; Row 2: RS Deep Minnow, Foxie Clouser—Chub, Coyote Clouser, Foxie Clouser—Darter; Row 3: FS Deep Minnow, River Puff, Jig Clouser—Golden Shiner, Sparkle Grub—Olive; Row 4: Tube Jig Fly, Fur Piece. JIMMY CHANG PHOTO

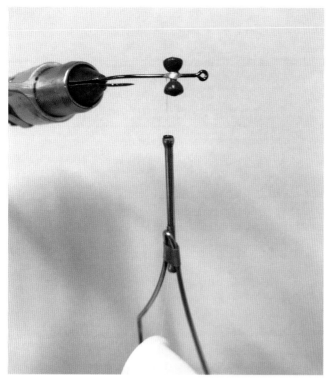

The eyes need to be perpendicular to the hook shank. Crisscross thread wraps to secure the eyes to the top of the shank, so the fly rides inverted with the hook up. JERRY DARKES PHOTO

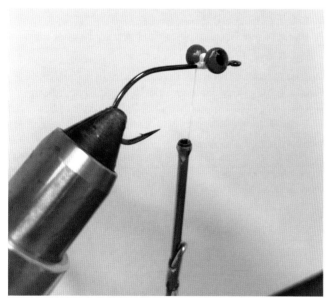

The eyes should be level when completed. Even with the glue gel, they can be knocked out of alignment after catching several fish. Be sure to check the position of the eyes regularly while fishing. JERRY DARKES PHOTO

The chartreuse/white with red eyes shown on the fly plate is a worldwide favorite. All white, olive/white, and gray/white are also popular combinations.

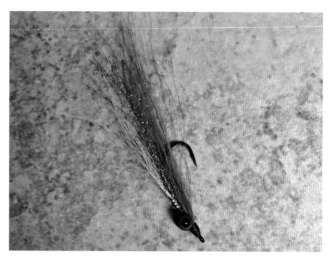

Here is a properly tied and proportioned Deep Minnow. In this silver shiner version it will catch fish across the Great Lakes and Midwest. You can fish it in a range of sizes, but #4 and #2 are most common. JERRY DARKES PHOTO

## HALF AND HALF

*Originated by Lefty Kreh, tied by Jerry Darkes*

- **Hook:** #2/0-4 Gamakatsu B10S
- **Thread:** 140-denier UTC, color to match back
- **Eyes:** Barbell-style, size to hook
- **Tail:** Two to four saddle hackles
- **Belly:** Bucktail
- **Back:** Krystal Flash, bucktail over top

**Notes:** The addition of the saddle hackle from Lefty's Deceiver gives a larger visible profile and a bit of additional color and movement. The fly shown on the plate fly was tied using Krinkle Mirror Flash. Different types of flash have different looks in the water and can be altered as desired or needed. On any given day, this may affect the fly's appeal to fish. Saddle hackle type and color can be adjusted along with the color of the bucktail.

## DOUBLE DEEP MINNOW

*Originated and tied by Jerry Darkes*

- **Hook:** #2/0-4 Gamakatsu B10S
- **Thread:** 140-denier UTC, color to match back
- **Eyes:** Barbell-style, size to hook
- **Tail:** Bucktail
- **Belly:** Bucktail
- **Back:** Krinkle Mirror Flash, bucktail

**Notes:** The Deep Minnow is subject to an extensive assortment of variations. In this version, adding the bucktail as a tail gives a long, slender profile and allows an additional color to be brought in if desired. Make the tail around three times the length of the hook shank. Again, keep the bucktail sparse for best results.

Although usually grouped as a warmwater pattern, the Deep Minnow will catch plenty of trout. It can be tied in both natural and attractor color combinations as a productive trout streamer. JERRY DARKES PHOTO

## FLASHTAIL DEEP MINNOW

*Originator unknown, tied by Jerry Darkes*

- **Hook:** #1-6 Gamakatsu B10S
- **Thread:** 140- or 70-denier UTC, color to match back
- **Eyes:** Barbell-style, size to hook
- **Tail:** Holographic Flashabou
- **Belly:** Bucktail
- **Back:** Bucktail

**Notes:** In open-water situations, extra flash can help attract fish from a longer distance. Holographic Flashabou is used here to enhance this. This may resemble a crippled baitfish on the retrieve, or perhaps just the flash itself attracts fish. Lake trout, steelhead, brown trout, and smallmouth have all responded to this pattern fished from a boat or breakwall. A perch coloration is shown here. You can match local baitfish or create attractor combinations.

## RS DEEP MINNOW

*Originated and tied by Jerry Darkes*

- **Hook:** #1/0-2 Gamakatsu B10S
- **Thread:** 140-denier UTC, color as desired
- **Eyes:** Barbell-style, size to hook
- **Tail:** Rabbit strip
- **Belly:** Bucktail
- **Back:** Bucktail, Krinkle Mirror Flash

**Notes:** This fly has caught more suspended Lake Erie walleye than any other pattern I have tried. The rabbit strip certainly gives a lot of movement on the drop and when retrieved. It has also caught largemouth in deeper water, which will hang on and chew the rabbit strip before taking the whole fly. Tie the rabbit strip in with the fur side up, then coat ½ to 1 inch of the hide side from the hook bend with Zap-A-Gap or a similar product to stiffen it, which

minimizes tangling over the hook when casting. You could also tie a small loop of stiff 20-pound mono at the hook bend to help keep the rabbit strip from tangling. I hesitate to state a specific flash material as there are so many options. Coloration can be natural forage or attractor.

## FOXIE CLOUSER—CHUB

*Originated and tied by Jon Uhlenhop*

- **Hook:** #4-6 TMC 200R
- **Thread:** Red 140-denier UTC
- **Eyes:** Red Real Eyes, small
- **Belly:** White Arctic fox
- **Back:** Pearl Krystal Flash, opal Lateral Scale, coyote fur over top

**Notes:** For smaller-size Deep Minnow patterns, altering the hook style and hair used can be a help. The softer hair condenses into a slim profile when wet, but gives more movement and makes a better imitation of a smaller baitfish.

## COYOTE CLOUSER

*Originated and tied by Jerry Darkes*

- **Hook:** #4-6 Mustad 3366 or equivalent
- **Thread:** Tan 140-denier UTC
- **Eyes:** Red barbell-style, size to hook
- **Belly:** Coyote tail fur
- **Back:** A mix of gold and copper grizzly Krystal Flash, coyote tail fur over top

**Notes:** Coyote tail fur has several really fishy qualities. First, the long guard hairs are flexible and have dark tips similar to the tails on many darker baitfish. Also, the underfur is long enough to give a bit of bulk at the head of the fly, again like natural baitfish. This has been a good pattern in warmwater rivers. This particular fly was tied with a Mustad 3366 hook. It is usable, but I would opt for the Gamakatsu B10S whenever possible.

## FOXIE CLOUSER—DARTER

*Originated and tied by Jon Uhlenhop*

- **Hook:** #4-6 TMC 200R
- **Thread:** Red 140-denier UTC
- **Eyes:** Red Real Eyes, small
- **Belly:** Orange Arctic fox
- **Back:** Root beer Krystal Flash, gold Holographic Flashabou, coyote fur over top

**Notes:** There are numerous darter species found in rivers across the Midwest that are targeted by gamefish. An entire series of darter patterns colored to local species could be created based off this pattern design. Again, the softer hair allows a small, realistic pattern to be created.

## FS DEEP MINNOW

*Originated and tied by Jerry Darkes*

- **Hook:** #2-4 Gamakatsu B10S
- **Thread:** Olive 140-denier UTC
- **Belly:** White or chartreuse bucktail
- **Throat:** Red bucktail
- **Back:** Olive Krinkle Mirror Flash, olive bucktail over top
- **Head:** Gold Flymen Fish-Skull, medium

**Notes:** Here the keel bottom of the Fish-Skull takes the place of the barbell eyes to invert the hook and have it ride upside down. This is a productive color scheme, but can be varied as needed or desired.

## RIVER PUFF

*Originated and tied by Austin Adduci*

- **Hook:** #4 TMC 200R
- **Thread:** Chartreuse 70-denier UTC
- **Eyes:** Red barbell-style, small
- **Tail:** White bucktail
- **Body:** White marabou plume
- **Collar/Head:** Chartreuse schlappen

**Notes:** This is the fly fishers version of a marabou jig, only much more refined. It breathes in the water with the slightest movement. The marabou is tip-wrapped to add durability to the fly. The schlappen is wrapped both behind and in front of the eyes. Flash could be added with the tail. This is a favored color combination, but options are endless.

## JIG CLOUSER—GOLDEN SHINER

*Originated and tied by Jim Sharpe*

- **Hook:** #1/0 Gamakatsu 60-degree jig hook
- **Thread:** White 140-denier UTC
- **Eyes:** Gold barbell-style, large
- **Belly:** White bucktail
- **Back:** Gold Flashabou, yellow bucktail over top

**Notes:** The late Jim Sharpe created this to work in the weedy areas of Lake Erie's Presque Isle Bay in Pennsylvania. By placing the eyes back toward the bend of the hook, the fly will drop straight down, and even "back up" a bit and stay right in the cover before the retrieve is started. It also gives a bit of tippet protection from toothy critters.

## SPARKLE GRUB—OLIVE

*Originated and tied by Karl Weixlmann*

- **Hook:** #4-6 Daichi 1750
- **Thread:** White 3/0 Danville
- **Eyes:** White or red barbell-style, small
- **Tail:** Olive Arctic fox, olive Krinkle Mirror Flash
- **Body:** Olive Cactus Chenille or Estaz

**Notes:** This is a productive general-purpose warmwater pattern. Other key colors are white (pearl), chartreuse, black, and brown.

## TUBE JIG FLY

*Originated and tied by Jerry Darkes*

- **Hook:** #4-8 Daichi 1710
- **Thread:** 140-denier UTC, color to match body
- **Eyes:** Red barbell-style, large (#4), medium (#8)
- **Tail:** Sili Legs, to match body color
- **Body:** Estaz

**Notes:** This is fun to tie and has been productive for an assortment of warmwater species. Attach the barbell eyes as with the Deep Minnow. Double over three to four sets of Sili Legs for the tail and trim fairly short. If they tangle into the hook when casting, trim back more. Be sure to wrap the Estaz around the barbell eyes. Base colors to use are chartreuse, pearl, and olive, or you can be creative!

## FUR PIECE

*Originated and tied by Steve Madewell*

- **Hook:** #2-6 Daichii 1720
- **Thread:** White 140-denier UTC
- **Eyes:** Barbell-style, large or medium
- **Tail:** White saddle hackle tips, yellow black-flecked Sili Leg on each side
- **Body:** Crosscut rabbit strip, red Krystal Flash, yellow black-flecked Sili Leg

**Notes:** This pattern has caught everything from Grand River, Ohio, smallmouth and steelhead to Lake Superior brook trout. The white coloration as shown is Madewell's favorite color, with olive and black running a close second. I'm not sure what it resembles, but fish like it. Use two saddles per side for the tail and attach so they curve outward. With dyed barred rabbit and dyed grizzly saddles, some interesting color combinations are possible.

# Group 13: Mostly Baitfish

These are all baitfish imitations that will catch a variety of species. A variety of materials and construction techniques are used to create these patterns. A few of these flies have saltwater roots, but are productive wherever they are fished and transfer well to fresh water. Some are tied on stainless hooks. There are a number of standard hook options to replace those if desired. The Gamakatsu B10S is a favorite for this use.

## LAKE ERIE EMERALD SHINER

*Originated and tied by Steve Brugger*

- **Hook:** #1-4 Daiichi 2546
- **Thread:** White 140-denier UTC
- **Belly:** White bucktail
- **Wing:** Pearl Krinkle Mirror Flash or Lateral Scale, white bucktail, chartreuse bucktail, olive bucktail
- **Head:** Flymen Fish Skull, size to hook

**Notes:** Steve Brugger grew up in Erie, Pennsylvania, fishing Lake Erie's Presque Isle Bay. Emerald Shiners are a primary, year-round forage species targeted by all gamefish. This pattern also transfers over to saltwater use well.

## ICE OUT ALEWIFE

*Originated and tied by Dustan Harley*

- **Hook:** #2 Gamakatsu Octopus
- **Thread:** White 70-denier UTC
- **Shank:** 45 mm closed eye
- **Eyes:** Barbell-style, large or medium
- **Connector to Shank:** 50 lb. braid
- **Tail:** White marabou
- **Body:** Small pearl Cactus Chenille, white schlappen
- **Wing:** Olive hanked Lite Brite or Ripple Ice Fiber, 10 to 12 peacock herls
- **Head:** Bronze peacock Lite Brite on top, polar pearl Lite Brite on bottom

**Notes:** Dustan Harley guides tributaries on the southern end of Lake Michigan. This area has nearly year-round fishing for a seasonal assortment of species. When creating the body, the schlappen is palmered over the Cactus Chenille. This pattern also replaces a long hook shank by putting a short-shank hook on a braid loop to eliminate leverage for a large fish to work free.

## SIM'S DOUBLE THUNDER

*Originated and tied by Jim Simonelli*

- **Hook:** #1-4 Daiichi 2546 or similar
- **Thread:** White 140-denier UTC
- **Belly:** White bucktail
- **Back:** Chartreuse bucktail, pearl Flashabou
- **Eyes:** Stick-on
- **Head:** Epoxy, Clear Cure Goo, or similar material over bucktail and thread

**Notes:** Veteran Lake Erie angler and fly tier Jim Simonelli fishes this in the waters around Erie, Pennsylvania. Note that the bucktail is reverse-tied to create the head. Olive/white, olive/orange, chartreuse/orange, and all white are productive color combinations, but you can create your own favorite variation. This pattern is easy to cast and fishes well.

## CROSS DRESSER

*Originated and tied by Jim Simonelli*

- **Hook:** #2-4 Mustad 34007
- **Thread:** White 140-denier UTC
- **Tail:** White saddle hackles, silver Krystal Flash
- **Body:** Pearl Estaz
- **Pectoral Fins:** White with silver fleck Sili Legs
- **Head:** Red Estaz

**Notes:** This pattern represents a larger, crippled baitfish. Use three saddle hackles on each side and tie them in to splay (curve) outward. There is plenty of flash and movement to simulate an injured fish. Be sure to attach it with a loop knot and use a jerky retrieve!

## BOBBLE-HEAD BAITFISH

*Originated and tied by Ted Kraimer*

- **Hook:** #1 Mustad S74SZ
- **Thread:** Gray 6/0 Uni
- **Weight:** Eight to ten wraps of .030-inch-diameter lead wire
- **Tail:** Four white rooster saddle hackles, pearl Angel Hair
- **Belly:** White bucktail
- **Back:** White marabou
- **Collar:** Mallard flank
- **Throat:** Red Krystal Flash
- **Head:** White ram's wool on bottom, gray ram's wool on top
- **Eyes:** 3D

**Notes:** This also imitates an injured baitfish. In this instance, the lead wire is wrapped from halfway down the bend of the hook up, then secured with thread. Be sure to coat with Zap-A-Gap to secure the wire. Attaching the lead wire in this way makes the fly fall like a dying fish—an easy meal for a predator. The tail saddle hackles are then attached right in front of the wire. The ram's wool is trimmed to shape the head. Kraimer says to wet the fly thoroughly before fishing so that it sinks right away.

**(Left to right)** Row 1: Lake Erie Emerald Shiner, Ice Out Alewife, Sim's Double Thunder, Cross Dresser; Row 2: Bobble-Head Baitfish, Great Lakes Phantom Minnow, Mike's Murdich, Cosmic Minnow; Row 3: Bucky Minnow, High and Tight Baitfish, Bart-O Minnow; Row 4: Bush Pig, Fin Clip. JIMMY CHANG PHOTO

## GREAT LAKES PHANTOM MINNOW

*Originated and tied by Eli Berant*

- **Hook:** #1/0-2 Daiichi 2546
- **Thread:** White 140-denier UTC
- **Belly:** White SLF Flash blend
- **Back:** Olive SLF Flash blend
- **Eyes:** 3D

**Notes:** Eli Berant owns greatlakesfly.com and is a commercial tier of oversized streamers to target big fish. His patterns have been used successfully in both rivers and the big water of the Great Lakes. Both the belly and back material is reverse-tied and then trimmed to length and shape. The Phantom Minnow is best used in clear water, where its translucency gives it a very realistic look.

## MIKE'S MURDICH

*Originated and tied by Mike Schultz*

- **Hook:** #1 Daiichi 2546 or similar
- **Thread:** White 140-denier UTC
- **Weight:** .030-inch-diameter lead wire
- **Tail:** White bucktail, silver holographic Flashabou
- **Collar:** White CCT Wrap or Minnow Body Wrap (optional: spot on collar)
- **Head/Body:** Estaz
- **Eyes:** 3D

**Notes:** Mike Schultz of Schultz Outfitters ties this simplified version of Bill Murdich's Minnow. Originally a saltwater pattern, it works well across the Midwest. The tail and collar are tied in at the hook bend. A large dark spot can be added to the collar on each side, as some baitfish have these and they can be a strike trigger. The weight is then added. Double wrap the Estaz to create the head. Tie it in at the hook eye, then wrap it back to the collar and forward again. Weighting the head makes the fly dart erratically on a fast retrieve. Chartreuse, pearl, pink, and olive Estaz can all be used for the head. Schultz uses Loctite gel to attach the eyes. Be sure to tie this on with a loop knot!

## COSMIC MINNOW

*Originated and tied by Charlie Piette*

- **Hook:** #1-2 Gamakatsu SC15
- **Thread:** Red 140-denier UTC
- **Tail:** White bucktail
- **Body:** Red Palmer Chenille
- **Wing:** Opal Mirage Flashabou, black Flashabou, gray Extra Select Craft Fur on top
- **Collar/Head:** Two bunches of gray Senyo Laser Dub

**Notes:** This multi-use minnow design can be used in any situation where a baitfish pattern is needed. It is lightweight and easy to cast, absorbing a minimal amount of water. Tie the tail in forward of the hook bend. As we have seen before, the Laser Dub bunches are tied down in the middle first, then pulled back and secured with the thread in front. Colors are simple to adjust, but this is Piette's favorite combination.

## BUCKY MINNOW

*Originated and tied by Nate Sipple*

- **Hook:** #1/0 TMC 811S
- **Thread:** White 140-denier UTC
- **Tail:** White ostrich (pictured) or white schlappen, pearl Krinkle Mirror Flash
- **Body:** Gray EP Craft Fur Brush
- **Rattle:** Small glass
- **Collar:** Black/red Senyo Barred Predator Wrap
- **Head:** Gray EP Craft Fur Brush

**Notes:** This is the first pattern we have seen that incorporates a rattle into its construction. Sound may play an important part at times to trigger strikes to a fly. The use of rattles is a fairly new concept, and they add another dimension beyond color, flash, and movement to attract gamefish. The rattle is secured to the hook shank in front of the tail. Put a bit of Super Glue gel on top of the shank, set the rattle in place, then wrap the thread over the top ten to twelve times. The Craft Fur Brushes are wrapped to form the body and head. The head is then trimmed to give a baitfish shape.

## HIGH AND TIGHT BAITFISH

*Originated and tied by Ted Kraimer*

- **Hook:** #1 Mustad S74SZ
- **Thread:** Gray 6/0 Uni
- **Tail:** Four white saddle hackles, pearl Angel Hair
- **Body:** Pearl Sparkle Braid or similar
- **Underwing:** Gray bucktail
- **Wing:** Four gray saddle hackles, gray bucktail, mix of silver Speckled Flashabou and black Holographic Flashabou
- **Throat:** White marabou, red Krystal Flash
- **Eyes (optional):** 3D

**Notes:** This pattern imitates a number of larger, silvery baitfish. The use of saddle hackles provides abundant movement, and the fly holds its profile well. There is plenty of flash to attract a gamefish from a long distance. Adding eyes to a baitfish pattern is not an absolute necessity, but many anglers feel that the eyes help trigger strikes.

## BART-O MINNOW

*Originated and tied by Bart Landwehr*

- **Hook:** #6 TMC 8089 nickel
- **Thread:** White 100-denier GSP
- **Tail:** White bucktail, mix of pearl and silver Flashabou
- **Wing:** Gray, olive, or tan Icelandic Sheep, with 2 peacock herls on each side
- **Throat:** Red rabbit fur
- **Collar:** White Ice Fur on top and bottom
- **Head:** White chenille, pearl EP Sparkle Brush, colored with Prismacolor marker (gray, olive, brown)

**Notes:** Bart Landwehr of Tight Lines Fly Fishing in DePere, Wisconsin, created this pattern primarily for smallmouth bass. While most fly patterns are best seen only from a side view, this is more of a 3D design and has a realistic view from any angle. Because of this, Landwehr likes to fish it high in the water column where gamefish will get a good view of it from underneath. To create the head, wrap the chenille first and then wrap the Sparkle Brush over the top.

## BUSH PIG

*Originated by Earl Hamilton, tied by Jeremiah Knudsen*

- **Hook:** #2/0-2 Gamakatsu SL12S
- **Thread:** White 140-denier UTC
- **Body:** White or polar white DNA Holofusion
- **Head:** DNA Holofusion
- **Eyes:** 3D

**Notes:** This pattern comes to use from way Down Under. Earl Hamilton created this for use on a host of Australian gamefish. Its use transfers well as a pattern for the Great Lakes, where it has been used to target a host of species, being particularly effective on lake trout. The body is created by working forward from the hook bend with bunches of the DNA Holofusion. The head is usually a different color, such as chartreuse, blue, yellow, or brown, and reverse-tied. The head and body are trimmed to shape. By varying the amount and length of material used on the hook and how it is trimmed, the profile can be changed. The eyes are stuck to the head, and then eyes and head are coated with Clear Cure Goo or other UV cure material.

## FIN CLIP

*Originated and tied by Ted Kraimer*

- **Hook:** #1/0-2 Gamakatsu B10S
- **Thread:** Olive dun 6/0 Uni
- **Weight:** .030-inch-diameter lead wire strips
- **Tail:** White bucktail
- **Belly:** Shad gray and white Icelandic Sheep
- **Back:** Silver gray Icelandic Sheep, barred with a Sharpie marker, olive brown Icelandic Sheep over top
- **Sides:** Pink Angel Hair or Krystal Flash, pink bucktail
- **Throat:** White calf tail
- **Eyes:** ⅜-inch 3D

**Notes:** When rainbow trout are stocked for put-and-take, larger fish take note and will target them. The freshly planted trout make for an easy meal. The Fin Clip is designed for those situations. Weight is added by tying five pieces of wire underneath the hook shank to form a triangle, then coating with Zap-A-Gap. This fly can also be tied in variety of color schemes to imitate a wide range of prey. Kraimer likes to use the flexible, gluelike Liquid Fusion to attach the eyes, especially when larger sizes are used, as in this case.

## Group 14: Gobies and Such

The Round Goby is an invasive species in the Great Lakes. They look very similar to a sculpin and are native to the Black and Caspian Seas. Gobies entered the lakes through the discharge of ballast water from oceangoing freighters. Their impact has not been totally negative, as they now provide a significant food source for sportfish such as smallmouth bass, walleye, brown trout, lake trout, and others, which consume them with great relish. Gobies also feed on several other notorious Great Lakes invasives—the zebra mussel and quagga mussel.

**(Left to right)** Row 1: Moby Goby, Crafty Sculpin; Row 2: Goby Wan Kenobi, Red Neck Goby, Goblin; Row 3: Great Lakes Goby. JIMMY CHANG PHOTO

### MOBY GOBY

*Originated and tied by Karl Weixlmann*

- **Hook:** #4-6 TMC 200R
- **Thread:** Brown flat waxed nylon Danville
- **Eyes:** Red barbell-style, small
- **Tail:** Gray marabou
- **Body:** Dubbed gray and cream rabbit fur mix
- **Wing/Back:** Pine squirrel fur strip, gray marabou, root beer Krystal Flash
- **Pectoral Fins:** Gray partridge feathers
- **Head:** Black, then brown wool

**Notes:** This a realistic imitation of a small goby and has caught everything from carp to coho across the Great Lakes. It is also a good sculpin pattern for river use. The barbell eyes are attached on the top of the hook so it rides inverted in the water. The pine squirrel strip is attached by pushing the hook through the hide, then secured over the top and just in front of the body. Leave a length of the fur strip extending back over the tail. The wool for the head is spun loosely around the shank. It is then trimmed into shape.

## CRAFTY SCULPIN

*Originated and tied by Steve May*

- **Hook:** #2 Gamakatsu B10s
- **Thread:** White 140-denier UTC
- **Eyes:** Gold barbell-style, medium
- **Underbody:** .030-inch-diameter lead wire
- **Tail:** White Polar Fiber, brown Polar Fiber, barred with Sharpie marker
- **Collar:** Tan grizzly schlappen
- **Head:** White CCT Body Wrap or Minnow Body Wrap, colored with brown and black markers

**Notes:** This pattern can serve as either a sculpin or goby. Tie it so the hook rides inverted. The wrap material for the head is trimmed to shape, leaving some a bit longer in back in front of the collar. It has a great 3D profile, looking realistic when viewed from any angle. This is an easy one to tie, and it looks great in the water.

## GOBY WAN KENOBI

*Originated and tied by Jerry Darkes*

- **Shank:** Aqua 33mm Round Eye Shank
- **Thread:** Brown 140-denier UTC
- **Braid:** 40-50 lb.
- **Hook:** #2 Aqua Talon Swing Hook
- **Tail:** Two or three brown grizzly marabou feathers
- **Body:** Two natural emu feathers, grizzly brown schlappen
- **Pectoral Fins:** Three or four brown rubber legs on each side
- **Eyes:** Red plastic bead chain, large
- **Collar/Head:** Brown ram's wool

**Notes:** This pattern is a variation of Kevin Feenstra's Emulator. It has taken Great Lakes brown trout, steelhead, and smallmouth. Tying it on the shank minimizes leverage for large fish to work free. After looping the braid on the hook, tie the grizzly marabou to the hook. The braid is then secured to the shank with the hook eye right at the back end of the shank. The emu feathers are wrapped together to make the body, then the grizzly schlappen is palmered over the top. If there is enough schlappen, add several extra wraps in front to form a collar. The rubber hackle is added, then the wool for the head.

## RED NECK GOBY

*Originated and tied by Karl Weixlmann*

- **Hook:** #4-6 Daiichi 1750
- **Thread:** Brown flat waxed nylon
- **Eyes:** Red barbell-style, medium
- **Tail:** Gray rabbit fur
- **Body:** Dubbed gray rabbit fur
- **Wing:** Pine squirrel strip
- **Collar:** Rainbow Krystal Flash, gray partridge

**Notes:** The hook is pushed through the pine squirrel strip, leaving a hook length or so extending back. It is then secured over the top of the body over the eyes. This pattern works best slow-stripped close to the bottom. Its slim profile casts well and sinks rapidly. Olive and brown versions are also productive.

## GOBLIN

*Originated and tied by Ted Kraimer*

- **Hook:** #4 Daiichi 2451
- **Thread:** Camel 6/0 Uni
- **Eyes:** Red barbell-style, small
- **Wing:** Black-barred gold variant rabbit strip
- **Collar:** Brown schlappen
- **Pectoral Fins:** Brown hen hackles
- **Head:** Sculpin olive ram's wool on top, cream on bottom

**Notes:** Push the hook through the rabbit strip, leaving a hook length extending back, and secure in front. Trim the ram's wool at the head to shape. As the name implies, this pattern is a cross between a sculpin and a goby and is a terrific smallmouth pattern. Great Lakes carp will also take it. Give it try for stream trout, too!

## GREAT LAKES GOBY

*Originated and tied by Austin Adduci*

- **Hook:** #2 TMC 765
- **Thread:** Tan 140-denier UTC
- **Eyes:** Black nickel 3/16-inch IBalz
- **Tail:** Tan rabbit strip
- **Body:** Olive Estaz, everglades EP Fibers over top
- **Head:** Two to three bunches of tan ram's wool

**Notes:** Adduci created this pattern to combat gear anglers fishing tube jigs for smallmouth in southern Lake Michigan. Standard barbell eyes can also be used. The EP Fibers on the body can be trimmed short. The ram's wool is spun and trimmed to form the head. This pattern will work wherever gobies are found. This is the most popular color, but it can be varied as desired.

# Group 15: Flashy Attractors

These patterns incorporate flash and color to trigger strikes. Sizes vary considerably, but they are all fished with a rapid, erratic retrieve. They are geared toward steelhead and salmon, but you can never tell what might strike.

## FLASHTAIL DECEIVER— TUTTI FRUITI

*Originated by Mark Sedotti, tied by Russ Maddin*

- **Hook:** #1 Gamakatsu Octopus
- **Thread:** Fluorescent pink 140-denier UTC
- **Eyes:** Barbell-style, small
- **Tail:** Mint green bucktail, mix of pearl DNA Holo Fusion and pearl Magnum Flashabou
- **Back:** Pink bucktail, 8 to 10 peacock herls, mint green bucktail
- **Belly:** Pink bucktail

**Notes:** This pattern was originally tied for striped bass in the northeast United States. Note that in this case, the barbell eyes are secured on the underside of the hook shank. It can be colored in a variety of combinations as a baitfish or attractor. This is Maddin's favorite color when targeting Great Lakes chinook salmon before they enter tributaries.

## FLASH FLY (2 COLORS)

*Originated and tied by Jeff Liskay*

- **Hook:** #4 Daiichi 2461
- **Thread:** Fluorescent orange 70-denier UTC
- **Eyes:** Real Eyes, small or medium
- **Body:** Chartreuse or pink medium Palmer Chenille
- **Wing:** Two long, thin, silver doctor blue or chartreuse saddle hackles, silver Holographic Flashabou over top
- **Belly:** Mix of pearl Flashabou and silver Holographic Flashabou
- **Head:** UV fluorescent pink or UV chartreuse Ice Dub over top of eyes

**Notes:** Lake Erie guide-extraordinaire Jeff Liskay fishes this from piers and breakwalls and at tributary mouths for steelhead. He uses a sinking-head line from piers and breakwalls and an intermediate head at shallower river mouths. Strip fast!

## KREELEX MINNOW

*Originated by Chuck Kraft, tied by Montana Fly Co.*

- **Hook:** #2-6 Daiichi 1720
- **Thread:** White flat waxed nylon Danville
- **Eye:** Barbell-style, ³⁄₁₆ inch, so that hook is inverted
- **Tail:** MFC Kreelex Flash
- **Belly:** MFC Kreelex Flash
- **Top:** MFC Kreelex Flash

**Notes:** This pattern comes out of the state of Virginia from guide Chuck Kraft, who designed it as a smallmouth

bass and trout streamer. It works around the Great Lakes and Midwest for a host of species. The belly is tied in front of the eyes, pulled back over and secured behind the eyes, then trimmed to length just past the bend of the hook. The top is tied in over the eyes and trimmed to the length of the belly. It looks too simple and basic to work, but it does—and catches just about anything. The material is the key. It is super flexible, with a unique shine to it in the water. All silver, gold/silver (pictured), and copper/gold have been favorite colors, but Montana Fly Company now has this material in about 40 different colors, so possibilities are endless.

## CHARTREUSE THING

*Originated and tied by John Uhlenhop*

- **Hook:** #2/0 Gamakatsu Octopus
- **Thread:** White 140-denier UTC
- **Tail:** Chartreuse bucktail, gold Holographic Flashabou
- **Body:** Chartreuse Estaz
- **Head:** Black nickel Cross-Eyed Cone, large

**Notes:** This pattern is used to target chinook salmon. It is used when fish are staging around harbor areas before moving into tributaries. Tie it on with a loop knot and use an erratic retrieve. Uhlenhop also fishes a variation called Pink Thing.

Large, flashy streamers are best to attract open-water gamefish like this brown trout. The waters of the Great Lakes can be fished successfully with these types of patterns. Color these patterns similar to what gear anglers are finding successful. JERRY DARKES PHOTO

**(Left to right)** Row 1: Flashtail Deceiver—Tutti Fruiti, Flash Fly (2 colors); Row 2: Kreelex Minnow, Chartreuse Thing, Ken's Cleo; Row 3: Green Lantern, Flash Attack. JIMMY CHANG PHOTO

This Lake Ontario lake trout took a Green Lantern streamer fished on a sinking line. Use large, flashy patterns to attract free-swimming predators in open water. JERRY DARKES PHOTO

## KEN'S CLEO

*Originated and tied by Ken Collins*

- **Hook:** #2-4 Partridge Salmon Hook or similar
- **Thread:** Blue or black 70-denier UTC
- **Tag:** Chartreuse Diamond Braid
- **Body:** Silver UV Palmer Chenille
- **Wing:** Silver blue Farrar Flash
- **Collar:** Blue guinea hackle

**Notes:** Ontario guide Ken Collins has found this a good fly to swing for steelhead in cold, clear river conditions. A super-flexible flash material is used for maximum material movement. MFC Kreelex Flash is nearly the same as the Steve Farrar Flash. The chartreuse tag provides a good target for a fish to strike.

## GREEN LANTERN

*Originated by Paul Castellano, tied by Jerry Darkes*

- **Hook:** #1/0 Gamakatsu Octopus
- **Braid:** 50 lb.
- **Shank:** Green 40 mm Senyo Shank
- **Back/Belly:** A mix of chartreuse Pearl Flashabou, chartreuse Mirage Flashabou, and chartreuse Krinkle Mirror Flash
- **Head:** #5 or #6 Flymen Fish Mask, with 3D eyes

**Notes:** This fly has caught big brown trout and lake trout in the open waters of the Great Lakes. Fished on a sinking line, it can draw fish from a long distance. Although this is the only color scheme I have used so far, it could be colored and fished a variety of ways.

## FLASH ATTACK

*Originated and tied by Jerry Darkes*

- **Hook:** #1 Gamakatsu B10S
- **Thread:** White 140-denier UTC
- **Eyes:** Chartreuse barbell-style, large
- **Body:** UV chartreuse Ice Dub
- **Belly:** A mix of pearl and chartreuse Krinkle Mirror Flash
- **Back:** Chartreuse Krinkle Mirror Flash with peacock black Krystal Flash

**Notes:** This pattern has caught steelhead off Lake Erie piers and breakwalls. Endless combinations of materials and colors are possible. As the steelhead tributaries continue to become more crowded, fly anglers are exploring other opportunities offered by the big water of the lakes.

# Group 16: Recent Developments

In the ongoing process of fly tying, we see patterns continue to evolve. New ideas are born as new materials come on the market, and the creative process continues. These patterns are some of the more recent developments that have appeared on the scene. Several are developed from earlier patterns and others are new creations. We will also see new hook designs.

## DRUNK AND DISORDERLY

*Originated and tied by Tommy Lynch*

- **Front Hook:** #2/0-4/0 Gamakatsu Jig 60 Degree Flat Eye
- **Rear Hook:** #1-2 Gamakatsu B10S
- **Thread:** White or black 100-denier GSP
- **Connector:** Rio Powerflex Bite Wire, with two or three 8 mm 3D beads
- **Tail:** Two extra-webby schlappen feathers, regular or Holographic Flashabou
- **Rear Body:** UV Polar Chenille, thin rabbit strip
- **Overwing:** Mallard flank
- **Front Body:** Regular or Holographic Flashabou, rabbit strip, UV Polar Flash, medium rattle, Holographic Flashabou over top
- **Overwing:** Two mallard flank feathers
- **Collar:** Rabbit strip, deer body hair
- **Head:** Deer body hair
- **Head Coating:** Clear Cure Goo Hydro on top and bottom
- **Eyes:** 3D

**Notes:** Michigan guide Tommy Lynch (thefishwhisperer .com) is known for his ability to catch big trout. We have seen the downsized version of this pattern earlier. This is the original design that was created to mimic the action and sound of a large crankbait.

For both the rear and front body, a thin rabbit strip is wrapped. On the front body, the first section of Flashabou should cover the connector. The deer body hair for the head and collar is spun. The head is trimmed into a wedge shape, flat on top and bottom. This gives the fly its movement. The rattle and eyes are secured with Super Glue gel, with thread wraps over the rattle in addition.

This pattern has caught BIG trout everywhere, along with a host of other large predators. It is a bit time consuming to tie, but worth the effort. Colors can be varied as desired for all components. Fish this size with an 8-weight-minimum outfit on a matching sinking-head line with a short, stout leader and hang on! You can find a detailed video of Tommy tying this pattern at schultzoutfitters.com.

## LAFKAS'S SUSPENDING NICKEL

*Originated and tied by Alex Lafkas*

- **Front Hook:** #3/0 Partridge Aberdeen Predator
- **Rear Hook:** #1 Gamakatsu B10S
- **Thread:** Black 110-D GSP
- **Connector:** Senyo Intruder Wire with two 3D beads
- **Tail:** Four feathers
- **Sides:** Three strands of Holographic Flashabou on each side, bucktail bunch
- **Rear collar:** Bucktail
- **Front Body:** Bucktail with Senyo Predator Wrap, two clumps of reverse-tied bucktail, then Grizzly Flashabou over top, then a webby saddle or large hen hackle to imitate pectoral fins
- **Collar/Head:** 1-inch SLF Brush

**Notes:** Alex Lafkas is another big-fish guru, and this pattern can be used to target large trout and other predators. It is very lightweight for its large size, with minimal water retention, making it easy to cast. Use long, thin saddle feathers for the tail as they give more movement when the fly is stalled. Secure the bucktail on the rear collar and two clumps of bucktail in front of the Predator Wrap. The bucktail covering the connector is tied in as normal. Wrap the saddle/hen hackles on the front hook. The SLF Brush is trimmed into a rounded head. Always fish this with a loop knot and a lot of rod tip movement while stripping to give maximum action. This fly can be scaled larger and is an excellent muskie pattern. Colors are up to the tier and can be either natural, imitative or attractor schemes.

## DITCH PIG

*Originated by Bob Linsenman, tied by Pacific Fly Group*

- **Hooks:** #4 Daichii 2220
- **Thread:** 140-denier UTC, match to fly
- **Connectors:** 20 lb. Maxima monofilament
- **Rear Body:** Marabou plume tips, Krystal Flash on each side
- **Middle Body:** Same as rear body
- **Front Body:** Marabou plume tips, Krystal Flash
- **Head:** Several bunches of ram's wool

**Notes:** This was likely the first multi-articulated pattern created and available commercially. Unfortunately, it was only used locally on Michigan's lower AuSable River and never received the notoriety of later similar patterns. It was also created prior to the availability of many of the latest materials; hence it is quite simple compared to later designs.

**(Left to right)** Row 1: Drunk and Disorderly, Lafkas's Suspending Nickel, Ditch Pig; Row 2: Game Changer, Finesse Changer, Chromatic Nut; Row 3: Brush Hog, Bucktail Game Changer, Lafkas's Modern Deceiver. JIMMY CHANG PHOTO

The old adage "big flies for big fish" often holds true in fishing streamers for brown trout. The largest flies can trigger strikes from fish that might otherwise ignore smaller offerings. JON RAY PHOTO

On each hook a series of marabou plume tips are tied in going forward. The rear hook is cut at the bend, leaving only the shank with materials. On the front hook the marabou plumes only go two-thirds up the shank. After the Krystal Flash is added, the ram's wool bunches are spun on and then trimmed. This pattern is lightweight, casts well, is easy to tie, and catches fish. Olive /tan as shown is a popular color along with all black. Color combinations are endless, and it can be altered and customized many ways. Tie and fish some!

## GAME CHANGER

*Originated by Blane Chocklett, tied by Justin Pribanic*

- **Front Hook:** #1/0 Gamakatsu B10S
- **Rear Hook:** #1 Partridge Attitude
- **Thread:** White 70-denier UTC or similar
- **Tail:** 15 mm Fish Spine with grizzly hackle tips, pearl Filler Flash
- **Rear Bodies:** Two 15 mm Fish Spines and rear hook wrapped with 1 inch Baitfish Brush
- **Front Bodies:** Two 20 mm Fish Spines and half of front hook wrapped with 2 inches Baitfish Brush
- **Pectoral Fins:** Grizzly hackles
- **Head:** 2 inches Baitfish Brush
- **Eyes:** 8-10 mm 3D

**Notes:** This pattern from Virginia guide/fly designer Blane Chocklett has revolutionized the streamer game. The use of the Fish Spines creates a multiple-articulated fly that swims realistically in the water. This basic pattern makes a fly around 6 inches in length. Trim the head into a round

shape, then taper the body so that it gradually gets thinner toward the tail. Color as desired using waterproof markers.

The Game Changer is normally fished with a saltwater-style, hand-over-hand retrieve. The fly is time consuming to tie and a bit difficult to cast due to air resistance, but these factors are usually overlooked due to the productivity of the fly.

## FINESSE CHANGER

*Originated by Blane Chocklett, tied by Justin Pribanic*

- **Hook:** #1/0 Partridge Attitude Extra
- **Thread:** White 70-denier UTC
- **Tail:** Eastern Trophies Game Changer/Popper Tail, with Chocklett Game Changer Chenille on a 10 mm Fish Spine
- **Body Sections:** Four 10 mm Fish Spines with Chocklett Game Changer Chenille
- **Connector:** 50 lb. mono
- **Front Body:** Chocklett Game Changer Chenille on the hook
- **Eyes:** 3D

**Notes:** Justin Pribanic is an uber-talented guide and commercial tier who covers Michigan, Ohio, and Pennsylvania chasing both coldwater and warmwater species. This version of the Game Changer was developed due to the need for a smaller version of that pattern. Steam to expand all the body material fibers. Then trim the head to shape and taper the body. Color if desired with waterproof markers.

## CHROMATIC NUT

*Originated and tied by Russ Maddin*

- **Front Hook:** #1 Ahrex Trout Predator
- **Rear Hook:** #4 Ahrex Trout Predator
- **Thread:** 70-denier UTC, color to match fly
- **Tail:** 10 mm Fish Spine, marabou, Holographic Flashabou, Palmer Chenille
- **Second Section:** 15 mm Fish Spine with UV Polar Chenille, rabbit strip wrapped
- **Rear Hook (body):** Senyo Chroamtic Brush, UV Polar Chenille, Sili Legs
- **Connector:** 30 lb. Maxima with two 3D beads
- **Front Hook (body):** UV Polar Chenille, Sili Legs on each side, 2 colors Senyo Chromatic Brush, schlappen
- **Weight:** Pseudo Eyes, large, on bottom of hook shank
- **Head:** Senyo Laser Dub

**Notes:** Russ Maddin pays particular attention to how materials and colors work and blend together. This updated version of his Circus Peanut incorporates a full range of new materials on the tying scene. All his designs are well tested before he presents them to the public. This pattern can be done in a range of color combinations and various hook sizes, both smaller and larger.

## BRUSH HOG

*Originated and tied by Russ Maddin*

- **Front Hook:** #2 Ahrex Nordic Salt Deep Streamer
- **Rear Hook:** #4 Ahrex Trout Predator
- **Thread:** 70-denier UTC, color to match fly
- **Tail:** Three or four saddle schlappen feather tips, Holographic Flashabou, Palmer Chenille on a 10 mm Fish Spine
- **Next Section:** 15 mm Fish Spine with UV Polar Chenille, schlappen
- **Rear Hook (body):** 3-inch EP Senyo Chromatic Brush, EP Sparkle Brush, schlappen
- **Connector:** 30 lb. Maxima with two 3D beads
- **Front Hook (body):** EP Sparkle Brush, EP Senyo Chromatic Brush
- **Pectoral Fins:** Grizzly hen feathers
- **Weight:** Small double-bead chain
- **Head:** EP Senyo Chromatic Brush

**Notes:** Flash and movement are the primary components of this pattern. Again, all of Maddin's flies receive extensive, on-water testing to determine maximum effectiveness. Videos of a number of Maddin's patterns can be seen on mangledfly.com

## BUCKTAIL GAME CHANGER

*Originated by Blane Chocklett, tied by Justin Pribanic*

- **Front Hook:** #1/0 Partridge Predator X
- **Rear Hook:** #2 Partridge Attitude Extra
- **Thread:** 140-denier UTC, color to match fly

- **Tail:** Three or four saddle hackle tips, opal Mirage Flashabou, Chocklett Filler Flash on a 15 mm Fish Spine
- **Second Section:** Chocklett Filler Flash, Senyo Predator Wrap, bucktail on a 15 mm Fish Spine
- **Rear Hook (body):** Chocklett Filler Flash, trimmed Predator Wrap, bucktail
- **Next Sections:** Two 15 mm Fish Spines, repeat body as previously
- **Connector:** 20 mm shank secured and glued on top of shank
- **Front Hook (body):** Ten to twelve wraps of .025-inch-diameter lead wire, Filler Flash, bucktail, leaving front one-third of shank clear
- **Pectoral Fins:** Grizzly Flutter Legs
- **Collar/Head:** Deer belly hair

**Notes:** Getting a proper balance of materials and weight is important for this pattern to swim properly. The bucktail is reverse tied and lengthens as you work forward on each section of the fly. Use ten to twelve wraps of wire, secured well at the hook bend. This fly is light and extremely buoyant, so the weight on the front hook shank serves as both a keel and rudder so that the fly doesn't flip or spin. The deer hair for the collar and head are spun, packed, and trimmed the same as the Zoo Cougar. This is a popular color combination, but there are numerous other options.

## LAFKAS'S MODERN DECEIVER

*Originated and tied by Alex Lafkas*

- **Front Hook:** #3/0 Ahrex Aberdeen Predator
- **Rear Hook:** #2 Ahrex 600SP
- **Thread:** White 140-denier UTC or similar
- **Tail:** Four 3-inch saddle hackles, opal Mirage Flashabou, wrapped saddle hackle on a 10 mm Fish Spine
- **Next Section:** Chocklett Filler Flash, schlappen, on a 15 mm Fish Spine
- **Rear Hook (body):** XL pearl Cactus Hackle, bucktail in front
- **Next Body Sections:** Two 20 mm Fish Spines with XL pearl Cactus Hackle and bucktail
- **Connector:** 50 lb. mono
- **Front Hook (body):** Eight to ten wraps of .025-inch-diameter lead wire, XL pearl Cactus Hackle, bucktail in front, 10 to 12 peacock herls

**Notes:** The front hook is weighted with eight to ten wraps of lead wire starting at the bend, and then six sections of lead wire are formed into a triangle secured to the bottom of the shank. This recipe gives an overall length of around 8 inches, which is Lafkas's favorite for large brown trout. The bucktail should be lengthened ¼ inch on each section to give the fly a natural taper. The fly can be made longer by lengthening the saddle hackles at the tail. Again, weighting the front gives the fly stability on a fast retrieve. If a dark color is desired, Lafkas says to substitute colored Chocklett Filler Flash and change the bucktail colors as desired.

4

# Free Swimmers and Bottom Crawlers

## INTRODUCTION

There are various aquatic organisms beyond insects and baitfish that can be an important food source in rivers, lakes, and streams. Leeches are predatory worms, actually quite similar to earthworms, and are found in a wide range of

water conditions. There are a number of different species across the waters of the Midwest.

General leech size varies from about ½ inch to 2½ inches. They are usually a black or brown color, but various colors are seen, and some have spotted or striped patterns on them.

Hundreds of square miles of flats in the Great Lakes offer sight-fishing opportunities for carp and smallmouth. Both swimming and bottom-crawling patterns can be fished depending on the situation. LEO WRIGHT PHOTO

Some live around rocks or submerged logs while others burrow in soft bottom areas. Leeches swim in an undulating motion and generally avoid sunlight. They are important to fly anglers locally, as some waters have higher numbers than others. Leeches are fished regularly in the streams of the Driftless area.

Leech patterns vary in size considerably depending on the application. The Red Eye Leech (top) is used as more of a large, dark attractor. The Turkey Leech (bottom) is a more realistic leech imitation and used mainly on trout waters. JIMMY CHANG PHOTO

Crayfish are crustaceans that are found in rivers, streams, ponds, and lakes across the Midwest. They are also present in all the Great Lakes and are a primary food source for a host of gamefish, especially in the summer. Crayfish are bottom dwellers and can vary widely in color, often matching their surroundings as a form of protective camouflage. Adults are most active at night, when they emerge from their protective surroundings to feed. When disturbed, they will rapidly kick their tails to move backwards away from danger.

Most crayfish species are not tolerant of pollution and require clean water for survival. They can, however, tolerate a wide range of temperatures, allowing a wide range of distribution. Molting crayfish that have outgrown and shed their outer shell attract particular attention. Called "softshells," they are particularly vulnerable at this stage before the new shell hardens.

Smallmouth bass and carp are particularly fond of crayfish. Both are often seen rooting under rocks and other debris in search of this tasty shellfish. An interesting symbiotic relationship has been observed in some areas, where smallmouth bass will follow feeding carp and snatch up crayfish and other organisms disturbed by the carp.

## Group 1: Leeches

This assortment of patterns shows a wide range of sizes. Often any fly that is long, thin, and dark-colored is generically called a "leech." Those designed to specifically imitate leeches are often much smaller and simple in design. The larger versions may also imitate a lamprey. The sea lamprey is a Great Lakes invasive and spawns in tributary streams. There are also native lamprey species.

### TURKEY LEECH

*Originated by Tom Wendelburg, tied by Jerry Darkes*

- **Hook:** #6-14 Daiichi 1720
- **Thread:** Black 70-denier UTC
- **Weight (optional):** Lead wire, brass bead, or glass bead
- **Tail/Body:** Wild turkey down feather

**Notes:** A Wisconsin original, this pattern is true simplicity. The tip of the feather is secured at the hook bend and wrapped forward up the hook shank to the eye. You can fish it as nymph, let it swing, or strip it in slow current. You can twist the feather into the tying thread to give added strength. It can also be ribbed with wire to add durability and a hint of color.

### MARABOU LEECH

*Originated by Tom Wendelburg, tied by Jerry Darkes*

- **Hook:** #6-14 Daiichi 1720 streamer
- **Thread:** 70-denier UTC, to match marabou color
- **Weight:** Lead wire, size to hook shank
- **Tail:** Marabou plume tip
- **Body:** Marabou

**Notes:** Use lead wire of a similar diameter to your hook size and wrap over the front half of the hook. Tie the tip of the marabou plume in at the bend of the hook, but don't trim. The back half of the body is the upper part of the marabou plume from the tail, twisted and wrapped. The front half of the body is marabou dubbed to the thread and wrapped to create a larger diameter at the front of the fly. This same tying process could also be used for the Turkey Leech presented previously. Black, olive, brown, and gray are the key colors for this pattern.

**(Left to right)** Row 1: Turkey Leech, Marabou Leech, Olive Leech, Lazy Leech, Leechinator; Row 2: Pine Squirrel Leech, Red-Eyed Leech, Lamprey Leech; Row 3: Simpleech (3 colors). JIMMY CHANG PHOTO

Leech patterns often work well for Great Lakes steelhead. It may be that they feed on them as juvenile lamprey.
JERRY DARKES PHOTO

## OLIVE LEECH

*Originated and tied by Matt Zudweg*

- **Hook:** #8 Daiichi 1710
- **Thread:** Olive 6/0 Uni
- **Weight:** 1/8-inch copper or gold bead
- **Tail:** UV olive Ice Dub fibers
- **Body:** Dubbed UV olive Ice Dub
- **Underwing:** Copper Ice Dub fibers
- **Wing:** UV olive Ice Dub fibers

**Notes:** Matt Zudweg ties this pattern specifically for use on Michigan's Muskegon River system. He fishes it for trout when no hatch activity is present. I suspect it will also work in other places.

## LAZY LEECH

*Originated and tied by Charlie Piette*

- **Hook:** #6-8 Daiichi 2460
- **Thread:** Black 70-denier UTC
- **Bead:** Metallic red, 5/32 inch
- **Tail:** Black pine squirrel strip
- **Body:** Black/red leech yarn

**Notes:** Charlie Piette is a specialist on the spring creeks of the Driftless region. This pattern is a favorite of his. It has plenty of movement while the body yarn is very translucent in the water.

## LEECHINATOR

*Originated and tied by Craig Amacker*

- **Hook:** #6-8 Daiichi 1710
- **Thread:** Black 70-denier UTC
- **Cone:** Gold, small or medium
- **Tail:** Chartreuse marabou, gold Flashabou
- **Body:** Fine olive chenille
- **Wing:** Olive pine squirrel strip
- **Rib:** Copper wire
- **Collar:** Webby olive saddle hackle

**Notes:** The copper wire rib is used to secure the pine squirrel strip to the top of the fly. This can also be done in black and brown variations, functioning as both a leech and a dark-colored baitfish imitation. The chartreuse tail gives good contrast and attention-getting visibility in the water.

## PINE SQUIRREL LEECH

*Originated and tied by Charlie Piette*

- **Hook:** #6-8 Daiichi 2461
- **Thread:** Red 8/0 Uni
- **Bead:** Copper or gold, 1/8 inch
- **Tail/Wing:** Olive pine squirrel strip, bead, 2 strips of copper Speckled Flashabou
- **Collar:** Olive grizzly marabou

**Notes:** This leech variation may also resemble a small baitfish in this color. The pine squirrel strip is tied in Zonker-style, secured at the bend of the hook, then pulled over and secured in front of the body. It can also be tied in black and brown versions. This pattern will also take smallmouth, carp, and a number of panfish species in addition to trout.

## RED-EYED LEECH

*Originated and tied by Mike Schultz*

- **Hook:** #1 Daiichi 2546 (Gamakatsu B10S would be the non-stainless steel substitute)
- **Thread:** Black 100-denier GSP
- **Weight:** Red Pseudo Eyes, medium or large
- **Tail:** Black rabbit strip, gold or copper Speckled Flashabou
- **Body:** Black rabbit strip
- **Collar:** Mallard flank dyed wood duck
- **Head:** Black Australian opossum fur

**Notes:** Although it is called a leech, this is really a dark-colored attractor pattern. The rabbit strip is wrapped to make the body. The head is formed by putting the Australian opossum fur in a dubbing loop. This can also be tied in olive or brown variations. It is a great early season smallmouth pattern, but catches everything. It's especially productive in high or stained water.

## LAMPREY LEECH

*Originated and tied by Ted Kraimer*

- **Hook:** #4 TMC 200R
- **Thread:** Camel 6/0 Uni
- **Bead:** Copper

- **Tail:** Natural brown saddle hackles
- **Body:** Brown saddle hackle palmered halfway up shank, then a wrap of UV Palmer Chenille, then ginger and golden brown marabou wrapped
- **Collar:** Mallard flank dyed wood duck
- **Head:** Rust-colored sheep wool

**Notes:** This pattern could have also gone under general purpose streamers, except for the name. It actually represents a chestnut lamprey, which is a native species of lamprey, not the invasive sea lamprey. The chestnut lamprey is well distributed from Hudson Bay down into the central and eastern United States.

## SIMPLEECH (3 COLORS)

*Originated and tied by Dave Pinczkowski*

- **Hook:** #4-6 Gamakatsu B10S
- **Thread:** 70-denier UTC, color to match fly
- **Eyes:** Red barbell-style, small or medium
- **Wing:** Black, olive, or brown barred or solid rabbit strip

**Notes:** Another super-simple design that catches fish. The barbell eyes are attached to invert the hook. The hook is pushed through the rabbit strip and secured over the top of the eyes. There are plenty of creativity options here if wanted, to add flash, a body, or rubber legs. If the rabbit strip tangles when cast, trim it a bit shorter.

# Group 2: Crayfish

For smallmouth fly fishers, discovering a perfect crayfish pattern is akin to finding the Holy Grail. It is something that may or may not exist. Patterns that really look like a crayfish in hand often fail in the water due to materials that are too stiff. The fly might spin in the water or have no lifelike movement to it. When tying, it is critical to consider what the fly looks like in the water.

Crayfish flies are thought of as primarily for smallmouth and carp, but big trout also actively target and eat them. Crayfish are too abundant and too good a food source to be ignored by most gamefish. I have even seen muskie and steelhead nose under rocks trying to force crayfish out.

In their own ways, the following patterns resemble crayfish and have proven productive across the region. Several have quite simple construction, while others are more involved to tie. Give these a try and pick your own favorite(s).

## CLOUSER CRAYFISH

*Originated and tied by Bob Clouser*

- **Hook:** #2-8 TMC 5263
- **Thread:** 6/0 Uni, to match Furry Foam color
- **Weight:** Lead wire, same diameter as hook shank
- **Tail:** Pheasant tail fibers, hen pheasant or hen mallard body feather fibers over top
- **Back:** Tan or olive Furry Foam strip
- **Head:** Tan Antron dubbing, built up heavy
- **Claws:** A hen pheasant or hen mallard body feather on each side
- **Body:** Tan Antron dubbing, cree, or barred ginger saddle hackle
- **Rib:** Tying thread

**Notes:** This was one of the first crayfish imitations that actually worked consistently. It was designed to be fished as a nymph, being dead-drifted or slowly swung across the current. In this configuration, it did not work well stripped rapidly or crawled on the bottom. As we shall see, later patterns addressed these issues.

The lead wire is wrapped on the front half of the hook. The Furry Foam is tied in over the top of the tail fibers and pulled down over the head in front of the claws and tied down. After making the body and palmer wrapping the saddle hackle over the top, take the thread back to just behind the head. Pull the remaining Furry Foam down over the body and secure it by wrapping the tying thread as a rib forward to the eye. Leave a bit of Furry Foam to look like a tail.

**(Left to right)** Row 1: EZ Craw (2 colors), Clawdad; Row 2: May's Full Motion Crayfish (2 colors), May's Clear Water Crayfish V1 and V2; Row 3: SF Crayfish, Jon's Crayfish; Row 4: Cray Z. JIMMY CHANG PHOTO

The Clouser Crayfish is often fished more like a nymph than actively stripped. Designed for smallmouth bass, it will also catch trout and a variety of other species.
JERRY DARKES PHOTO

## E-Z CRAW (2 COLORS)

*Originated and tied by Jerry Darkes*

- **Hook:** #4 Daiichi 1710 or 1760
- **Thread:** 70-denier UTC, to match body
- **Weight:** Barbell-style, small or medium
- **Antennae:** Two Sili Legs
- **Pincers/Tail:** Clawdad Tails (available from Eastern Trophies Fly Fishing)
- **Body:** Cross-cut rabbit

**Notes:** I've tied and fished this pattern for nearly twenty years. When I first saw Chuck Kraft's products, the Clawdad Tails jumped right out and grabbed me! They are found in a variety of colors in several sizes. Olive, rusty brown, and tan have been my go-to colors. This pattern can be stripped fast or slow, swung across the current, or dead-drifted.

## CLAWDAD

*Originated by Chuck Kraft, tied by Eastern Trophies Fly Fishing*

- **Hook:** #2-6 Mustad R74
- **Thread:** 140-denier UTC, color to match body
- **Weight/Eyes:** Barbell-style, small or mediun
- **Head:** Medium chenille wrapped halfway around the hook bend and back
- **Pincers/Tail:** Clawdad Claws
- **Body:** Medium chenille
- **Legs:** Round rubber hackle, to match body color

**Notes:** Though not as well know as some imitations, this may be one of the best crayfish patterns out there for actually catching fish. It has caught countless big

smallmouth, brown and rainbow trout, and carp, too. Fish hit this pattern consistently when it is on the drop.

Tie the barbell eyes on so the hook rides inverted. After making the head, the hook point is pushed through the hole in the Clawdad Claws and the tapered point is pulled over the head and tied down. The chenille is wrapped forward, then around the eyes, and tied off at the hook eye. Restart the thread halfway up the body. Tie in a small bunch of rubber hackle in the middle on both the top and bottom of the hook, so that it spreads all around the hook, and tie off. Trim the rubber hackle so it extends past the bend of the hook in back, shorter in front, as pictured.

Several YouTube videos showing the tying process are worth viewing, as there are a few tricks for this pattern. The Clawdad has numerous ways to tweak and customize it, but the basic pattern seems to work just fine. Again, check Eastern Trophies Fly Fishing for the claws and more.

## MAY'S FULL MOTION CRAYFISH (2 COLORS)

*Originated and tied by Steve May*

- **Hook:** #4-8 TMC 200R
- **Thread:** 140-denier UTC (#4, #6) or 70-denier UTC (#8), color to match fly
- **Eyes:** Barbell-style, size to hook
- **Tail:** Pheasant tail fibers, then rabbit fur
- **Eyes:** Plastic bead chain
- **Back/Carpace:** Furry Foam strip
- **Head:** Zonker strip, Sili Legs on each side
- **Body:** Tying thread

**Notes:** This pattern looks good in hand and fishes great, too. It could be called an inverted version of the Clouser Crayfish, as it turns that fly over and allows it to be stripped more effectively. The construction steps are similar to that of the Clouser Crayfish, with a few additions. The barbell eyes are secured on top of the hook, behind the eye. Add the bead chain eyes over the top of the tail fibers. Here the Zonker strip is wrapped to simulate the claws and legs. Using tying thread as ribbing, secure the rest of the Furry Foam to the hook shank, tie off, and trim Furry Foam even with hook eye. Brown, olive, and tan are always key patterns, but black as shown here often works very well, too. This should be in every smallmouth angler's fly box.

## MAY'S CLEAR WATER CRAYFISH V1

*Originated and tied by Steve May*

- **Hook:** #6-8 Daiichi 1720
- **Thread:** 70-denier UTC, color to match body
- **Weight:** Barbell-style, small or extra small
- **Tail:** Pheasant tail fibers, then pinch of rabbit fur
- **Eyes:** Mono
- **Back:** Long turkey tail feather fibers
- **Head:** Chenille, then a pheasant rump or hen hackle on each side as claws, turkey tail fibers
- **Body:** Chenille, saddle hackle, turkey tail fibers
- **Rib:** Medium copper or gold wire

**Notes:** This pattern gives a realistic-colored, small crayfish that is more like a nymph than streamer. As the name implies, this is best in clear water situations where the fish gets a chance to inspect the fly closely. The turkey tail fibers are pulled down over the head just past the claws. The rib is then tied in, and after the body chenille and saddle hackle are wrapped, the remaining turkey tail fibers are pulled over the top, secured at the eye, and trimmed just past the eye. The rib is then wrapped over the body to the eye.

## MAY'S CLEAR WATER CRAYFISH V2

*Originated and tied by Steve May*

- **Hook:** #4 or #6 UFM S506H
- **Thread:** 140-denier UTC, color to match body
- **Weight:** Barbell-style, medium or small

**Notes:** The materials and tying process are the same as the previous version. The jig hook gives a little different swimming movement in the water and is better suited toward the larger size.

## SF CRAYFISH

*Originated and tied by Mike Schultz*

- **Hook:** #1-#2 Daiichi 2546
- **Thread:** Black 100-denier GSP
- **Eyes:** Gold Pseudo Eyes, large
- **Antenna/Tail:** Olive orange-tipped Sili Legs, gold or copper Speckled Flashabou
- **Claws:** Two gold variant rabbit strips, one on each side, olive orange-tipped Sili Legs
- **Body:** Rusty orange rabbit strip
- **Collar:** Mallard flank
- **Head:** Gold variant rabbit fur

**Notes:** This is Mike Schultz's key crayfish pattern for high water in rivers. When flows are up, fish will move into softer current areas closer to shore. The fly should be heavy to get in the zone quickly and moved fast to trigger strikes. Substitute a Gamakatsu B10S hook if you do not want to use the stainless hook. The rabbit strip used for the body is wrapped while the rabbit fur used at the head is spun into a dubbing loop and wrapped through the eyes. This is the original color of this pattern, but any of the natural variant rabbit colors are usable.

The Clawdad can be stripped, crawled, or hopped. This smallmouth took the fly while being hopped under an indicator. LEO WRIGHT PHOTO

This hefty Lake St. Clair smallmouth took a Cray Z pattern. Depending on the mood of the fish, this fly can be stripped at different speeds or cast and let sink. When bass are in a neutral mood, a slow-sinking pattern can be effective. JERRY DARKES PHOTO

## JON'S CRAYFISH

*Originated and tied by Jon Uhlenhop*

- **Hook:** #1-4 Gamakatsu 60-degree flat-eye jig hook
- **Thread:** 140-denier UTC, to match overall color scheme of fly
- **Weight:** Black nickel Dazl Eyes, size to hook
- **Antennae:** Olive and orange Fly Enhancer Legs or Sili Legs, black Krystal Flash
- **Eyes:** Black mono, large
- **Head:** Orange Ice Dub
- **Claws:** Gold variant rabbit strip, one each side
- **Body:** Olive Estaz, tan grizzly saddle, mottled brown or olive Thin Skin or similar in mottled
- **Rib:** Medium copper wire
- **Legs:** Olive and orange Fly Enhancer Legs or Sili Legs

**Notes:** This pattern is best in a big-water or high, off-color situation where it is necessary to attract fish with color and movement. It gives a realistic crayfish profile in the water. The barbell eyes are tied so the hook rides inverted. After the body Estaz is wrapped, the saddle feather is palmer wrapped. Then the Thin Skin is pulled over the top and secured with the rib. To work closer to the bottom, tie on the jig hook; if stripping in mid-water column, the Gamakatsu B10S hook can be used.

## CRAY Z

*Originated and tied by Brian Meszaros*

- **Hook:** #1, #2 Daiichi 2461
- **Thread:** Olive 140-denier UTC
- **Cone:** Large black
- **Tail:** Two full olive marabou plumes, tied split
- **Body:** Peacock Ice Dub, spun in a loop and wrapped to make a full body

**Notes:** This is a true "guide fly" creation. Capt. Brian Meszaros has fished this pattern with great success on Lake St. Clair and lower Detroit River areas. It is stripped rapidly to trigger strikes from smallmouth and other gamefish. Additional color combinations would be brown marabou/golden brown Ice Dub and burnt orange marabou/rusty brown Ice Dub.

## Group 3: Crayfish and More

Here we find additional crayfish patterns and then present an assortment of bottom-crawling patterns. While most of these can attract a number of different fish, smallmouth and carp are the primary targets. The two species are quite similar in their favorite forage items for much of the year.

### LANTZ'S BUNNY CRAW

*Originated and tied by Josh Lantz*

- **Hook:** #4 TMC 200R or similar
- **Thread:** Olive brown 140-denier UTC
- **Eyes:** Barbell-style, medium
- **Tail:** Brown Krystal Flash, trimmed short
- **Claws:** Splayed olive grizzly hackle tip on each side
- **Body:** Olive rabbit strip, olive or brown speckled Sili Legs
- **Head:** Olive rabbit strip, brown Krystal Flash on top

**Notes:** The body is formed by wrapping the rabbit strip. A set of Sili Legs is secured in the front and back of the body. The rabbit strip is wrapped through the eyes to form the head. This fly has plenty of movement, even when stationary. It also flutters enticingly on the drop when first cast and in between strips. This can be an important feature when a first retrieve is not working. A brown or tan color scheme is a worthwhile variation of this pattern.

### ROUGH DUB CRAYFISH

*Originated and tied by Chris V*

- **Hook:** #2-4 Gamakatsu B10S
- **Thread:** 140-denier UTC, color to match fly
- **Weight:** Black bead chain, medium or large
- **Head:** A ball of Crawfish Dub at bend of hook
- **Pincers:** A bunch of fox squirrel tail hairs on each side of hook shank
- **Body:** Crawfish Dub in dubbing loop

**Notes:** This pattern comes out of Missouri, but it has become a go-to fly for sight-fishing carp in the Great Lakes. It appears simple, but there are several key details to construct it properly. When setting the squirrel tail hair for the pincers, do not even the ends. Also, make a parachute-post wrap around each bunch to help separate and secure them to the shank. Form a large-diameter body with the Crawfish Dub, wrap through the eyes, then brush the dubbing out around the whole fly and trim flat on the bottom. A search on YouTube will find several tying demos for this pattern. Tie it in the various shades of Crawfish Dub to match different crayfish colorations.

The Rough Dub Crayfish scores on the flats near Lake Michigan's Beaver Island. Stalking Great Lakes carp in the shallows draws anglers from around the world. Lake Michigan has abundant flats and crystal-clear water.
JERRY DARKES PHOTO

**(Left to right)** Row 1: Lantz's Bunny Craw, Rough Dub Crayfish, Chewey's Crayfish; Row 2: Conrad's Crayfish, Terror Cray, Simple Crayfish, Cheesy Poof; Row 3: Baby Crayfish, Spicy Crab, Coyote Ugly; Row 4: Warm Water Charlie (2 sizes, 2 colors). JIMMY CHANG PHOTO

## CHEWEY'S CRAYFISH

*Originated and tied by Jon Stefanchew*

- **Hook:** #2 Gamakatsu B10S
- **Thread:** Olive 140-denier UTC
- **Eyes:** Barbell-syle, large
- **Tail/Antennae:** Two olive orange-tipped Sili Legs
- **Pincers:** Barred orange rabbit strip with fur trimmed off lower half
- **Body:** Olive copper UV Polar Chenille
- **Collar:** Olive schlappen in front of eyes

**Notes:** Capt. Jon Stefanchew, aka Chewey, guides out of the Traverse City, Michigan, area. I have a soft spot for this fly because it caught my largest freshwater fish on a fly, a carp that weighed 40 to 45 pounds. Great Lakes carp will often take flies while they are cruising. It takes an accurate cast to get a fly to flutter down into their sight window. This pattern is great for that application and also working the bottom. You can change the color of the pincers, but leave the body and collar. Fish this for smallmouth, too!

The author's largest freshwater fish on a fly took a Chewey's Crayfish on Lake Michigan's Grand Traverse Bay. The carp was estimated at over 40 pounds and inhaled the fly on the drop. JON RAY PHOTO

## CONRAD'S CRAYFISH

*Originated and tied by Jeff Conrad*

- **Hook:** #2 Mustad 3366
- **Thread:** Brown 140-denier UTC
- **Weight:** Barbell-style, medium or large
- **Tag:** A ball of orange Senyo Laser Dub
- **Pincers:** A bunch of fox squirrel tail hairs on each side of tag
- **Body:** Brown Estaz, brown schlappen, brown Thin Skin
- **Rib:** Black medium wire
- **Wing:** Brown Flexi Floss

**Notes:** Here is another productive pattern from Jeff Conrad. It has a good profile and movement in the water and fishes well stripped or crawled. This is Conrad's primary color for this fly. We have seen this construction process before. After the body Estaz is wrapped, palmer with schlappen, pull down the Thin Skin, and secure with the rib.

## TERROR CRAY

*Originated and tied by Austin Adduci*

- **Hook:** #6 TMC 8089
- **Thread:** Burnt orange 6/0 Uni
- **Tail:** Orange-tipped Sili Legs
- **Head:** Olive Estaz
- **Eyes:** Red barbell-style, medium
- **Body:** Olive copper UV Polar Chenille, brown schlappen
- **Overbody:** Flymen Crawbody

**Notes:** There a few interesting things with this pattern. First, the eyes are mounted at the hook bend instead of near the eye. This makes the fly drop straight down instead of diving, which is a realistic movement in crayfish. Next, the Crawbody is secured to the back with the tying thread and gives the appearance of a crayfish in a defensive position.

## SIMPLE CRAYFISH

*Originated and tied by Nick Pionessa*

- **Hook:** #8 Daiichi 1260
- **Thread:** Burnt orange 8/0 Uni
- **Pincers:** A clump of fox squirrel tail
- **Eyes:** Black bead chain, small
- **Body:** Coarse brown or tan dubbing

**Notes:** New York guide and angler Nick Pionessa fishes this pattern to mudding carp on the flats of the upper Niagara River. It is a good shallow-water fly because it hits gently and sinks slowly. Try to get it into the fish's line of movement and strike at any quick movement of the fish forward. This will also take smallmouth in the same manner, as well as rock bass and perch.

Tie in the fox squirrel tail and split with a series of "X" wraps, then wrap over the butt ends of the squirrel tail to the eye of the hook. Trim the hair to extend just past the eye. Wrap the dubbing through the pincers and eyes and then to the hook eye.

## CHEESY POOF

*Originated and tied by Nick Pionessa*

- **Hook:** #8 Gamakatsu C-14S
- **Thread:** Tan 70-denier UTC
- **Eyes:** Gold or black bead chain, medium
- **Body:** Red fox body fur, a single strand of gold Krystal Flash on each side

**Notes:** This is another stealthy pattern for mudding, shallow-water carp. Carp are generally opportunistic feeders, so the fly needs to look alive, but not be an imitation of anything particular. Again, the goal is to drop the fly into the sight line of the feeding fish. Sink rate is determined by the size of the bead chain. The fox fur is spun into a dubbing loop and combed out.

## BABY CRAYFISH

*Originated and tied by Charlie Chlysta*

- **Hook:** #8 Daiichi 1710
- **Thread:** Tan 70-denier UTC
- **Bead:** Copper, ⅛ inch
- **Tail:** Pheasant tail fibers, tan grizzly marabou
- **Body:** UV brown Ice Dub, tan grizzly schlappen or webby saddle hackle
- **Rib:** Copper wire, Brassie size

**Notes:** Chlysta is a retired biology teacher and explains that crayfish hatchlings are a favorite food of a host of freshwater fish. When large numbers are present, fish can become selective to the hatchlings. For most Midwest species, eggs hatch when water temperatures reach 74 degrees F. Full size is reached after three to four months. Fish this pattern in early summer in areas where crayfish are known to nest. Be sure that the tail fibers extend past the grizzly marabou.

## SPICY CRAB

*Originated and tied by Kevin Feenstra*

- **Hook:** #4 Daiichi 1710
- **Thread:** Tan 70-denier UTC
- **Eyes:** Barbell-style, medium
- **Antenna:** Brown with gold-flecked Sili Legs
- **Body:** A small bunch of orange deer belly hair, then a bunch of olive, golden brown, or olive brown Ice Dub on top and bottom
- **Legs:** Brown with gold-flecked Sili Legs, secured behind eyes on bottom of hook

**Notes:** This fly is an example of one that looks very nondescript when in hand, but changes once it is fished. This pattern is simple to tie and becomes very lifelike in the water. Crawl it slow or strip it fast—it will catch fish.

## COYOTE UGLY

*Originated and tied by Dave Pinczkowski*

- **Hook:** #4-6 Gamakatsu B10S
- **Thread:** Tan 70-denier UTC
- **Eyes:** Red barbell-style, small
- **Tail:** Coyote or red fox tail with underfur and guard hairs, Micro Opal Mirage Flashabou
- **Body:** Olive Petite Estaz
- **Legs:** Orange and black speckled Sili Legs
- **Wing:** Light brown deer body hair

**Notes:** Dave Pinczkowski fishes this fly on the Lake Michigan flats around Door County, Wisconsin, for carp. It sinks slowly with great action on the drop and will often be taken before it hits bottom. It's also a good pattern for stubborn smallmouth. Trim the front of the deer hair wing to create a tail.

## WARM WATER CHARLIE (2 SIZES, 2 COLORS)

*Originated and tied by Jon Uhlenhop*

- **Hook:** #4-6 TMC 200R
- **Thread:** 70-denier UTC, to match fly color
- **Eyes:** Black nickel barbell-style, machined, small and medium
- **Tail:** Grizzly marabou, 2 Sili Legs
- **Body:** Sparkle Yarn, 3 sets of Sili Legs, Ice Dub
- **Collar:** Pheasant rump or hen hackle, wrapped
- **Wing:** Arctic fox tail

**Notes:** Jon Uhlenhop has found that a tan and olive version of this pattern works best. Select your materials for these color schemes. A variety of warmwater species will take this pattern. It has great movement and life in the water. It can be fished in a stillwater application or cast and stripped while swinging across the current.

# Group 4: Bottom Crawlers

This is a mix of patterns that are mainly carp focused. Carp behave differently depending on the environment they are in. In smaller streams it is critical to find actively feeding fish in order to have consistent success with flies. As this expands to large rivers, reservoirs, and lakes, and finally the waters of the Great Lakes, cruising fish seem more likely to move for a fly. If feeding fish are present, always target them first. In all cases, accurate casting and getting the fly into the fish's sight line is critical.

## ROCK HOPPER

*Originated and tied by Austin Adduci*

- **Hook:** #6 TMC 200R
- **Thread:** Tan 70-denier UTC
- **Eyes:** Red barbell-style, medium
- **Tail:** Two brown grizzly marabou plumes
- **Body:** Grizzly marabou
- **Head:** Cream or ginger rabbit fur top and bottom

**Notes:** Austin Adduci has extensive experience chasing Lake Michigan carp with flies from the southern end of the lake to the flats of Beaver Island. This pattern sinks quickly for deeper-feeding fish. This is his preferred color, but an olive or tan design can also work.

## ANDERSON'S HAMMERHEAD

*Originated and tied by Ian Anderson*

- **Hook:** #4 Mustad R74
- **Thread:** Black 210-denier UTC
- **Weight:** .035-inch-diameter wire
- **Tail:** Pumpkin Sili Legs with a mix of green and yellow glow-in-the-dark Flashabou
- **Rear Body:** Dark-colored yarn
- **Front Body:** Crawfish orange magnum rabbit strip
- **Eyes:** Large bead chain, 2 on each side

**Notes:** Indiana-based fly tier Ian Anderson designed this fly for the flats of Lake Michigan's Beaver Island. The multiple bead chain eyes add a bit of rattle to the fly. This color combination is the original, but can be altered as desired, as this pattern will also take both smallmouth and largemouth bass. Weight the front half of the hook with wire and wrap the rabbit strip for the front body.

## RL HELMET BUGGER

*Originated and tied by Jerry Darkes*

- **Hook:** #4 Daiichi 1760
- **Thread:** Black 70-denier UTC
- **Tail:** Marabou plume tip
- **Body:** Olive Estaz, olive grizzly Bugger Hackle
- **Legs:** Speckled Sili Legs, 3 to 4 on each side
- **Head:** Small Flymen Sculpin Helmet

**Notes:** The curved 1760 hook pairs perfectly with the small Sculpin Helmet, creating a pattern with a stand-up profile that fishes well along the bottom. This is a good color scheme, but brown and even an orange mix would work, too. Many other color combinations are also possible.

## GREAT LAKES CARP DREDGER

*Originated by Steve Martinez, tied by Austin Adduci*

- **Hook:** #4 TMC 200R
- **Thread:** Brown 140-denier UTC
- **Belly:** Sparse olive bucktail, copper grizzly Krystal Flash, sparse white bucktail
- **Back:** White bucktail, everglades EP Fibers
- **Collar:** Mallard flank feather dyed wood duck
- **Head:** Flymen Sculpin Helmet

**Notes:** Steve Martinez is part of Indigo Guide Service, based near Ludington, Michigan. He uses this pattern for deep-water carp in Lake Michigan's Beaver Island archipelago. Carp and smallmouth are the normal targets, but this pattern has also taken Great Lakes coho, brown trout, and lake trout in other areas.

## TED'S SWIMMING HEX

*Originated and tied by Ted Kraimer*

- **Hook:** #6 Mustad C49S or similar
- **Thread:** Camel 6/0 Uni
- **Weight:** Extra-small to small lead barbell or medium bead chain
- **Tail:** Tan, ginger, tan-barred brown rabbit strip, pheasant rump feather
- **Thorax:** Golden stone dubbing blend
- **Legs:** Pumpkin black Sili Legs
- **Wing Case:** Peacock herl

**Notes:** This fly could have been put in the Wets and Nymphs chapter. I placed it here because Kraimer says it is his best pattern for carp on the Grand Traverse Bay flats around Traverse City. Just looking at it, you can see it is usable for smallmouth and even trout. It is probably taken as a small goby or sculpin, too. The pheasant rump feather is wrapped in front of the rabbit strip as part of the tail. Also, the tail shouldn't be more than an inch long or it will tangle when cast. FYI: Kraimer has tying instructions for all of his patterns that I have presented in this book at current-works.com.

**(Left to right)** Row 1: Rock Hopper, Anderson's Hammerhead, RL Helmet Bugger; Row 2: Great Lakes Carp Dredger, Ted's Swimming Hex, Morlock's Tailer Teaser; Row 3: Carp Charlie, Bottom Scratcher, Morlock's Carp Breakfast; Row 4: Morlock's Beast Bait, Carp Bunny, Carp Nymph. JIMMY CHANG PHOTO

## MORLOCK'S TAILER TEASER

*Originated and tied by Kevin Morlock*

- **Hook:** #4 Mustad R74
- **Thread:** Black 140-denier UTC
- **Eyes:** Yellow or red barbell-style, medium
- **Tail:** Orange Krystal Flash, everglades EP Fibers over top
- **Weight:** .025-inch-diameter lead wire
- **Body:** Brown Estaz
- **Head:** Orange Estaz
- **Legs:** Brown and black Juicy Legs or Sili Legs

**Notes:** Kevin Morlock owns Indigo Guide Service. This is one of its top-producing patterns for the waters surrounding Beaver Island. By adjusting the amount of lead wire on the body and the size of the barbell eyes, the fly can be made to sink at various rates. This is also a good big-water pattern for smallmouth and freshwater drum.

## CARP CHARLIE

*Originated by Russ Maddin, tied by Pacific Fly Group*

- **Hook:** #4 Daiichi 1550
- **Thread:** Black 70-denier UTC
- **Eyes:** Bead chain, small or medium
- **Body/Underwing:** Copper Krystal Flash
- **Wing:** Brown marabou with grizzly hackle tip on each side

**Notes:** Russ Maddin creates more than just streamers. This saltwater-like fly is used successfully for carp on the flats near Traverse City, Michigan. The Krystal Flash is twisted and wrapped as the body and around the eyes. It is then tied over the eyes as the underwing. It works best when the fish are up in skinny water and a subtle presentation is needed. Olive and tan marabou versions are also good.

## BOTTOM SCRATCHER

*Originated and tied by Austin Adduci*

- **Hook:** #10 TMC 8089
- **Thread:** Olive 70-denier UTC
- **Weight/Eyes:** Barbell-style, plain lead, medium
- **Tail:** Four strands of gold Holographic Flashabou, olive black-tipped rabbit strip
- **Belly:** Small clump of tan Arctic fox
- **Back:** Front part of rabbit strip from tail
- **Collar:** Olive copper UV Polar Chenille, mallard flank feather dyed wood duck, gold Mini-Flashabou over top
- **Head:** Same color rabbit fur in a dubbing loop

**Notes:** This fishy pattern is a crayfish, or sculpin, or goby—whatever you want it to be. It is a good template to create a number of variations by changing the hook size and colors. Black, tan, and brown variations all work, or feel free to blend colors as desired. The hook is pushed through the tail rabbit strip with a bit extending forward

Carp Charlie scores. Wading Great Lakes flats provides a very saltwater-like experience, as you can stalk and sight-cast to large cruising fish. JERRY DARKES PHOTO

as the back of the fly. After the rabbit fur dubbing loop is made, wrap this in front of the collar and through the eyes, too.

## MORLOCK'S CARP BREAKFAST

*Originated and tied by Kevin Morlock*

- **Hook:** #4 TMC 200R
- **Thread:** Black 70-denier UTC
- **Eyes:** Yellow barbell-style, medium
- **Tail:** Light olive marabou, 6 to 8 strands of red Krystal Flash
- **Body:** Peacock herl
- **Rib:** Medium copper wire
- **First Collar:** Yellow mallard flank feather, red Krystal Flash
- **Second collar:** Brown schlappen

**Notes:** This another of Morlock's favorite patterns. It is tied in four variations: brown, black, olive, and tan. It will catch carp and other bottom feeders all across the Great Lakes and beyond.

Kevin Feenstra searches for a target on a Lake Michigan flat. It's easy to imagine you're at a tropical paradise at many locations around the Great Lakes. Just as in salt water, keen eyesight and accurate casting are needed for success. JERRY DARKES PHOTO

## MORLOCK'S BEAST BAIT

*Originated and tied by Kevin Morlock*

- **Hook:** #2-4 Mustad R90
- **Thread:** Black 140-denier UTC
- **Eyes:** Yellow barbell-style, medium
- **Tail:** Yellow rabbit strip
- **Collar:** Smolt blue Krystal Flash on back and belly, then brown schlappen
- **Head:** Brown yarn or dubbing, wrapped around the eyes

**Notes:** This color scheme has produced some of Morlock's largest carp. Color variations can also be tied and fished for just about anything. This is a great pattern template that is open to a wide range of interpretation. The hook is pushed through the rabbit strip and the front tied in halfway up the hook shank.

The Great Lakes have hundreds of square miles of fishable flats. The bottom ranges from mud to hard white sand to flat rock, gravel, and boulders. Some areas are easily waded while others are best fished from a boat. Carp and smallmouth are the main species found in these areas. JERRY DARKES PHOTO

## CARP BUNNY

*Originated and tied by Mike Exl*

- **Hook:** #4 Gamakatsu SL45
- **Thread:** Tan 70-denier UTC
- **Eyes:** Chartreuse and nickel Eyebalz, medium
- **Tail:** Orange Arctic fox, black-barred brown rabbit strip
- **Body:** Red Cohen's Carp Dub
- **Collar:** Burnt orange grizzly marabou

**Notes:** Mike Exl is a partner in Moving Waters Outfitters of Indianapolis, Indiana. He fishes nearby rivers and lakes regularly for carp and other species. This is a favorite pattern of his design for this use. He also ties it in olive and other natural color variations.

## CARP NYMPH

*Originated and tied by Mike Exl*

- **Hook:** #8 Gamakatsu SL45
- **Thread:** Tan 70-denier UTC
- **Bead:** Baetis green, $5/32$ inch
- **Tail:** Tan grizzly marabou
- **Abdomen:** Tan Ice Dub
- **Rib:** Green Flashabou
- **Legs:** Medium tan/grizzly Centipede Legs
- **Thorax:** Olive Cohen's Carp Dub

**Notes:** Exl finds this the most productive color combination for the pattern. The contrasting leg colors and green bead help draw attention to the fly when it is presented to a mudding fish. If any movement of the fish toward the fly is seen, tighten up the line to check if the fish is on. Don't wait to feel a strike. A single Centipede Leg is used on each side and tied in the middle to create the "V" shape. The Carp Dub is then wrapped around and through the legs.

This carp was stationed under a tree eating mulberries. A clipped deer hair pattern "plopped" in front of the fish got a positive feeding response. JERRY DARKES PHOTO

# Warmwater Patterns

**5**

## INTRODUCTION

When we refer to warmwater fly patterns, it means patterns designed to target warmwater species. By definition these are fish that spawn in water temperatures above 60 degrees F. This includes bass, sunfish, and some other species such as catfish. Things get blurred a bit, as this puts fish such as northern pike

and muskellunge in the coldwater category, where most of us picture only trout. Perhaps a coolwater category is needed?

Flies for warmwater use can be very simple, like a rubber spider for bluegill. They can also be intricate and time consuming to tie, as we will see in a number of the deer hair designs presented. I'll go out on a limb and say that the most

Rick Kustich shows a beautiful Lake Erie smallmouth bass. Smallmouth reign as the primary warmwater species targeted by Midwest and Great Lakes fly fishers. They are found in small inland creeks all the way into the waters of the Great Lakes. Fly anglers love smallies, as they feed through the entire water column, from the surface to the bottom, and are often less selective than finicky trout. NICK PIONESSA PHOTO

An assortment of patterns for warmwater use. Fly style and size vary greatly depending on the species targeted and time of year. JERRY DARKES PHOTO

Northern pike cross water temperature lines easily. They take flies readily and are found in the slower parts of many trout waters, as well as in many regular warmwater environments. JON RAY PHOTO

artistic patterns presented in this book are in this category. From a fish-catching standpoint this may not be necessary, but the pure creativity and tying skill exhibited is certainly aesthetically pleasing.

Learning to spin, stack, blend, and trim deer hair is an art in itself. Making a fishable bug is fairly simple, but it takes time and practice to achieve the artistic level of some of these patterns. Some of the best instructional videos to teach this came from the late Chris Helm of Toledo, Ohio. Helm taught hundreds of students the art of tying with deer hair. A search on YouTube will also find numerous video clips on working with deer hair.

Dr. James Henshall is often credited with creating the first hair bugs for catching bass in the late 1800s. However, there are references to indigenous people of the American South using hair "bobs" on a long pole in the late 1700s for catching largemouth bass. Mary Orvis Marbury presented a number of fly plates with bass-specific patterns in her *Favorite Flies and Their Histories*, published in 1892. Warmwater patterns have been around for a long time.

Minnesota's Larry Dahlberg may be the most influential force in warmwater patterns as we know them today. His diver designs revolutionized both tying and fishing for a host of species including bass, pike, muskie, and more. Dave Whitlock expanded on Dahlberg's designs and added more of his own to the mix. Bill Sherer increased the offerings for toothy critters. Pat and Jared Ehlers have added numerous patterns with a Midwest flavor. One thing for certain: Bass bugging is a true American creation.

You will notice that some of the patterns are tied with a weedguard. This is mostly an optional—but often practical—step, depending on where you are fishing. A weedguard is certainly helpful when working the fly through any sort of cover. We will see several different ways weedguards are constructed.

Warmwater fly fishing has grown significantly in the past decade. Smallmouth bass and muskie have been the primary focus. There is a growing cadre of influential young anglers, guides, and tiers focused on these species and taking this activity to the next level.

Two patterns tied by the late Chris Helm of Toledo, Ohio. Helm was renowned for his fly-tying skills. He was an artist in the selection and use of deer hair and taught many tiers how to best use this versatile material. JIMMY CHANG PHOTO

# Group 1: Deer Hair Topwater

Deer hair has proven to be a very functional fly-tying material. We have seen it in numerous dry flies and streamer designs. Here we find another application as a spun or stacked body material that is then trimmed to a specific shape. The final shape is based on a specific function.

## CHRIS'S MOUSE

*Originated and tied by Chris Helm*

- **Hook:** #2/0-2 Daiichi 2461
- **Thread:** White or black 100-denier GSP
- **Tail:** Microsuede
- **Body:** Deer belly hair
- **Ears:** Microsuede
- **Whiskers:** Moose body hair
- **Eyes:** Dot with black Sharpie

**Notes:** The late Chris Helm was a master in the use of deer hair. From tying techniques to selecting hair for specific uses, few people matched his knowledge. Fortunately, much of this has been chronicled through his many students and a series of tying DVDs. This was his signature pattern—simple in design, artistic in appearance, and functional in use—and he spent nearly 20 years perfecting this fly.

## TY'S TANTILIZER

*Originated by Tim England, tied by Chris Helm*

- **Hook:** #2/0 Gamakatsu B10S
- **Thread:** White or black 100-denier GSP
- **Tail:** Centipede Legs
- **Legs:** Three large rooster hackles on each side, Krystal Flash
- **Body:** Red or orange Cactus Chenille or Estaz
- **Collar:** Deer belly hair
- **Head:** Deer belly hair
- **Eyes:** 5 mm solid doll eyes

**Notes:** The unique trimmed design of the head on this pattern allows it to both pop and dive and trail a large bubble stream. The head has to be tightly packed in order to be trimmed correctly and to function properly. Colors can vary, but the frog version pictured here is the most popular. This is the first time we have seen solid doll eyes being used. After the eye stem is removed, a space in the deer hair is either trimmed or burned to set in the eyes, which are best secured with Liquid Fusion.

## STEVE'S POP CHARGE

*Originated and tied by Steve Wascher*

- **Hook:** #3/0-1 Daiichi 2461
- **Thread:** White or black 100-denier GSP
- **Rear Hook:** #1 Mustad 3366
- **Rear Body:** White marabou, pearl Krystal Flash, pearl Palmer Chenille colored with permanent marker
- **Connector:** 10 mm (#1-1/0 hook), 15 mm (#2/0-3/0 hook) Flymen Fish Spine
- **Collar:** Deer belly hair
- **Body:** Deer belly hair
- **Eyes:** ¼-inch solid doll eyes
- **Front:** Coat with Flexament

**Notes:** Steve Wascher is a master of deer hair. His creations are practical artwork; all are fish catchers, but exquisitely constructed. A seasoned fly angler, Wascher studied under Chris Helm and is often seen at fly-tying and fly-fishing expos. The tips of the deer hair are left on the collar. For the body, the hair is spun, stacked, and packed super tight and then trimmed into a cylinder shape. The stems of the doll eyes are removed and they are glued into a recess burned into the hair.

**Hint:** Coating the front of deer hair poppers with Flexament or similar flexible cement (Liquid Fusion, Shoe Goo) stiffens and protects the hair. It stays rigid and will make a louder "pop" during the retrieve.

## TAP'S BUG

*Originated by H. G. Tapply, tied by Chris Helm*

- **Hook:** #2/0-1 Chris Helm Gaelic Supreme Bass
- **Thread:** White or black 100-denier GSP
- **Tail:** Yearling elk or deer belly hair
- **Body:** Yearling elk or deer belly hair

**Notes:** This classic pattern was a favorite of the late Chris Helm to both tie and fish. It is a good one to learn and practice and will catch fish. Vary the colors as desired. The tail hair is stacked by color. The body is spun, packed, and trimmed. It is unlikely you will easily locate the hook specified in the recipe; substitute with the Gamakatsu B10S.

**Hint:** Helm created a tool called the Brassie to help tiers pack deer hair. It is available from most fly shops and tying material suppliers.

**(Left to right)** Row 1: Chris's Mouse, Ty's Tantilizer; Row 2: Steve's Pop Charge, Tap's Bug; Row 3: Baby Bass Popper, Steve's Chain Gang Popper; Row 4: Frog Popper. JIMMY CHANG PHOTO

## BABY BASS POPPER

*Originated and tied by Nick Pionessa*

- **Hook:** #4 Daiichi 2461
- **Thread:** White 6/0 Uni for tail, 100-denier GSP for body
- **Tail:** White bucktail, pearl Polar Flash
- **Back:** Olive and black stacked deer belly hair
- **Belly:** White stacked deer belly hair
- **Eyes:** 7 mm doll eyes

**Notes:** The small profile of this pattern allows it to be cast with a lighter-weight line. It makes a lot of noise when retrieved, despite its small size. Be sure to pack the deer hair tightly as you work up the shank. The body is trimmed straight on the sides and should end up approximately ⅜ inch wide. Use a razor blade to form the body, as it is easier to trim the hair as short as needed. Make some in all white, too!

## STEVE'S CHAIN GANG POPPER

*Originated and tied by Steve Wascher*

- **Hook:** #2/0 Gamakatsu B10S
- **Thread:** Red 70-denier UTC for segments, 100-denier GSP for body
- **Tail:** Flashabou glued with Flexament, trimmed to a paddle shape
- **Segments:** Four 15 mm Fish Skull Fish Spines, Palmer Chenille, grizzly hen wrapped in front
- **Connector:** 15 mm Fish Spine
- **Fins:** Grizzly hen saddle feathers, 1 on each side
- **Collar:** Deer belly hair
- **Body:** Deer belly hair
- **Eyes:** ¼-inch solid doll eyes with stem removed, glued

**Notes:** This creation from Steve Wascher has great swimming movement to it and makes plenty of noise on the retrieve.

## FROG POPPER

*Originator unknown, tied by Jerry Darkes*

- **Hook:** #2/0-1 Gamakatsu B10S
- **Thread:** White or chartreuse 140-denier UTC
- **Tail:** Short white marabou, pearl Krystal Flash
- **Legs:** White, then chartreuse, then olive grizzly large rooster neck hackle on each side
- **Collar:** Olive over white deer belly hair
- **Body:** Orange, white, olive deer belly hair
- **Weedguard (optional):** 25 lb. hard mono
- **Eyes:** 7 mm plastic doll eyes

**Notes:** The deer hair frog popper is a "must-have" pattern for warmwater fly fishers. Much like the Adams dry fly for trout, frog poppers are a mainstay for bass fly anglers. This is a generic design that has been catching bass for decades. Even with my meager deer hair skills, I can make a functional fly. Using this same design template, unlimited color combinations can be made.

The belly hair is both stacked and spun, packed, and then trimmed to shape. Liquid Fusion is used to coat the front and secure the eyes. A bit hard to see on the fly plate, this is the first instance of a weedguard in a fly in this section. Here a length of 20-pound hard mono is flattened with smooth pliers at one end and bent 90 degrees. This is secured underneath the hook eye, then trimmed off in front of the eye and just past the hook gap on the bottom.

**Hint:** Your deer hair patterns can be sprayed with Scotchguard to minimize water absorption. This keeps the fly on the surface and reduces extra water weight.

# Group 2: More Topwater

Here we transition from deer hair body designs to various types of foam being used for flotation. Closed-cell foam materials have helped to revolutionize fly tying for a wide range of species and have a wide range of applications in fly construction. In many cases they simplify the tying process, but the aesthetic look may be lost.

## STEVE'S SLOP SLIDER

*Originated and tied by Steve Wascher*

- **Hook:** #2/0-1 Gamakatsu B10S
- **Thread:** White 100-denier GSP
- **Weedguard:** 25 lb. hard mono
- **Tail:** Round rubber hackle
- **Body:** Deer belly hair
- **Eyes:** 7 mm solid doll eyes

**Notes:** There are times when loud, popping bugs will not attract fish. Slider-style bugs make a minimal amount of noise when retrieved and have a more darting-style movement to them, often diving a bit and moving side to side. The deer hair can be both stacked and spun, and then is trimmed into a rounded wedge shape. Be sure to tie this on with a loop knot! Here the weedguard is tied in on each side of the hook, partway around the bend, then tied off at the eye after the fly is completed. This allows the fly to be crawled through the thickest of weeds, brush, and lily pads. Some strikes will be missed with this design, but it is needed to work the fly in cover.

## ST. PAUL SLIDER

*Originated and tied by Paul Hansen*

- **Hook:** #1/0-4 Gamakatsu B10S
- **Thread:** Black 6/0 Uni
- **Tail:** Marabou with Krystal Flash
- **Body:** EVA foam, pre-shaped and painted
- **Legs:** Rubber hackle

**Notes:** Minnesota-based angler and tier Paul Hansen creates a wide assortment of foam-bodied flies. They are formed from EVA foam block that he shapes and paints. The frog coloration here is most popular, but a baitfish color works, too. The slider shape darts through the water with minimal noise.

**Hint:** Zuddy's Leg Puller simplifies getting the legs through the body. You can find this useful tool in most fly shops. If you plan to work with foam, it is well worth the investment.

The use of closed-cell foam and rubber hackle has simplified the construction of topwater patterns. The foam is easier to work with and lasts longer than cork, is available in a variety of colors, and can be colored with markers if desired. JIMMY CHANG PHOTO

## ZUDBUBBLER POPPER (2 COLORS)

*Originated and tied by Matt Zudweg*

- **Hook:** #3/0 Daiichi 2720 or similar
- **Thread:** Red 6/0 Uni
- **Tail:** Marabou plume tip, Centipede Legs
- **Collar:** Ice Dub
- **Body:** Zudbubbler foam body, Centipede Legs

**Notes:** This is a signature pattern of Michigan guide and tier Matt Zudweg. It combines features of the classic Gerbubble Bug and the Blockhead Popper, described later. Having less surface area, it is easier to cast than the original Blockhead Popper. Fish the Zudbubbler slowly and let the legs work.

For the initial body prep, using a dubbing needle or leg puller (Check out Zuddy's Leg Puller!), push a hole through the Zuddbubbler body (centered as much as possible). Lay a thread base on the hook shank and coat with Zap-A-Gap or similar glue. Use the leg puller to bring the Centipede Legs through the body. Color the body with a Sharpie marker.

**Hint:** Due the popularity of foam poppers, most bodies are now available pre-drilled in the center.

**(Left to right)** Row 1: Steve's Slop Slider, St. Paul Slider; Row 2: Zudbubbler Popper (2 colors); Row 3: Baby Blockhead, Blockhead Popper; Row 4: Hula Frog, J Hook Popper. JIMMY CHANG PHOTO

## BABY BLOCKHEAD

*Originated by Sheldon Bolstad, tied by Paul Hansen*

- **Hook:** #6 TMC 8089
- **Thread:** White 6/0 Uni
- **Tail:** Rooster hackle tips, marabou, Krystal Flash mixed in
- **Collar:** Wrapped rooster hackle
- **Body:** Foam block, 12 mm x 12 mm x 8 mm
- **Eyes:** 7 mm plastic doll eyes

**Notes:** For this pattern, the body is attached by cutting a slit the length of the foam block in the middle. The hook shank is covered with thread and the body slid over. The fly is turned over and Zap-A-Gap is put into the foam slit. It is then centered level on the hook, and the foam sides are pinched together until they hold. The body can be colored as desired with a Sharpie. This downsized version of a Blockhead Popper is small enough to hook panfish, but makes enough noise to attract larger fish. It can be cast on a lighter (6-weight) outfit.

## BLOCKHEAD POPPER

*Originated by Sheldon Bolstad, tied By Great Lakes Fly Shop*

- **Hook:** #2/0-1 Gamakatsu B10S or similar
- **Thread:** 3/0 Uni, color to match body
- **Tail:** Marabou plume tip, Flashabou
- **Weedguard:** 20 lb. hard mono
- **Collar:** Schlappen
- **Body:** Foam block, 20 mm x 20 mm x 10 mm
- **Eyes:** 12 mm plastic doll eyes

**Notes:** This pattern is a well-recognized, upper Midwest original that catches *lots* of fish. It is designed to float forever and make a lot of noise, drawing fish from a long distance. It has a large surface area, so needs to be cast on a heavier-weight outfit (8-weight) and a stout leader to turn over. Measure the length of the body back from the hook eye and start your thread there, tying in the weedguard, tail, and collar. The body is prepared as on the Baby Blockhead: Make a slit on the bottom, slide it over the threaded hook shank, and glue with Zap-A-Gap or similar. Color with Sharpie or similar marker if desired. The weedguard is tied off at the hook eye as the final step.

## HULA FROG

*Originated and tied by Paul Hansen*

- **Hook:** #1/0 Gamakatsu B10S
- **Thread:** Black 6/0 Uni
- **Tail:** Rooster hackles, 2 per side
- **Body:** Shaped EVA foam, painted or colored with waterproof markers

**Notes:** Paul Hansen makes and fishes a number of shaped-foam patterns. They are lightweight, durable, and float indefinitely. The foam is prepped with a hole in it to slide over the thread-covered hook shank. Stiffer rooster saddles are best for the tail, as they minimize tangling in the hook when cast. This shape refers back to a well-known casting surface lure.

## J HOOK POPPER

*Originator unknown, tied by Jerry Darkes*

- **Hook:** #1 Daiichi 4350
- **Thread:** 70-denier UTC, match color scheme of the popper
- **Body:** 5 mm foam strip, 30 mm long x 12 mm wide
- **Tail:** Small bunch of Craft Fur and 2 rooster neck hackles on each side.
- **Collar:** Rooster neck, hackle, wrapped
- **Eyes:** 7 mm plastic doll eyes

**Notes:** Tony Pagliei of Lansing, Michigan, showed me this interesting design, but he was not the originator. The "J" hook is used in conventional angling, and it adapts well to this fly design. To seat the body properly, find the middle of the foam and push the hook through. Slide the foam back toward the hook bend and tight to the collar. Then fold and glue with Zap-A-Gap or similar (you can add rubber legs, if desired, before folding over). This is a fun pattern to make and a productive fish catcher.

Popper in mouth, a surface-hooked largemouth takes to the air. Catching bass on topwater flies is the ultimate in the sport for many anglers. Action like this is available across the Great Lakes and Midwest.
KEVIN FEENSTRA PHOTO

## Group 3: Even More Topwater

Here are some additional topwater patterns that function a bit differently than what we have seen. Gurglers make a soft noise when retrieved. It is enough to attract attention, but not too loud to scare off fish in a neutral feeding mood. Jack Gartside is credited with the first gurgler design for saltwater use. Like many saltwater flies, it transfers over to warmwater use very well. Also, as noted earlier, it can also be an effective trout pattern.

With their long silhouette, pencil poppers generally imitate a crippled baitfish. These also have a saltwater origin, but adapt well to warmwater use—particularly for bass. They are easier to cast, having less air resistance than most standard popper designs.

(**Left to right**) Row 1: Eyed Gurgler; Row 2: Stunned Minnow Popper; Row 3: Gartside Gurgler; Row 4: St. Joe Gurgler.
JIMMY CHANG PHOTO

Topwater flies are generally worked along some sort of cover. When the fly gets too far away from the area, it is picked up and cast again. It is important to have an outfit with a line weight suitable to carry the size flies you are casting. JERRY DARKES PHOTO

## EYED GURGLER

*Originated and tied by Nick Pionessa*

- **Hook:** #4 Daiichi 1720
- **Thread:** White 6/0 Uni
- **Tail:** White Super Hair, green Ice Wing Fiber
- **Back:** 3 mm white foam strip, same width as hook gap
- **Body:** Pearl green Ice Dub
- **Head:** Same strip used for back
- **Eyes:** Small solid doll eye or 3D stick-on

**Notes:** Here the end of the foam strip is tied in at the tail and left extending forward. It is pulled over and tied down at the front of the body, then pulled back over the hook eye to form the head. The strip is tied off at the front of the body again and trimmed at an angle. The stem of the solid doll eye can be clipped short and inserted into the fold of the foam and glued. A 3 to 5 mm 3D eye can also be used.

This is a great crippled emerald shiner imitation. It makes a bit of noise and has a darting motion on the retrieve. It will work for any bright silver baitfish. Be sure to tie this on with a loop knot for maximum movement.

## STUNNED MINNOW POPPER

*Originator unknown, tied by Rick Kustich*

- **Hook:** #2 Mustad 33903
- **Thread:** Gray 70-denier UTC
- **Tail:** Four white saddle hackles, splayed two on each side
- **Collar:** Grizzly schlappen, rubber hackle
- **Body:** Preformed and painted hard foam or balsa body

**Notes:** This is a fun pattern to fish for smallmouth cruising rocky flats. The baitfish design is used most of the time, but there are many color combinations.

## GARTSIDE GURGLER

*Originated by Jack Gartside, tied by Charles Chlysta*

- **Hook:** #2 Daiichi 2461
- **Thread:** 3/0 Danville or Monocord, to match color scheme of fly
- **Tail:** Marabou plume, Sili Legs (optional), per color scheme of fly
- **Body:** Estaz or Cactus Chenille, grizzly saddle hackle, per color scheme of fly
- **Back:** 2 mm closed-cell foam
- **Legs:** Sili Legs, 4 on each side

**Notes:** This pattern is also listed in the Dry Flies chapter. In addition to being a night trout guru, Charlie Chlysta, aka Picket Pin, is also a smallmouth bass addict. His version of the Gurgler is a great pattern for both smallmouth and largemouth. The dark shade shown here is for low light or after dark. During the day a brighter-colored version is often better.

The foam for the back is tied in over the tail, then the body is wrapped with the grizzly saddle palmered over the Estaz or Cactus Chenille. The foam is then pulled over and tied down right in front of the body, just behind the eye. Sili Legs are added on each side and the thread is tied off. Leave about ½ inch of the foam extending forward and trim in a curved shape. Straight foam can be used or it can be precut using the River Road Creations Frog Cutter.

## ST. JOE GURGLER

*Originated and tied by Doug Taylor*

- **Hook:** #6 TMC 8089
- **Thread:** White 6/0 Uni
- **Tail:** Bucktail
- **Back:** Two layers of 2 mm foam, same width as hook gap
- **Body:** UV Polar Chenille

**Notes:** Pull the foam over the top of the body and trim just behind the hook eye. Trim the top foam strip about ½ inch past the hook eye and the bottom one ¼ inch. Illinois angler/tier Doug Taylor uses a switch rod to skate his gurgler variation downstream and across for river smallmouth. Switch rods are a great tool for river fishing, and smallmouth bass are usually willing participants. The "dark day/dark color, bright day/bright color" axiom works well here.

# Group 4: Diver Patterns

Subsurface patterns for warmwater use have gotten a lot of attention in recent decades. This is due to several reasons. First, general interest and awareness in warmwater fly fishing has grown. Next, there have been advances in equipment—especially in fly lines that allow anglers to present flies through the water column. Finally, there is a group of younger anglers and guides who are focusing most of their attention on warmwater species.

Larry Dahlberg has been a continuing influence in the Midwest and beyond. His original patterns have stood the test of time along with variations created by anglers such as Dave Whitlock. They have inspired a group of innovative younger anglers such as Michigan's Mike Schultz, Tim Landwehr in Wisconsin, and others. There has been a new focus, on the water, behind the fly shop counter, and at the vise, to take warmwater fly fishing to another level.

Here we will look at some now "classic" subsurface patterns, along with others that incorporate the latest in materials and methods to create a new generation of flies.

## RABBIT STRIP DIVER

*Originated by Larry Dahlberg, tied by Jerry Darkes*

- **Hook:** #2/0-4 Gamakatsu B10S
- **Thread:** 140-denier UTC, color to match fly
- **Weedguard (optional):** 20-30 lb. stiff mono (depends on hook size)
- **Tail/Back:** Rabbit strip, Krinkle Mirror Flash
- **Legs (optional):** Sili Legs or round rubber
- **Collar:** Palmer Chenille, deer belly hair
- **Head:** Deer belly hair

**Notes:** This is a jazzed-up version of Dahlberg's legendary pattern. If you like to fish streamers, you should have an assortment of these. Color choices are endless. Trim the deer head flat on the bottom. Leave a sizable secondary deer hair collar on the back half of the head. Coat the front of this collar with Flexament. Though it is considered a surface pattern, you can fish the Rabbit Strip Diver on both intermediate and sinking-head lines. Be sure to tie it on with a loop knot. You can get it to hover in the mid-depth water column in between strips, and bass often find it irresistible. Trout love this fly, too!

## DAHLBERG DIVER

*Originated by Larry Dahlberg, tied by Jerry Darkes*

- **Hook:** #1-4 Gamakatsu B10S
- **Thread:** 140-denier UTC, color to match fly
- **Weedguard (optional):** 20-30 lb. stiff mono (depends on hook size)
- **Tail:** Short marabou plume tip, Krinkle Mirror Flash, rooster neck hackles
- **Collar:** Palmer Chenille (optional), deer belly hair
- **Head:** Deer belly hair

**Notes:** This is another of Dahlberg's fish-catching classics with an updated look. I prefer this in the baitfish coloration presented, but it can be colored as desired. There are many types of flashy strand materials on the market. Krystal Flash is probably used most often. When looking for a brighter sparkle, consider Krinkle Mirror Flash, Lateral Scale, or Holographic Flashabou.

**(Left to right)** Row 1: Rabbit Strip Diver, Dahlberg Diver, Frog Diver; Row 2: Articulated Diver (2 colors); Row 3: Swingin' D Changer; Row 4: Steve's Chain Gang Diver, Mini Swingin' D. JIMMY CHANG PHOTO

Smallmouth as well as largemouth bass love diver patterns. This chunky Lake Erie specimen found a Rabbit Strip Diver irresistible. Vary both fly color and type of retrieve until the right combination is found. JERRY DARKES PHOTO

## FROG DIVER

*Originated by Larry Dahlberg/Dave Whitlock, tied by Jerry Darkes*

- **Hook:** #1/0-4 Mustad Signature Stinger or similar
- **Thread:** Olive brown 140-denier UTC
- **Weedguard (optional):** 30 lb. stiff mono
- **Tail:** White Arctic fox, olive Arctic fox over top, olive Krystal Flash
- **Legs:** Two grizzly olive, then white rooster neck hackles on each side
- **Collar:** Deer belly hair, chartreuse and olive on top, white on the bottom
- **Legs:** Round rubber hackle, mix yellow, olive, grizzly olive
- **Head:** Deer belly hair—olive on top, white or yellow on bottom
- **Eyes:** 7 mm plastic doll eyes

**Notes:** This is my take on a timeless pattern. The Mustad Signature Stinger is a bit longer than the B10S, making it easier to add all the materials. The diver head is created as in previous patterns. In this pattern I substituted Arctic fox tail fur for marabou. Marabou is fairly fragile, and the Arctic fox is nearly indestructible with similar movement in the water. In heavy-duty use, it will last much longer.

## ARTICULATED DIVER (2 COLORS)

*Originated and tied by Pat Ehlers*

- **Front Hook:** #2 Gamakatsu B10S
- **Rear Hook:** #4 down-eye streamer hook cut at bend
- **Thread (rear body):** 6/0 Uni, to match color
- **Thread (front body):** White or black 100-denier GSP
- **Rear Body:** Marabou plume, ¼-inch length of ¼-inch-diameter foam
- **Connector:** Thin nylon-coated wire with 1 small glass bead
- **Wing (on front hook):** Single large or several smaller marabou plumes, Flashabou
- **Collar:** Deer body hair
- **Throat:** Red deer body hair
- **Head:** Deer belly hair

**Notes:** Wisconsin's Pat Ehlers is a well-known fly shop owner, angler, and tier. For the rear body, the marabou plume is wrapped and the foam cylinder glued to the cut-off end of the hook. This helps the fly suspend and stops rust from forming on the exposed metal of the cut end. The head is constructed similar to other diver heads. This pattern has unlimited movement and can be fished from top to bottom by varying the line used. Having a neutral buoyancy, it is a fly angler's version of a jerk bait.

The Dahlberg Rabbit Strip Diver design has morphed into more modern creations including Mike Schultz's Swingin' D. Here the definition between a fly and a fly rod lure starts to blur. As long as it is cast by the weight of the line, can we still call it a fly? JIMMY CHANG PHOTO

## SWINGIN' D CHANGER

*Originated and tied by Mike Schultz*

- **Front Hook:** #2/0 Partridge Universal Predator
- **Rear Hook:** #2 Partridge Universal Predator
- **Thread:** White 70-denier UTC, or match color scheme of fly
- **Rear Body:** Two saddle hackles, small pearl Lateral Scale, pearl Palmer Chenille, wrapped grizzly saddle, mallard flank
- **Mid-Body:** Two 20 mm Fish Spines with pearl Palmer Chenille and wrapped grizzly saddle
- **Connector:** 25 mm Fish Spine
- **Rattle:** 5 mm glass rattle secured to front hook
- **Front Body:** Ten to twelve turns of .030-inch-diameter wire, pearl Palmer Chenille, grizzly saddle hackle to cover connector up to rattle, sparse Senyo Predator Wrap, wrapped marabou tip, Krinkle Mirror Flash, grizzly hackle on each side
- **Collar:** Small pearl Lateral Scale, large Palmer Chenille
- **Head:** Rainy's Foam Diver Head, small or medium

**Notes:** There is a lot going on with this pattern, and it blurs the line between a fly and lure. The amount and placement of the lead wire is critical to the balance and swimming movement of the fly. The front body and collar should go almost to the hook eye. Super Glue gel is applied over the top of this material and the diver head is slid on. This is usually tied in baitfish color schemes—all white, white/olive mix, white/gray mix—but can be colored as desired. Chartreuse as pictured here is also a good one! It was designed for smallmouth and pike, but everything eats it—trout, too! You can find several videos detailing construction on YouTube.

This is best fished on an intermediate line to keep it in the upper part of the water column and visible to gamefish.

Remember, most of our gamefish feed upward. Few have a subterminal mouth (like carp) directing them downward.

## STEVE'S CHAIN GANG DIVER

*Originated and tied by Steve Wascher*

- **Hook:** #2/0-2 Gamakatsu B10S
- **Thread:** Red 6/0 Uni for Fish Spines, white 100-denier GSP for head
- **Tail:** 10 mm Fish Spine, marabou plume tip, Krinkle Mirror Flash, grizzly hen
- **Mid-Body:** One each 15 mm then 20 mm Fish Spines, Chocklett's Filler Flash, grizzly hen
- **Connector:** 25 mm Fish Spine
- **Collar:** Two grizzly hen hackles on each side, deer belly hair
- **Head:** Deer belly hair
- **Eyes:** 1/4-inch solid doll eyes

**Notes:** The use of the Fish Spines gives this fly a lot of extra movement. The rear sections have a great wiggle to them on the retrieve and allow the back of the fly to flex and bend in between strips. The diver head is constructed as we have seen before, with the collar hair tips extending back and the head stacked, packed, and trimmed. Color combinations are endless, but a bright color, a light shade, and a dark shade will cover most needs.

## MINI SWINGIN' D

*Originated and tied by Mike Schultz*

- **Hook:** #1/0-1 Partridge Universal Predator
- **Thread:** White 70-denier UTC, to match color scheme of fly
- **Rear Body:** 20 mm Fish Spine, 2 saddle hackles, Flashabou, Palmer Chenille, rabbit strip, mallard flank
- **Connector:** 30 lb. hard mono with 3D bead
- **Front Body:** Rabbit strip, small rattle, large Palmer Chenille
- **Collar:** Tip-wrapped marabou plume, grizzly saddle on each side, Senyo Predator wrap, large Palmer Chenille
- **Head:** Small Rainy's Foam Diver Head

**Notes:** This downsized version of a Swingin' D is for lighter lines and when the fish are keyed on smaller bait. The diver head is secured with Super Glue gel. It is fished on intermediate and even sinking-head lines.

## TODD'S WIGGLE MINNOW

*Originated by Todd Boyer, tied by Jerry Darkes*

- **Hook:** #6 TMC 8089
- **Thread:** White 140-denier UTC
- **Tail:** Loop of 20 lb. hard mono over hook bend, Polar Fiber or Craft Fur, Krystal Flash
- **Body:** 1½-inch length of 5/16-inch or 3/8-inch-diameter foam cylinder
- **Eyes:** 3D or solid doll eyes

**Notes:** This can also be tied on a #2-4 Gamakatsu B10S hook. Cover the shank with thread and tie off. Take the foam cylinder, cut one end to a 45-degree angle, cut a slit halfway into the cylinder on the bottom, then take a dubbing needle and make an angled hole from the front of the cylinder into the slit. Open the slit in the cylinder and push it over the eye of the hook through the hole in front, then seat the slit over the hook shank. Turn it over and put Zap-A-Gap, Super Glue, or similar into the slit, pinch until the slit stays closed, then color the cylinder as desired with waterproof markers. The eyes are attached with Super Glue gel.

OK, this is not really a fly, but a fly rod lure. It has a saltwater origin, but will catch a host of freshwater species. When constructed properly, it will dive a foot or so with a noticeable side-to-side movement. Fish it on floating, intermediate, or sinking lines to various depths in the water column. As a fly rod crankbait or jerk bait, it is particularly effective on smallmouth bass, where letting the "fly" hover or float up in between strips can be irresistible to them. Be sure to fish this (and most other divers and streamers) with a loop knot for maximum action. A Duncan Loop or Rapala Knot both work well for this.

Todd's Wiggle Minnow. JERRY DARKES PHOTO

## JUKE AND JIVE DIVER

*Originated and tied by Austin Adduci*

- **Front Hook:** #2 TMC 8089
- **Thread:** Fluorescent red 70-denier UTC
- **Rear Hook:** #4 TMC 105
- **Rear Body:** Two to four white saddle tips, pearl Flashabou, silver UV Polar Chenille, white schlappen, mallard flank feather
- **Connector:** 50 lb. braid with three 8mm plastic beads
- **Front Body:** White tip-wrapped marabou, pearl Flashabou, red UV Polar Chenille, white schlappen, mallard flank feather
- **Head:** 3/8-inch white foam cylinder

**Notes:** To complete the head, cut the cylinder to 45 degrees in front, trim to fill the length of the hook, put a slit in the bottom, then slide it over the hook shank and glue with Super Glue gel. This pattern combines features of the Wiggle Minnow and Swingin' D or Double D patterns shown earlier. The use of the braid as a connector allows more movement to the back part of the fly. Obviously, this is a baitfish-color version. Other colors can be used as desired. This was designed mainly as a smallmouth fly, but it will work for trout and other species, too.

Juke and Jive Diver. JERRY DARKES PHOTO

# Group 5: Forage Species

This group of patterns covers some of the common forage species found in warmwater environments across the Midwest. These can be used to target the larger natural predators such as bass, pike, and muskie as well as introduced species such as striped bass and striper/white bass hybrids.

## PMS PERCH

*Originated and tied by Jerry Darkes*

- **Hook:** #1/0-4/0 Daiichi 2461
- **Thread:** Chartreuse 140-denier UTC
- **Wing:** Yellow Icelandic Sheep, chartreuse Icelandic Sheep, gold Holographic Flashabou, barred with a brown Sharpie
- **Back:** Chartreuse or olive bucktail
- **Belly:** Orange bucktail
- **Collar:** Deer belly hair, chartreuse or olive on top, orange on bottom
- **Head:** Deer belly hair, chartreuse or olive on top, orange on bottom
- **Eyes:** 7 mm 3D

**Notes:** The PMS stands for Pike Muskie Special. The belly hair on the collar and head is stacked. Leave the tips on the collar hair. Trim to a rounded fish-head shape. The eyes are attached with Super Glue gel. The Icelandic Sheep hair compresses down when out of the water, making the fly easier to cast. Increase the size through the season. The perch color is key and can be varied from almost golden brown to olive on the back, depending on location. Bass as well as toothy critters will hit this pattern.

PMS Perch. JERRY DARKES PHOTO

## BIG EYE BLUEGILL

*Originated and tied by Karl Weixlmann*

- **Hook:** #1/0-2 Mustad Signature Stinger
- **Thread:** White flat waxed nylon
- **Tail:** White or cream EP Fibers with opal Mirage Flashabou, colored with permanent marker
- **Belly:** White or cream EP Fibers, colored with permanent marker
- **Back:** Olive EP Fibers with opal Mirage Flashabou, barred with permanent marker
- **Eyes:** Gold 7 mm 3D

**Notes:** This pattern presents a large profile and can be used wherever bluegill are found. The materials do not hold much water, so it is easy to cast. Be sure to soak it good prior to casting so it will sink.

## PAT'S SUNFISH

*Originated by Pat Ehlers, tied by Rainy's Flies*

- **Hook:** #6 TMC 8089 or similar
- **Thread:** Orange flat waxed nylon
- **Weedguard:** 20 lb. hard mono
- **Belly:** Orange marabou
- **Back:** Olive marabou, with copper Krystal Flash
- **Collar:** Olive deer body hair
- **Throat:** Red deer belly hair, sparse
- **Head:** Olive deer body hair on top, orange deer belly hair on bottom, trimmed
- **Eyes:** 4 mm 3D

**Notes:** The weedguard is tied in around the bend of the hook as the first step and tied off at the head as the last step. The deer belly hair is stacked, packed, and trimmed as with other patterns we have seen. This is a fun pattern to both tie and fish. Largemouth bass are the main target, but pike and muskie have also eaten this fly. A number of different sunfish species can be imitated by adjusting the colors.

**(Left to right)** Row 1: Big Eye Bluegill, Pat's Sunfish; Row 2: Shad-O; Row 3: Super Shad. JIMMY CHANG PHOTO

## SHAD-O

*Originated and tied by Brian Meszaros*

- **Hook:** #1/0 Gamakatsu B10S
- **Thread:** White 140-denier UTC
- **Tail (tied on hook):** Two grizzly saddle hackles extending beyond bucktail, 2 sections of white bucktail, pearl Krystal Flash
- **Front Body:** 15 mm Senyo Shank with a single section of white bucktail on top and bottom, pearl Krystal Flash, root beer Krystal Flash over top
- **Eyes:** ¼-inch 3D

**Notes:** The bucktail in this pattern is all reverse-tied to add a larger profile with a minimal amount of material. To increase durability, primary thread wraps—where the bucktail is reverse-tied, at the head, and to secure the eyes—are coated with Clear Cure Goo Hydro. This is a great big-water pattern or wherever shad or large silver shiners are present. It can also be tied in attractor colors as desired. Largemouth, pike, and muskie are the primary targets. It is a good choice for inland stripers and hybrids, too.

## SUPER SHAD

*Originated and tied by Ryan Ratliff*

- **Hook:** #2/0-2 Partridge Attitude Extra
- **Thread:** White 140-denier UTC
- **Tail:** Natural white Arctic Runner or Icelandic Sheep
- **Body:** White Arctic Runner or Icelandic Sheep, sparse mix of pearl ¹⁄₆₉-inch Lateral Scale, opal Mirage Flashabou, and UV pearl Angel Hair
- **Overbody:** Gray Extra Select Craft Fur
- **Lateral Line:** Grizzly saddle
- **Topping:** Peacock herl
- **Head:** White Extra Select Craft Fur
- **Eyes:** 10 mm 3D

**Notes:** Ryan Ratliff works for Mad River Outfitters in Columbus, Ohio. An accomplished fly fisher and tier, he uses this pattern to target pike, stripers, and hybrid stripers in area rivers, as well as largemouth bass in lakes. The body, overbody, and head materials are all reverse-tied, which increases the profile of the fly. The materials absorb little water and compress well when wet for easy casting. The head is coated with Clear Cure Goo or Loon UV Clear Fly Finish. This also secures the eyes.

Largemouth bass are distributed all across the Great Lakes region, and are normally found around soft-bottom areas near weeds and woody cover. They are a primary fly rod target and respond to a wide range of patterns. This hefty specimen took a Shad-O fly.
JERRY DARKES PHOTO

## Group 6: Pat Ehlers Patterns

Pat Ehlers has been a driving force in warmwater fly fishing for several decades. As owner of The Fly Fishers in Milwaukee, Wisconsin, Ehlers has helped promote fly fishing in general and develop numerous patterns for a wide range of species. He is a contract tier for Rainy's Flies. Ehlers has also made a significant contribution in the design and use of subsurface patterns for largemouth bass. We have already seen several of his designs; here are more of his signature patterns.

### PAT'S FOAMTAIL SUPERWORM

*Originated by Pat Ehlers, tied by Rainy's Flies*

- **Hook:** #2/0 Gamakatsu Wide Gape J Hook
- **Thread:** Black 6/0 Uni
- **Weedguard:** 25 lb. hard mono
- **Tail:** Rabbit fur, Holographic Flashabou, Centipede Legs
- **Body:** Hareline Krystal Hackle, large, with Holographic Flashabou
- **Legs:** Centipede Legs
- **Wing:** Magnum rabbit strip, ½-inch x 1-inch-chartreuse foam strip
- **Eyes:** Red barbell-style, large

**Notes:** The hook is pushed through the rabbit strip and the front covers the body. The foam strip is glued to the end of the rabbit strip with Tear Mender glue. This pattern is designed to ride hook up. It is mainly crawled on the bottom, but can be stripped in the mid-depth water column like a streamer. It's fished similar to a plastic worm; if missing strikes, let the fish chew on the rabbit strip a bit before setting the hook. Black and purple are key colors, but it can be done in many variations.

### PAT'S GRIM REAPER (3 COLORS)

*Originated by Pat Ehlers, tied by Rainy's Flies*

- **Hook:** #3/0 Gamakatsu Extra Wide 60-degree jig hook
- **Thread:** 3/0 Uni, color to match fly
- **Tail:** Cascade Crest Hyper Reaper Tail, large
- **Body:** UV Polar Chenille
- **Legs:** Sili Legs
- **Weedguard (optional):** Single strand of 25 lb. hard mono
- **Eyes:** Red barbell-style, medium

**Notes:** Designed to fish as a "jig and pig" replacement, this has been one of Ehlers's best bass patterns. It has also taken pike, muskie, salmon, and steelhead. It can be tied in numerous color schemes, but dark, bright, and crayfish combination, as pictured, cover most needs. The Sili Legs should go all around the body like a skirt. The weedguard should extend a bit past the bend in the hook. The Reaper Tail can be accented with a waterproof marker (spots, stripes, etc.) to enhance the appearance of the fly.

### PAT'S J PIG (2 COLORS)

*Originated by Pat Ehlers, tied by Rainy's Flies*

- **Hook:** #2 bend-back design (see notes)
- **Thread:** 6/0 Uni, color to match fly
- **Weedguard (optional):** 25 lb. hard mono
- **Tail:** A mix of Krystal Flash, Flashabou, and mini rubber legs
- **Body:** Cactus Chenille or Estaz
- **Wing:** Krystal Flash
- **Collar:** Round rubber legs
- **Eyes:** Red or chartreuse barbell-style, large

**Notes:** This fly duplicates many of the rubber-skirt jigs fished by conventional anglers. These hooks are hard to find, but it is easy to make your own. Hold a 2xl to 3xl straight-eye hook (Daiichi 2460, for example) just behind the eye with a pair of needle-nose pliers, with the hook pointed up, and push down until there is a bend of about 15 degrees. If done correctly, the flat part of the hook shank should be in line with the hook barb. The weedguard is tied in at the bend and tied off at the eye. Ehlers fishes this in the two colors shown, but there are many color options. The hook rides up, so this pattern can be fished in various types of fish-holding cover.

### PAT'S LONG STRIP CRAYFISH (2 COLORS)

*Originated by Pat Ehlers, tied by Rainy's Flies*

- **Hook:** #2 Gamakatsu B10S
- **Thread:** 6/0 Uni, color to match fly
- **Tail:** Olive or brown orange-tipped Sili Legs with Krystal Flash
- **Eyes:** Red barbell-style, large
- **Body:** Olive or root beer Estaz
- **Wing:** Barred olive or crayfish orange rabbit strip, olive or copper Krystal Flash
- **Weedguard (optional):** Single strand of 25 lb. hard mono

**Notes:** This fly is based on Pat's Long Strip Bonefish Fly, listed at the end of this section. Primary crayfish colors are presented. The eyes are attached with the standard crisscross wrap at the bend of the hook so that the hook is inverted. This placement of the eyes makes the fly sink straight down. The rabbit strip is pushed over the hook point, extending back over the tail. The wire rib is used to secure the rabbit strip on top of the body and is wrapped over the top of the strip to the hook eye and secured. This has caught a wide range of species including largemouth, smallmouth, carp, pike, and muskie—plus it's a good trout fly, too!

**(Left to right)** Row 1: Pat's Foamtail Superworm, Pat's Grim Reaper (2 colors); Row 2: Pat's J Pig, Pat's Long Strip Crayfish, Pat's J Pig; Row 3: Pat's Crazi Craw, Pat's Long Strip Crayfish, Pat's Fat Boy Crab, Pat's Bonefish Reaper; Row 4: Pat's Crazi Craw, Pat's Long Strip Bonefish Fly, Pat's Grim Reaper. JIMMY CHANG PHOTO

## PAT'S CRAZI CRAW (2 COLORS)

*Originated by Pat Ehlers, tied by Rainy's Flies*

- **Hook:** #2 Gamakatsu B10S
- **Thread:** Olive or brown 6/0 Uni
- **Eyes:** Red Pseudo Eyes, medium
- **Weedguard (optional):** 25 lb. hard mono
- **Tail:** Four olive or crayfish orange Micro Pine Squirrel Zonker Strips, olive or root beer Krinkle Mirror Flash
- **Body:** Olive copper or copper UV Polar Chenille
- **Legs:** Olive or orange Centipede Legs

**Notes:** This impressionistic crayfish pattern works wherever these crustaceans are found. These are the two primary colors needed, and the exact material recipe is given. Anything that eats crayfish will take this fly.

## PAT'S FAT BOY CRAB

*Originated by Pat Ehlers, tied by Rainy's Flies*

- **Hook:** #2 or #6 Daiichi 2546 (Gamakatsu B10 for freshwater use)
- **Thread:** Chartreuse 6/0 Uni
- **Eyes:** Small (#2 hook) or extra small (#6 hook)
- **Body:** Tan CCT Body Fur
- **Legs:** Tan Centipede Legs with pearl Krystal Flash, trimmed short
- **Mouth:** Tan marabou plume tip

**Notes:** This is a saltwater pattern by design, to simulate a crab fleeing from a permit. It has proven effective for both carp and smallmouth, with a noticeable fluttering motion to it on the drop that both of these species find irresistible at times. You can also tie this in an olive or brown variation. The CCT Body Fur is wrapped and trimmed top and bottom. For strictly freshwater use, tie on the Gamakatsu B10S.

## PAT'S BONEFISH REAPER

*Originated by Pat Ehlers, tied by Rainy's Flies*

- **Hook:** #2-4 Daiichi 2546
- **Thread:** Pink 6/0 Uni
- **Eyes:** White barbell-style, medium or small
- **Tail:** White medium or small Reaper Tail, colored with tan permanent marker
- **Body:** Tan rabbit fur in a dubbing loop
- **Wing:** Tan Krystal Flash, 3 sets of pink Sili Legs

**Notes:** This is another saltwater pattern and has proven effective for carp on hard-white flats. It is also a good fly for crappie, and don't be surprised if a bass grabs it. This is another pattern where the fly can be done in olive and black versions on the Gamakatsu B10S hook and catch fish.

Smallmouth bass may be the widest distributed of all sportfish across the Great Lakes and Midwest, found from the big water of the Great Lakes to small tributary streams. They are a perfect fly rod fish.
KEVIN FEENSTRA PHOTO

## PAT'S LONG STRIP BONEFISH FLY

*Originated by Pat Ehlers, tied by Rainy's Flies*

- **Hook:** #2 Daiichi 2546
- **Thread:** Tan 6/0 Uni
- **Eyes:** White barbell-style, medium or small, tied in at bend of hook
- **Tail:** Two sets of tan Centipede Legs, tan Krystal Flash
- **Body:** Pearl Estaz or Cactus Chenille
- **Wing:** Tan rabbit strip, tan Krystal Flash over top
- **Rib:** Stainless wire
- **Weedguard (optional):** 25 lb. hard mono extending past hook point

**Notes:** The saltwater version of this pattern presented here has also worked well for carp on a hard, light-colored bottom. It can be stripped as a baitfish imitation for multiple species, too. This is constructed as the previous versions. Substitute the Gamakatsu B10S hook if no saltwater fishing is in your future.

# Group 7: Miscellaneous Patterns

This is an assortment of foam-bodied patterns mainly for bass and panfish. Several imitate specific insects while others are just suggestive of different life forms. As mentioned earlier, the use of foam materials has had a significant impact on modern fly tying.

## BLUE DAMSEL

*Originated and tied by Charlie Chlysta*

- **Hook:** #6 Mustad R50
- **Thread:** White 6/0 Euro
- **Tail:** Blue Extra Select Craft Fur, smolt blue Krystal Flash
- **Shellback:** 3 mm blue foam
- **Body:** SLF Prism Electric Blue Dubbing three-quarters up hook shank
- **Legs:** Two sets of white Centipede Legs, white saddle hackle

**Notes:** This fly was designed for smallmouth bass on Midwest rivers, but will also work for trout-eating damsels. The use of the Craft Fur and Centipede Legs gives more movement to the fly. The shellback is cut with a River Road Creations STP Frog Cutter, medium, then tied in over the tail by the narrow end. After the body is dubbed and wrapped, the shellback is tied down and the legs and hackle added at that point.

## MINI GURGLER

*Originated and tied by Charlie Chlysta*

- **Hook:** #8-10 Daiichi 1100
- **Thread:** 70-denier UTC, color to match fly
- **Tail:** Two sets of Grizzly Micro Legs
- **Back:** 2 mm foam cut with small River Road Creations Beavertail Cutter
- **Body:** Wrapped foam strip
- **Legs:** Two sets of Micro Grizzly Legs on each side

**Notes:** This pattern serves as both a hopper imitation and a simple gurgler depending on coloration and how you fish it. It is designed for panfish, but will also attract trout. Large bass have eaten it, too. Brown back/yellow belly is a hopper, all black a cricket. Chartreuse and white versions are great for panfish.

Patterns imitating damselflies and dragonflies should be worked along the edge of weed beds. The insects emerge in these areas, and when they are active, fish will be close by. JERRY DARKES PHOTO

**(Left to right)** Row 1: Blue Damsel, Mini Gurgler; Row 2: Dragon Wiggly, Ol' Mr. Wiggly; Row 3: BT (2 colors); Row 4: Foam Spider (2 colors). JIMMY CHANG PHOTO

## DRAGON WIGGLY

*Originated and tied by Charlie Piette*

- **Hook:** #2-4 Daiichi 2461
- **Thread:** Black 70-denier UTC
- **Body:** Peacock black Ice Dub
- **Back:** Peacock ¼-inch-wide Foam Skin
- **Legs:** Brown Buggy Nymph Legs, 3 sets per side
- **Wings:** Gray with blue flake Sili Legs, 5 sets per side
- **Sighter:** Small yellow foam strip

**Notes:** This is a great dragonfly imitation designed to target bass. The abundant rubber legs give it plenty of life on the water. The back is doubled over and tied down in sections over the body. The folded end serves as the head. Trim the back end to a point just past the hook bend. The legs are secured at the second section behind the head and trimmed short. The Sili Legs forming the wings are tied in behind the head. Colors can be altered to match those of your local bugs.

## OL' MR. WIGGLY

*Originated and tied by Charlie Piette*

- **Hook:** #2-6 Daiichi 2461
- **Thread:** Brown 70-denier UTC
- **Body:** Golden brown Ice Dub
- **Back:** ¼-inch-wide 2 mm yellow foam strip
- **Tail:** Orange Sili Legs, 1 strand on each side
- **Legs:** Brown or tan Micro Sili Legs, 2 sets on each side

**Notes:** This pattern can be done in a wide range of color combinations, but this is Piette's favorite. The foam strip for the back is doubled over and tied down in sections over the body. The folded end is the head. Trim the back end to a point just past the hook bend. The tail is secured in between the foam sections. The legs are secured at the other tiedown points for the back.

Fish it slow so the legs get plenty of opportunity to move. Both bass and panfish will take it.

## BT (2 COLORS)

*Originated and tied by Chad Miller*

- **Hook:** #4 TMC 200R
- **Thread:** Black 70-denier UTC
- **Back:** Two strips of ⅜-inch-wide Glitter Foam
- **Body:** Pearl Diamond Braid to match foam color
- **Wing:** Flash N' Slinky
- **Legs:** Round rubber
- **Sighter:** 2 mm orange foam

**Notes:** The BT name of this pattern refers to "Bass Terrestrial." Indiana-based angler/tier Chad Miller loves to fish for smallies on hot summer days "when they are not feeding." He will target shaded areas along grassy banks or under overhanging trees and find smallmouth sipping an assortment of terrestrial bugs including ants, beetles, hoppers, and crickets. The versions shown are his favorite colors, with black running a close third.

The Glitter Foam is tied in so that the sparkly side is exposed. After the body is wrapped, the Glitter Foam is pulled over the top and tied down in two sections and the rest of the assembly takes place. White/clear Hi-Viz can replace the Flash N' Slinky for the wing. Also, as the TMC 8089 hook in size 12 is now available again, Miller recommends this as the best hook for the pattern.

When dragonflies and damselflies are active, blue becomes a key color for surface-feeding smallmouth. A variety of surface patterns can be used in a blue coloration and produce strikes. JERRY DARKES PHOTO

## FOAM SPIDER (2 COLORS)

*Originator unknown, tied by Jerry Drake*

- **Hook:** #10-#12 standard dry fly
- **Thread:** Red 70-denier UTC
- **Body:** 2 mm foam cut with River Road Creations Beetle Cutter
- **Legs:** White rubber hackle

**Notes:** The first closed-cell foams came on the market in the 1960s, and foam spiders appeared shortly after. This is likely the oldest foam pattern and has caught countless bluegill and other panfish, along with a surprising number of large bass. You can buy pre-cut bodies, but if you plan to use lots of these, the River Road Creations cutters are a good investment. After cutting the foam, tie it in at the tab at the back of the body, wrap thread a bit behind the eye, then pull the foam over and secure. Add legs, then tie down the foam at the hook eye, trim and tie off. You can vary the color of the tying thread if desired. This makes a durable fly that will last for numerous fish. They are much more durable than most commercial spiders.

Small flies can produce big results. Largemouth are opportunistic feeders and can take small flies targeted for panfish. JERRY DARKES PHOTO

# Group 8: Panfish Specials

For many of us, our first fly rod fish was a bluegill or sunfish. Often grouped generically as "sunfish," these fish are found across the Midwest, from small creeks to the Great Lakes. Bluegill are the most common type caught on a fly, but there are a host of other species of sunfish that can show up. Both largemouth and smallmouth bass are considered part of the sunfish family.

Redear sunfish, rock bass, pumpkinseed, and green sunfish are found in a variety of Midwest waters. Crappie are common across the region, but a bit more difficult to catch on a fly as their main habitat is larger, deeper lakes and they rarely come to the surface. The male longear sunfish in breeding colors is one of the most beautiful of freshwater fishes.

These fish are targeted by most fly anglers while they are spawning in shallow water. This occurs in late spring and early summer across the region, when they will be concentrated and easy to locate, eagerly taking most small flies. Post-spawn, they can disperse into deeper water and become very selective as to what they eat.

There is a small group of Midwest fly fishers who target panfish—especially bluegill and crappie—all season long. They are often very secretive about the locations they fish and the flies they use. Here are a few patterns for use through the season.

## BLUEGILL SPARROW

*Originated by Jack Gartside, tied by Jerry Drake*

- **Hook:** #8-12 Mustad 94831
- **Thread:** Olive, gray, or black 8/0 Uni
- **Weight:** Ten to fifteen turns of .015-inch-diameter lead wire
- **Tail:** Fluff from ringneck pheasant rump feather
- **Body:** Olive, caddis green, golden brown, or peacock black Ice Dub
- **Collar:** Ringneck pheasant rump feather
- **Head:** Aftershaft from ringneck pheasant rump feather

**Notes:** Jerry Drake hails from Indiana and is a season-long "panfish junkie." This variation of Jack Gartside's Sparrow Nymph is a great searching pattern for suspended bluegill and crappie. Using a leader with an extra-long, light tippet (10 feet of 5X), the fly is counted down and slowly retrieved.

## PF ANT

*Originated and tied by Jerry Drake*

- **Hook:** #8-12 Mustad 3399A or similar
- **Thread:** Black 8/0 Uni
- **Tail:** Small bunch of hackle fibers (yellow, red, chartreuse, orange, and black are all used)
- **Body:** Dubbed fine black fur like rabbit or beaver
- **Hackle:** Black saddle

**Notes:** Yes, this is a simple ant pattern, but here is why this pattern is presented. Over the years, Drake has found that big bluegills can become very selective when surface feeding in open water after spawning. Just a change in the tail color can trigger strikes from otherwise stubborn fish. The same is true for 'gills and other sunfish found stationed under overhanging tree limbs where ants are dropping into the water; they can become as cautious as a brown trout. Fish it just below the surface at times, too.

(**Left to right**) Row 1: Bluegill Sparrow, PF Ant, DJ Dredger; Row 2: Steve's Twin Tail; Row 3: Crappie Streamer (3 colors). JIMMY CHANG PHOTO

There are very few places that don't have bluegill close by. They are a great fish to learn fly fishing, as they're usually willing to take a fly. Big bluegill can become as selective as trout after spawning time. KEVIN FEENSTRA PHOTO

## DJ DREDGER

*Originated and tied by Jerry Drake*

- **Hook:** #10-12 Mustad 3399A
- **Thread:** Flat waxed nylon Danville
- **Weight:** Twelve to fifteen wraps of .015-inch-diameter lead wire
- **Body:** Peacock herl or peacock Ice Dub, hen hackle wrapped, tying thread

**Notes:** This is another pattern to count down and retrieve slowly for suspended fish. The thread can be varied to alter the body color. Yellow and chartreuse have proven effective, but darker colors (olive, black) can also be used. It is likely that fish take this fly as a larger chironomid (midge) larva.

## STEVE'S TWIN TAIL

*Originated and tied by Steve Wascher*

- **Hook:** #8-12 Daiichi 1120 or similar
- **Thread:** 70-denier UTC, to match body
- **Tail:** Chartreuse, orange, or white round rubber hackle
- **Body:** Caddis green, olive, chartreuse, or peacock black Ice Dub
- **Hackle:** Mottled hen

**Notes:** Steve Wascher lives on the shores of New York's Chautauqua Lake. In addition to his other interests, Wascher loves to chase panfish with a fly. This buggy design has taken bluegill, sunfish, crappie, and yellow perch for him. It can be cast to bedded fish or used as a searching pattern.

## CRAPPIE STREAMER (3 COLORS)

*Originated and tied by Jerry Drake*

- **Hook:** #8 Mustad 9672
- **Thread:** Flat waxed nylon, match tail color
- **Weight:** Ten to fifteen wraps of .015-inch-diameter lead wire
- **Tail:** Chartreuse, white, pink, blue, or gray marabou plume tip
- **Body:** Silver mylar braid
- **Head:** Tying thread

**Notes:** This simple pattern imitates an assortment of small baitfish, the main forage for crappie. It is another pattern that can be used on suspended fish with a countdown technique. Although crappie are the main target, large bass have been taken on this fly, and it will also take trout in lakes.

Rock bass, also known as red eye or goggle eye, take flies readily. They are found from small creeks to large lakes across the region. Look for them around hard-bottom areas. JERRY DARKES PHOTO

# 6

# Patterns for Migratory Species

## INTRODUCTION

For the most part, the migratory species of the Great Lakes are trout and salmon. Their history here is an interesting one. There are actually no true trout that are natural to the lakes. The true natives are brook trout and lake trout, which are actually classified as char; and Atlantic salmon that ascended the St. Lawrence River into Lake Ontario, as well as a land-locked population.

The history of all three is a sad one. Due to a variety of factors—overfishing, loss of habitat, and pollution—all suffered through the late nineteenth and most of the twentieth centuries. The lake-dwelling coaster brook trout were eliminated from Lake Huron and maintained a tenuous hold in Lake Superior. Luckily, these fish received some protection before it was too late, and they are making a slow but steady comeback in part of their historic range in Lake Superior.

The use of two-hand and switch rods to swing flies has become common across Great Lakes tributaries. There has also been a movement toward more traditional fly designs as seen in the Pacific Northwest. JIMMY CHANG PHOTO

The coaster brook trout of Lake Superior were almost wiped out by the late 1900s. They are genetically the same as stream brookies, but behave very differently. Coasters inhabit a narrow shoreline zone in the lake and are constantly on the move. Some spawn in the lake while others ascend tributaries. JERRY DARKES PHOTO

Special regulations have made a significant difference in coaster populations in the Ontario waters of Lake Superior. They have expanded their range along with a noticeable increase in both size and numbers. This is a fishery management success story. JERRY DARKES PHOTO

Lake trout (actually a char) are native to all five of the Great Lakes. Populations are being reestablished in all the lakes after decades of depletion. They hit flies aggressively and come into range of fly anglers early and late in the season. JERRY DARKES PHOTO

Lake trout are present in all five of the Great Lakes. Much of their depletion has been due to an invasive species—the sea lamprey, which was first noticed in Lake Ontario around 1830. The Welland Canal and later the Soo Locks allowed their passage into all of the Great Lakes. With no natural defense to these parasitic predators, lake trout and other deep-water fish suffered the most.

The native salmon of Lake Ontario suffered from a host of impacts—overfishing, habitat loss, deforestation, dam

Atlantic salmon are being stocked in both Lake Huron and Lake Ontario. The plantings in Lake Huron have had successful survival with fish returning consistently in the St. Marys River and several other locations. Restoration efforts in Lake Ontario have had minimal success.
PHIL COOK PHOTO

Whether you call them steelhead or rainbow trout, these fish are well established in all of the Great Lakes. There are both wild, self-sustaining populations and those maintained by regular stockings. These trout have established themselves as the premier sportfish of the region. JERRY DARKES PHOTO

construction, and pollution among them. By the end of the nineteenth century, they were gone. There are attempts at reestablishing self-sustaining populations in some areas. Various stocking programs have had fish survive and return, mainly in the St. Marys River and most recently along the eastern shoreline of Lake Huron. However, establishing self-sustaining populations has not happened so far.

Pacific salmon were introduced in the 1960s to control populations of the invasive alewife. They quickly established themselves and, through both continued stocking and natural reproduction, created a sport fishery that still exists. Three of the five main species are present: chinook, coho, and pink. Both coho and pinks eat flies readily. Great Lakes chinook will occasionally take a fly, and they do present opportunities when ascending tributaries to spawn and, at times, in the lakes.

McCloud River (California) rainbow trout were stocked in the lower AuSable River near Oscoda, Michigan, in 1873. These fish thrived and by the turn of the century were well distributed around the Great Lakes. Localized, self-sustaining populations became established. There are both stream-dwelling and migratory populations of these fish, and over the last one hundred years a number of different strains of rainbows have been stocked.

Here we call rainbows that drop to the big water "steelhead." West Coasters say we can't do that because our fish don't go to salt. Regardless, they are here. To keep the peace, we can also call them Great Lakes migratory rainbows, and I will use both names interchangeably. They have been present in the lakes for nearly 150 years. These fish take flies as eagerly as their saltwater-based relatives.

Brown trout have been present in the Great Lakes since 1883, first planted in Michigan's Pere Marquette River. There is movement of these fish into tributaries in some locations and limited natural reproduction. They can also be targeted

Brown trout are also found in all five of the Great Lakes and are an added bonus for near-shore anglers. There are several areas around the lake with significant populations of browns. They can be caught on a variety of fly patterns, from large, flashy streamers to small, natural-looking designs. JERRY DARKES PHOTO

by fly anglers in harbor and river mouth environments. Several big-water strains of browns have been stocked that have resulted in world record–size fish in recent years.

Fly patterns for these various migratory species have gone through a series of evolutions. At first, patterns reminiscent of West Coast designs were used with some success. With the return of salmon to tributaries throughout the 1960s, a resurgence of interest in targeting migratory rainbows occurred, along with the observation of lake-run browns.

While Pacific salmon did not feed, they did hit flies at times. The trout, however, were a different story. They fed heavily on eggs from spawning salmon, just as in their native waters, and would also target a variety of stream-based forage. Various egg/attractor designs emerged along with nymph and baitfish patterns that proved successful on the trout.

It is interesting to note that there are also migratory populations of smallmouth bass across the Great Lakes. These are lake-dwelling fish that ascend tributaries to spawn. It is likely a survival mechanism that provides an ongoing breeding stock in case lake spawning is impacted. Very little is known about these fish, except that certain ones come into a tributary, spawn, and then drop back to their home lake.

In recent decades there has been a move toward the use of more traditional methods to target Great Lakes trout using flies similar to those currently used for Pacific steelhead. This has proven quite successful and is now a common technique. This chapter will provide a comprehensive look at this evolution of flies, from early examples to the most recent designs.

Perhaps the most significant patterns to emerge recently are the shank designs with the hook set back on a loop of wire or Kevlar braid. This allows a "long-shank" fly with a short-shank hook that eliminates the leverage given from a long hook for a fish to work loose. The earlier Waddington shanks accomplished this to a certain extent, but current shank patterns are much more versatile. These were previously mentioned in the Streamer Patterns chapter, but the shanks were developed for the steelhead fishery.

We will also see a number of tube fly patterns. This style of tying emerged in the UK in the late 1940s. Again, the idea is to eliminate a long hook shank to minimize leverage helping a hooked fish get loose. Many conventional streamer patterns can convert to a tube design, and it is actually more versatile than using a shank. There are proponents of this tying method in North America, but the components are hard to find. It remains mainly a European approach.

## Group 1: Great Lakes Classics

In 1979, Great Lakes fly angler and writer Dave Richey published the first book devoted to fly patterns for Great Lakes steelhead. There were 900 copies of *Great Lakes Steelhead Flies* printed. The book features several West Coast patterns and an assortment of Great Lakes creations based on western designs. They are nearly all attractor-style flies.

When reviewing these designs, we need to keep in mind that the anglers, tiers, and guides of that time were working with the materials they had available. There was a very limited assortment of synthetics to work with along with minimal knowledge of the feeding habits of the migratory rainbows. Although anglers fished bait for them, the fly patterns used for steelhead had not made that jump yet.

Richey's book helped usher in a new awareness of this great gamefish and brought it back into the focus of fly fishers. Of the patterns presented here, few are seen anymore. One pattern has survived the test of time. Spring's Wiggler is still found across Michigan in bait and fly shops. Considered a Hex nymph imitation, it likely also imitates crayfish, and you can find it in both natural and attractor colors.

### SPRING'S WIGGLER

*Originated by Ron Springs, tied by Jerry Darkes*

- **Hook:** #6-8 Mustad 36890
- **Weight:** Six to eight wraps of .020-inch-diameter lead wire
- **Thread:** Black 6/0 Danville
- **Tail:** Fox squirrel tail
- **Body:** Cream yarn or chenille for original pattern, brown hackle
- **Back:** Fox squirrel tail

**Notes:** This is considered a late winter to early spring pattern. It may also be tied on modern hooks such as the Daiichi 1710, and bright-colored chenille is often used for the body. It can be dead-drifted and swung through suspected holding water. With a tan or olive body, the Wiggler will also catch summertime smallmouth.

Spring's Wiggler. JERRY DARKES PHOTO

**(Left to right)** Row 1: Richey's Platte River Pink; Row 2: Little Manistee, Orange PM Special. JIMMY CHANG PHOTO

## RICHEY'S PLATTE RIVER PINK

*Originated by George Richey, tied by Jerry Darkes*

- **Hook:** #4-8 Mustad 36890
- **Weight (optional):** .020-inch-diameter lead wire
- **Thread:** Orange 6/0 Danville
- **Tail:** Pink synthetic fur
- **Body:** Fluorescent pink chenille, ribbed with silver tinsel
- **Rib:** Medium silver tinsel
- **Wing:** White calf tail
- **Throat:** Pink synthetic fur

**Notes:** This pattern dates back to 1973 and is a true attractor pattern. Reminiscent of many West Coast designs, it is one to try in fast-moving water with some color to it. If weight is added, keep it on the front part of the shank.

*Great Lakes Steelhead Flies* by Dave Richey was the first book focused on flies designed specifically for the migratory rainbows of the Great Lakes. Most of the patterns reflect a significant Pacific Northwest influence, as very little was known about how to target these fish on flies. Most were either caught on bait or as an incidental catch when targeting other fish. JERRY DARKES PHOTO

## LITTLE MANISTEE

*Originated by Dave Borgeson, tied by Jerry Darkes*

- **Hook:** #4-8 Mustad 36890
- **Weight (optional):** .020-inch-diameter lead wire
- **Thread:** Red 6/0 Danville
- **Tag:** Silver tinsel
- **Tail:** Hot orange calf tail
- **Body:** Pink chenille on rear two-thirds, black chenille on front one-third
- **Wing:** Hot orange calf tail, then yellow calf tail with hot orange calf tail on top
- **Throat:** Hot orange calf tail

**Notes:** This pattern dates back to 1968 and presents an assortment of colors. It is considered an excellent all-around fly for a variety of water conditions.

## ORANGE PM SPECIAL

*Originated by David Borgeson, tied by Jerry Darkes*

- **Hook:** #4-8 Mustad 36890
- **Thread:** Orange 6/0 Danville
- **Tag:** Medium silver tinsel
- **Tail:** Hot orange calf tail
- **Butt:** Medium silver tinsel
- **Body:** Orange or yellow chenille on rear two-thirds, black chenille on front one-third
- **Wing:** Yellow calf tail with orange calf tail over top
- **Throat:** Orange calf tail

**Notes:** This fly was developed by Borgeson in 1967. It functions as both an attractor and is also used when trout are feeding on eggs.

# Group 2: Eggs and Attractors

All trout eat fish eggs. This is particularly true of rainbows. As much as we like to think of them daintily sipping mayflies or other insects, they will target eggs when present. There is just too much food value there for trout to pass them up. In the Great Lakes tributaries, these can be eggs from salmon, trout, various species of suckers, walleye, and others.

Some of these patterns are specific egg imitations. Others are suggestive of eggs by shape and/or color. The specific pattern used by the angler is a function of time of year, location, and water conditions.

## TWO EGG SPERM FLY

*Originated by Dave Whitlock, tied by Jerry Darkes*

- **Hook:** #6 Mustad 36890
- **Thread:** Fluorescent red 6/0 Danville
- **Body:** Two ball-shaped sections of flame orange chenille separated by medium silver tinsel
- **Wing:** White marabou
- **Throat:** Red hackle fibers

**Notes:** This pattern could have been put in the Great Lakes Classics section. It is one of the earliest egg-specific designs. From the early 1970s, it was fished behind spawning salmon. Rainbows will follow salmon in from the big water and station behind them to feast on drifting eggs. Lake-run and resident brown trout will also feed on salmon eggs.

## MCFOAM EGG (2 COLORS)

*Originator unknown, tied by Jerry Darkes*

- **Hook:** #8-14 Daiichi 1120
- **Thread:** Fluorescent red, fluorescent orange, or chartreuse 70-denier UTC
- **Body:** McFly Foam yarn

**Notes:** For a #10 hook, a bunch of yarn approximately two times the diameter of a pencil and 1½ inches long is needed. You can adjust this for other hook sizes. Some tiers prefer using 50-denier GSP thread now that it is available. The drawback is only two color choices: black

or white. For true egg imitations, colors can be pale yellow, orange, or pink. It can also be tied in bright colors for visibility as an attractor. McFly Foam is a much easier material to use than the original Glo Bug Yarn. McFly Foam compresses easily and can be tied with lighter thread; it is also much easier to trim. Check out YouTube to see tying instructions and ways to increase speed and minimize material waste.

## EYED EGG (2 COLORS)

*Originator unknown, tied by Jerry Darkes*

- **Hook:** #8-14 Daiichi 1120
- **Thread:** Fluorescent red, fluorescent orange, or chartreuse 70-denier UTC
- **Body:** Large bunch of McFly Foam yarn, small section of contrasting color on top (cheese with flame, chartreuse with flame, steelhead orange with flame are popular)

**Notes:** This imitates an egg with the yolk or "eye" present. There are multiple ways to tie this, and YouTube again is a great resource to see the tying process. I like using the wide-gap hook because it hooks and holds better in smaller sizes.

(**Left to right**) Row 1: Two Egg Sperm Fly; Row 2: McFoam Egg, Eyed Egg, Clown Egg, Nuke Egg; Row 3: McFoam Egg, Eyed Egg, Clown Egg, Nuke Egg; Row 4: Eggstacy Egg (2 colors), Sucker Spawn, Blood Dot, Egg Cluster; Row 5: Scrambled Egg, Bear's Crystal Egg (2 colors); Row 6: Bear's Rag Egg (3 colors). JIMMY CHANG PHOTO

## CLOWN EGG (2 SIZES)

*Originator unknown, tied by Jerry Darkes*

- **Hook:** #8-14 Daiichi 1120
- **Thread:** White 50-denier GSP
- **Body:** Four to six small, different color bunches of McFly Foam yarn combined to form one large bunch

**Notes:** This pattern presents a variety of colors. If steelhead are showing a color preference, it is likely something that can trigger a strike. It may also resemble an egg beginning to discolor as it tumbles down the current. With the larger amount of yarn being used, the 50-denier GSP thread allows you to compress the yarn more when securing it to the hook.

**Hint:** Prepackaged clown egg yarn assortments are available, which save you from deciding what colors to select. Trim a few so that the yarn is oversized and give it a try in dirty water or when nothing else works

## NUKE EGG (2 COLORS)

*Originator unknown, tied by Jerry Darkes*

- **Hook:** #8-12 Daiichi 1120
- **Thread:** Fluorescent orange or fluorescent red 70-denier UTC
- **Body:** McFly Foam yarn, trimmed short
- **Veil:** White or light-colored McFly Foam, Egg Veil, or similar surrounding the body, trimmed just past bend of hook

**Notes:** There are numerous variations of this pattern; I think this is the easiest version. It works best in faster flows where fish get a quick look at the fly before it is past them. Other hooks can be used, such as the TMC 2457 or Daiichi 1530, for example. Just be sure it is a heavy shank hook with a good point to hold a hard-fighting steelhead.

## EGGSTACY EGG (2 COLORS)

*Originated by unknown and tied by Jerry Darkes*

- **Hook:** #10-12 Daiichi 1120
- **Thread:** Fluorescent orange 70-denier UTC
- **Body:** Eggstacy Yarn, in various egg and attractor colors

**Notes:** Eggstacy Yarn is a newer material for egg patterns. It is built on a core, wraps like chenille, and soaks up water quickly. It also has a great translucent look in the water. Use a colored brass or glass bead to make an eyed-egg design and help it sink faster.

Brown trout will also take advantage of eggs as a food source. They will often stage behind spawning salmon and eat eggs that drift past the salmon redd.
JERRY DARKES PHOTO

## SUCKER SPAWN

*Originator unknown, tied by Jerry Darkes*

- **Hook:** #10-16 Daiichi 1120
- **Thread:** Red 70-denier UTC
- **Body:** Cream Angora yarn

**Notes:** This fly originated in the trout streams of central Pennsylvania and dates back to at least the 1960s. It was used to target early season trout feeding on the eggs from spawning suckers. It migrated north to Lake Erie tributaries where it has become a must-have for steelhead all season long. This pattern will produce across the Great Lakes and beyond, wherever trout are feeding on eggs. This is the original coloration of this fly.

As simple as it looks, there are a couple tricks to this pattern. First the yarn is separated into individual strands and then it is tied down in a series of loops going up the hook shank. Any heavy wet-fly hook is usable, but I favor the Daiichi 1120. It is strong and sharp, and the wide gap holds better in smaller sizes. Fish over 10 pounds can be landed readily (and quickly), even on the #16.

## BLOOD DOT

*Originated by Jeff Blood, tied by Jerry Darkes*

- **Hook:** #10-14 Daiichi 1120
- **Thread:** Fluorescent orange 70-denier UTC
- **Body:** Pale yellow Angora yarn, steelhead orange yarn spot

**Notes:** Pennsylvania fly angler/tier Jeff Blood has popularized this variation of the Sucker Spawn fly. It is designed to resemble a group of several eyed trout or salmon eggs clustered together. Again, this is the original version of the fly; yarn color can be varied from pale orange to pale pink. The yarn spot is added after the second set of angora loops are secured.

## EGG CLUSTER

*Originator unknown, tied by Jerry Darkes*

- **Hook:** #10-14 Daiichi 1120
- **Thread:** Fluorescent orange or fluorescent red 70-denier UTC, or color to body
- **Body:** Single strand of egg yarn or a yarn other than Angora, tied down in loops over hook shank

**Notes:** Here we see that other types of yarn can be tied down in loops. It is thought that the yarn loops get caught in the trout's teeth, making it harder to reject the fly.

## SCRAMBLED EGG

*Originator unknown, tied by Jerry Darkes*

- **Hook:** #10-14 Daiichi 1120
- **Thread:** Fluorescent orange or fluorescent red 70-denier UTC
- **Body:** Two to three strands of different color egg yarn, tied down in loops over hook shank

**Notes:** This can be tied in a mix of natural egg colors or attractor colors for use in various water conditions. A version made with strands of Crystal Braid or Pearl Diamond Braid material tied down in loops is referred to as a Crystal Meth pattern.

## BEAR'S CRYSTAL EGG (2 COLORS)

*Originated by Bear Andrews, tied by Jerry Darkes*

- **Hook:** #8-12 TMC 105
- **Thread:** Fluorescent range 70-denier UTC
- **Tail:** Pearl Crystal Flash
- **Body:** Orange, chartreuse, or pink Estaz
- **Wing:** White egg yarn

**Notes:** This is a signature pattern of noted Michigan fly tier Bear Andrews. It works best in faster flows or when the water is a bit off-color. It can be classified as an attractor pattern as much as a true egg. Bottom line: It catches fish. The white egg yarn wing is tied in as a veil around the hook and then combed out, giving a noticeable translucent look in the water.

## BEAR'S RAG EGG (3 COLORS)

*Originated and tied by Bear Andrews*

- **Hook:** #6-10 TMC 105
- **Thread:** Red 70-denier UTC
- **Tail:** Pearl Krystal Flash
- **Body:** Estaz
- **Collar:** Three to four colors of egg yarn spread around the hook

**Notes:** This is an upsized version of the Crystal Egg. It generally works better in higher flows and when the water is off-color. Much like the Clown Egg, multiple colors are presented to help trigger strikes.

This angler is fighting a steelhead hooked on an egg pattern drifted under an indicator. Dead-drift presentations are the most productive way to fish both egg and nymph patterns for Great Lakes rainbows. JERRY DARKES PHOTO

# Group 3: Steelhead Nymphs

There was a period of time when it was thought that migratory trout did not feed when they entered tributaries, similar to spawning salmon. We know that Great Lakes rainbows do follow spawning salmon and will stage behind them to eat eggs as the salmon spawn. This behavior is well known in the Pacific Northwest and Alaska.

Depending on when trout enter tributaries to spawn, there can be feeding activity associated. They may not need to feed during this time period and can live off stored body fat for an extended time. But if there is a food source readily available to them, or if food is presented to them, trout will take advantage of it.

Feeding likely shuts down during the actual spawning period, but pre-spawn and particularly post-spawn feeding takes place. Nymph patterns presented in a natural manner may be the best way to catch these fish consistently. Exact imitations are not always necessary. As long as the pattern is buggy-looking it can work. Color can be an important factor, or often an extra touch of color beyond the natural will help trigger strikes.

## SYNDENHAM PEACOCK

*Originated and tied by Jay Passmore*

- **Hook:** #10-14 Daiichi 1560
- **Thread:** Black 70-denier UTC
- **Tail:** Black schlappen fibers
- **Abdomen:** Peacock herl
- **Thorax:** Peacock herl
- **Wing Case:** Black schlappen fibers
- **Legs:** Black schlappen fibers from wing case

**Notes:** This is a basic, fish-catching pattern that has been tied in Ontario for a long time. The iridescence of peacock works in a wide range of water conditions. The pattern can also be tied in a beadhead variation. The peacock herl in the abdomen is overwrapped with tying thread for added strength. The same schlappen fibers that form the wing case are split and tied on each side as legs. Any quality nymph hook is usable.

## PURPLE PEACOCK

*Originated and tied by Steve May*

- **Hook:** #10-14 Daiichi 1560
- **Thread:** Black 70-denier UTC
- **Tail:** Dyed purple peacock herl
- **Abdomen:** Dyed purple peacock herl
- **Rib:** Black Ultra Wire, Brassie size
- **Thorax:** Black brass bead, size to hook, with purple peacock herl
- **Wing Case:** Black schlappen fibers
- **Legs:** Black schlappen fibers from wing case

**Notes:** Steelhead can distinguish colors. Often small changes in color can draw strikes from reluctant trout. A bit of purple in the fly can often trigger strikes if other colors are not working. Purple has good visibility in dirty water and is not overpowering in clear water. Any quality nymph hook can be used. Tying a bead in at the thorax of a nymph is another way to add weight. Depending on the effect you are looking for, a flashy bead or dull color can be used.

## STEELHEAD PT (2 COLORS)

*Originator unknown, tied by Steve May*

- **Hook:** #10-14 Daiichi 1120
- **Thread:** Black 70-denier UTC
- **Tail:** Natural pheasant tail fibers
- **Abdomen:** Natural pheasant tail fibers
- **Rib:** Copper wire, Brassie size
- **Thorax:** Ice Dub in pheasant tail or peacock colors
- **Wing Case:** Pheasant tail fibers
- **Legs:** Pheasant tail fibers

**Notes:** Steve May likes this pattern for skittish fish in low, clear water. Using the heavy scud hook in smaller sizes strengthens the wire and gives a larger gap to help hold hard-fighting steelhead. The TMC 2457 can be substituted for the hook. I have had good success using bright colors of Ice Dub in the thorax on larger-size hooks (#10) when then water is stained. Also, don't forget purple!

## ICE PT

*Originated and tied by Steve May*

- **Hook:** #8-12 Daiichi 1560
- **Thread:** Black 70-denier UTC
- **Tail:** Pheasant tail fibers
- **Abdomen:** Pheasant tail Ice Dub, brown Scud Back over top
- **Rib:** Copper wire, Brassie size
- **Thorax:** Ice Dub from body, hen hackle, hot orange Ice Dub
- **Wing Case:** Brown Scud Back

**Notes:** This pattern has a small amount of bright dubbing at the front to attract attention and trigger strikes. Any quality nymph hook can be used. The design can be done in a variety of color combinations depending on water conditions. This version seems to work best in tannic-colored flows.

**(Left to right)** Row 1: Syndenham Peacock, Purple Peacock; Row 2: Steelhead PT (2 colors); Row 3: Ice PT, Ice Stone V1, Ice Stone V2; Row 4: Fried Shrimp, Linsenman's Mayfly Nymph; Row 5: Ken's Steelhead Caddis, Green Caddis Larva, JQ Caddis; Row 6: Antron Caddis, Green Rock Worm. JIMMY CHANG PHOTO

Great Lakes steelhead may ascend tributaries most any month of the year. Several strains of migratory rainbows are present and move into tributaries at different times. The majority are winter run/spring spawners. Depending on the specific locale, spawning can start as early as late February, but can also extend into early June.
ROBERT SCHOELLER PHOTO

## ICE STONE V1

*Originated and tied by Steve May*

- **Hook:** #10-14 Daiichi 1120
- **Thread:** Black 70-denier UTC
- **Tail:** Black goose biots
- **Abdomen:** Black Ice Dub, black Scud Back over top
- **Rib:** Black wire, Brassie-size
- **Thorax:** Black schlappen fiber legs on each side, purple Ice Dub
- **Wing Case:** Black Scud Back

**Notes:** The Ice Dub colors normally used are peacock, peacock black, purple, or olive, but you can be creative as desired. Once again, slight color changes can make a difference on any given day. Don't be afraid to experiment. The TMC 2457 or any quality heavy scud hook can be substituted.

## ICE STONE V2

*Originated and tied by Steve May*

- **Hook:** #8-14 Daiichi 1560
- **Thread:** Black 70-denier UTC
- **Tail:** Black goose biots
- **Abdomen:** Peacock Ice Dub, black Scud Back over top
- **Rib:** Black wire, Brassie-size

- **Thorax:** Black goose biot on each side, peacock Ice Dub, black Scud Back over top

**Notes:** Once again, colors can be varied—black, brown, and golden variations cover the primary stonefly colors found around the Great Lakes. Any quality nymph hook is usable.

## FRIED SHRIMP

*Originated and tied by Steve May*

- **Hook:** #12 Daiichi 1120
- **Thread:** Cream 70-denier UTC
- **Tail:** Cream Antron yarn
- **Body:** Gold or peach Petite Estaz
- **Back:** Cream Antron yarn
- **Eyes:** Black plastic bead chain, small

**Notes:** This is not a true nymph, although it is usually fished that way. A generalist design, it may be taken as a trout fry, baitfish, or freshwater shrimp. Regardless, it catches fish. This is also a good pattern for bluegill and other panfish. It can be tied larger and smaller, too.

Patterns for Migratory Species | 189

## LINSENMAN'S MAYFLY NYMPH

*Originated and tied by Bob Linsenman*

- **Hook:** #8-12 Daiichi 1710
- **Thread:** Tan 70-denier UTC
- **Tail:** Tan Hungarian partridge fibers
- **Abdomen:** Tan nymph blend ribbed with pearl Krystal Flash
- **Rib:** Three to four pearl Krystal Flash fibers
- **Thorax:** Peach Petite Estaz
- **Wing Case:** Tan Swiss Straw, a single strand of pearl Krystal Flash down the center
- **Legs:** Tan Hungarian partridge

**Notes:** Bob Linsenman also ties this in black and olive variations. The color used is often dependent on daily water and weather conditions. On a bright day and clear water, start with tan. On a dark day or dirty water, use black. Olive is a good choice when conditions are in between.

## KEN'S STEELHEAD CADDIS

*Originated and tied by Ken Collins*

- **Hook:** #6-14 Daiichi 1150
- **Thread:** Fine monofilament tying thread
- **Body:** Chum green, chartreuse, or olive Diamond Braid
- **Back:** Peacock herl, pull over body
- **Rib:** Mono thread
- **Head:** Peacock herl

**Notes:** Often called the Green Rock Worm, *Rhyacophila* species caddis are found across the Great Lakes. Their color varies from olive to bright green depending on species and water chemistry. They are free-living, meaning they do not build a case, and are subject to drift during low-light periods, making them easily available to trout. Substitute any quality upturned-eye scud hook.

## GREEN CADDIS LARVA

*Originated and tied by Mike Veatch*

- **Hook:** #10-14 Daiichi 1560
- **Thread:** Olive 70-denier UTC
- **Weight:** Black brass bead, size to hook
- **Underbody:** Fine olive dubbing, taper heavier toward eye
- **Body:** Chartreuse Vinyl Rib, colored olive on back with permanent marker
- **Head:** Peacock Ice Dub

**Notes:** Angler/tier Mike Veatch fishes this pattern on Pennyslvania and New York tributaries. It is normally fished in tandem with an egg pattern and dead-drifted under an indicator. This pattern can be tied with most any quality wet, scud, or nymph hook.

## JQ CADDIS

*Originated by Joe Quarandillo, tied by Jerry Darkes*

- **Hook:** #10-14 Daiichi 1120
- **Thread:** Black 70-denier UTC
- **Bead:** Black brass, size to hook
- **Underbody:** Chartreuse 140-denier UTC
- **Body:** Chartreuse Stretch Tubing
- **Head:** Black Hare's Ear Plus dubbing in a dubbing loop

**Notes:** This has been a favorite pattern of mine for many years. It has taken countless migratory rainbows across the Great Lakes as well as a few Atlantic salmon in the St. Marys River. Where two flies are legal, it is usually fished in tandem with an egg pattern or black stone nymph. The dubbing at the head should be brushed out to give the appearance of legs.

## ANTRON CADDIS

*Originator unknown, tied by unknown*

- **Hook:** #6-10 Daiichi 1530
- **Thread:** Black 70-denier UTC
- **Body:** Caddis green Antron dubbing in a loop
- **Head:** Peacock Ice Dub

**Notes:** This is about as simple as a fly gets. I'm not sure who originated this. The basic design came out of western Michigan, and the fly is a staple around the Great Lakes. I'm also not sure who tied this particular fly. Antron is a bit difficult to finger dub, so twisting it in a loop is the best way to use it for a body. Be sure to brush out both the body and head when finished. You can change hook type and size, body color, or add a bead to make numerous variations.

## GREEN ROCK WORM

*Originated and tied by Scott Thorpe*

- **Hook:** #10-12 Daiichi 1120
- **Thread:** Olive 6/0 Uni
- **Tail:** Three to four strands of root beer Krystal Flash
- **Body:** Chartreuse Vinyl Rib
- **Head:** Peacock herl

**Notes:** Guide Scott Thorpe fishes Minnesota's North Shore tributaries of Lake Superior. This is a standard springtime pattern for him. Any quality scud hook can be used.

# Group 4: Steelhead Nymphs and Wets

This large group has an assortment of patterns that both simulate and imitate a wide variety of food forms along with some attractor-type patterns. One of the factors in chasing migratory rainbows is that we don't need to have exact imitations for them to take a fly. Often a food-like silhouette will work, and then the actual color may be more of a factor. We find a little of both elements in this grouping.

Several noted steelhead guide/tiers are represented. Minnesota's Scott Thorpe, Ohio's Patrick Robinson, and Bear Andrews from Michigan all have multiple patterns that present different fly styles from across the Great Lakes. These flies will tempt steelhead across the region.

## STEELHEAD PINK SQUIRREL

*Originated and tied by Scott Thorpe*

- **Hook:** #4-8 Daiichi 1160
- **Thread:** Black 6/0 Uni for body, pink 6/0 Uni for head
- **Bead:** Copper, 3/32 inch
- **Tail:** Pearl Krystal Flash, trimmed short
- **Body:** Squirrel nymph blend in a dubbing loop
- **Rib:** Copper wire, Brassie-size
- **Head:** Fluorescent pink chenille

**Notes:** This beefed-up version of the Bethke Pink Squirrel could be termed an "attractor nymph" in this application. Thorpe fishes this in the fast-running, tannic tributaries of Lake Superior, where fish need to make a quick decision to take a fly or let it pass. It has a nymph outline and a trigger color.

## STEELHEAD PT SOFT HACKLE

*Originated and tied by Scott Thorpe*

- **Hook:** #8-10 Daiichi 1560
- **Thread:** Black 6/0 Uni
- **Bead:** Copper, size to hook
- **Weight:** .020-inch-diameter lead wire
- **Tail:** Pheasant tail fibers
- **Abdomen:** Pheasant tail fibers, wrapped
- **Rib:** Fine copper wire
- **Thorax:** Peacock Lite Brite or Ice Dub
- **Legs:** Partridge or hen hackle

**Notes:** This version of a Pheasant Tail Nymph is designed to get down quick in fast water. The lead wire is wrapped in the thorax area tight up to the bead. No wing case is needed with the wrapped soft hackle. The heavy wire hook helps hold hard-fighting trout in heavy current. A variety of heavy-wire nymph hooks are usable.

## BASIC STONE FLY

*Originated and tied by Scott Thorpe*

- **Hook:** #6-10 Daiichi 1710
- **Thread:** Black 6/0 Uni
- **Weight (optional):** .020-inch-diameter lead wire
- **Tail:** Brown or black goose biots
- **Abdomen:** Black wool yarn
- **Rib:** Small clear Vinyl Rib
- **Thorax:** Brown chenille
- **Legs:** Round black rubber hackle
- **Wing Case:** Black Swiss Straw
- **Antennae:** Brown or black goose biots

**Notes:** Stonefly nymphs are a key pattern for Great Lakes migratory rainbows. This pattern presents a great silhouette for this important insect.

## STEELHEAD SAN JUAN

*Originated and tied by Scott Thorpe*

- **Hook:** #6-10 TMC 200R
- **Thread:** Pink 6/0 Uni
- **Body:** Tying thread, fluorescent pink Ultra Chenille, hot pink waterproof marker
- **Rib:** Fine copper wire

**Notes:** Earthworms do get washed into tributaries and are eaten by steelhead. Here we have a worm shape in a visible color for stained, high-water conditions. The body has a base of tying thread over the hook shank, with Ultra Chenille colored on the top half of the body and front chenille section with waterproof marker.

## WIGGLER NYMPH VARIANT

*Originated by Ron Springs, tied by Scott Thorpe*

- **Hook:** #8-10 Daichii 1710
- **Thread:** Olive 6/0 Uni
- **Weight:** .020-inch-diameter lead wire
- **Tail:** Fox squirrel tail
- **Body:** Olive chenille, grizzly saddle hackle
- **Back:** Fox squirrel tail

**Notes:** This updated version of Spring's Wiggler is presented in Thorpe's favorite color. Again, this pattern is suggestive of several food forms and gives a generic, "buggy" appearance. Weight only the front half of the hook.

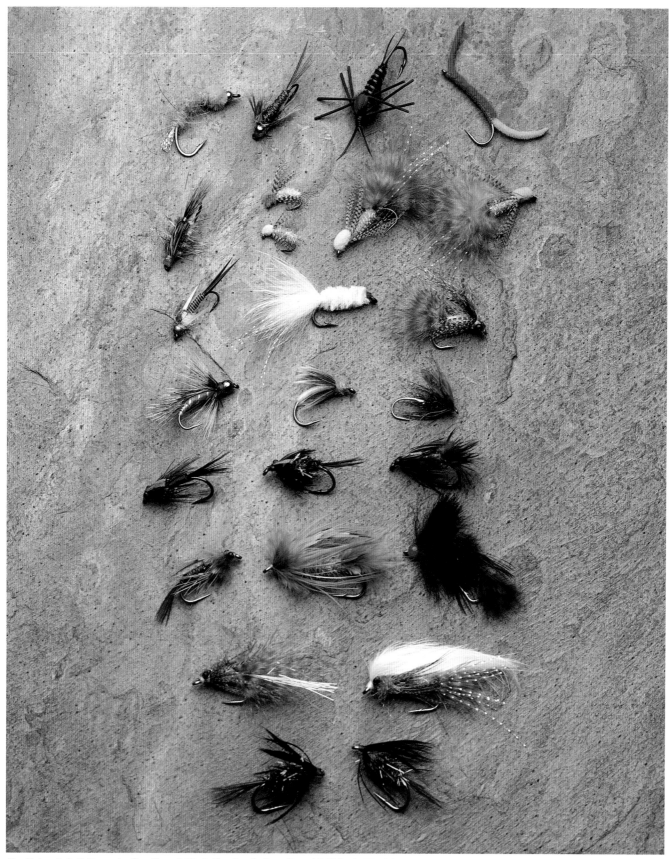

**(Left to right)** Row 1: Steelhead Pink Squirrel, Steelhead PT Soft Hackle, Basic Stone Fly, Steelhead San Juan; Row 2: Wiggler Nymph Variant, Robinson's Chicken Hawk (2 colors), Robinson's Chicken Little (2 colors); Row 3: Robinson's Psychedelic Smurf Stone, Robinson's Money Fly, Fonzi Fry; Row 4: Red Neck Surveyor, Bear's PM Caddis, Steelie Soft Hackle; Row 5: Bear's Neon Stone, Ben Stone, Bear's Peacock Fuzzbuster; Row 6: Bear's Pheasant Tail, Bear's French Hex, Dr. J; Row 7: Bear's Crossdresser, Bear's Strip Fry; Row 8: Dr. K (2 colors). JIMMY CHANG PHOTO

Prospecting for steelhead on Minnesota's North Shore. Nearly all Lake Superior steelhead are wild, stream-bred fish.
JERRY DARKES PHOTO

## ROBINSON'S CHICKEN HAWK (2 COLORS)

*Originated and tied by Patrick Robinson*

- **Hook:** #14 Daiichi 1120
- **Thread:** White 6/0 Uni
- **Body:** Midge Cactus Chenille
- **Collar/Legs:** Waterfowl flank feather or partridge
- **Head:** McFly Foam yarn

**Notes:** This caddis-like pattern falls into the attractor nymph scheme and has proven productive on Lake Erie tributaries and heavily pressured fish. Robinson varies colors depending on water clarity and amount of sunlight. In clear water and bright sun, muted colors are used. In low light, brighter combinations come into the mix. The collar/legs are set by trimming the feather to a "V." The tip is cut out and the fuzz and unwanted fibers removed from the bottom of the feather. The feather is secured on the hook, then set to length and wrapped in position. Trim off any excess to the front.

## ROBINSON'S CHICKEN LITTLE (2 COLORS)

*Originated and tied by Patrick Robinson*

- **Hook:** #8 Daiichi 1530
- **Thread:** White 6/0 Uni
- **Tail:** Sand or tan grizzly marabou, pearl Krystal Flash
- **Body:** Bonefish tan Midge Cactus Chenille

- **Collar:** Mallard flank dyed wood duck color
- **Head:** Pink or orange McFly Foam yarn

**Notes:** This pattern falls into several groupings. It may be an attractor nymph or possibly a baitfish. Regardless, it catches fish. Set the collar/legs the same as in the previous pattern. This basic design also allows for a wide range of color interpretation.

## ROBINSON'S PSYCHEDELIC SMURF STONE

*Originated and tied by Patrick Robinson*

- **Hook:** #10 Daiichi 1560
- **Thread:** Chartreuse 6/0 Uni
- **Bead:** Brass, 1/8 inch
- **Tail:** Black goose biots
- **Abdomen:** Hot yellow and blue Ultra Wire, wrapped together
- **Thorax:** Chartreuse Ice Dub
- **Wing Case:** Steelie blue Ice Dub
- **Legs:** White goose biots

**Notes:** This may be the ultimate attractor-nymph design. The stonefly silhouette features a contrasting combination of colors to trigger strikes from reluctant fish. It is also a good choice in high, stained water, where it sinks quickly and is visible to the fish.

## ROBINSON'S MONEY FLY

*Originated and tied by Patrick Robinson*

- **Hook:** #8 Daiichi 1560
- **Thread:** Hot pink 6/0 Uni
- **Tail:** White rabbit fur, pearl Krystal Flash
- **Underbody:** Tying thread
- **Body:** White rayon chenille, medium
- **Head:** Build up with thread

**Notes:** This is a true attractor pattern. Cover hook shank completely with tying thread several times to make the underbody, which is an important component of this fly. When the chenille gets wet, it becomes a bit translucent, and the pink underbody becomes visible and appears to "glow" through the chenille.

## FONZI FRY

*Originated and tied by Ted Kraimer*

- **Hook:** #8 TMC 2457
- **Thread:** Gray 6/0 Uni
- **Tail:** Grizzly marabou
- **Body:** UV pearl Ice Dub
- **Collar:** Teal flank feather
- **Back:** UV pearl Ice Dub with peacock Ice Dub over top, both tied in as strands, not dubbed
- **Eyes:** Black plastic bead chain, small

**Notes:** Where there is natural reproduction of salmon, fry become an important source of food as the eggs hatch and the fry develop. Both migratory and resident trout will feed heavily on them. This pattern can be fished dead-drifted and also swung down and across as a traditional wet fly.

## RED NECK SURVEYOR

*Originated and tied by George McCabe*

- **Hook:** #8-10 Daiichi 1560
- **Thread:** Red 6/0 Uni
- **Bead:** Black nickel, 5/32 inch
- **Tag:** Small oval silver tinsel
- **Tail:** Groundhog guard hairs
- **Body:** 1/8-inch-wide strip of pink surveyor tape, wrapped
- **Rib:** Medium oval silver tinsel
- **Wing:** Groundhog guard hairs
- **Collar:** Badger saddle

**Notes:** This fun pattern from Ohio fly fisher George McCabe is a great example of material creativity. It incorporates a totally unexpected body material into an effective, classic-looking pattern. It has become a favorite of McCabe's after taking a trout over 13 pounds on its first outing. If you don't have groundhog fur, substitute with sparse fine deer body hair.

## BEAR'S PM CADDIS

*Originated and tied by Bear Andrews*

- **Hook:** #6-14 TMC 2457
- **Thread:** Tan 6/0 Uni
- **Body:** Chartreuse Larva Lace
- **Collar:** Brown hen hackle
- **Head:** Natural hare's ear

**Notes:** Named for Michigan's Pere Marquette River, a #8 is the standard size for this pattern, but it can be adjusted depending on local water conditions. A simple pattern to tie, this has been around for a number of years and will take fish wherever *Rhyacophila* caddis are found. Vinyl Rib is an acceptable substitute for the Larva Lace. This pattern could have been in the previous group, but was placed here with the other Bear Andrews nymphs.

**Hint:** Dead-drift with an egg pattern for an extra-effective combination.

## STEELIE SOFT HACKLE

*Originated and tied by Jon Ray*

- **Hook:** #6-10 Daiichi 1710
- **Thread:** Brown 6/0 Uni
- **Abdomen:** Opal Mirage Tinsel
- **Thorax:** UV black Ice Dub
- **Collar:** Brown partridge

**Notes:** Jon Ray guides anglers year-round on the rivers of northwest Michigan. Based on a traditional soft-hackle design, don't be fooled by the nondescript appearance of this fly. The feather is tip-wrapped and includes a bit of the marabou "fuzz" at the base of the feather. With just a bit of sparkle to attract attention, Ray finds it is particularly effective in clear water for both spring steelhead and resident trout.

This beautiful Great Lakes rainbow is fresh from the big water, showing the silvery coloration that gives the name steelhead. The first blush of pink color is showing on the gill plates. ROBERT SCHOELLER PHOTO

## BEAR'S NEON STONE

*Originated and tied by Bear Andrews*

- **Hook:** #8-14 Daiichi 1530
- **Thread:** Black 8/0 Uni
- **Tail:** Pheasant rump fibers
- **Abdomen:** Black peacock Ice Dub
- **Rib:** Black biots
- **Wing Case:** Pheasant tail
- **Thorax:** Peacock herl
- **Eyes:** Black mono
- **Hackle:** Black pheasant rump

**Notes:** Bear Andrews's steelhead nymphs are legendary across the Great Lakes tributaries. This pattern has a bit of attention-getting sparkle to accompany a very natural design. Size is adjusted depending on water flow speed and color. Treat the wing case with Flex Seal or Flexament to minimize shredding by steelhead teeth.

## BEN STONE

*Originated and tied by Bear Andrews*

- **Hook:** #6-10 Daiichi 1530
- **Thread:** Black 8/0 Uni
- **Tail:** Black pheasant rump fibers
- **Abdomen:** Black 28-gauge wire
- **Wing Case:** Pheasant tail
- **Thorax:** Peacock herl or peacock Ice Dub
- **Hackle:** Black pheasant rump
- **Eyes:** Black mono, small

**Notes:** With a slim profile and heavy body, this pattern was designed for deep, fast flows. It is fished in larger sizes to sink as efficiently as possible. Again, treat the wing case.

## BEAR'S PEACOCK FUZZBUSTER

*Originated and tied by Bear Andrews*

- **Hook:** #8 Daiichi 1530
- **Thread:** Brown 8/0 Uni
- **Tail:** Brown dyed grizzly hen saddle
- **Abdomen:** Peacock herl or peacock Ice Dub
- **Back/Wing Case:** Pheasant tail
- **Ribbing:** Mono
- **Thorax/Hackle:** Peacock herl, dyed brown grizzly hen saddle
- **Eyes:** Black mono, small

**Notes:** This is an effective, buggy pattern that doesn't imitate anything in particular but has a lot of movement in the water. It can be dead-drifted and also swung down and across, wet-fly style. The grizzly hen saddle is wrapped over the peacock herl thorax, and don't forget to treat the wing case. Andrews also ties this in black.

## BEAR'S PHEASANT TAIL

*Originated and tied by Bear Andrews*

- **Hook:** #6-10 Daiichi 1530
- **Thread:** Brown 8/0 Uni
- **Tail:** Pheasant tail
- **Abdomen:** Pheasant tail
- **Rib:** Copper wire
- **Wing Case:** Pheasant tail
- **Thorax:** Peacock herl
- **Hackle:** Pheasant rump with aftershaft
- **Eyes:** Black mono

**Notes:** This design takes the Pheasant Tail Nymph to a whole new level. It is more a combination of the Sparrow Nymph and Pheasant Tail and has plenty of movement, but muted natural colors. Use this in clear water on a bright day.

## BEAR'S FRENCH HEX

*Originated and tied by Bear Andrews*

- **Hook:** #6 Daiichi 1730
- **Thread:** Tan 8/0 Uni
- **Tail:** French partridge
- **Body:** Sulphur Squirrel Blend Dubbing
- **Hackle:** French partridge with aftershaft

**Notes:** This oversized version of a Sparrow Nymph works well where there is an abundance of Hex mayflies. It likely also resembles a variety of small baitfish. You can dead-drift, swing, and even trip this pattern for migratory and resident trout. No French partridge around? Use ringneck pheasant rump instead.

## DR. J

*Originated and tied by Bear Andrews*

- **Back Hook:** #6 Daiichi 1530
- **Front Hook:** #4 TMC 105
- **Thread:** Black 8/0 Uni
- **Connector:** 20 lb. hard mono
- **Tail:** Base of a black-dyed pheasant rump
- **Rear Body:** Black dubbing brush or dubbing
- **Rear Hackle:** Black pheasant rump and aftershaft
- **Front Body:** Orange $3/16$-inch tungsten bead collared with black pine squirrel

**Notes:** This mini version of an Egg Sucking Leech can also be done with a black bead to become a baby lamprey or regular leech pattern.

## BEAR'S CROSSDRESSER

*Originated and tied by Bear Andrews*

- **Hook:** #4 TMC 105
- **Thread:** White 8/0 Uni
- **Tail:** Natural grizzly Chickabou with a few wisps of pearl Angel Hair or Krystal Flash on sides
- **Back:** Peacock herl
- **Body:** Pearl Ice Dub on two-thirds, red Ice Dub on one-third
- **Hackle:** Teal flank
- **Eyes:** Black mono, small

**Notes:** This pattern can function as a Hex nymph or a baitfish fry pattern. Both steelhead and resident stream trout can target this fly. Fish down and across on a swing, letting it rise and hang at the end of the swing.

## BEAR'S STRIP FRY

*Originated and tied by Bear Andrews*

- **Hook:** #4 TMC 3761
- **Thread:** White 8/0 Uni
- **Tail:** Grizzly Chickabou and pearl Krystal Flash
- **Body:** Pearl Ice Dub

- **Wing:** White Micro Rabbit Strip, tied in Zonker-style
- **Collar:** Teal flank
- **Yolk Sac:** Hot orange Ice Dub
- **Eyes:** Black bead chain, small

**Notes:** This is another salmon fry pattern that is productive in the late winter/early spring time frame. Again, both migratory and stream trout will hit this fly. It can also be fished during other time periods as a crippled baitfish.

## DR. K (2 COLORS)

*Originated and tied by Bear Andrews*

- **Hook:** #4-6 Daiichi 1530
- **Thread:** Hot orange 8/0 Uni
- **Tail:** Black pheasant tail fibers
- **Abdomen:** Peacock herl, dubbing brush, or Ice Dub
- **Thorax:** Pearl blue Estaz (for blue phase)
- **Hackle:** Black hen saddle, collared

**Notes:** This is more of a traditional-style wet fly to swing across and downstream. The wine color phase uses a wine-colored Estaz for the thorax. These work best in water temperatures above 40 degrees F, when fish are more apt to chase a swung pattern.

# Group 5: Great Lakes Originals

Throughout the remaining groupings in this chapter, we will see a combination of wet and streamer patterns for swung fly use. These will cover a range of different fly styles, including traditional designs, shank, and tube patterns. Swinging flies has become increasingly popular in Great lakes tributaries to target mainly steelhead, but it will also produce migratory browns and occasionally salmon.

This starting group is an interesting combination of patterns that vary greatly in appearance. Pattern selection for Great Lakes rainbows often varies depending on time of year and water conditions.

## THUNDERSTICK BOSS

*Originated and tied by Matt Supinski*

- **Hook:** #3-5 Alec Jackson Blue Water Nickel Hook
- **Thread:** Black 6/0 Uni
- **Weight:** Silver bead chain
- **Tail:** Pearl Krystal Flash
- **Body:** Black Vinyl Rib, copper Cactus Chenille in front
- **Collar:** Chartreuse, then orange schlappen, orange Glow-in-the-Dark Flashabou Accent over top
- **Eyes (optional):** Jungle cock

**Notes:** The use of Thunderstick lures is an effective way to catch Great Lakes chinook. This pattern is based on the traditional Boss fly design from the 1940s that incorporates bead chain for weight. The use of the Glow-in-the-dark Flashabou is for low light and after dark. Great Lakes chinook will take a swung fly at times under these conditions.

## FUNKY COPPER COLD MEDINA

*Originated and tied by Matt Supinski*

- **Hook:** #1-4 Daiichi 2151
- **Thread:** Black 6/0 Uni
- **Weight:** Silver bead chain
- **Tail:** Two black-barred copper Sili Legs with copper Flashabou
- **Body:** Wrapped copper Flashabou, then copper Cactus Chenille
- **Collar:** Olive copper UV Polar Chenille, black schlappen
- **Eyes (optional):** Jungle cock

**Notes:** Color combinations of copper and black are productive in the tannic-color conditions of northern Great Lakes tributaries. This traditional design highlights this color scheme. Vary the fly size to the size of the tributary being fished.

**(Left to right)** Row 1: Thunderstick Boss, Funky Copper Cold Medina, BTS; Row 2: Troutfitter Spey (2 colors); Row 3: Steelhead Spey Soft Hackle (2 colors). JIMMY CHANG PHOTO

## BTS (BETTER THAN SPAWN)

*Originated and tied by Kevin Feenstra*

- **Front Hook:** #6 Daiichi 1120
- **Thread:** White 140-denier UTC
- **Rear Hook:** #10 4xl straight-eye streamer
- **Connector:** 20 lb. mono
- **Tail/Rear Body:** Natural grizzly marabou
- **optional:** cut off bend of the rear hook
- **Eyes:** Black plastic bead chain, large
- **Front Body:** Small bunch of Australian opossum fur, silver Holographic Flashabou (don't trim in front), then UV pink Ice Dub
- **Back:** Silver Holographic Flashabou
- **Pectoral Fins:** Silver Holographic Flashabou

**Notes:** This is another long-standing salmon fry pattern and a favorite springtime pattern of Kevin Feenstra's. The grizzly marabou is tied in as a tail on the rear hook and then the remainder of the feather is wrapped to make the body. The same bunch of silver Holographic Flashabou is pulled over the UV pink Ice Dub and tied down as the back, tied in front of the eyes, and then pulled back and trimmed as the pectoral fins. Substitute pearl or olive Ice Dub for the UV pink and you have a very viable small baitfish design.

## TROUTFITTER SPEY (2 COLORS)

*Originated and tied by Ken Collins*

- **Hook:** #1/0-4 standard salmon-style
- **Thread:** Orange 6/0 Uni
- **Tag:** Silver mylar tinsel
- **Underbody:** Silver mylar tinsel
- **Abdomen:** Edge Brite
- **Thorax:** Large Cactus Chenille or Estaz to match Edge Brite color
- **Collar:** Mallard flank

**Notes:** From Ontario, this pattern is designed to be bright and visible in the high flows of spring. Fished on a sinking-tip line, it has minimal weight to snag and stays at fish eye level through the swing. Chartreuse, pink, and orange are the primary colors.

## STEELHEAD SPEY SOFT HACKLE (2 COLORS)

*Originated and tied by Kim Benbow*

- **Hook:** #8 Daiichi 1760
- **Thread:** Black 8/0 Veevus
- **Body:** Three colors of Holographic Tinsel (silver, chartreuse, red, silver, purple, and orange are favorites), then peacock herl
- **Collar:** Extra-long partridge hackle

**Notes:** This is designed for selective fish in low, clear conditions. Again, subtle changes often trigger strikes. If you know steelhead are holding in an area and not spooking from your presentation, change colors if they do not take the fly after a dozen or so swings.

# Group 6: More Great Lakes Originals

This section contains additional patterns for use on Great Lakes tributaries and connecting waters. In the fall, both salmon and trout enter tributaries, including Atlantic salmon and Pacific salmon species, along with rainbow, brown, and in some areas brook and lake trout. In the spring, a wide range of species enter tributary streams, such as rainbow trout, walleye, smallmouth bass, and a variety of rough fish species.

## BOA LEECH (2 COLORS)

*Originated and tied by Jerry Darkes*

- **Hook:** #4-8 Daiichi 1710
- **Thread:** Fluorescent orange or fluorescent red 70-denier UTC
- **Tail:** Black or purple marabou plume tip
- **Back:** Black or purple Holographic Flashabou
- **Body:** Black or purple Boa Yarn or Pseudo Herl
- **Head:** UV shrimp pink or UV pink Ice Dub

**Notes:** This has been a consistent fish catcher for me across the Great Lakes that works well in stained water. It is quick and simple to tie, durable, and productive. To create the back, the Holographic Flashabou is tied forward at the eye, then pulled back a few strands at a time and secured as the body is wrapped forward.

## BOA MINNOW

*Originated and tied by Jerry Darkes*

- **Hook:** #4-8 Daiichi 1710
- **Thread:** Chartreuse or white 70-denier UTC
- **Tail:** Chartreuse or white marabou plume tip
- **Back:** Pearl Krinkle Mirror Flash or Lateral Scale
- **Body:** White Boa Yarn or Pseudo Herl
- **Head:** Pearl or chartreuse Ice Dub

**Notes:** This baitfish version in the Boa series will catch a wide range of species. It can be stripped or swung depending on the situation. It works best when there are schools of small baitfish present.

**(Left to right)** Row 1: Boa Leech (2 colors), Boa Minnow; Row 2: Rabbit Strip Spey, Cranberry Spey; Row 3: Crustacean Spey, Grass Stain. JIMMY CHANG PHOTO

Smallmouth bass in the Great Lakes have been documented to follow schools of baitfish as they migrate back toward the shallows in the fall. This gives anglers an additional opportunity to catch trophy-size smallies on a fly. A number of harbor areas receive big concentrations of fish. JEFF LISKAY PHOTO

## RABBIT STRIP SPEY

*Originated and tied by Jerry Darkes*

- **Hook:** #2-4 Daiichi 2161
- **Thread:** 70-denier UTC, color to match fly
- **Tail:** Rabbit strip
- **Body:** Flat braid
- **Rib:** Brassie-size wire to match body
- **Wing:** Rabbit strip, Krystal Flash or Krinkle Mirror Flash over top
- **Collar:** Schlappen, mallard
- **Eyes (optional):** Jungle cock

**Notes:** This is the first fly of my own design that took a steelhead on the swing. That was 20 or so years ago, and this pattern still catches plenty of fish. I usually tie it in a baitfish color scheme, but dark and bright colors also work. The rabbit strip wing should blend smoothly into the tail strip for the fly to swim properly; the curved shape of the hook is important for this—a straight-shank hook will not work.

## CRANBERRY SPEY

*Originated and tied by Kevin Feenstra*

- **Hook:** #2 Daiichi 2161
- **Thread:** Gray 6/0 Uni
- **Body:** Wrapped pearl Flashabou
- **Underwing:** Flashabou from body, pulled back and tied down
- **Thorax:** Emerald green Ice Dub, blue-eared pheasant
- **Wing:** Cranberry Holographic Flashabou

**Notes:** While Kevin Feenstra is best known for his large, flashy steelhead streamers, he also has a number of smaller, lesser-known patterns that are very productive. His color blends are a result of careful observation under various water and light conditions. This pattern is an interesting blend of natural and synthetic materials on a traditional-style template. The blue-eared pheasant is wrapped through the Ice Dub and then in front of it.

## CRUSTACEAN SPEY

*Originated and tied by Jerry Darkes*

- **Hook:** #3-5 Daiichi Alec Jackson Spey Fly Hook
- **Thread:** Olive 70-denier UTC
- **Tail/Antennae:** Olive-dyed pheasant tail fibers, curving downward
- **Eyes:** Plastic bead chain, small
- **Rostrum:** Olive hackle fibers
- **Body:** Olive or olive brown Craw Dub in a loop, grizzly olive saddle
- **Wing:** Bronze mallard flank
- **Hackle:** Olive-dyed pheasant rump or blue-eared pheasant

**Notes:** I have tied this fly for a long time. The inspiration for it came one fall as I watched steelhead eating crayfish that were migrating to their wintering areas. This pattern has a great, traditional look to it and can be tied in all the various Craw Dub shades. Both olive and an orange variation have taken numerous fish in British Columbia as well as across the Great Lakes.

## GRASS STAIN

*Originated and tied by Kevin Feenstra*

- **Hook:** #2 Daiichi 2161
- **Thread:** Light olive 6/0 Uni
- **Body:** Yellow Holographic Flashabou, wrapped
- **Underwing:** Yellow Holographic Flashabou
- **Thorax:** Golden brown Ice Dub, blue-eared pheasant
- **Wing:** Magnum copper Flashabou, kelly green Flashabou over top

**Notes:** This pattern has a noticeable amount of flash and movement in the water and often triggers strikes from otherwise reluctant fish. Tie it the same as the Cranberry Spey. Copper and green color combinations have proven productive in many of the tannic-colored tributaries of the northern Great Lakes.

# Group 7: Still More Great Lakes Originals

Here is another group of proven producers for Great Lakes migratory rainbows and brown trout. These vary widely in design and appearance, but all are proven patterns.

Migratory smallmouth bass are an interesting Great Lakes phenomenon. There are a number of locations where runs of bass ascend tributaries to spawn and then drop back to the big water. The smallmouth generally come in as the steelhead are dropping back. This makes for a unique species overlap in the spring. Several flies presented here are effective for these fish, as well as trout.

## EMULATOR

*Originated and tied by Kevin Feenstra*

- **Hook:** #2 Daiichi 2461
- **Thread:** Tan 6/0 Uni
- **Tail:** Two grizzly marabou feathers
- **Body:** Two to three emu feathers, brown or grizzly schlappen
- **Collar:** Mallard flank feather
- **Pectoral Fins:** Grizzly marabou feathers, 1 on each side
- **Head:** Clump of Australian opossum body fur

**Notes:** This is one of the earliest Great Lakes patterns designed to be swung on sinking-tip lines. Kevin Feenstra's home base, Michigan's Muskegon River, is loaded with sculpin, and both resident and migratory trout eat them with gusto. This pattern has proven itself in other areas for an assortment of species. Keep the stiffer center stem of the grizzly marabou when tying in the tail and have the feathers curve away from each other. For the body, wrap the emu feathers and then palmer with the schlappen feather. The Australian opossum fur is tied on similar to ram's wool. Attach it in the middle, letting it spread around the hook, then tighten wraps to secure it.

Pull the clump back, move the thread in front, and secure. If needed, trim the fur to a rounded shape.

**Hint:** Scale the Emulator down to size 4 and fish it for smallmouth! You can also add a bit of gold or copper flash.

Now considered an old-school pattern, the Emulator still catches plenty of fish. It can be swung or cast for several different species including steelhead, brown trout, and smallmouth. JERRY DARKES PHOTO

**(Left to right)** Row 1: Emulator, Mr. Red Eye, Joe's Leech; Row 2: Aquatic Nuisance, The Fly; Row 3: Flat Brim Spey (3 colors). JIMMY CHANG PHOTO

The Great Lakes contain lake-spawning smallmouth as well as populations that spawn in tributaries. Tributary spawners will hit swung flies aggressively when they first enter the streams. JERRY DARKES PHOTO

## MR. RED EYE

*Originated and tied by Jeff Liskay*

- **Front Hook:** #4-6 Daiichi 1530
- **Rear Hook:** #6-8 Daiichi 1710
- **Thread:** Black 70-denier UTC or similar
- **Rear Body:** Olive black-barred marabou, olive copper UV Polar Chenille in front
- **Connector:** 40-50 lb. braid
- **Front Body:** Copper olive UV Palmer Chenille, mallard flank
- **Back:** Four to six peacock herls
- **Eyes:** Red plastic bead chain

**Notes:** Liskay has fished this pattern around the Great Lakes with success for both resident and migratory trout. Imitating both sculpin and an assortment of darker-colored baitfish, it can be both swung and stripped on a sinking-tip line. This is another pattern to use for smallmouth, too!

## JOE'S LEECH

*Originated and tied by Joe Penich*

- **Hook:** #1-4 Daiichi 2161 or similar
- **Thread:** Black 70-denier UTC
- **Underbody:** Lead wire
- **Body:** Black Ice Dub
- **Wing:** Black rabbit strip with bronze, copper, red, or blue Flashabou added
- **Collar:** Black Arctic fox strip, wrapped, or put in a dubbing loop then spun and wrapped

**Notes:** Simple to tie and good looking in hand, this pattern is effective for migratory and resident trout under a wide range of water conditions. Pick your favorite Flashabou colors to accent it—mine are bronze or copper! The lead wire is tied parallel to the hook shank on each side rather than wrapped. The rabbit strip is tied down in the back and front Zonker-style. Another good one for smallmouth, too!

## AQUATIC NUISANCE

*Originated and tied by Kevin Feenstra*

- **Hook:** #2 Daiichi 2460 or 2461
- **Thread:** Tan or gray 6/0 Uni
- **Tail:** Dark olive rabbit strip
- **Body:** Black Ice Dub, dark brown schlappen
- **Wing:** A mix of copper, black, and kelly green Flashabou
- **Collar:** Mallard flank feather
- **Head:** Clump of Australian opossum body fur

**Notes:** This is one of Feenstra's earliest "flashy" designs and still one of his favorites. The Australian opossum head gives extra movement to the fly and also creates a "mini-vortex" behind it to give extra movement to the Flashabou. This pattern transfers well to both shank and tube fly variations.

## THE FLY

*Originated and tied by Dave Barkman*

- **Hook:** #2 TMC 9395 or similar
- **Thread:** Burnt orange 70-denier UTC
- **Tail:** Black marabou plume tip
- **Body:** Brown UV Polar Chenille
- **Wing/Belly:** Copper Flashabou
- **Sides:** Wood duck or mallard flank dyed wood duck
- **Head:** Black marabou, wrapped

**Notes:** Michigan guide Dave Barkman favors combinations of black and copper for rivers like Michigan's Big Manistee. The contrast of a black background with copper flash works well in tannic-colored waters. This pattern also has plenty of movement on a swing.

## FLAT BRIM SPEY (3 COLORS)

*Originated and tied by Jon Uhlenhop*

- **Hook:** #2-4 Daiichi 2151
- **Thread:** Red 8/0 Uni
- **Body:** Ice Dub, stiff-fiber hackle, 4 to 6 strands of Holographic Flashabou
- **Collar:** Two colors of tip-wrapped marabou, with natural or dyed guinea
- **Wing:** Mallard flank or pheasant rump, natural or dyed to match fly color scheme

**Notes:** Baitfish, bright, and natural color combinations are shown here. The stiff hackle should be about half the hook gap when wrapped. It is used to keep the collar and top wing from collapsing in the current, giving the fly a great 3D profile. The wing should be tied to lie flat on top of the fly. Tie this one in your favorite colors.

## Group 8: Robert Schoeller Eurostyle Patterns

Robert (Uncle Bobbie) Schoeller has a unique take on fishing Pennsylvania's Lake Erie tributaries. With a graduate degree in fisheries and extensive experience chasing Atlantic salmon and sea trout in Europe, Schoeller combines this knowledge in his pursuit of lake-run rainbows, brown trout, and more in the waters around Erie, Pennsylvania. His patterns reflect European sea trout and Atlantic salmon designs, but work well in his local waters.

This is a great example of "thinking outside the box" when it comes to pattern design. Much of the steelhead tradition of the Pacific Northwest can trace its roots to European Atlantic salmon flies and techniques. However, few of us are familiar with that tying style. Likewise with the sea trout of Europe. These are migratory brown trout that enter tributaries from the ocean to spawn.

Several of these patterns are quite intricate and time consuming. They are made to Schoeller's specific requirements for the waters he fishes, but would certainly be applicable to other locales around the Great Lakes.

Great Lakes brown trout respond well to traditional European sea trout patterns. These have proven most productive during low-light conditions in clear, shallow water around creek mouths. A quiet, stealthy setup and presentation is required. ROBERT SCHOELLER PHOTO

**(Left to right)** Row 1: Uncle Bobby's Irish Shrimp, Great Lakes Spottail Shiner—Night Variation; Row 2: Uncle Bobby's Shrimp #1, Great Lakes Spottail Shiner—Day Variation; Row 3: Uncle Bobby's Shrimp #2, Pregnant Mysis.

JIMMY CHANG PHOTO

## UNCLE BOBBY'S IRISH SHRIMP

*Originated and tied by Robert Schoeller*

- **Hook:** #11-13 black Partridge Salar Double
- **Thread:** White 16/0 Veevus, finish head with black 12/0 Veevus
- **Tag:** Pearl Krystal Mirror Flash
- **Tail:** Golden pheasant rump fibers, tied long
- **Antennae:** Boar bristles, tied to splay, strand of pearl Flashabou on each side
- **Body:** Pearl Mini Flat Braid
- **Rib:** Fine silver wire
- **Collar:** Orange then purple soft hackle
- **Eyes/Carapace:** Two small jungle cock

**Notes:** This is a favorite pattern and color of Schoeller's that can be altered easily by changing the hackle colors. This fly is swung on a variety of sinking-tip line and poly leader combinations depending on water conditions. The double hook holds fish extremely well in small sizes and adds a bit of weight to the fly. They may be difficult to find, so a small single hook, like the Daiichi 2421, can also be used. It's unlikely most of us will have boar bristles. These can be replaced with stripped hackle stems. The collar can be wrapped hackle or small groups of hackle fibers tied down. The jungle cock eyes are tied in the form and angled roof over the hackle.

**Hint:** Using a strong, super-thin thread minimizes bulk when it is not wanted.

## GREAT LAKES SPOTTAIL SHINER—NIGHT VARIATION

*Originated and tied by Robert Schoeller*

- **Hook:** #5-#7 black Partridge Salar Single
- **Thread:** White 16/0 Veevus, finish with red 12/0 Veevus at head
- **Tag:** Pearl Crystal Mirror Flash
- **Tail:** UV pearl Spirit River Crystal Mirror Splash
- **Butt:** Black ostrich or peacock herl
- **Body:** White Glow-in-the-Dark Flashabou, wrapped on rear one-third; shrimp glow EP Dubbing Brush, wound on front two-thirds
- **Rib:** Fine silver wire
- **Underwing:** Untrimmed portion of EP Dubbing Brush, white Glow-in-the-Dark Flashabou over top
- **Wing:** Gray or olive EP Fibers, sparse
- **Sides:** Purple Fluoro Flash, Micro Crystal Flash UV, and pearl Fire Fly Flash, length of the wing, several strands per side
- **Head:** UV olive Ice Dub, sparse
- **Eye:** 3 to 4 mm 3D

**Notes:** Trim the EP Brush fibers from the body short on the bottom and at the front just on top to set the wing properly. The eyes are secured with Clear Cure Goo. Schoeller is a big proponent of fishing the pre-dawn period, especially early in the season when fish are staging at the tributary mouths. Fish will often be in the main plume, often in ankle-deep water. As soon as it gets light or you start wading, they drop into deeper water. The fly can be "shot" with a camera flash to charge the materials for visibility. It is then swung across the current with a long leader and floating line. Be sure to point your flash away from the water when charging flies for nighttime use. The flash of light can push fish away from the shallows and out of reach.

The spottail shiner is a common but lesser-known Great Lakes baitfish. They have a purplish flash to them as opposed to the green of the emerald shiner. Both are important forage species for most Great Lakes sportfish.

## UNCLE BOBBY'S SHRIMP (2 COLORS)

*Originated and tied by Robert Schoeller*

- **Hook:** #12-14 Patridge CS1 Salar Double or similar, or #6 heavy curved scud hook
- **Thread:** White 16/0 Veevus
- **Tail:** Two boar bristles, splayed outward, then 1 strand each pearl Krystal Flash and UV Flash on each side
- **Rostrum:** Soft-hackle fibers to contrast with body color
- **Eyes:** Black mono, small
- **Body:** White or cream wool, tapering heavier to thinner toward eye
- **Rib:** Fine silver wire
- **Carapace/Back:** Pearl Prismatic Pliable Sheet Back, shaped to an elongated point
- **Head/Throat:** Colored Fluoro Fiber
- **Coating:** Clear Cure Goo, heaviest back by eyes

**Notes:** Although marine-size shrimp are not present in the Great Lakes, migratory trout still seem to have an affinity for them. This pattern is not as difficult to tie as it sounds, and is actually quite easy after becoming familiar with it. Again, substitute stripped hackle stems for the boar bristles. Fino Skin, Thin Crystal Skin, or Prism Scale Film can also be used for the carapace and back. (These are carried by Hareline.) Prep several back pieces before starting to tie. The Fluoro Fiber is wrapped up to the hook eye, then pulled back and tied down underneath the eye.

Great Lakes steelhead will also hit small, traditional patterns. These are a good option for use in low, clear water when standard patterns are being ignored. ROBERT SCHOELLER PHOTO

## GREAT LAKES SPOTTAIL SHINER—DAY VARIATION

*Originated and tied by Robert Schoeller*

- **Hook:** #5-7 nickle Partridge Salar Single
- **Thread:** White 16/0 Veevus, finish with red 12/0 Veevus at head
- **Tag:** Silver Crystal Mirror Flash
- **Tail:** UV pearl Crystal Mirror Flash
- **Butt:** Black ostrich or peacock herl
- **Body:** UV pearl Flat Braid (Lagartun) on rear one-third, blue pearl EP Dubbing Brush on front two-thirds
- **Rib:** Fine silver wire
- **Underwing:** Pearl Fire Flash, white EP Minnow Fiber, sparse tan Ice Fur
- **Sides:** Several strands of purple Fluoro Fiber on each side
- **Head:** Olive Ice Dub, sparse
- **Eyes:** 3 to 4 mm 3D

**Notes:** This is a super-realistic representation of a spottail shiner for clear-water use. It is designed to be swung across the current, through the deeper flows that trout move to when the sun is up. Be sure to give a few strips at the end of the swing before picking up to recast. This may trigger any fish that followed the fly on the swing to strike. The EP Dubbing Brush is again wound to form the front of the body, then trimmed short on the bottom and short at the front on top. The eyes are set with Clear Cure Goo. This is also a good pattern to target lake-run smallmouth.

## PREGNANT MYSIS

*Originated and tied by Robert Schoeller*

- **Hook:** #14 Partridge Salar Double
- **Thread:** White 16/0 Veevus
- **Antennae/Tail:** Six to eight strands of pink Fluoro Fiber in a "V" shape
- **Eyes:** Black mono, extra small
- **Body:** Glo green Brilliance Luminous Sewing Thread, pink Madiera Embroidery Thread
- **Rib:** Silver wire

**Notes:** The Daiichi 1530 can be used as a substitute for the hard-to-find double hook. The body should taper from heavy at the hook bend to thin at the eye. The threads described here should be available at most fabric stores. If you cannot locate these, with a bit of creativity you can come up with substitute materials that will give a similar effect. For example, wrap a tapered underbody with white dubbing, then overwrap with Krystal Flash in pearl then pink. Coat with Clear Cure Goo.

## Group 9: Greg Senyo Favorites

Greg Senyo grew up fishing the waters of northwest Pennsylvania. An Orvis Fly Tier of the Year Award winner in 2008, he is well known for his fly patterns and material development with Hareline Dubbin. Senyo's designs have produced across the Great Lakes, Pacific Northwest, Canada, and Alaska. Many are outlined in his book, *Fusion Fly Tying*. Here are some of his key steelhead patterns. All of these can be tied in multiple color schemes; Senyo's favorites are given.

**(Left to right)** Row 1: Predator Scandi; Row 2: Artificial Intelligence; Row 3: Flow Rider, Stray Dog; Row 4: Tropic Thunder. JIMMY CHANG PHOTO

## PREDATOR SCANDI

*Originated and tied by Greg Senyo*

- **Shank:** Black or blue 40 mm Flymen Fishing Co. Senyo Steelhead/Salmon Shank
- **Thread:** Blue 70-denier UTC
- **Loop:** Senyo Intruder Wire or 50 lb. Fireline Braid
- **Hook:** #1-4 Octopus-style
- **Tag:** Silver Flat Diamond Braid
- **Tail:** Chartreuse Fluoro Fiber
- **Body:** Blue Flat Diamond Braid, blue berry 1.5-inch EP Senyo Chromatic Brush
- **Rib:** Gold medium French tinsel over Diamond Braid
- **Underwing:** Senyo UV Barred Predator Wrap
- **Wing:** Blue Arctic fox tail, mixed pearl Lateral Scale and blue Flashabou
- **Collar:** Blue guinea
- **Eyes (optional):** Jungle cock, real or artificial

**Notes:** This pattern is based on Temple Dog and Scandinavian-style designs. It is a fairly simple tie, with a great teardrop profile, and has plenty of flash and movement. Despite its size, it is easy to cast as there is minimal water absorption. This recipe is for a blue color scheme, but it can be adjusted to many different colors as desired.

## ARTIFICIAL INTELLIGENCE

*Originated and tied by Greg Senyo*

- **Shank:** Green 25 mm Flymen Fishing Co. Senyo Salmon/Steelhead Blank Shank
- **Thread:** Olive 70-denier UTC
- **Loop:** Senyo Intruder Wire or 50 lb. Fireline Braid
- **Hook:** #1-4 Octopus-style
- **Weight:** Small bead chain (2 beads on each side)
- **Hot Spot:** Chartreuse Krystal Flash Chenille
- **Body:** Copper olive UV Polar Chenille
- **Underwing #1:** Section of chartreuse Lady Amherst Center Tail Feather
- **Underwing #2:** Ten to twelve strands of black Senyo's Barred Predator Wrap
- **Overwing #1:** Twelve to fifteen strands of mixed gold and kelly green Flashabou
- **Overwing #2:** Twelve to fifteen strands of mixed speckled copper and kelly green Flashabou
- **Collar:** Brown schlappen, chartreuse guinea in front
- **Eyes (optional):** Jungle cock, real or artificial

**Notes:** Greg Senyo calls the Artificial Intelligence his confidence pattern and it is well suited to the varying water conditions of Great Lakes tributaries. The pattern has easy-to-find materials, great movement and visibility in the water, and is very durable. Senyo prefers baitfish color combinations for fresh-run fish and more natural colors as river time increases. This mix of copper, gold, and kelly green has become a favorite of many anglers. The Predator Wrap is tied in a bit longer than the Lady Amherst with the tips uneven. The first wing is tied in ¼ inch longer than the Predator Wrap and the second wing ¼ inch longer than the last.

## FLOW RIDER

*Originated and tied by Greg Senyo*

- **Shank:** Black 40 mm Flymen Fishing Co. Senyo Steelhead/Salmon Shank
- **Thread:** Black 70-denier UTC
- **Loop:** Senyo Intruder Wire or 50 lb. Fireline Braid
- **Hook:** #1-4 Daiichi Octopus
- **Tail:** Hot orange Fluoro Fiber
- **Rear Wing:** Gray Arctic fox tail, bronze Flashabou on top
- **Rear Collar:** Natural guinea feather
- **Body:** Orange Flat Diamond Braid, natural guinea feather
- **Rib:** Gold medium French tinsel
- **Eyes:** Silver bead chain, 2 per side
- **Front Wing:** Gray Arctic fox tail, bronze Flashabou on top
- **Front Collar:** Natural guinea feather
- **Eyes (optional):** Jungle cock, real or artificial

**Notes:** This fly has a large profile for high flows and stained water. It combines a Scandinavian up-wing pattern with an Intruder body for maximum visibility with lots of movement. This color scheme is called classic gray ghost. Black ghost and green butt skunk are others to fish.

## STRAY DOG

*Originated and tied by Greg Senyo*

- **Shank:** Black 25 mm Flymen Fishing Co. Senyo Salmon/Steelhead Shank
- **Thread:** Black 70-denier UTC
- **Wire:** Senyo Intruder Wire or 50 lb. Fireline Braid
- **Hook:** #2 Daiichi Octopus
- **Body:** Pink pearl Flat Braid
- **Weight:** Gold bead chain, large
- **Underwing:** Mountain blueberry Senyo Aqua Veil Chenille
- **Wing:** White Arctic fox tail with gray Arctic fox tail over top
- **Accent:** Senyo UV Barred Predator Wrap
- **Flash:** Pearl Lateral Scale
- **Collar:** Blue guinea feather
- **Eyes:** Jungle cock, real or artificial

**Notes:** This is a simplified version of a Temple Dog pattern that retains the characteristics of the original design. It is a good choice for someone getting into the swing game and looking for an effective, simple-to-tie pattern. The blue version is given here, but this template can be easily adjusted to a variety of colors.

## TROPIC THUNDER

*Originated and tied by Greg Senyo*

- **Shank:** Blue 40 mm Flymen Fishing Co. Senyo Salmon/Steelhead Shank
- **Thread:** Blue 70-denier UTC
- **Loop:** Senyo Intruder Wire or 50 lb. Fireline Braid
- **Hook:** #1-4 Daiichi Octopus
- **Tail:** Blue black-barred ostrich plume herls
- **Body:** Chartreuse Flat Diamond Braid, blue 3-inch EP Senyo Chromatic Brush
- **Rib:** Gold medium French tinsel
- **Wing/Belly:** Chartreuse barred ostrich plume herls, spaced around the shank, mix of pearl Lateral Scale and silver Flashabou on top
- **Collar:** Purple guinea feather
- **Eyes (optional):** Jungle cock, real or artificial

**Notes:** This pattern is tied with a minimal amount of material to give a maximum amount of action. This is a key color scheme along with orange/pink/chartreuse. These combinations have caught everything from Great Lakes steelhead to European sea trout to Alaska kings. It has been a consistent producer in water temps below 40 degrees F.

**Important:** After the fly is completed, turn it upside down by the hook and stroke all the fibers down to expose the junction of the Diamond Braid and EP Senyo Brush, then apply a thin bead of Clear Cure Goo or Loon Flow Fly Finish to the base of the brush at the body and harden it. This will flare the material and keep it from collapsing.

# Group 10: Jon Uhlenhop Intruders

Manager of Chicago Fly Fishing Outfitters, Jon Uhlenhop is a very gifted fly tier we have met before. He has tied for nearly any fly-fishing situation imaginable for himself or clients of the store. This is Uhlenhop's interpretation of an Intruder-style pattern for Great Lakes applications

## GREAT LAKES INTRUDER (3 COLORS)

*Originated and tied by Jon Uhlenhop*

- **Shank:** 40 mm Senyo Steelhead/Salmon Shank
- **Thread:** Red 140-denier UTC
- **Loop:** Senyo Intruder Wire
- **Hook:** #1-4 Daiichi Octopus
- **Rear Section:** A ball of Ice Dub, Senyo Laser Dub around shank, with rhea and Lady Amherst pheasant fibers
- **Body:** Pearl Mylar Flat Braid
- **Weight:** Gold Dazl Eyes, ⅛ inch
- **Front Section:** Senyo Laser Dub around shank, with rhea and Lady Amherst pheasant fibers
- **Topping:** Two grizzly hackles, pearl Krinkle Mirror Flash
- **Collar:** Guinea feather, wrapped
- **Eyes (optional):** Jungle cock

**Notes:** Ed Ward's Intruder pattern revolutionized fly designs for Pacific salmon and steelhead. The idea of the Intruder is a fly with a big profile in the water that casts easily, sinks quickly, and has lots of life and movement. Ward's design has spread worldwide and has found a place on the tributaries of the Great Lakes where it is tied in both natural and attractor color combinations.

**(Top to bottom)** Great Lakes Intruder (3 colors: chartreuse, purple, pink). JIMMY CHANG PHOTO

# Group 11: Assorted Shank Streamers

This group of patterns are mainly for swung-fly applications, but several can also be stripped as desired. All are proven producers designed mainly for migratory trout, but can be used to target other species, too.

## CONVERTIBLE

*Originated and tied by Jerry Darkes*

- **Hook:** #1-4 Daiichi 2161
- **Thread:** 70-denier UTC, color to match fly
- **Loop:** Senyo Intruder Wire
- **Trailer Hook:** #1-4 Daiichi Octopus
- **Body:** Ice Dub
- **Collar:** Tip-wrapped marabou plume
- **Wing:** Rabbit strip, Krystal Flash on top
- **Eyes:** 3D glued or jungle cock

**Notes:** The Convertible is open to lots of adjustment in design and color. You can fish it with two hooks, just the single front hook, or cut the front hook and fish it as a shank design. If you cut the front hook, coat the now-exposed hook material with a UV cure material to minimize rust. Color schemes are endless, so just tie it up in your favorite combinations.

## RED-EYED SCULPIN

*Originated and tied by Jerry Darkes*

- **Hook:** #2 Aqua Talon
- **Shank:** 35-40 mm Senyo Shank or Flymen Articulated Shank
- **Thread:** 70-denier UTC, color to match fly
- **Tail:** Brown, olive, or tan grizzly marabou, dressed on rear hook
- **Body:** Grizzly marabou to match tail, wrapped emu feathers, grizzly schlappen to match tail
- **Collar:** Grizzly schlappen
- **Eyes:** Red plastic bead chain or red barbell-style weighted eyes
- **Head:** Arctic fox tail fur, color to match marabou and schlappen

**Notes:** The dressed hook is slipped onto the loop of the shank, the loop is closed with tying thread, and then the fly is constructed. The Arctic fox is tied in fairly long to cover most of the shank. Pull the butt ends of the hair back in steps so that the base fur is secured, then trim the base fur wide and flat. I usually tie this as a single main color, but you could mix the three colors given. This pattern can be swung or stripped for steelhead, resident trout, and smallmouth. It has been a good pattern for the migratory smallmouth of Lake Erie as well as migratory trout in a number of locales from the Great Lakes to Alaska.

## METAL DETECTOR

*Originated and tied by Kevin Feenstra*

- **Shank:** 25 mm Senyo Shank
- **Thread:** Tan or white 6/0 Uni
- **Loop:** 50 lb. Fireline Braid
- **Hook:** #1-2 Daiichi Octopus
- **Tail:** Olive pine squirrel strip
- **Wing:** Mix of red and gold Holographic Flashabou
- **Collar:** Orange deer belly hair
- **Eyes:** Silver bead chain, extra small, 2 per side
- **Head:** UV pink Ice Dub on bottom, chartreuse Ice Dub on top

**Notes:** An online search shows several different Metal Detector–named flies. This pattern from Kevin Feenstra has a lot of flash with color contrast for off-color water conditions. Incorporating deer hair gives a bit of buoyancy to help keep the fly above the bottom and minimize snags. It is a good one to swing above areas with a lot of bottom debris or rocks of different sizes.

## GRAPEFRUIT HEAD LEECH

*Originated and tied by Kevin Feenstra*

- **Shank:** 40 mm Senyo Shank or Flymen Articulated Shank
- **Thread:** Black 6/0 Uni
- **Loop:** 50 lb. braid
- **Hook:** #1-2 Daiichi Octopus
- **Tail:** Black marabou plume tip, with red Flashabou
- **Body:** Black tip-wrapped marabou, black schlappen
- **Collar:** Mallard flank feather
- **Wing:** Silver Flashabou, then blue Flashabou, top with kelly green Flashabou
- **Head:** Pink Cactus Chenille or Estaz, chartreuse Ice Dub
- **Eyes (optional):** Silver bead chain tied in between Cactus Chenille and Ice Dub

**Notes:** This is likely Feenstra's most dependable and productive cold-weather pattern. It is a "must-have" to swing in clear conditions and water temps below 40 degrees F. You can fish this wherever migratory trout are found.

**(Left to right)** Row 1: Convertible, Red-Eyed Sculpin; Row 2: Metal Detector, Grapefruit Head Leech; Row 3: Swingin' Sculpin, Shrew Sculpin. JIMMY CHANG PHOTO

Shank-style designs allow a fly with length to be used with a short-shank hook. This minimizes the leverage from a traditional long-shank hook that makes it easier for a large fish to work free. With some adjustments, shank designs can be both swung and stripped as needed. KEVIN FEENSTRA PHOTO

## SWINGIN' SCULPIN

*Originated and tied by Jon Uhlenhop*

- **Shank:** 25 to 35 mm Waddington-style shank
- **Thread:** Orange 10/0 Veevus
- **Loop:** 30 lb. Senyo Intruder Wire
- **Hook:** #2-4 Daiichi Octopus
- **Butt:** Chartreuse chenille
- **Rear Body:** Chocolate 3-inch Senyo Chromatic Brush
- **Front Body:** Copper UV Polar Chenille with pearl Polar Flash, then tip-wrapped olive and brown marabou in front
- **Collar:** Tip-wrapped olive and brown marabou, olive pheasant rump
- **Top:** Pheasant rump feather

**Notes:** The heavier shank gives a bit of extra weight without having to add bead chain or barbell eyes. The body materials provide support to the marabou and allow the fibers to hold their shape and move freely without flattening down to nothing. The UV Polar Chenille will "glow" through the marabou, giving a very lifelike look in the water.

## SHREW SCULPIN

*Originated and tied by Kevin Feenstra*

- **Shank:** 35 mm Flymen Articulated Shank
- **Thread:** Black 6/0 Uni
- **Loop:** 50 lb. braid
- **Hook:** #2 Daiichi Octopus
- **Tail:** Olive pine squirrel strip with several strands of red Holographic Flashabou
- **Body:** Olive grizzly marabou feathers
- **Pectoral Fins:** Olive pine squirrel strip
- **Eyes:** Gold plastic bead chain, medium
- **Head:** Peacock Ice Dub

**Notes:** This nondescript pattern has produced a surprising number of large steelhead for Feenstra. It is quick and simple to tie and also attracts smallmouth and stream trout. Tie several olive grizzly marabou feathers in a tent shape to make the body.

# Group 12: More Shank Patterns

Here are several more shank designs for consideration. The Fusion Dub Sculpin is specific in its coloration while the other two patterns can be adjusted as desired to a variety of natural and attractor colorations. Water color and temperature, weather conditions, and time of year can all influence fly color selection.

## MUTTON CHOP

*Originated and tied by Ted Kraimer*

- **Shank:** 25 mm Senyo Shank
- **Thread:** Brown 8/0 Uni
- **Loop:** 50 lb. braid
- **Hook:** #4 Daiichi Octopus
- **Body:** Copper UV Polar Chenille, brown schlappen
- **Wing:** Brown Arctic fox tail, copper Flashabou and copper Speckled Flashabou over top
- **Collar:** Mallard flank feather dyed brown
- **Eyes:** Black bead chain
- **Head:** Copper Ice Dub

**Notes:** This is a simple shank pattern that can be tied quickly, but is super fishy in the water. It has a sculpin-like appearance in this color scheme, but can be altered as desired to cover a wide range of applications.

## RABBIT STRIP SHANK FLY— EMERALD SHINER

*Originated and tied by Mike Veatch*

- **Shank:** 25 mm Senyo Shank
- **Thread:** Olive 70-denier UTC
- **Loop:** Senyo Intruder Wire
- **Butt:** Pearl Estaz or Cactus Chenille
- **Rear Body:** Pearl Senyo Predator Wrap
- **Front Body:** Silver UV Polar Chenille
- **Eyes:** Silver bead chain, medium, 2 per side
- **Wing:** Olive rabbit strip

**Notes:** This is another easy-to-tie, fish-catching pattern. It is usually done in baitfish colors, with the olive or a chartreuse or white rabbit strip wing. Colors can be easily adjusted if needed to fit a wide range of situations.

## FUSION DUB SCULPIN

*Originated and tied by Greg Senyo*

- **Shank:** 40 mm Senyo Shank
- **Thread:** Black 140-denier UTC
- **Loop:** Senyo Intruder Wire or 50 lb. Fireline Braid
- **Hook:** #2-4 Daiichi Octopus
- **Tail:** Olive marabou plume tip, copper Speckled Flashabou
- **Body:** Pepperoni Senyo Aqua Veil
- **Collar:** Fiery brown schlappen with brown guinea in front
- **Flash:** Pearl Lateral Scale
- **Head:** Tobacco, midnight, emerald Senyo Fusion Dub

(**Top to bottom**) Mutton Chop; Rabbit Strip Shank Fly— Emerald Shiner; Fusion Dub Sculpin. JIMMY CHANG PHOTO

**Notes:** This pattern is designed to imitate a variety of bottom-dwelling baitfish including sculpin, gobies, madtoms, chubs, and others. In the water, this fly has a large head and slender body profile. To form the head properly, tie in the Fusion Dub one clump at a time; each centered, folded back, and secured, then combed back to get the colors to blend. The marabou tail provides movement, and the blend of colors gives the appearance of all the above-listed critters. This can be both swung and stripped for a wide range of species.

## Group 13: Tube Flies

It is a bit surprising that tube flies are not more popular in North America, especially for streamer patterns. The ease of adjusting hook styles and sizes, plus the ability to drop a hook any desired distance behind the body, gives tubes a positive nod. Shanks serve a similar function, but do not really allow a hook to be changed out easily or numerous times without affecting the wire or braid loop.

There are a number of tube fly proponents across the region. Some of these individuals utilize both shanks and tubes depending on the situation and specific pattern. Most of these patterns focus on steelhead and salmon, but can cross over into other applications.

There are numerous tubes on the market. All-plastic tubes are common and have several characteristics: small diameter, slow melting, and do not compress when thread is wrapped on them. Metal tubes of copper, brass, and aluminum are also available. These are lined with a plastic tube to prevent the tippet from being cut on any sharp edges. The ends of the plastic liner tube are melted to form a lip holding the liner inside the metal tube.

Some sort of a short-shank hook is used with the tube. It can be set up different ways. If the tube diameter is large enough, the hook is tied to the tippet and pulled to seat the eye in the tubing. When the tube is too small for this, another section of tubing called the junction is attached to the rear of the tube to secure the hook eye. The junction can also be colored and then becomes part of the fly body. The photo at the end of this section shows an assortment of tubes and hook setup options.

A wide assortment of usable hooks are available for tube patterns. The TMC 105 and Daiichi 1640 and 2451 are popular in smaller sizes, up to #6. For #4 hooks and larger, the Aqua Talon, Owner Live Bait, and Mosquito hooks are favorites. Other similar designs can be used. Upturned-eye hooks, such as the Octupus-style, can be used if the tippet is tied so that it comes through the center of the eye, as in a Turle Knot. Otherwise it sits in the junction at an angle and can ruin the swimming motion of the fly. As hook choices vary due to personal preference and specific application, they are not included in the pattern recipes.

### BLACK LAKE LEECH

*Originated and tied by Tim Pearson*

- **Tube:** 1-inch small-diameter plastic with junction tube
- **Weight:** Large silver cone
- **Thread:** Black 6/0 Uni
- **Wing:** Black rabbit strip, black Flashabou
- **Collar:** Mallard flank feather dyed heron gray
- **Sides:** Black opal Lateral Scale, 2 pieces per side

**Notes:** Guide Tim Pearson fishes this pattern along Minnesota's North Shore for coaster brook trout, steelhead, and salmon. His favored hook to use is the Daiichi 2451.

### BETTER MINNOW

*Originated and tied by Nick Pionessa*

- **Tube:** 1-inch plastic with junction tube
- **Thread:** White 6/0 Uni
- **Body/Belly:** White Arctic fox, spun in a loop and wrapped
- **Flash:** DNA Holo Chromosome Flash, several strands per side
- **Eyes:** Barbell-style, small
- **Back:** Gray Finn raccoon, natural gray ostrich herl on top

**Notes:** Nick Pionessa fishes this in the Niagara River and various Lake Erie tributaries. The main targets are lake-run trout and smallmouth bass. This pattern can be swung or stripped. The Arctic fox for the body/belly is spun in a loop and wrapped. The Finn raccoon is reverse-tied. Use short-shank, straight-eye hooks to seat in junction tubing. The Daiichi 1640 and TMC 105 are good choices, but most any hook of this type is usable.

### DEVIL'S ADVOCATE

*Originated and tied by Rick Kustich*

- **Tube:** HMH 2-inch copper with junction tube
- **Thread:** Red 6/0 Uni
- **Body:** Purple Flat Braid
- **Collar:** Tip-wrapped white marabou, with 3 to 4 strands of silver Holographic Flashabou on each side

**Notes:** Rick Kustich fishes this in the lower Niagara River for steelhead coming in from Lake Ontario. The copper tube adds weight to get the fly down in the fast current. Copper tubes are the heaviest, then brass, with aluminum being lightest. This is a smelt coloration, but the color can be varied as desired.

### ICE MAN MINNOW

*Originated and tied by Greg Senyo*

- **Tube:** ⅜-inch small-diameter plastic
- **Thread:** Red 6/0 Uni
- **Belly:** Senyo Laser Dub
- **Wing:** Ice Dub
- **Head:** Senyo Fusion Dub
- **Eyes:** 3 to 4 mm 3D

**Notes:** This simple pattern can be colored as desired. It works extremely well fished under an indicator as an injured or stunned baitfish and will catch a wide range of species. It can also be fished in tandem with a larger fly and stripped. You'll notice that there is no junction tubing. You can seat the hook knot in the body instead.

**(Left to right)** Row 1: Black Lake Leech; Row 2: Better Minnow; Row 3: Devil's Advocate, Ice Man Minnow; Row 4: Emerald Shiner Tube. JIMMY CHANG PHOTO

Essential Flies for the Great Lakes Region

## EMERALD SHINER TUBE

*Originated and tied by Robert Schoeller*

- **Tube:** 10 mm stainless micro
- **Thread:** White 16/0 Veevus
- **Wing:** From bottom, all sparse: 8 strands of Glow-in-the-Dark Flashabou Accent, UV pearl Ice Wing, white EP Minnow Fiber, topped with EP Fiber in light olive or gray
- **Sides:** Mix a few strands each of pink, green, and purple Fluro Flash and mother of pearl Gliss and Glow, 1 each side
- **Eyes:** 3 mm 3D
- **Head:** Red 6/0 Uni

**Notes:** This is a key pattern of Schoeller's for fishing his favored pre-dawn time period at tributary river mouths in Lake Erie. He usually adds a small (#12-14) double or treble as the hook. This has given him the highest hook-up to landed ratio. Migratory trout, smallmouth, and even walleye have taken this fly. In shallow river-mouth situations, it often pays to match the size of the baitfish that are present. This can vary depending on time of year, so pay attention.

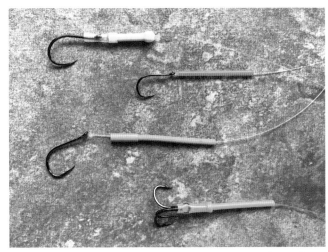

Hook versatility is a primary factor with tube flies. The hook can be varied for style and size as required. It can also be seated into junction tubing or set back from the fly to target short-striking fish. JERRY DARKES PHOTO

## Group 14: More Tube Flies

This series of patterns shows both European influence and also some recent development. Both imitative and attractor designs are presented, which allow a wide range of colors to be used.

### LAKE ERIE RAINBOW SMELT

*Originated and tied by John Nagy*

- **Tube:** Extra-small Wurm Micro Tungsten bottle tube with clear Canadian Tube Fly Co. FlexTube, 1½ inch
- **Thread:** White 8/0 Uni
- **Tail:** Pearl Krinkle Mirror Flash, 5 strands through and 2 inches past FlexTube
- **Body:** Pearl Ice Dub over front part of FlexTube and on to bottle tube
- **Wing:** On bottle tube, bottom to top, all sparse: pearl Krinkle Mirror Flash, white T's Fur, then silver Angel Hair, white T's Fur, plum Angel Hair, smolt blue SLF Hank, plum Angel Hair, dark olive T's Fur, rusty olive Angel Hair, finish with 8 peacock herls
- **Head:** Polar pearl Lite Brite with 5 mm 3D eyes

**Notes:** John Nagy has published several editions of the very successful *Steelhead Guide* for Lake Erie tributaries. Rainbow smelt were introduced into the Great Lakes and are still an important forage species in some areas. Although this layering of wing materials may seem excessive, it does an excellent job of representing the colors of a living specimen. Lake Erie gamefish certainly agree.

### CRYSTAL INTRUDER TUBE

*Originated and tied by John Nagy*

- **Tube:** Canadian Tube Fly Co. FlexTube, 1½ inch
- **Thread:** White 8/0 Uni
- **Rear Hackle:** White schlappen, olive Lady Amherst fibers
- **Body:** Pearl Crystal Chenille, white saddle hackle, chartreuse Krinkle Mirror Flash
- **Front Hackle:** Olive Lady Amherst fibers, white schlappen
- **Sides:** Two grizzly yellow saddles on each side
- **Eyes:** Nickel barbell-style, small or medium

**Notes:** This design shows the interpretation of a shank fly on a tube. The favored color scheme for this pattern is presented, but it can be done in any combination desired. Plenty of movement and flash is present in this design, and it can be used in a wide range of situations.

**(Left to right)** Row 1: Lake Erie Rainbow Smelt; Row 2: Crystal Intruder Tube; Row 3: Temple Dog Tube; Row 4: Glitzy Girl, Flame Fly. JIMMY CHANG PHOTO

Tube patterns can be fished successfully around much of the Great Lakes region. They can be adapted to most streamer patterns and allow adaptability in hooks used. Tube flies can be fished for a wide range of species.
JERRY DARKES PHOTO

## TEMPLE DOG TUBE

*Originated and tied by John Nagy*

- **Tube:** Silver Eumer Teardrop brass tube, large
- **Thread:** White 12/0 Bennechi
- **Tail:** Red or orange Fluoro Fiber
- **First Wing:** Bottom to top, all sparse: silver Angel Hair, white bucktail, silver Fire Fly, white saddle hackle
- **Second Wing:** Bottom to top, all sparse: silver Angel Hair, white Temple Dog fur, silver Fire Fly, white saddle, with blue Krinkle Mirror Flash over top
- **Third Wing:** Kingfisher blue T's Fur or similar, peacock Fire Fly, kingfisher blue teal feather, wrapped
- **Top Wing:** Dark blue T's Fur or similar, peacock Fire Fly, topped with black ostrich herl
- **Eyes (optional):** Jungle cock

**Notes:** The layering of wings in this manner creates a Scandinavian-style pattern with a baitfish silhouette. The white saddle hackle is wrapped in front of the first two wings, then the teal feather is wrapped in front of the third wing. The combination of white/blue/silver is effective on sunny days. This same pattern template can be done in various colors to adjust to weather and water conditions.

## GLITZY GIRL

*Originated and tied by Scott Currie*

- **Tube:** 1-inch small-diameter plastic with junction tube
- **Thread:** Black 6/0 Uni
- **Body:** Silver Holographic Uni Flat Braid tinsel, medium chartreuse cone

- **Wing:** Purple Arctic fox tail or Temple Dog with a mix of purple, blue, and green Flashabou over top, finish with black Arctic fox or Temple Dog
- **Collar:** Black schlappen, then purple
- **Eyes (optional):** Jungle cock
- **Head:** Ultralight Monster Cone

**Notes:** Scott Currie fishes this in the St. Marys and other Ontario rivers for salmon and steelhead. Adding the cone underneath the wing gives a bit of color and weight. The front disc-shape cone creates an extra push of water behind it, adding more movement to the materials as the fly is swinging.

## FLAME FLY

*Originated and tied by Robert Schoeller*

- **Tube:** 13 mm brass Shumakov Skittle Tube with orange junction tube
- **Thread:** Black 16/0 Veevus
- **Wing:** Bottom to top: fluorescent yellow Arctic fox, pearl gold Lite Brite, hot orange Arctic fox, hot orange Lite Brite, finish with fiery brown Arctic fox
- **Throat:** Orange soft hackle
- **Sides:** A few strands of pearl Mirage Flashabou on each side
- **Eyes (optional):** Jungle cock

**Notes:** This pattern is designed for visibility in dirty water. The bottle tube serves as both weight and a body. Material buildup is minimized by using a very thin, strong thread.

# Group 15: Still More Tube Flies

These additional tube designs feature both imitator and attractor patterns. All are open to a wide range of color variation. With all designs, color, movement, and flash trigger fish to hit. In addition to water clarity, water temperature, and weather being influencers, the personal whims of the tier are a major factor in the final fly appearance.

## HOT HEAD TRIPLE TAIL

*Originated and tied by Jeff Liskay*

- **Tube:** 1-inch small-diameter plastic tube with junction tube
- **Thread:** 70-denier UTC, color to match head
- **Tail:** Three schlappen feather tips
- **Body:** UV Polar Chenille
- **Wing:** Mix 3 colors including 1 each of Flashabou, Holographic Flashabou, and Mirage Flashabou
- **Head:** Senyo Laser Dub

**Notes:** Jeff Liskay fishes these under a wide range of water conditions and has taken steelhead across the Great Lakes as well as the Pacific Northwest on this pattern. The use of contrasting colors gives the fly good visibility to fish, and the flash mix gives a unique look. Favorite colors are black feathers/chartreuse or orange head, purple feathers/chartreuse or pink head, and olive feathers/orange head. The flash mix is usually copper Flashabou, opal Mirage Flashabou, and Holographic Flashabou to match the feather colors.

## RIPPLE ICE CRUSH HANG TUBE

*Originated and tied by Matt Supinski*

- **Tube:** 1½-inch small-diameter plastic tube (junction tube optional)
- **Thread:** Orange 6/0 Uni
- **Tail:** Black rabbit strip with short section of junction tubing tied in
- **Body:** Black rabbit strip
- **Back:** Copper Flashabou, chartreuse Krinkle Mirror Flash
- **Belly:** Copper Flashabou, chartreuse Krinkle Mirror Flash
- **Head:** Pink Ripple Ice Fiber
- **Eyes (optional):** Jungle cock
- **Weight (optional):** Lead barbell

**Notes:** This combination of movement, flash, and color is designed to pull fish from a long distance or have maximum visibility in dirty water. The black rabbit strip at the tail is wrapped for the body. The addition of a junction tube in the tail allows the hook to be set back and secured. In coldwater temps, trout tend to nip the back end of the fly. This gives an increased chance to hook these fish.

Small treble hooks can be added to tubes for light-striking fish. This is often the case in coldwater temperatures. Fish will still hit flies, but their metabolism is slower and the strikes less aggressive.
ROBERT SCHOELLER PHOTO

## HYBRID SCULPIN

*Originated and tied by Nick Pionessa*

- **Tube:** HMH 1-inch copper with junction tube
- **Thread:** Olive 8/0 Uni or similar
- **Wing:** Olive rabbit strip, 4 to 6 strands of gold Holographic Flashabou per side
- **Collar:** Tip-wrapped olive marabou
- **Head:** Olive rabbit fur

**Notes:** While not an exact imitation, this pattern gives a perfect sculpin profile with the marabou adding extra movement. The rabbit fur at the head is spun into a loop and wrapped. This pattern will catch pretty much any gamefish species found in the Great Lakes. You can add brown and black color variations into the mix.

## ICED RABBIT

*Originated and tied by Jerry Darkes*

- **Tube:** 1-inch small-diameter plastic (junction tube optional)
- **Thread:** Black 70-denier UTC
- **Wing:** Rabbit strip with pearl Krinkle Mirror Flash on top
- **Collar:** Tip-wrapped marabou plume
- **Head:** Ice Dub

**Notes:** Similar to Nick Pionessa's previous design, this pattern will catch a wide assortment of fish species

**(Left to right)** Row 1: Hot Head Triple Tail; Row 2: Ripple Ice Crush Hang Tube; Row 3: Hybrid Sculpin, Iced Rabbit; Row 4: Arctic Wiggler—Emerald Shiner, EZ Leech. JIMMY CHANG PHOTO

including migratory trout. A colored junction can be added as a body or the hook set back on a loop. The rabbit can be trimmed to length, if needed, during setup. Colors can be varied as desired for dark-, bright-, or contrast-color schemes. This purple/chartreuse combination has become a favorite of mine.

## ARCTIC WIGGLER—EMERALD SHINER

*Originated and tied by Jerry Darkes*

- **Tube:** Yellow Eumer Ball Tube (junction tube optional)
- **Thread:** Chartreuse 70-denier UTC
- **Tail:** White Arctic fox tail, chartreuse Arctic fox tail, a few strands each of olive Krinkle Mirror Flash and olive Krystal Flash
- **Body:** Olive Estaz
- **Collar:** White schlappen, olive Palmer Chenille
- **Eyes (optional):** Jungle cock

**Notes:** Eumer out of Finland has a complete series of painted brass tubes that were available for a period of time in the United States. These are great tube fly platforms to easily give extra weight and color. Unfortunately, they are not being distributed at the present time, but can be found on some online material sites. The Ball Tube was a favorite. This pattern can be varied in color for most any situation.

## EZ LEECH

*Originated and tied by Jerry Darkes*

- **Tube:** Hot orange Eumer Ball/Body Tube (junction tube optional)
- **Thread:** Black 70-denier UTC
- **Body:** Black Ice Dub or Petite Estaz
- **Wing:** Black rabbit strip
- **Collar:** Black schlappen

**Notes:** This is a simple, easy-to-tie Egg Sucking Leech variation with built-in weight and contrast color. The Ball/Body Tube is a great tying platform that allows pattern creation for a wide range of applications. By varying tube, rabbit, and schlappen colors, plenty of variations can be created.

## Group 16: Peter Humphries Patterns

Originally from the United Kingdom, Peter Humphries lives in western Michigan and is a well-known Spey casting instructor and guide on the Muskegon River. Humphries has extensive experience fishing for Atlantic salmon in the UK and steelhead in British Columbia. He brings that influence and experience to this series of patterns for migratory species of the Great Lakes.

Post-spawn steelhead begin to feed aggressively as they drop back to big water. This fish hit a tube pattern in an emerald shiner color scheme. JERRY DARKES PHOTO

**(Left to right)** Row 1: Big Dog, Cheerleader; Row 2: Baby Dog, Cheerleader; Row 3: Cheerleader, Big Dog.

JIMMY CHANG PHOTO

## BIG DOG (2 COLORS)

*Originated and tied by Peter Humphries*

- **Tube:** Short plastic with colored junction tube
- **Thread:** Black 8/0 Uni or similar
- **Body:** Medium-size cone, slid on tube, held in place by junction tubing
- **Wing:** Three sparse layers of Temple Dog fur or Arctic fox tail, with Flashabou blend in between
- **Collar:** Schlappen
- **Eyes (optional):** Jungle cock

**Notes:** This pattern is similar to the Cheerleader, but without the Monster Cone. It is a bit lighter in weight with a more streamlined shape on the swing. The junction tube comes into play adding additional color.

## CHEERLEADER (3 COLORS)

*Originated and tied by Peter Humphries*

- **Tube:** Short plastic (junction tube optional)
- **Thread:** Black 8/0 Uni or similar
- **Body:** Medium-size cone
- **Wing:** Temple Dog fur or Arctic fox tail, a blend of Flashabou, Temple Dog fur, or Arctic fox tail, sparse Flashabou
- **Collar:** Schlappen

- **Eyes (optional):** Jungle cock
- **Head:** Monster Cone, color as desired

**Notes:** The body cone is slid to the back of the tubing and all materials added in front. This pattern is open to a wide range of color schemes. Humphries favors olive, yellow, and chartreuse combinations with copper and kelly green flash for the Muskegon's normally clear tannic waters. Black and blue with silver and blue flash works in cold water. If the junction tube is eliminated, the hook is set on a loop the desired distance back under the wing.

## BABY DOG

*Originated and tied by Peter Humphries*

- **Tube:** Short plastic with colored junction tube
- **Body:** Small cone
- **Thread:** Black 8/0 Uni or similar
- **Wing:** Single color of Temple Dog fur or Arctic fox tail, with a few strands of Flashabou
- **Collar:** Schlappen
- **Eyes (optional):** Jungle cock

**Notes:** This is a scaled-down version of the Big Dog—smaller in size with less material for low, clear water and spooky fish. The junction tube plays a significant role adding color to the fly.

# Group 17: Low Water and Trout Spey

This grouping of patterns has crossover application to target both migratory trout and resident trout. In low, clear conditions, Great Lakes steelhead may refuse or even run from standard swing designs. Downsized patterns in natural colors can often tempt these fish. Resident fish may also respond to these designs and others more imitative of the natural food forms they are used to.

## MINI INTRUDER

*Originated and tied by Greg Senyo*

- **Shank:** 23 mm Senyo Micro Shank
- **Thread:** Brown 70-denier UTC
- **Hook Loop:** 30 lb. braid
- **Rear Body:** 3D everglades EP Fibers, tan Lady Amherst fibers, natural ostrich plume fibers
- **Center:** Copper Mini Flat Braid
- **Front Body:** 3D everglades EP Fibers, 2 strands of opal mirage Lateral Scale, tan Lady Amherst fibers, natural ostrich plume fibers
- **Eyes (optional):** Jungle cock
- **Hook:** #4 Aqua Talon

**Notes:** In this color scheme, a small sculpin, crayfish, darker baitfish, or possibly a Hex nymph is imitated. This pattern has plenty of life to it and can be both swung and stripped. Colors can be varied as wanted—muted tones are normally used. For both bodies, the EP Fibers are tied down in a bunch and trimmed short.

## MICRO SPEY FLY

*Originated and tied by Greg Senyo*

- **Shank:** 17 mm Senyo Micro Shank
- **Thread:** Brown 70-denier UTC
- **Hook Loop:** 30 lb. braid
- **Hook:** #4 Aqua Talon
- **Body:** Orange Mini Flat Braid, sparse 3D everglades EP Fibers
- **Topping:** Black-barred UV Senyo Predator Wrap fibers, sparse and short
- **Collar:** Mallard flank feather dyed tan
- **Eyes (optional):** Jungle cock

**Notes:** This color scheme is a small variation of the previous pattern. There is a hint of brighter color and a bit of UV for extra attraction. Fish it down and across as a traditional wet fly. Again, this can also be done in additional muted color tones such as olive or gray.

**(Left to right)** Row 1: Mini Intruder, Micro Spey Fly; Row 2: Lady Muraski, Blue Moon Tube; Row 3: Wolverine, The Ghost Who Walks. JIMMY CHANG PHOTO

In low water, downsizing patterns can often tempt reluctant steelhead to strike. More natural colors are generally most effective. The type of tip and even the weight of tippet will likely also need to be adjusted.
ROBERT SCHOELLER PHOTO

## LADY MURASKI

*Originated and tied by Kim Benbow*

- **Shank:** 17 mm Senyo Micro Shank
- **Thread:** Black 8/0 Veevus
- **Hook Loop:** .018-inch nylon coated wire
- **Hook:** #4-6 Daiichi Octopus
- **Body:** Pink Ice Chenille
- **Eyes:** Black bead chain, small
- **Underwing:** White Arctic fox tail
- **Wing:** Purple Arctic fox tail with black Arctic fox tail over top, a single strand of pearl Krystal Flash on each side
- **Collar:** Purple guinea
- **Head:** Pink 8/0 Veevus

**Notes:** Once again, this gives crossover use to both resident and migratory trout. This pattern has a great profile in the water with lots of movement and a bit of flash. Plenty of color options, but this is a favored combination. The Arctic fox for the underwing is reverse-tied to keep the wing from collapsing. Most fur, natural, and synthetic hair materials can be reverse-tied to help them hold their shape.

## BLUE MOON TUBE

*Originated and tied by Kim Benbow*

- **Tube:** Chartreuse ¼-inch small-diameter plastic
- **Thread:** Black 8/0 Veevus
- **Tag:** Medium oval silver tinsel
- **Body:** Neon chartreuse floss and black floss, chartreuse Estaz
- **Rib:** Medium oval silver tinsel
- **Wing:** Turkey wing fibers, winter-run purple New Age Holo Flash, a few strands of gold Holo Flash
- **Collar 1:** A wrap of black Mirror Flash, natural teal flank in front
- **Collar 2:** Tip-wrapped peacock blue marabou, blue Lady Amherst fibers, purple guinea wrapped

**Notes:** This pattern easily crosses over to use for migratory trout. Kim Benbow has found it to be productive for wintertime brown trout in Michigan rivers. Be sure that you are fishing an open area during the winter!

## WOLVERINE

*Originated and tied by Kim Benbow*

- **Hook:** #9 Alec Jackson Steelhead Iron
- **Thread:** Black 8/0 Uni
- **Tag:** Small oval silver tinsel, yellow floss
- **Tail:** Golden pheasant crest feather
- **Body:** Black floss ribbed with medium oval silver tinsel
- **Rib:** Medium oval silver tinsel
- **Hackle:** Kingfisher blue saddle
- **Wing:** Gray squirrel

**Notes:** This is a variation of the Blue Charm Atlantic salmon fly. It delivers a traditional look in a package suited for trout. Trout, both migratory and resident, sometimes find blue irresistible.

## THE GHOST WHO WALKS

*Originated and tied by Kim Benbow*

- **Hook:** #18 Daiichi Klinkhammer Emerger Hook
- **Thread:** Black 8/0 Uni
- **Body:** Dark purple floss
- **Rib:** Fine silver tinsel
- **Thorax:** Peacock herl
- **Collar:** English grouse, wrapped

**Notes:** This a true soft-hackle pattern. It is fished across and down as a traditional wet fly. Benbow has found this effective on the Mason tract of Michigan's AuSable River, and it will catch stream trout everywhere.

# Group 18: More Low Water and Trout Spey

Ryan Ratliff is a talented tier who works at Mad River Outfitters in Columbus, Ohio. Here are additional patterns that can be used for several different applications. He fishes these mainly for trout, but they will also catch steelhead and smallmouth.

The Sunken Fox series of patterns shows how various minor adjustments in material and color can make a significant change to a fly. The main template does not change, but appearance varies noticeably.

## CC SHINER TUBE

*Originated and tied by Ryan Ratliff*

- **Tube:** 1-inch small-diameter plastic tube with junction tube
- **Thread:** White 70-denier UTC
- **Rear Section:** Dubbed ball of pearl Ice Dub, pearl EP Sparkle Brush, teal or mallard flank
- **Center Section:** Pearl Ice Dub
- **Front Section:** Pearl EP Sparkle Brush
- **Eyes (optional):** Jungle cock, real or imitation
- **Head:** Pearl Ice Dub and white Senyo Laser Dub, 50/50 mix

**Notes:** Intruder-style designs adapt well to being tied on tubes, as seen here. Size can be adjusted by the length of the body tube. This color scheme is for a bright baitfish, but can be varied as desired.

## CC SHINER SHANK

*Originated and tied by Ryan Ratliff*

- **Shank:** 23 mm Senyo Micro Shank
- **Thread:** White 70-denier UTC
- **Hook Loop:** Senyo Intruder Wire, thin
- **Hook:** #8 Daiichi 2553
- **Rear Section:** Small, barbell-style weight, dubbed pearl Ice Dub, mallard flank feather
- **Center Section:** Pearl Ice Dub
- **Front Section:** Mallard flank, pearl EP Sparkle Brush
- **Head:** Pearl Ice Dub, white Senyo Laser Dub, 50/50 mix

**Notes:** Here is the shank variation of the previous pattern. Most streamer designs can be adapted to tying on both a shank or tube platform. Either style helps eliminate the leverage advantage given to the fish by a long-shank hook design. Eyes are optional.

## BUCK NASTY (TUBE VERSION)

*Originated and tied by Ryan Ratliff*

- **Tube:** HMH 1-inch rigid plastic with junction tube
- **Thread:** Brown 70-denier UTC
- **Rear Section:** Yellow bucktail kept sparse, copper EP Sparkle Brush fibers, pheasant rump feather
- **Center:** Yellow Mini Flat Braid or Senyo Laser Dub
- **Front Section:** Dubbed ball of brown Angora goat, yellow bucktail, copper EP Sparkle Brush
- **Collar:** Tip-wrapped MFC black-barred brown marabou

**Notes:** This pattern imitates any number of darker baitfish. It can also be adapted to a shank quite easily. The yellow bucktail on both sections is reverse-tied to keep a wider profile and help support the marabou. Barred marabou plumes are now available in a full range of sizes. They can be used to give a more lifelike appearance in many patterns.

## SUNKEN FOX—ALL BLACK

*Originated and tied by Ryan Ratliff*

- **Hook:** #4-8 Daiichi 2161
- **Thread:** Black 70-denier UTC
- **Body:** Silver and blue UTC Brassie wire
- **Thorax:** Peacock Ice Dub, black ½-inch Chocklett's Body Tubing
- **Wing/Belly:** Black Arctic fox tail fur, black EP Sparkle Brush fibers
- **Collar:** Black schlappen

**Notes:** This pattern functions as an oversized soft hackle. Reverse-tie the fox fur to keep shape and schlappen from completely collapsing due to the pressure of the current. The wire body allows it to sink and hold a bit of depth on the swing.

**(Left to right)** Row 1: CC Shiner Tube, CC Shiner Shank; Row 2: Buck Nasty (Tube Version); Row 3: Sunken Fox (3 variations); Row 4: Sunken Fox—Baitfish. JIMMY CHANG PHOTO

Downsizing standard patterns is a key technique for low-water steelhead. These patterns can also be used to target regular stream trout in most situations. ROBERT SCHOELLER PHOTO

## SUNKEN FOX—BLACK AND WHITE

*Originated and tied by Ryan Ratliff*

- **Hook:** #4-8 Daiichi 2161
- **Thread:** Black 70-denier UTC
- **Body:** Silver and black UTC Brassie wire
- **Thorax:** Peacock Ice Dub, black ⅛-inch Chocklett's Body Tubing
- **Wing/Belly:** Black Arctic fox, black EP Sparkle Brush fibers
- **Collar:** Natural guinea feather, wrapped

**Notes:** Again, the Arctic fox is reverse-tied for extra support. The use of the guinea feather gives this fly a lot more "pop" than the all-black version. The use of dyed guinea allows a number of other color schemes to be created.

## SUNKEN FOX—OLIVE

*Originated and tied by Ryan Ratliff*

- **Hook:** #4-8 Daiichi 2161
- **Thread:** White 70-denier UTC
- **Body:** Flat silver tinsel
- **Rib:** Small oval gold tinsel
- **Thorax:** Cream Angora goat
- **Wing/Belly:** Olive Arctic fox

**Notes:** This version of the Sunken Fox uses shorter guard hairs and a bit more reverse-tied Arctic fox underfur to function as "hackle." It can imitate baitfish fry or a large, emerging insect in this color scheme.

## SUNKEN FOX—BAITFISH

*Originated and tied by Ryan Ratliff*

- **Hook:** #4-8 Daichii 2161
- **Thread:** White 70-denier UTC
- **Body:** Silver tinsel
- **Rib:** Small oval gold tinsel, fine olive wire
- **Thorax:** Cream Angora goat
- **Wing/Belly:** White Arctic fox tail
- **Collar:** Mallard or teal flank feather

**Notes:** Again, reverse-tie the Arctic fox. This version gives an example of how ribbing can be used to accent body color, and how the barred feather color adds a natural, lifelike look of spotting or bars on a small baitfish.

## Group 19: Surface Patterns

The main strains of migratory trout in the Great Lakes are winter-run, spring spawners. Because of this, surface opportunities are at a minimum. There are short time periods in both the fall and spring when some steelhead can be tempted to take a fly on the surface, but it would be hard to predict this with any dependability.

There are some summer-run steelhead present, and these will take a surface pattern under the right conditions. This is a bit more predictable, but the locations are very limited. Bottom line: Catching a Great Lakes steelhead on a surface fly is not a regular occurrence, but if you are willing to put in the time, it can be accomplished.

**(Left to right)** Row 1: Orange Belly Skater; Row 2: October Caddis, Orange Drew Dog; Row 3: Tarantula Mysis; Row 4: Tribulator. JIMMY CHANG PHOTO

End of the day on a Great Lakes creek mouth. Low-light conditions are the best times to explore these areas as fish move in closer to feed. At times they may be in ankle-deep water sitting in the current. JEFF LISKAY PHOTO

## ORANGE BELLY SKATER

*Originated and tied by Rick Kustich*

- **Tube:** 1-inch plastic with diameter that will hold the hook eye or knot, hole added to each side at front of tube so it can be skated from the side
- **Thread:** Black 8/0 Uni
- **Tail:** Black Arctic fox tail
- **Body:** Dubbed orange Angora goat
- **Collar:** Orange schlappen
- **Back:** Two sections of 2 mm black foam

**Notes:** Rick Kustich has had some success skating for steelhead on Ontario's Grand River in the early fall for fresh-run fish. This system has natural, stream-bred fish that spend a minimum of a year in the rivers before dropping to Lake Erie. There is abundant insect life, and these fish learn to feed on the surface and retain this memory. It is also possible to tempt springtime, drop-back steelhead to take a surface pattern or a fly fished "damp," or just under the surface.

## OCTOBER CADDIS

*Originated and tied by Rick Kustich*

- **Hook:** #6 Daiichi 2421
- **Thread:** Black 8/0
- **Body:** Orange Ice Dub, grizzly dry fly hackle
- **Wing/Head:** Deer body hair

**Notes:** This gives a natural imitative pattern to attract steelhead to the surface. *Pycnopsyche* species caddis are present across the Great Lakes region. Also referred to as the Great Brown Autumn Sedge, they hatch from mid-July through October. This pattern can trigger a natal reaction from a stream-bred fish or, at times, influence a surface take from a stocked fish.

## ORANGE DREW DOG

*Originated and tied by Matt Supinski*

- **Hook:** #6-10 Daiichi 1120
- **Thread:** White 8/0
- **Body:** Orange Ice Dub
- **Back:** Orange foam strip, white hackle
- **Legs:** Orange black-barred Nymph Legs
- **Hackle:** White saddle

**Notes:** This terrestrial-like pattern is effective for summer-run steelhead found in the St. Joseph River. Matt Supinski has spent many years guiding this system. It seems counterintuitive to use a heavy-wire hook for a dry fly. However, it is needed to avoid springing the small hook open on hard-fighting fish.

## TARANTULA MYSIS

*Originated and tied by Matt Supinski*

- **Hook:** #8-10 Daiichi 1120 or similar
- **Thread:** Orange 8/0
- **Tail/Abdomen:** Pearl Midge Diamond Braid, wrapped as an extended body
- **Thorax:** Pearl Ice Dub, 3 sets of white Grizzly Micro Legs
- **Back:** Clear Senyo Barred Predator Wrap, pulled over thorax and trimmed to extend a bit past hook eye
- **Eyes:** Black mono, extra-small

**Notes:** This is another design to target St. Joe summer-run steelhead. These fish feed on mysis shrimp while in Lake Michigan. This fly is designed as a reminder of that instinctive behavior. Dress the fly with floatant before fishing it. This can also be fished just below the surface and take fish.

## TRIBULATOR

*Originated and tied by Jerry Darkes*

- **Hook:** #6-8 Daiichi 2421 Low Water Salmon
- **Thread:** Black 70-denier UTC
- **Tail:** Moose body hair
- **Wing:** A single post of chartreuse calf body hair or similar
- **Body:** Stiff, black dry fly hackle, width of hook gap to wing
- **Rib:** Fine silver wire
- **Hackle:** Stiff, black dry fly hackle, sized normally in front of wing

**Notes:** This pattern can be dead-drifted and then skated or fished damp on the swing. It has accounted for a number of Lake Erie rainbows over the years and has also been effective in British Columbia. I also tie this with grizzly hackle.

This migratory rainbow took an all-black foam skater. Taking Great Lakes steelhead on the surface usually requires a lot of persistence. As the majority of fish are winter-run, there are minimal opportunities to find them looking at the surface. JEFF LISKAY PHOTO

The muskellunge is the apex predator in most situations around the Great Lakes and Midwest. They respond well to flies and are present across the region in a wide range of waters, from inland rivers and creeks, to large impoundments, to the big water of the Great Lakes. RICK KUSTICH PHOTO

# Apex Predator Patterns

**7**

## INTRODUCTION

An apex predator is also called the alpha predator. By definition, it is the top organism of the food chain in a given system. In freshwater environments this can be occupied by several different fish species depending on time of year, location, and other factors. It is also possible that several species may fill this role.

Across most of the Midwest and Great Lakes, the muskellunge is considered the ultimate apex predator where present. In some instances, this badge may be given to the northern pike or possibly even largemouth bass. Both of these species assume the role quite well.

In coldwater situations, where trout are the primary species, brown trout usually take the alpha predator position. If brown trout are not present, it may be steelhead or even chinook salmon that take this status. Again, much of this is dependent on location.

Fly patterns targeting the top of the food chain are almost always streamers of some sort. As we have seen, these designs may imitate a wide range of food forms or just trigger strikes by movement, color, and flash. They are usually larger flies that have active movement imparted by the angler, with larger fish the primary target.

Apex patterns are oversized compared to standard flies, to target the largest fish. Size can vary depending on time of year. In another version of "match the hatch," anglers look to imitate various baitfish and may increase fly size through the season as the forage species increase in size. The only real limitation on fly size is how big we can effectively cast for any period of time on the equipment we have.

Most of these flies require a minimum 8-weight outfit to cast and work properly. More often a 9-weight or a 10-weight will be required. Remember, the mass of the fly line needs to overcome the mass and air resistance of the fly in order to cast. Sinking-head lines are employed to hold the fly at depth with a fast retrieve. These outfits require a bit of strength conditioning in order to cast them for an extended period of time.

Flies for top-level predators should correspond with the size of prey. This is an important factor, especially progressing through summer into fall when prey size is at its largest. It is unlikely one could tie a fly too big for use. The limiting factor is the ability to cast it.
JON RAY PHOTO

The ultimate reward for this work is a trophy-size fish. For most of us it will be either a muskie or a brown trout. One is native to the region while the other is an introduced species. Success is the culmination of what is normally a long process of education, preparation, and practice. The process is often similar to taking a big game animal, except here we have the option to release our trophy after it has been captured.

# Group 1: Mixed Mega Streamers

These patterns can be used to target most any larger, freshwater species. Several of them have traceable saltwater roots, mainly to the Northeast striper fishery. Fishing any big body of water in the Midwest for larger species has a saltwater feel to it. Similar equipment is often used and both sight-fishing as well as blind casting may be involved.

## GREAT LAKES DECEIVER

*Originated and tied by Eli Berant*

- **Hook:** #3/0 Daiichi 2546
- **Thread:** 140-denier UTC, to match color scheme
- **Tail:** Four to six schlappen feathers
- **Back/Belly:** Three to four sets of bucktail
- **Sides:** Mix of Flashabou and Krystal Flash on each side
- **Eyes:** 7 mm 3D

**Notes:** Eli Berant of greatlakesfly.com has been tying this pattern for many years. The chartreuse/white as pictured is the most popular combination, but can be varied as needed. This pattern has taken everything from river brown trout to muskie. The sets of bucktail for the back and belly are all reverse-tied for maximum action and to maintain a large profile.

## ELECTRIC YELLOW

*Originated and tied by Scott Currie*

- **Hook:** #4/0 TMC 800 SP
- **Thread:** Clear monofilament
- **Belly:** White SF Blend
- **Back:** Chartreuse SF Blend
- **Gills:** Hot orange Fluoro Fiber
- **Eyes:** 10 mm 3D

**Notes:** Despite its large profile, this pattern is easy to cast as the materials do not hold much water, and it condenses in size when wet. There is plenty of movement here with a visible gill and a large, predator-attracting eye.

## ANGEL HAIR BAITFISH

*Originated and tied by Scott Currie*

- **Hook:** #4/0 TMC 100 SP
- **Thread:** Monofilament
- **Belly:** White Slinky Fiber, pearl Flashabou
- **Sides:** Olive Angel Hair
- **Back:** Black Slinky Fiber
- **Gills:** Hot orange Fluoro Fiber
- **Eyes:** 10 mm 3D

**Notes:** The visible gill on any of these patterns helps to simulate an injured baitfish. Combined with an erratic retrieve, these features along with ample flash give the illusion of a crippled fish turning on its side. Currie fishes these two patterns around his home waters in Ontario for pike and muskie.

## GRAPEFRUIT HOLLOW FLY

*Originated and tied by Pat Kelly*

- **Hook:** #4/0 Gamakatsu SL12S
- **Thread:** Black or white 100-denier GSP
- **Tail:** White flatwing rooster saddles, pearl Lateral Scale, and opal Mirage Flashabou
- **Body:** Mix of white, pastel pink, fluorescent yellow, pastel pink, silver holographic EP Sparkle Fiber, tied in with each color change

**Notes:** Hollow-tied bucktail differs from a standard reverse-tie in that the tip ends are evened before tying in. This allows the tier to make a uniform taper as the bunches are tied in surrounding the hook. Also, the hair bunches are kept sparse, giving the fly a translucent look and the illusion of bulk. Despite appearing bulky, these patterns have minimal material and are easy to cast.

## HOLLOW DECEIVER

*Originated and tied by Pat Kelly*

- **Hook:** #4/0-1 Partridge Universal Predator
- **Thread:** Black or white 100-denier GSP
- **Tail:** White flatwing rooster saddles
- **Body:** White bucktail, white bucktail with silver Holographic Flashabou, white bucktail with chartreuse grizzly Flashabou, orange bucktail, olive bucktail with opal Mirage Flashabou on top
- **Lateral Line:** Grizzly saddle

**Notes:** The sparse, hollow-tie technique with bucktail allows for an interesting blending of colors. The grizzly saddle is put in on each side after the second bucktail bunch. Pat Kelly is a master of this technique that was originated by saltwater guru Bob Popovics.

**(Left to right)** Row 1: Great Lakes Deceiver, Electric Yellow, Angel Hair Baitfish; Row 2: Grapefruit Hollow Fly, Hollow Deceiver; Row 3: Pike Pirate, Deep Creeper. JIMMY CHANG PHOTO

## PIKE PIRATE

*Originated and tied by Steve Wascher*

- **Hook:** #3/0 Daiichi 2546 or similar
- **Thread:** Red 140-denier UTC
- **Tail:** White bucktail, silver Krystal Flash
- **Body:** Silver holographic EP Sparkle Brush
- **Topping:** White Arctic fox tail fur, red Arctic fox tail fur in front
- **Belly:** White Arctic fox tail fur
- **Sides:** White Lady Amherst tippet feather
- **Eyes (optional):** Jungle cock or 3D

**Notes:** The use of the brush for the body of this fly helps give it a better 3D silhouette and supports the materials in front. The Lady Amherst feather gives a good imitation of a gill cover. This can be downsized a bit, and it makes a good pattern for largemouth bass. This is a favored color for pike, but can be varied as desired.

## DEEP CREEPER

*Originated and tied by Jerry Darkes*

- **Hook:** #4/0-2/0 Gamakatsu Weedless Worm Hook
- **Thread:** 140-denier UTC, color to match fly
- **Tail:** Arctic fox tail fur
- **Body:** Estaz, then 2 sets of rubber legs on each side
- **Eyes:** Barbell-style, large
- **Back:** Magnum rabbit strip, Zonker-style

**Notes:** This pattern is a takeoff on an old Russ Maddin design. It has taken a number of muskie, some big pike, and largemouth bass. Using the premade weedless hook is strictly a convenience factor. This has been a productive color, but combinations are endless.

## Group 2: More Mega Streamers

Size increases as we get into this grouping. I am not sure how to specifically define a "mega streamer." I would say anything starting in the 8-inch-long range. These patterns go a step further, getting into the 10-inch-long category. Several also have larger rattles as part of their makeup.

All of this becomes important when considering how to efficiently cast flies like this, and how to do it for an extended period of time. Material selection becomes a factor as to the amount of water-retaining material that can be incorporated into the design. A balance needs to be struck with these various components as to how practical the pattern really is to use.

**(Left to right)** Row 1: Foosa, Dahlberg Mega Diver; Row 2: Jared's Outlaw; Row 3: Figure 8; Row 4: CAT 5.

JIMMY CHANG PHOTO

## FOOSA

*Originated and tied by Eli Berant*

- **Hook:** #4/0 Ahrex Predator Stinger
- **Thread:** 210-denier UTC, to match fly color
- **Tail:** Six saddle hackles, single color or mixed, Finn raccoon, opal Mirage Flashabou
- **Body:** 5 mm glass rattle, cover with Estaz
- **Collar:** Bucktail
- **Sides:** Crystal Mirror Splash, red Holographic Flashabou
- **Head:** Finn raccoon with underfur
- **Eyes:** 10 mm 3D

**Notes:** This pattern has some bulk but condenses well when wet. It has a great swimming profile in the water. Reverse-tie the bucktail. This is a favored attractor color scheme that has proven productive. Black/red head, white/red head, and olive/orange head are all good, too.

**Hint:** Adding barred coloring can completely change the look on many solid-colored patterns. Do this with a Sharpie or other permanent marker and use more than just black. Brown, olive, and even some brighter colors can make a big difference.

## DAHLBERG MEGA DIVER

*Originated by Larry Dahlberg, tied by Jerry Darkes*

- **Hook:** #3/0-5/0 Gamakatsu Weedless Worm Hook
- **Thread:** 140- or 210-denier UTC, color to match head
- **Tail:** Big Fly Fiber, Flashabou
- **Sides:** Grizzly saddles
- **Collar:** Deer belly hair
- **Head:** Deer belly hair

**Notes:** This was one of the original toothy-critter patterns from Larry Dahlberg. It seems odd that it has fallen out of favor in recent years, as it is still a great fish-catching design. Fished on a sinking-head line, it is deadly. It is maybe the easiest of these patterns to cast, swims wonderfully, and is open to a wide range of color interpretation. The weedless worm hook again is a convenience if you don't want to build your own weedguard. Be sure to include the curly ends of the Big Fly Fiber when you construct the fly. Check out the updated Big Fly Fiber with Curl, which has color blends and flash built in!

## JARED'S OUTLAW

*Originated by Jared Ehlers, tied by Rainy's Flies*

- **Hook:** #3/0 Gamakatsu SP113L3H
- **Thread:** Black or red 210-denier UTC
- **Tail:** 8-inch length of Holographic Flashabou in a bunch
- **Back/Belly:** 3-inch x ½-inch strip of Extra Select Craft Fur
- **Sides:** One large grizzly rooster hackle on each side
- **Collar:** Enhancer Wrap or Senyo Predator Wrap
- **Throat:** Marabou
- **Eyes:** 10 mm 3D

**Notes:** A Wisconsin native, Jared Ehlers guided for giant Alaskan pike for a number of years and is an expert on toothy critters. This pattern was designed for muskie and has plenty of application across the Great Lakes region and beyond. Again, we see minimal water retention with these materials, minimizing casting difficulty. Black/orange as shown, yellow/olive, and purple are his go-to colors. Many other variations can be created.

## FIGURE 8

*Originated by Bill Sherer, tied by Pacific Fly Group*

- **Hook:** #4/0-2/0 Daiichi 2461
- **Weedguard:** Preformed .030-inch-diameter nylon-coated wire (available from wetieit.com)
- **Tail:** Bucktail, Krystal Flash over top
- **Body:** UV Polar Chenille
- **Wing:** Icelandic Sheep, Krystal Flash, Holographic Flashabou
- **Belly:** Bucktail
- **Back:** Bucktail with Krystal Flash over top
- **Eyes:** 3D

**Notes:** This pattern has been around for a long time and updated several times. It has probably caught more toothy critters than almost any other fly. The use of the Icelandic Sheep gives length and great movement, but compresses down to nothing when casting. The fire tiger/perch color is a favorite, but can be varied as desired. The eyes are set in Clear Cure Goo. Use several layers to secure the eyes and cover the thread.

## CAT 5

*Originated and tied by Eli Berant*

- **Front Hook:** #4/0 Gamakatsu SL12S
- **Rear Hook:** #3/0 Gamakatsu Round Bend Worm Hook
- **Thread:** 210-denier UTC, to match fly
- **Connector:** .020-inch-diameter nylon-coated wire with four 8mm beads
- **Rear Body:** Six schlappen feathers, then 3 sections of bucktail with Krystal Flash, pearl Flashabou at front
- **Front Body:** Three sections of bucktail with Krystal Flash, pearl Flashabou
- **Eyes:** 10 mm 3D

**Notes:** This pattern is a great choice for the largest of predators. Be advised that it becomes more difficult to cast when a big, articulated, double-hook pattern is used. This is a true 10-weight fly that requires at least a 450-grain line to carry it. Learning the technique of water-hauling to cast larger flies like this is a great tool to add to your bag of casting tricks. The perch pattern shown here is a primary color, but can be varied as needed. All the bucktail sections are reverse-tied.

## Group 3: Additional Mega Streamers

This is another grouping of flies of different design concept, but similar application. The color combinations pictured feature mainly yellows and browns with lots of grizzly saddles and flash. These can imitate various sucker species, smallmouth bass, and perch. All become fair game as food for marauding muskies, especially in late season.

(**Top to bottom**) Steve's Esox Muddler, Double Optic Minnow, Double Nickel. JIMMY CHANG PHOTO

### STEVE'S ESOX MUDDLER

*Originated and tied by Steve Wascher*

- **Hook:** #4/0 Partridge Absolute Predator
- **Thread:** White or black 100-denier GSP
- **Tail:** Mix of brown and yellow EP 3D Minnow Fiber, gold and bronze Flashabou, 2 each yellow and grizzly brown saddles, peacock Angel Hair on top, yellow Angel Hair on bottom
- **Belly:** Brown bucktail
- **Back:** Cream or yellow bucktail
- **Pectoral Fins:** Three ringneck pheasant body feathers on each side
- **Collar/Head:** Mix of yellow and brown shades of deer belly hair
- **Eyes:** 7 mm doll eyes

**Notes:** This pattern highlights Steve Wascher's deer hair skills and practical fly design. The bucktail is reverse-tied, while the deer hair is stacked, packed, and trimmed into the rounded shape. This pattern is very lightweight, but does incorporate some air resistance that may affect casting. The lightweight hook helps to reduce weight, but will still effectively hook and hold large predators.

Most anglers carry several primary color schemes in mega streamers. Favorite colors can vary depending on factors such as water color, time of year, water temperature, and more. A bit of research on the area you plan to fish can help you narrow down your selection and increase your odds of success. JON RAY PHOTO

## DOUBLE OPTIC MINNOW

*Originated by Brad Bohen, tied by Chris Willen*

- **Rear Hook:** #2/0 Gamakatsu B10S
- **Front Hook:** #4/0 Gamakatsu Heavy Wire Worm Hook
- **Thread (rear hook):** Red 140-denier UTC
- **Thread (front hook):** Black 210-denier UTC
- **Connector:** .020-inch-diameter nylon-coated wire with four 8 mm 3D beads
- **Rear Body:** White bucktail, mix of pearl, black, and gold Holograhic Flashabou, add 3 yellow grizzly saddles per side, brown bucktail
- **Front Body:** Three sections of bucktail in brown, white, brown, one yellow grizzly saddle between second and third bucktail section
- **Head:** Copper/gold Sparkle Fibers
- **Eyes:** 12 mm 3D

**Notes:** Wisconsin guide/angler Brad Bohen introduced this design a number of years ago. All the bucktail is reverse-tied, which helps add the illusion of bulk without the need for a lot of extra material. Adding saddles and flash outside the reverse-tied sections enhances the movement of these materials. Coat the eyes with a UV cure such as Clear Cure Goo.

## DOUBLE NICKEL

*Originated and tied by Chris Willen*

- **Rear Hook:** #3/0 Gamakatsu Heavy Worm Hook
- **Front Hook:** #4/0 Gamakatsu Heavy Worm Hook
- **Thread:** White or black 150-denier GSP
- **Connector:** .020-inch-diameter nylon-coated wire
- **Rear Body:** White bucktail, black Holographic Flashabou, 3 yellow grizzly saddles per side with mix of black Holographic Flashabou, opal Mirage Flashabou, and pearl Krystal Flash, white bucktail, finish with yellow reverse-tied bucktail, single yellow grizzly saddle per side
- **Front Body:** Two sections of white bucktail, black Holographic Flashabou, pearl Krystal Flash and 2 yellow grizzly saddles per side, yellow bucktail, black Holographic Flashabou
- **Head:** Ends of final bucktail bunch, alternating sections of white, yellow, and black deer belly hair
- **Eyes:** Aluminum Deep Sea Eyes, large, added between deer belly hair sections

**Notes:** Chris Willen is a full-time guide for muskie and smallmouth bass. Based in Illinois, he covers a significant part of the Midwest. As with all these patterns, the bucktail sections are reverse-tied and the deer hair at the head is stacked, packed, and trimmed. This is Willen's signature pattern and can be done as shown, with additional color schemes using white, black, chartreuse, rust, and olive as base colors. He will also reduce the size for smallmouth, and has found this to be an effective trout streamer in smaller sizes, too.

## Group 4: Even More Mega Streamers

Here are a couple additional patterns that approach one foot in length. These are single-hook designs making them a bit easier to cast. Muskie, in particular, often "t-bone" a fly, hitting it cross-ways at the head, minimizing the need for a trailer or stinger hook. Adding the extra hook may possibly result in hooking an additional fish or two over a period of time. The drawback is the extra time and materials need in construction along with the extra weight added when casting.

(**Top to bottom**) Optimus Swine, Fauxford JIMMY CHANG PHOTO

### OPTIMUS SWINE

*Originated and tied by Eli Berant*

- **Hook:** #5/0 Gamakatsu Spinnerbait
- **Thread:** White or black 100-denier GSP
- **Rattle:** Plastic jig rattle on a rubber arm
- **Tail:** Rattle, Syn Yak with grizzly saddles on each side, Holographic Flashabou, Syn Yak, Holographic Flashabou
- **Body:** Chartreuse Rainy's popper head reversed, alternating 4 bunches of bucktail on top, 3 bunches of bucktail on bottom
- **Sides:** Holographic Flashabou, Crystal Mirror Splash
- **Head:** Senyo Laser Dub
- **Eyes:** 12 mm 3D

**Notes:** This is a proven pattern for the largest toothy critters. The fire tiger pattern shown can be easily interpreted and doesn't have to be an exact match to be successful. The chartreuse Rainy's popper head is pushed back and secured over the tail thread with Loctite gel. *Do not* reverse-tie the bucktail this time. The eyes are attached with Loctite gel. Black/red, brown/orange (sucker color), and olive/orange (perch color) are all good colors. Berant also scales this pattern down to a #2/0 for bass.

# FAUXFORD

*Originated and tied by Brian Smolinski*

- **Hook:** #4/0 Gamakatsu Heavy Worm Hook or similar
- **Thread:** Fluorescent orange 140-denier UTC
- **Tail:** White bucktail
- **Body:** Cream Misfit Wampa Hair, mixed gold, crawdad, and cranberry Holographic and Magnum Holographic Flashabou
- **Sides:** Two grizzly saddles on each side
- **Collar:** Red Icelandic Pony or Snow Runner
- **Head:** Burnt orange Extra Select Craft Fur

**Notes:** Reverse-tie the bucktail around the shank. The Craft Fur is spun similar to deer hair at the head, which is a rarely seen, unique way to work the Craft Fur. This pattern really comes to life in the water. Despite the massive 3D profile, there is very little water weight. No matter what angle it is seen from, there is visible bulk to the body. This is another pattern that is easily scaled down in size for other applications.

Capt. Brad Petzke enjoying a rare day off in the fall. Based in Michigan's Upper Peninsula, Petzke favors flies in orange and a contrasting dark color with plenty of gold flash mixed in. This is a proven combination for use in the area's tannic-colored waters. JERRY DARKES PHOTO

## Group 5: More Pat Ehlers Patterns

Pat Ehlers has a few more additions here in the Apex Predator lineup. These target mainly toothy critters—especially pike, but also catch muskie, and even largemouth bass. They are moderately sized and can be handled on an 8- or 9-weight outfit.

**(Left to right)** Row 1: Midnight Sun (2 colors); Row 2: Gator Done (2 colors). JIMMY CHANG PHOTO

### MIDNIGHT SUN (2 COLORS)

*Originated by Pat Ehlers, tied by Rainy's Flies*

- **Hook:** #3/0 Gamakatsu SP113L3H
- **Thread:** Red 140-denier UTC
- **Back:** Magnum rabbit strip, Krinkle Mirror Flash
- **Collar:** Egg yarn or similar type material
- **Eyes:** 6 mm 3D

**Notes:** This pattern was developed at Midnight Sun Trophy Pike Adventures in Alaska for the huge, 50-plus-inch northerns there. The eyes are set and then the entire head is coated with Clear Cure Goo or other UV cure material. The egg yarn is tied around the hook shank, extending past the hook bend; it sticks to fish teeth like Velcro, making it hard for the fly to be ejected. Ehlers's favorite colors are shown, but there are endless combinations that can be created. This pattern can be scaled up to #5/0 and also smaller as needed.

### GATOR DONE (2 COLORS)

*Originated by Pat Ehlers, tied by Rainy's Flies*

- **Hook:** #3/0 Gamakatsu SP113L3H or similar
- **Thread:** Red 140-denier UTC
- **Wing:** Ice Fur, mix of Flashabou, Krystal Flash, and Lateral Scale
- **Sides:** One grizzly saddle per side
- **Collar:** Bucktail
- **Eyes:** 6 mm 3D

**Notes:** This is another pattern that was designed for pike but will also take muskie and big largemouth. Set the eyes then cover the entire head with a UV cure material. The bucktail at the collar is *not* reverse-tied and surrounds the hook, extending a bit past the bend. Ice Fur is available in a wide assortment of colors, allowing a variety of colors to be combined, so there are lots of possibilities with this fly. It can be easily downsized a bit if desired.

## Group 6: Lake St. Clair Favorites

As one of the best warmwater fisheries anywhere, Lake St. Clair has proven to be an excellent proving ground for fly pattern development. Capt. Brian Meszaros has fished the waters of Lake St. Clair all his life, and guided its waters for nearly three decades. Recently moved to the Florida Keys, he was one of the first fly-fishing guides to focus on the big water of the Great Lakes. Meszaros was also one of the earliest proponents of chasing muskie with flies. Here are a couple of his most productive fly patterns.

**(Top to bottom)** Articulated Black Death, Imperchinator. JIMMY CHANG PHOTO

### ARTICULATED BLACK DEATH

*Originated and tied by Brian Meszaros*

- **Hook:** #4/0 Gamakatsu SL12S
- **Shank:** 80 mm Flymen Big Game Shank
- **Thread:** Black 210-denier UTC
- **Connector:** 80 lb. Cross-Lock Snap Swivel
- **Rear Body/Hook:** Six grizzly red super saddles, red Flashabou, 3 sections of black yak hair
- **Front Body/Shank:** Four to five sections of reverse-tied black yak hair, red Flashabou
- **Eyes:** 14 mm 3D

**Notes:** The yak hair is all reverse-tied and trimmed to shape. Attach the eyes with Loctite gel. Secure the swivel through the loop on the shank; close the loop with thread and coat with Zap-A-Gap or similar cement. A main concept of this design is the ability to change out the rear hook section as needed, and colors can be quickly adjusted. For example, if you had three colors of head sections and three colors of hook sections, nine color combinations would be possible. This helps to simplify the number of flies needed. Also, the yak hair does not absorb water, so this pattern has a minimal amount of weight for its size. The black/red combination shown is a key color for muskies everywhere they are found.

### IMPERCHINATOR

*Originated and tied by Brian Meszaros*

- **Hook:** #7/0-6/0 Gamakatsu SL12S
- **Thread:** Black or orange 210-denier UTC
- **Tail:** Six olive or chartreuse (or mixed) grizzly super saddles, fire tiger Holographic Flashabou
- **Body:** Three sections of reverse-tied yak hair, olive on top, orange on bottom, fire tiger Holgraphic Flashabou
- **Eyes:** 10 to 12 mm 3D

**Notes:** This pattern as shown imitates one of a muskie's favorite foods, a yellow perch. Reverse-tie and trim the yak hair and add barring with a Sharpie. Attach eyes with Loctite Super Glue gel or similar. The Black Death coloration is important for this pattern, too, along with the sucker (brown/orange) coloration. Again, the yak hair minimizes water weight for casting and the super saddle feathers add an enticing swimming movement to the fly. As mentioned earlier, when casting any of these flies for an extended time period, learning the technique of water-hauling can make it much easier and reduce casting fatigue.

## Group 7: Adaptive Fly Favorites

Matt Grajewski operates Adaptive Fly and ties a variety of streamer patterns for big-water applications as well as moving water. Much of his developmental work has also been done on Lake St. Clair, but his patterns have proven productive anywhere they are fished. Capt. Eric Grajewski, Matt's brother, guides anglers on Lake St. Clair, so they have plenty of opportunity to test and refine Matt's patterns. Here are two of their favorites.

(**Top to bottom**) Slip n' Slide, Yard Sale. JERRY DARKES PHOTO

### SLIP N' SLIDE

*Originated and tied by Matt Grajewski*

- **Thread:** White or black 100-denier GSP
- **Rear Hook:** 4/0 spinnerbait hook
- **Rattle:** Large plastic rattle
- **Tail:** Bucktail base, synthetic yak hair, Flashabou
- **Body:** Bucktail and Senyo Predator Wrap
- **Connector:** 65 lb. Surflon with large beads
- **Front Hook:** 5/0 short-shank spinnerbait hook
- **Body:** Alternate bucktail and Senyo Predator Wrap
- **Cheeks:** Grizzly rooster hackle
- **Head:** Bucktail, Senyo Laser Dub veil
- **Eyes:** ½-inch 3D

**Notes:** Reverse-tie the bucktail for the rear and front hook bodies. The bucktail at the head is spun around the hook, then the ends are pulled back and tied down. The pattern as shown has an overall length of around 10 inches, but

can be varied from 4 inches up to 14 inches. Fly length is adjusted by changing hook sizes. Make sure the rear hook is always smaller than the front. Material length and component size are adjusted down and the hook size is reduced. This orange/brown color scheme is a favorite, but it can be varied as desired. A key to this fly is the hidden spun deer head, which gives it extra buoyancy. This pattern is extremely versatile and swims well on any retrieve—short strips, long strips, fast or slow, they all work.

### YARD SALE

*Originated and tied by Matt Grajewski*

- **Thread:** White or black 100-denier GSP
- **Rear Hook:** 5/0 spinnerbait hook
- **Rattle:** Large plastic rattle
- **Tail:** Schlappen feathers, Flashabou
- **Body:** Flash n' Slinky on top and bottom, Flashabou on sides

- **Wing:** Craft Fur
- **Connector:** 65 lb. Surflon with large beads
- **Front Hook:** 6/0 spinnerbait hook
- **Body:** Flash n' Slinky on top and bottom, Flashabou on sides
- **Wing:** Craft Fur
- **Head:** Senyo Laser Dub stacked on top and bottom
- **Eyes:** ½-inch 3D

**Notes:** The Flash n' Slinky is tied on in bunches ¼ inch apart and trimmed. The photo shows a favored color scheme, but it can be varied as desired. For big-water use, Grajewski ties all his flies with a lightweight design, with weight added to the rear hook. This is accomplished with a rattle as described or lead wraps in smaller sizes. This enhances the movement of the fly. This pattern is best fished with long strips, allowing the fly to sink during the pause. The next strip pulls the fly in the opposite direction. This gives a great side-to-side, swimming motion. The pattern will work in lengths from 3 to 13 inches.

## Group 8: Pat Kelly Designs

Ohio's Pat Kelly has a number of highly productive muskie and pike designs. Most of his fishing and guiding takes place on inland rivers across Ohio, Kentucky, and West Virginia. These patterns highlight both his creativity and tying ability.

**(Top to bottom)** Natural Born Killer, Muskie Charmer, Muskie Marauder. JIMMY CHANG PHOTO

Rick Kustich shows a late-season fish taken on a large, articulated pattern. This muskie shows an interesting coloration pattern. There are several strains of muskie across the Midwest and Great Lakes that have different color configurations. NICK PIONESSA PHOTO

## NATURAL BORN KILLER

*Originated and tied by Pat Kelly*

- **Front Hook:** #6/0 Gamakatsu SL12S
- **Rear Hook:** #4/0 Gamakatsu SL12S
- **Middle:** 40 mm Flymen Big Game Shank, connect to rear hook with .020-inch-diameter nylon-coated wire and two 8 mm beads
- **Rear Body:** Polar Pony Hair or Syn Yak and Big Fly Fiber, super saddle feathers, Holographic Flashabou, then bucktail and Krystal Flash in front
- **Middle Body:** Bucktail mixed with Flashabou, single grizzly super saddle feather on each side
- **Front Body:** Bucktail mixed with Flashabou
- **Sides:** Two or three super saddle feathers
- **Collar:** Finn raccoon
- **Head:** Deer belly hair
- **Eyes:** 12 mm 3D

**Notes:** This pattern measures out at 15 inches and is the largest fly we will see. The bucktail is hollow-tied in each section. The deer hair for the head is spun, packed, and trimmed into a square shape. Due to its size, only experienced casters will likely be able to handle a fly like this. Rather than trying to blind cast, it might be best to use this in a specific location known to hold a large fish or after a follow from a large fish that refused to take. The black/pink color scheme pictured is another productive muskie combination. The pattern can be adjusted to any colors desired.

## MUSKIE CHARMER

*Originated and tied by Pat Kelly*

- **Hook:** #4/0 Partridge Attitude Extra
- **Thread:** 100-denier GSP
- **Body Sections (back to front):**
- **Tail:** 20 mm Fish Spine, silver UV Polar Chenille, 4 schlappen feathers
- **Next:** 20 mm Fish Spine, silver UV Polar Chenille, then white bucktail
- **Next:** 28 mm Big Game Shank, silver UV Polar Chenille, white bucktail, 2 super saddles, clear Black Barred Flashabou
- **Next:** 40 mm Big Game Shank, 3 sections of ½-inch Chocklett's Body Tubing, bucktail, super saddles, opal Mirage Flashabou
- **Connector:** .020-inch-diameter wire
- **Hook:** UV Polar Chenille, then 2 sections of ½-inch Chocklett's Body Tubing, white bucktail
- **Front:** 40 mm Big Game Shank, 2 sections of ½-inch Chocklett's Body Tubing, white bucktail, opal Mirage Flashabou, clear Black Barred Flashabou

**Notes:** This is an oversized version of a Game Changer. There are minimal water-absorbing materials to affect casting, and this fly will give the illusion of size and bulk in the water while having a great swimming motion. The bucktail is all reverse-tied. This same basic template is open to a wide range of color interpretation. We have already seen a number of key muskie color schemes, but it's helpful to talk to conventional gear shops and anglers to find out if any particular baits or colors are "hot," or if there is anything out of the ordinary used in the area you plan to fish. Then make your initial fly selection(s) based on this info.

## MUSKIE MARAUDER

*Originated and tied by Pat Kelly*

- **Front Hook:** #4/0 Gamakatsu SL12S
- **Rear Hook:** #2/0 Gamakatsu SL12S
- **Thread (rear hook):** Chartreuse 210-denier UTC
- **Thread (front hook):** Hot orange 210-denier UTC
- **Connector:** .020-inch-diameter nylon-coated wire with three red 8mm beads

- **Rear Body:** Chartreuse Polar Pony or Syn Yak, chartreuse grizzly super saddles, fire tiger Holographic Flashabou, opal Mirage Flashabou, 3 sections of bucktail in chartreuse, orange, chartreuse
- **Front Body:** Four sections of bucktail in orange, chartreuse, orange, and olive, 1 orange grizzly super saddle per side, opal Mirage Flashabou after chartreuse section, red Krystal Flash after second orange section
- **Eyes:** 10 mm 3D

**Notes:** Though a bit time consuming, this pattern is fairly simple to make. Note that all the bucktail is hollow-tied. The eyes are glued to the thread head and then UV cure coated. It can be scaled down to create a pattern for a wide range of gamefish and becomes a great bass and even trout streamer. The hollow-tie technique gives the illusion of mass with a minimal amount of material. A fire tiger color scheme is shown, but the pattern can be tied in primary muskie colors and any other combinations you like.

## Group 9: Mega Tubes

Tube designs also interpret well to mega-size flies. There are several advantages with tubes in this application. The ability to alter or adjust the hook size and design can be important with larger flies. It is also possible to use a material-dressed hook with a tube to increase its size and also alter the appearance. Here are a couple basic design templates that can be adjusted for color as needed.

**(Top to bottom)** Cheesehead Seducer, Counting Sheep. JIMMY CHANG PHOTO

## CHEESEHEAD SEDUCER

*Originated and tied by Steve Wascher*

- **Tube:** HMH 2-inch hard plastic with junction tube
- **Thread:** Black 100-denier GSP
- **Tail:** Grizzly dyed yellow and grizzly dyed brown hackle feathers, 5 of each
- **Belly:** Pearl Angel Hair
- **Back:** Peacock Angel Hair
- **Sides:** Electric yellow Angel Hair, bronze Flashabou
- **Cheeks:** Brown hackle tip
- **Eyes:** 6 mm 3D
- **Cone:** Large brown

**Notes:** This pattern has a great profile in the water. The numerous small saddle feathers give plenty of movement in the water, and the flash can attract from a long distance or in off-color water. By changing the hackle and side Angel Hair colors, a variety of different looks are easily made. A strong straight-eye hook is used to set up to fish. Most any used in previous pattern recipes from this chapter are applicable. This varies depending on fly size, situation, and personal preference.

## COUNTING SHEEP

*Originated and tied by Rick Kustich*

- **Tube:** HMH 5-inch hard plastic (junction tube optional)
- **Thread:** Black 140-denier UTC
- **Tail:** Six white schlappen feathers
- **Back:** White SF Blend, silver Holographic Flashabou
- **Belly:** White SF Blend
- **Collar:** Long black Icelandic Sheep fur
- **Head:** Silver Cross-Eyed Cone, extra-large

**Notes:** Rick Kustich uses this design in the clear waters of the upper Niagara River and other clear-water locations. There are times that flash can be a hindrance and actually spook fish. This fly is tied "in the round," with materials distributed around the hook, and it gives a full profile from any angle. The white/black color contrast is visible from a long distance.

## Group 10: Mega Tubes Variations

These two patterns highlight a way to alter a fly design for a very specific purpose. In this case it is to create a weighted fly that drops quickly when the retrieve is stopped. This same concept could be applied to a large number of muskie fly patterns. Another advantage is the ability to substitute different hooks as desired. A final aspect of the versatility of a tube design would be to use hooks dressed in different colors and possibly different materials.

**(Top to bottom)** Black Death Mega Tube, Imperchinator Mega Tube. JIMMY CHANG PHOTO

Any muskie taken on a fly is an accomplishment. A number of factors contribute to success, including having the right fly, the ability to cast it, plus getting the fly to the right location and depth with a proper retrieve. Finally, the angler has to get the hook set and then keep the fish on and landed. JERRY DARKES PHOTO

## BLACK DEATH MEGA TUBE

*Originated and tied by Brian Meszaros*

- **Tube:** HMH 4-inch copper (junction tube optional)
- **Thread:** Black 210-denier UTC
- **Body:** 6 to 8 sparse sections of black yak hair, increasing in length as you go forward
- **Belly:** 6 to 8 sparse sections of black yak hair, increasing in length as you go forward
- **Sides:** Pearl Magnum Flashabou, red Flashabou
- **Eyes:** 12 mm 3D

**Notes:** Reverse-tie the front three yak hair sections. This fly is simple in design but with specific purpose. Muskies are notorious for following a fly or lure right to the boat. If you can keep a fly moving and hold the fish's interest, it may still strike. This is where the "figure 8" technique comes into play. Meszaros has found that most inexperienced anglers freeze when they see a large fish following the fly. The fly stops moving and the fish loses interest. With the fly on a copper tube, it will drop sharply if the retrieve is stopped. This quick change in direction can trigger a strike, giving the angler an extra opportunity to hook the fish.

## IMPERCHINATOR MEGA TUBE

*Originated and tied by Brian Meszaros*

- **Tube:** HMH 4-inch copper (junction tube optional)
- **Thread:** Chartreuse 210-denier UTC
- **Body:** 6 to 8 sparse sections of olive yak hair, increasing in length as you go forward, barred
- **Belly:** 6 or 8 sparse sections of orange yak hair, increasing in length as you go forward
- **Sides:** Fire tiger–colored Holographic Flashabou
- **Throat:** Red Krystal Flash
- **Top:** Black Holographic Flashabou
- **Eyes:** 12 mm 3D

**Notes:** The design function is the same as the previous one. The front sections of yak hair are reverse-tied. As always, color can be adjusted as desired, but these colors are key on Lake St. Clair as well as in many other locations. The hook is attached by running your bite tippet through the tube and securing with a crimped sleeve or knot depending on the type of wire being used. A large, short-shank single hook is generally attached (#4/0-6/0 Gamakatsu SL12S is popular); a large treble (#2/0) is also usable.

# Acknowledgments

I need to express a very sincere "thank you" to my editor, Jay Nichols, for his unending patience and understanding, as well as to the many contributors to this project.

Sincere thanks go out to everyone who contributed photos to this book. To Jimmy Chang for his beautiful fly plate photography and additional fly photos; I appreciate the many adjustments you were able to make in the plate photographs to help bring my vision to light. To my good friends, Kevin Feenstra and Jon Ray, for their contributions. They are not only top-notch guides, but also great photographers and creative tiers. Others including Phil Cook, Rick Kustich, Jeff Liskay, Nick Pionessa, and Leo Wright also contributed photos.

To Charlie Chlysta, Jerry Reagan, and Robert Schoeller for sharing both fly patterns, tying information, and photos. Each contributed a unique series of patterns that all of us should take note of. They could have kept this information private, but each was unselfishly willing to share this with everyone. To Jon Uhlenhop for his many contributions, always meticulously tied and perfect.

To Steve May for his time and effort in collecting patterns from a number of Canadian tiers. Others including Austin Adduci, Pat and Jared Ehlers, Ted Kraimer, Ed McCoy, Joe Penich, Charlie Piette, Dennis Potter, Patrick Robinson, Greg Senyo, Brian Smolinski, Steve Wascher, and Matt Zudweg contributed multiple patterns across a range of categories. To Gord Ellis for all the background info and help on the Nipigon River. Thank you all.

My most sincere thanks to everyone who contributed fly patterns. This book is about all of you. I will not try to list everyone as I will undoubtedly forget to include some of you. I hope you are adequately recognized in the body of the book. Most everyone took the time to write out recipes for their patterns, then package the flies and send them to me. I truly appreciate the information everyone provided to the content of the final work.

As always, I am thankful for the continuing support of my family on these projects. It would be impossible to assemble a book like this without their understanding. My wife, Lori, has tolerated fly boxes, stacks of books, papers, material catalogs, and more scattered across our basement for several years. Thank you for your acceptance of me as I am and letting me follow the unique path I have taken.

# Bibliography

## BOOKS

Bates, Joseph D., Jr. *Streamers and Bucktails*. New York, NY: Alfred A. Knopf, Inc., 1979.

Bates, Joseph D., Jr. *Streamer Fly Tying and Fishing*. Harrisburg, PA: The Stackpole Company, 1966.

Behnke, Robert J. *About Trout*. Guilford, CT: Lyons Press, 2007.

Borger, Gary. *Nymphing: A Basic Book*. Harrisburg, PA: Stackpole Books, 1979.

Darkes, Jerry. *Fly Fishing the Inland Oceans*. Mechanicsburg, PA: Stackpole Books, 2013.

Greenburg, Josh. *Rivers of Sand*. Guilford, CT: Lyons Press, 2014.

Hanley, Ken. *Tying Furled Flies*. New Cumberland, PA: Headwaters Books, 2008.

Karczynski, Dave, and Tim Landwehr. *Smallmouth: Modern Fly Fishing Methods, Tactics & Techniques*. Guilford, CT: Stackpole Books, 2017.

Kustich, Rick, and Jerry Kustich. *Fly Fishing for Great Lakes Steelhead*. Grand Island, NY: West River Publishing, 1999.

Linsenman, Bob, and Kelly Galloup. *Modern Streamers for Trophy Trout*. Woodstock, VT: The Countryman Press, 1999.

Marbury, Mary Orvis. *Favorite Flies and Their Histories*. Boston and New York: Houghton, Mifflin, and Company, 1892.

Miller, Ann R. *Hatch Guide for Upper Midwest Streams*. Portland, OR: Frank Amato Publications, Inc., 2011.

Mueller, Ross. *Upper Midwest Flies That Catch Trout*. Appleton, WI: R. Mueller Publications, 1995.

Nagy, John. *Steelhead Guide: Fly Fishing Techniques and Strategies for Lake Erie Steelhead*. Pittsburgh: Great Lakes Publishing, 2003.

Osborn, Jon. *Classic Michigan Flies*. Mechanicsburg, PA: Stackpole Books, 2013.

Perich, Shawn. *Fly Fishing the North Country*. Duluth, MN: Pfeifer-Hamilton, 1995.

Pobst, Dick. *The Orvis Vest Pocket Guide to Mayflies*. Guilford, CT: The Lyons Press, 2008.

Richey, David. *Great Lakes Steelhead Flies*. Grawn, MI: Sportsmans Outdoor Enterprises, Inc., 1979.

Schullery, Paul. *American Fly Fishing: A History*. New York: Nick Lyons Books, 1987.

Schwiebert, Ernest. *Nymphs*. New York: Winchester Press, 1973.

Senyo, Greg. *Fusion Fly Tying: Steelhead, Salmon, and Trout Flies of the Synthetic Era*. New York: Skyhorse Publishing, 2015.

Smith, Scott E. *Ontario Blue-Ribbon Fly Fishing Guide*. Portland, OR: Frank Amato Publications, Inc., 1999.

Snyder, Wayne. *The Golden Age: Fly Fishing in Michigan, 1860 to 1960, Edition 2*. Lexington, KY: Qw.e.s.t., 2013.

Swisher, Doug, and Carl Richards. *Selective Trout: A Dramatically New and Scientific Approach to Trout Fishing on Eastern and Western Rivers*. New York: Crown Publishers, 1988.

Valla, Mike. *The Founding Flies*. Mechanicsburg, PA: Stackpole Books, 2013.

## WEBSITES

www.frankenfly.com
www.globalflyfisher.com
www.michigandryflies.net

# About the Author

B ased in northern Ohio, Jerry Darkes has over five decades of fly-fishing experience in both fresh and salt water. He is recognized as an expert on fly fishing the waters of the Great Lakes and has extensive experience on the inland waters of the Midwest. He has been featured in books, radio, and television shows promoting fly fishing in the area. Darkes has two books to his credit: *Fly Fishing the Inland Oceans* and *Fly Tyer's Guide to Essential Flies for Bass and Panfish*, plus numerous magazine articles.

# Index